Embattled

EMBATTLED

*How Ancient Greek Myths
Empower Us to Resist Tyranny*

Emily Katz Anhalt

REDWOOD PRESS

Stanford, California

STANFORD UNIVERSITY PRESS
Stanford, California

Printed in the United States of America on acid-free, archival-quality paper

Library of Congress Cataloging-in-Publication Data
Names: Anhalt, Emily Katz, author.
Title: Embattled : how ancient Greek myths empower us to resist tyranny / Emily Katz Anhalt.
Description: Stanford, California : Redwood Press, 2021. | Includes bibliographical references and index.
Identifiers: LCCN 2021000152 (print) | LCCN 2021000153 (ebook) | ISBN 9781503628564 (cloth) | ISBN 9781503629400 (ebook)
Subjects: LCSH: Epic poetry, Greek—Themes, motives. | Greek drama (Tragedy—Themes, motives. | Mythology, Greek—Political aspects. | Power (Social sciences) in literature. | Democracy in literature.
Classification: LCC PA3092 .A545 2021 (print) | LCC PA3092 (ebook) | DDC 883/.010943219—dc23
LC record available at https://lccn.loc.gov/2021000152
LC ebook record available at https://lccn.loc.gov/2021000153

Cover design: Kevin Barrett Kane
Cover image: "Bronze cuirass (body armor)," 4th century BCE, The Met, Gift of Estée Lauder Inc., 1992.
Text design: Kevin Barrett Kane
Typeset at Stanford University Press in 10/15 ITC Galliard Pro

For my mother, Marilyn Ogus Katz (1933–2017)

ἥ γάρ σευ κλέος οὐρανὸν εὐρὺν ἱκάνει

Contents

A Note on the Text, Translations, and Endnotes

All adaptations, translations, and citations of the *Iliad*, *Odyssey*, *Oresteia*, and *Antigone* throughout this book are my own and derive from the Oxford Classical Texts of D. B. Monro and T. W. Allen (*Iliad*), T. W. Allen (*Odyssey*), D. Page (*Oresteia*), and A. C. Pearson (*Antigone*).

Homeric Greek is a literary composite of several dialects: primarily Aeolic and old-Ionic, with some Arcado-Cyprian, Attic, and non-Greek forms as well as some neologisms. This combination would have sounded somewhat strange and elevated even to audiences in the sixth and fifth centuries BCE. Sections of the tragedies also very likely sounded formal and stilted to their original audiences in the fifth century BCE. I have tried to paraphrase and, at times, to translate the Greek (into prose, not poetry) as literally as possible, while still yielding sense in English. When possible, I have sought to preserve some of the distance and elevated tone of the original Greek, particularly in passages of dialogue. To a contemporary reader, this may sound awkward at times.

Given the vastness of the scholarly bibliography, the endnotes, while undeniably exhausting, are far from exhaustive. Rather, I have aimed to offer a representative sample of relevant scholarship in English and to provide an impetus to further reading.

Embattled

CONFRONTING TYRANNY TODAY

Imagine a cool, overcast spring afternoon with a sharp breeze cutting through the branches of the olive trees. Sitting in the theater at Athens, you watch, apprehensively, as a father greets his son before the dark gates of an immense palace. The father is Creon, the new king of Thebes. He has condemned to death a young woman named Antigone, because she violated his ban on burying the body of a traitor. The son is Haemon, Antigone's fiancé. He has come to beg his father to spare the young woman's life. King Creon's elderly advisors anxiously watch and wait.

The son begins respectfully. With utmost tact, he insists that he values his father's success above all. He urges his father to be open to good advice: "Anyone who thinks that he alone has the capacity for thought or eloquence or reason, well, these men, once unfolded, are seen to be empty." There's nothing shameful in learning new things, Haemon explains. Trees that can bend survive storms, he points out. Whoever guides a ship but fails to loosen the sheet when necessary overturns his ship. Haemon implores his father to yield, and to stop being angry. He admits that he himself is young, but even an old person can't be right all the time and can learn from someone who speaks well.

The chorus of elderly advisors agrees. They think that both men can learn from one another.

But Creon reacts with astonishing and terrifying fury. "So at our age we will be taught to understand nature by a man of his age?" he asks. Does Haemon advise him to honor people who produce disorder? Hasn't Antigone been seized with just such a sickness?

I

Haemon manages to keep his voice calm. He points out that all the citizens are on his side.

Creon retorts that he is in charge, not the people. He confidently asserts that he rules exclusively in his own interest, since the city belongs to its ruler and to no one else.

Haemon now begins to lose control, too. Criticizing his father for sounding childish, he exclaims, "A city that belongs to one man is not a city!"

King Creon finds Haemon's statement incomprehensible. "Isn't the city thought to belong to the one who rules it?" he demands.

"Alone, you would rule nobly over a deserted land," Haemon sneers. But he continues to insist that he only wants to prevent his father from committing an injustice.

Disparaging his son as a woman's slave, Creon remains enraged that his son dares to criticize his father's knowledge of justice and his confidence in his own authority.

Haemon argues that Creon is dishonoring the gods and is thereby endangering himself along with his son and his son's fiancée.

Creon proceeds to denounce his son as a polluted character. Deaf to Haemon's arguments, he screams, "You will never marry this woman while she is living!"

"She will die, then," Haemon acknowledges. "And by dying, she will kill someone else."

"How dare you threaten me!" Creon cries.

"I'm not threatening you, just telling you my intention." Haemon intends to kill himself. He condemns his father's inability to listen, and he suggests that he is not thinking well.

The king responds with monstrous ferocity. "You know what?" he says. "You can watch her die." He orders Antigone to be brought forward so that Haemon can be present at her death.

"Don't expect me to watch her die," Haemon announces. "And you will never see me again. Go ahead and rave on among whoever of your friends are willing." *He stresses the word* philoi *(friends) ironically. Philoi also means blood relatives, but Creon has reduced it to mean only "political supporters." This misguided assessment has perverted the king's relationship with his own son. You,*

the audience, and the king's elderly advisors all watch in horror as Haemon rushes
away. They know that Creon's treatment of a traitor and a rebel aligns with stan-
dard practice. You know that this story is not going to end well.

TYRANNY BEGINS and ends in violence, intimidation, and oppression.
The brutality and greed of individuals wielding unfettered power, and
their replacement by equally brutal and rapacious successors, whether
by violence or by other means, inevitably fractures and crushes the
community. In English, "tyranny" is more or less synonymous with
"despotism," and in this book I use the two terms interchangeably to
refer to abusive, unrestrained, and unaccountable power. Abuses of
power—whether by one person, a few, or many—destroy individuals
and corrode communities.[1]

Today, worldwide, we are witnessing power grabs by corrupt strongmen and demagogues, including many who may even have been popularly
elected. To gain and maintain power, such individuals foster and exploit
tribal and partisan animosities. Their ability to flout the law has prompted
some of us to lose faith in democratic political ideals and institutions. Some
of us have given up on government altogether, preferring to rely on our
own resources, wits, and guns for survival. Still others, convinced that the
answer lies in expanding the power of majoritarian decision-making, seek
to remove any and all checks on the power of the people, sometimes called
"the popular will." All of these routes, history shows, lead more or less directly to dictatorship or various forms of authoritarianism. Autocrats thrive
on and promote the rejection of the rule of law, the rise of populism, and
the introduction or reintroduction of violence into the political process.
In the twenty-first century we are drifting—or, perhaps more accurately,
hastening—toward despotism.[2]

But arguably, this is not inevitable. History also provides an extraordinary example of the reverse trajectory: during the eighth through the fifth
centuries BCE, ancient Greece witnessed an unprecedented movement away
from tribalism and autocracy and toward civil society and broader forms of
political participation. Some Greek *poleis* (citizen-communities) instituted

oligarchic or, in some instances, democratic governments. Most famously, by the mid–fifth century BCE, Athens had developed radically democratic political institutions that made political decisions the responsibility of every individual citizen.[3]

Unaccountable and irresponsible power over other human beings proved not only grasping and cruel but also impermanent. No human being lives forever, and the *tyrannos* (tyrant), or perhaps his son, was always vulnerable to violent overthrow. As a result, tyranny began to seem unwise even for the tyrant. This impermanence and vulnerability of tyrannical rule caused the ancient Greeks to experience various types of political organization. It is no coincidence that they coined the terms *autocracy*, meaning power held by one person, *aristocracy*, meaning power held by the best people, and *democracy*, meaning power held by the people as a whole.[4] These compound words identify who has power, but not how they use it. The Greeks' political experiments revealed that thuggishness, intimidation, and oppression can take many forms. They discovered, as we have, that not only autocrats but also powerful groups small and large can behave tyrannically and commit atrocities.[5]

The Greeks' political experimentation did not occur in a cultural vacuum. Beginning more than three thousand years ago, the stories that we call Greek myths accompanied and advanced the ancient Greeks' preoccupation with political power and their ingenuity in devising novel forms of political organization.[6] Democracy did not exist as a concept until the Greeks coined the word and tried the experiment. Long before they did so, over the course of hundreds or maybe thousands of years, Greek epic tales and, later, Athenian tragic plays encouraged the Greeks to reject tyranny. Democratic political institutions developed as a consequence of gradual changes in social and political attitudes endorsed by epic and tragic reworkings of Greek myths over many centuries.[7] The ancient Greeks failed to create a just, humane society of political equals, but their epics and tragedies introduced justice, humanity, and equality as requirements for human survival and happiness. Stories told in epic and tragic poetry cultivated attitudes and skills required to progress toward these goals. The failures of the ancient Greeks in their own times cannot excuse ours. They never removed tyrannical abuses of power from their world or from themselves, but their stories show us why and how we might.

Many people witnessing the world's trajectory today are unaware of the valuable assistance available to us in the form of ancient Greek epic and tragic poetry. If you have never considered Homer, Aeschylus, or Sophocles relevant to contemporary concerns, this book is for you. (I include endnotes for scholars and individuals interested in pursuing particular topics further. I hope that others will feel free to ignore the endnotes.) Although ancient Greek tyrannical abuse often differed greatly from modern versions in structure and technique, the tales told in epic and tragic poetry nevertheless identify attitudes and skills crucial to preventing abuses of power today.

But why look to ancient Greek myths for insight and inspiration, you may well ask, since throughout the archaic and classical periods the Greeks themselves remained patriarchal, misogynistic, xenophobic, and bellicose bullies? Is it even ethical to read Greek literature at all? Although ancient Greek epics and Athenian tragedies condemn tyrannical behavior in all its forms, the ancient Athenians kept slaves. They treated women as property. They subjugated foreign communities, often with breathtaking brutality. They were more than willing to use violence in their relationships with outsiders and even, at times, with fellow Athenians.[8] At the same time the Athenian political system, though it excluded women, foreigners, and slaves from participation, nevertheless constituted a direct democracy: by the mid–fifth century BCE, nearly all political decisions were determined by what we might call referenda, direct votes by all male citizens.[9] In the same century, Athenians produced astounding innovations in art, architecture, and poetry. They devised historiography and moral philosophy. For a time, Athenians commanded a huge empire and amassed great wealth. None of this counterbalances the fact that the ancient Athenians never considered women, foreigners, slaves, or children equal to male citizens.[10]

We must condemn the Athenians for their slavery, misogyny, and abuse of power, as we must condemn the prejudice, misogyny, oppression, and tyrannical abuses of power that defile human societies of every time and place. At the same time, we can and must learn from the cultures of every human community. Every society offers both cautionary and salutary examples. I do not suggest that we read exclusively Greek literature, but only that we include it in our conversations about how we can and should treat one another, choose our leaders, and use our power. Ancient Greek literature focuses explicitly on these issues, and offers invaluable insights. The Athenians rejected autocratic government, and they broadened their political decision-making to include more people in the process than had ever been included anywhere in the world before.[11] The eloquent condemnation of tyranny in ancient Greek epic and tragic poetry identifies tools that are essential for confronting abuses of power today.

Unfortunately, ancient Greece has become a pawn in the culture wars of the twenty-first century, with experts and nonexperts of all ideological persuasions enlisting Greek literature and history in various creative and antithetical ways in the service of their own partisan political agendas. At one extreme, an unquestioning acceptance of distorted claims of ancient Greek cultural superiority undeniably cripples our capacity to confront tyranny. At the other extreme, a sweeping disdain for or rejection of Greek (and Roman) literature and history robs us of instructive examples. Recent debate often centers primarily on Roman sources. Extremists on all sides of the contemporary culture wars regularly overlook the extensive criticism of ancient Greek ideals and behavior that exists within Greek texts themselves.[12]

As in everything, so too in ancient Greek myths: extremist ideologies risk blinding us to reality. The ancient Greeks never achieved a free, egalitarian society, and in subsequent centuries the misguided assumption of their unchallenged cultural superiority has often promoted terrible oppression and exclusion. But during the eighth through fifth centuries BCE, ancient Greek epics and tragedies began to acknowledge the essential humanity of every human being. The Homeric epics, already reworking traditional tales from still earlier times, emphasized the one thing that we all share regardless of our gender, skin color, race, religion, nationality, or political convictions: Whether we are male, female, rich, poor, powerful, weak, old, or young, we are all vulnerable to suffering and death. As Athena, goddess of wisdom, explains, "Death, you know, is an impartial thing. Not even the gods can ward it off even from a man who is dear to them, whenever indeed the destructive fate of prostrating death overcomes him" (*Od.* 3.236–38). Could any insight be more fundamentally nonpartisan or egalitarian?

Every culture's narratives have political influence because they shape people's identity, aspirations, and interactions with one another. Over centuries, epic and tragic narratives kept retelling traditional ancient tales with evolving details and emphases. To Greeks of the sixth and fifth centuries BCE, these were stories of long ago about people now long dead. The epics and tragedies therefore held their characters' choices up for scrutiny by people with no direct vested interest in the details and outcome of the plot. Because, like Homer's earliest audiences, we don't star in these tales, we can judge the characters' behavior with less passion and partisanship than if we did. Crucially, the epics and tragedies don't invite us merely to admire and condemn but to analyze and reflect. The mortal characters are complicated people confronting challenging predicaments, some of their own making, some not. Because we are not them, we can see ourselves more clearly and objectively in them than we could by looking in a mirror. We are not them, but they are us.

Myths told and retold in ancient Greek epic and tragic poetry invited the Greeks to value reality and factual evidence; to admire human ingenuity, skepticism, self-restraint, and accountability; to distinguish vengeance from justice; and above all to despise tyranny. We must denounce ancient Greek culture (and its legacy) as patriarchal, misogynistic, bellicose, and bullying.[13] At the same time we must recognize that in doing so, we are judging the ancient Greeks by ideals that they themselves introduced, and that we are in danger of abandoning.[14]

Despite current political controversies over ancient Greece and its legacy, many people today do not know ancient Greek myths well or at all, and even fewer have the ability to read ancient Greek. But these stories can and must speak to us all. I have therefore opted to paraphrase some of the tales, staying as close to the Greek originals as possible in an effort to transmit insights visible to someone encountering the texts in Greek. In some sections I am in fact translating rather than paraphrasing. In italicized portions of the narratives, I address the reader directly in order to identify elements implicit but not explicitly stated in the texts. In retelling the tales

I attempt to encourage readers to imagine experiencing these stories as someone living in ancient times might have done, not in order to prevent evaluation from the perspective of the twenty-first century, but to suggest places where ancient and modern reactions might and might not align. I hope that readers encountering these stories for the first time will find the combination of narrative summary followed by analysis helpful. In Athens in the fifth century BCE, tales told in epic and tragic poetry had a vast, perhaps nearly universal audience. They shaped the attitudes and aspirations not of a segment of the population, but of the whole. The rejection of tyranny today requires the participation not of a few experts, but of everyone.

Rather than offering an historical account of a sociopolitical movement, I aim to expose vital political insights visible in selected epic and tragic tales. In the following chapters, I retell and then interpret stories from Homer's *Iliad* (c. 750 BCE), Homer's *Odyssey* (c. 700 BCE), Aeschylus's *Oresteia* (458 BCE), and Sophocles's *Antigone* (c. 443 BCE), drawing from them some useful tools for today's embattled and perilous political moment. My narratives and analyses derive not from other scholars' translations but from reading the Greek texts themselves. All translations are my own. Because I have discussed the *Iliad* at length in a previous book (*Enraged: Why Violent Times Need Ancient Greek Myths*), this book contains just one chapter on the *Iliad*, four on the *Odyssey*, and one each on the *Oresteia* and the *Antigone*. In focusing on the attitudes and skills accompanying the transition from autocracy to democracy, I have opted not to include any play by Euripides, since his surviving plays all date from the final third of the fifth century, well after the transition to radical democratic government in Athens was already complete.

Instead of attempting a broad cultural commentary on ancient Greek epic and tragic poetry, this book focuses on one theme: the abuse of power and the intellectual and emotional equipment required to prevent it. In choosing these particular texts and examining them specifically through that lens, I do not mean to suggest that the Greeks first recognized the risks of authoritarianism and then consciously used epic and tragic storytelling to produce broader political participation. Rather, these versions of Greek myths provide a window on the process of recognizing the dangers of all forms of tyranny, and they reveal intellectual insights and attitudes crucial to its defeat. The concept of sharing political power could well have been an unintended consequence. Undeniably, all archaic and classical Greek texts offer many valuable ideas in addition to the ones central to this book. Among their many illuminating aspects, Homer's *Iliad* and *Odyssey*, Aeschylus's *Oresteia*, and Sophocles's *Antigone* reveal potent tools for combating the abuse of power in ourselves and in others, whenever and wherever it threatens and in whatever form it takes.

This book is not about what Homer, Aeschylus, and Sophocles "intended." That we can never know. We don't even know who "Homer" was (the name is better understood as the name of a genre of poetic performance lasting many centuries), and we know little about the lives of Aeschylus and Sophocles.[15] In the absence of interviews, letters, or journal entries, we cannot determine from an epic poem or a play the motives or intentions of its author, let alone a 2,500-year-old one. (Perhaps Homer, Aeschylus, and Sophocles *intended* to write comedies but missed their target?) My book is about the *effect* of these stories in the form in which the texts have come down to us. It is about the warnings and advice that these reworkings of traditional mythical material offered their original audiences and can offer to us today.[16] This book is about the options that we face as human beings, and the insights and attitudes that ancient Greek epic tales and tragic plays reveal as survival skills. As the culture wars rage, these stories offer us more constructive ways of guiding our own decisions and governing our interactions with others.

Ancient Greek myths were transmitted first in the form of epic poetry, the oral tales in verse that coalesced into Homer's *Iliad* and *Odyssey* (c. eighth century BCE).[17] Not long after the Homeric epics were first written down in the mid–sixth century BCE, the Athenians overthrew their last tyrant and established a democratic government (508 BCE), giving political decision-making power to an assembly of all male citizens. Beginning in the late sixth century BCE and throughout the fifth, Athenian tragic plays retold many ancient tales, but with new details and emphases.[18] Both the archaic Homeric epics and the Athenian tragedies of the fifth century BCE exposed tyrannical behavior as self-defeating. Tragedies went even further in suggesting that democratic political institutions alone will not prevent and may even perpetrate tyrannical abuses. Athenian tragedies emphasized that the rejection of tyranny derives not merely from institutional changes, but from a transformation of values. Greek epics and tragedies prompt the realization that averting abuses of power requires asking not only "Who is to rule?" but also "With what methods and goals?" and "With what results?"[19]

Long before democracy existed even as a concept, the *Iliad* and *Odyssey* began to cultivate their audiences' capacity for critical reflection, rational judgment, and creative problem solving. Both epics depict a particular culture and a set of events involving both human beings and divinities. In the divine realm, Zeus's power is absolute. In the human realm, the *aristoi* ("best men," defined as wellborn, wealthy, and powerful) compete for *kratos* (power). All people are decidedly not equal.[20] By providing access to numerous viewpoints both mortal and immortal, however, both epics distinguish the audience's perspective from the characters' perspective. The *Iliad* even humanizes the Greeks' Trojan enemies. The epics' audience cannot ascertain with any certainty the intentions of the poet or the narrator, but the narrative emphasizes limitations in the characters' understanding by offering us the broader view. The wider perspective makes it possible for the audience, ancient or modern, to evaluate the values of Homer's characters and their consequences. The mortal characters largely attribute their own actions and experiences to divine agency, but Homer's audience sees that this is frequently not the case at all.[21]

This possibility of evaluating the world of the *Iliad* and *Odyssey* and its inhabitants' goals and actions was available to Homer's original audiences and to every later generation of hearers and readers of the epics. By observing the consequences of the characters' values and behaviors, the audience begins to question whether they are optimal: whether some of them are useful, but others not so much. The *Iliad* and *Odyssey* emphasize the vulnerability of the community to the greed and foolishness of self-centered and incompetent leaders, and both epics expose the vital interdependence between individual and group achievement, prosperity, and happiness. Both epics highlight the ambivalent potential of all human technology in its capacity to do great good and great harm. Both epics invite individuals to take responsibility for their own choices and actions, and to honor mutually beneficial obligations to one another. The *Odyssey* particularly emphasizes the value of reciprocal norms, as exemplified by *xenia* (guest-friendship), a set of conventions governing the behaviors of guests and hosts. Above all, the *Odyssey* portrays self-restraint, foresight, ingenuity, fact-based deductive reasoning, and rational deliberation as skills essential to survival and success.

Hundreds of years after Homer introduced the concept of the audience as critical moral thinker, as the first generations of Athenians were learning to wield democratic political institutions in the fifth century BCE, Athenian tragic playwrights continued to challenge traditional hierarchical (aristocratic) values while simultaneously critiquing newly emerging democratic political ideals. Their plays remind us that to challenge democratic values is to affirm them. By retelling many of the same stories with new emphases, the tragedies helped the Athenians to appreciate democracy as a mechanism for addressing individuals' needs, preferences, and grievances while maintaining communal stability and harmony.[22] In revising and repurposing an ancient tale of revenge, Aeschylus's *Oresteia* (458 BCE), urged the Athenians to distinguish justice from vengeance and to redefine victory as a win for all concerned. Sophocles's *Antigone* (c. 443 BCE), addressing the problem of conflict, warned contemporary Athenians to avoid the perils of polarization and to welcome good advice and creative solutions. By inviting discussion and debate, these tragic plays, then as now, promote the potential of democratic government to restrain destructive passions and to balance tribal allegiances with civic responsibilities.

One premise of my book is that the stories we read, watch, or tell shape our attitudes and choices. They teach us what to admire and what to condemn.[23] And the crucial lesson from the ancient Greeks and their stories is that you can make all the economic, institutional, and technological changes you want, but unless you address the human propensity for tyrannical behavior, you are not going to find yourself living in a desirable, flourishing community. In practice, as we know, democratic procedures and institutions can easily become the disguise donned by despots.[24]

Despite the ancient Greeks' own prejudices and exclusions, their epics and tragedies began to make moral reasoning the responsibility of every individual. Tales told in epic and tragic poetry present fact-based, rational decision making, caution, and self-restraint as admirable ideals of achievement. They emphasize the responsibilities of power (any power, whether derived from birth, wealth, personal talents, or numerical superiority), and they remind us that both the powerful and the powerless have obligations to one another. These stories cultivate the recognition that survival and success require an alignment (elusive, fragile, precarious, and shifting as it will inevitably be) between the needs of the individual and the needs of the community.[25] Revising and reinterpreting traditional ancient stories, ancient Greek epic and tragic poetry initiated a movement toward political and social equality that we in the twenty-first century have yet to accomplish. If we seek to eradicate tyranny in all its toxic forms, ancient Greek epics and tragedies point the way.

In a previous book, *Enraged: Why Violent Times Need Ancient Greek Myths* (Yale University Press, 2017), I have examined the critique of rage in Homer's *Iliad* and two fifth-century Athenian tragedies, Sophocles's *Ajax* (c. 448 BCE) and Euripides's *Hecuba* (c. 424 BCE). Encouraging the audience to evaluate the characters' choices, the *Iliad* exposes violent rage as self-destructive. Homer's characters attribute events to the gods' decisions or to fate, but the narrative enables the audience to realize that human choices and actions have reasonably predictable consequences and that human decisions, not the gods or fate, largely determine human experiences. Most crucially, the *Iliad* cultivates the audience's capacity to recognize the essential humanity of every human being, even an enemy. While Homer's characters frequently desire vengeance, the *Iliad* permits the audience to appreciate that empathy better serves an individual's own self-interest. Centuries later, Greek tragedies continue to emphasize that human attitudes and values—not the gods or fate, or even democratic institutions—determine the quality of life in any community. Sophocles's *Ajax* and Euripides's *Hecuba* both expose the capacity of a democratic voting process to validate injustice and even authorize atrocity. The *Iliad*, *Ajax*, and *Hecuba* all suggest that the transition from violent conflict to nonviolent, constructive group deliberation and decision making requires the ability to control one's own capacity for violent rage, and the wisdom to condemn the violent rage of others.

But that is only the beginning, and this book introduces essential next steps. Homer and the tragic playwrights all emphasize a direct causal relationship between an individual's priorities and skills and the survival and success of that individual and his or her community. The *Iliad, Odyssey, Oresteia,* and *Antigone* equip us to recognize and reject corrupt and incompetent leadership, to oppose the tyranny of the majority, and to resist the increasing use of violence and intimidation in the political process. Cultivating rational judgment and challenging unfounded certainties, they urge us to distinguish fact from fiction and good leadership from bad. In its effort to obliterate the concept of objective truth, tyranny strikes at the heart of democratic politics. If we cannot agree on factual evidence, then democratic debate and creative compromise cannot begin, let alone succeed. Ancient Greek epics and tragedies, however, offer antidotes to rapacious leadership and magical thinking by promoting empathy, fact-based logical deduction, and reasoned argument. Homer, Aeschylus, and Sophocles identify ethical and intellectual abilities crucial to egalitarian, compassionate, and constructive decision making in any society. They expose the destructiveness of tyranny and can help us to defeat it.

CHAPTER 1

LEADERSHIP (*ILIAD* 1–2)

Imagine yourself among the first people ever to hear tales of the Trojan War and the noble warriors who fought and died at Troy. Or maybe imagine yourself hearing these often-repeated tales hundreds of years later, but still long, long ago, long before smartphones and laptops and even long before books existed.

You are seated at a fine banquet and have eaten and drunk your fill. Conversation now ceases, as a singer steps forward. Accompanying himself on a lyre, a stringed instrument, he begins to sing tales of the Trojan War, a long-ago conflict well known to you, your father, your father's father, and his father too.

The singer is recounting the siege of Troy. A vast army of warriors, gathered from all over Greece, has been trying to recover Helen, stolen from Greece by the Trojan prince Paris. Warrior-kings each command their own bands of fighters, but all have agreed that Agamemnon is in charge of the entire Greek fighting force. It is now the tenth year of the siege, and King Agamemnon has quarreled with the warrior-king Achilles. Achilles is furious because Agamemnon took for himself a captive girl formerly allotted to Achilles as a prize for his great achievements in the war.

Achilles is the Greeks' very best fighter, but he is enraged now and has withdrawn from battle. He is refusing to defend his own allies. In his anger, he nearly killed Agamemnon, but the goddess Athena reminded him that he'd win greater prizes later if he restrained himself now. As a favor to Achilles's divine mother, a sea nymph, Zeus, king of the gods on Olympus, has agreed to Achilles's request to let the Greeks' enemies, the Trojans, prevail in battle for a while. Achilles wants the Greeks to see how vulnerable they are without his superior fighting abilities.

The singer's tale draws you in, making you feel present among the Greek warriors encamped on the shores of Troy. You are about to witness King Agamemnon's ineptitude firsthand.

It is the night following the quarrel between Agamemnon and Achilles. Agamemnon sleeps restlessly in his shelter, lying upon close-woven blankets. Suddenly, you alone see something marvelous: beside Agamemnon's head stands a dream figure, sent by Zeus, in the shape of the aged warrior and counselor Nestor, whom Agamemnon trusts and reveres. "Do you sleep?" the dream-Nestor asks Agamemnon. "A man with the burden of making plans, and the trust of his people, and so many cares should not sleep the whole night long. Quick, listen to me. I am Zeus's messenger. Zeus cares for you and pities you. He orders you to arm the Greeks as fast as you can, because today you could seize the city of Troy. All of the gods on Olympus have now agreed to let you win. Zeus is about to send terrible sufferings to the Trojans. But you—this is important: don't forget all of this once you awaken from sweet sleep."

Agamemnon wakes up certain that today is the day that he will capture Troy! *The narrator tells you that this dream is a trick, sent by Zeus to deceive Agamemnon, and you recently heard Zeus say that he plans to give greater honor to Achilles by destroying many Greeks. You know that Agamemnon is being duped.*

Agamemnon leaps up from his blankets. He dresses quickly, putting on his short tunic and throwing his long cloak over his shoulders. He straps beautiful sandals on his feet and slings his sword belt across his shoulders. Finally, he seizes his scepter, symbol of his acknowledged authority.

Standing beside the Greeks' ships, Agamemnon orders the heralds to call an assembly. The men are present in an instant. But first Agamemnon addresses only a council of high-minded elder warriors. He tells them his dream, remembering it word for word: the dream figure looking like Nestor, the command from Zeus to arm the men for battle, the promise that the gods are in unison, that today is the day the Greeks can capture Troy.

Clearly, Agamemnon hasn't forgotten the dream. But wait; what is he saying now? He's going to arm the Greeks, as the dream figure commanded, but first he's telling his council of elder warriors that he plans to test all of the other Greek fighters. He's going to tell them to flee from Troy, and then he'll see what they decide to do. Will they run away home or choose to remain in Troy and fight? *But why would they stay if their king tells them to flee? You wonder what exactly Agamemnon expects to "test" or prove by this tactic.*

Agamemnon's plan strikes you as strange, but the elderly counselor Nestor agrees to it because, he says, Agamemnon is not just anybody. He's the one who claims to be *aristos* (best) of the Greeks. If some other man had described such a dream, all would think it a lie. *Nestor, famed for wisdom though he is, does not question Agamemnon's bizarre decision to test his warriors' commitment to staying and fighting and capturing Troy.*

As the meeting concludes, the elders return to the other warriors, who swarm about them like bees hovering in throngs around flowers. When the warriors have assembled in order, Agamemnon addresses them, gripping his scepter. This scepter has a long history, and you get to hear its story before you hear Agamemnon speak. The god Hephaestus made it and gave it to Zeus, who gave it to Hermes, the messenger god. Hermes gave the scepter to Agamemnon's grandfather, who gave it to Agamemnon's father. Dying, Agamemnon's father gave it to Agamemnon's uncle, and he, dying in his turn, gave it to Agamemnon. *The scepter's long history reminds you that inherited power is no guarantee of sensible leadership, because now you see Agamemnon leaning upon this same scepter, the symbol of his inherited authority, as he implements his idiotic plan.*

"My own warriors, my friends, attendants of the war god Ares," Agamemnon begins grandly. "Zeus is harsh. He once promised me that I would capture Troy and then sail safely home. But now he orders me to return home in defeat and dishonor. It really is shameful: although we greatly outnumber the Trojans, we've been fighting them for nine years without success. Our ships are rotting, and our wives and children wait for us at home. Let's flee with our ships to our dear homeland. We will never capture Troy."

Agamemnon has scarcely finished speaking but the men are already in motion, roiling and shaking as a mass, like wind-whipped waves on the sea, or like fields of grain swept by the tumultuous west wind. The warriors are all racing to the ships, shouting to one another as they run. Agamemnon looks dismayed. His test has backfired. Did he expect his warriors to reassert their commitment to continuing the siege? Instead, they are dragging the ships down to the sea and readying them for the voyage home. *But how can this be? You know that the Greeks eventually sacked Troy. They can't have fled. Something is going terribly wrong.*

Suddenly, you are surprised to see two goddesses conversing. Hera is protesting to Athena that the Greeks are going to accomplish something "beyond fate." She means something that fate cannot or will not permit. They are going to sail safely home, leaving Helen to the Trojans and Troy unconquered. But of course this cannot happen. "Go now," Hera urges Athena. "Go among the people of the bronze-clad Greeks. With your kindly words, restrain each man, and do not allow him to drag the curved ships to the sea."

Without hesitating, gleaming-eyed Athena speeds down from the crests of Olympus and lands lightly near the Greeks' swift ships. She first approaches the wise Greek warrior Odysseus. He stands beside his ship but hasn't touched it. *Unlike the other warriors, Odysseus appears to want to remain and sack Troy.*

You alone see Athena address Odysseus. It isn't clear that he sees her, but he recognizes her voice. "Crafty Odysseus, are you going to jump into your ships and run away home?" she asks. "Will you leave Helen in Troy for the Trojans to boast about? Helen, for whose sake so many Greeks have died here in Troy so far from their own homeland?

"Go now," Athena continues, repeating to Odysseus Hera's command. "Go among the people of the Greeks. Don't withdraw any longer. With your kindly words, restrain each man, and do not allow him to drag the curved ships to the sea."

Odysseus instantly obeys. Tossing off his cloak, he sprints down the beach. Wordlessly, he grabs the immortal scepter from the inept king's hands. *Agamemnon just lets it go. Maybe he understands that he has lost control of his warriors?* Holding the scepter, symbol of Agamemnon's kingly power, Odysseus runs from ship to ship, man to man. Whenever he meets a king, or a preeminent fighter, he speaks softly and reasons with the man. He tries to restrain him with kindly words, as Athena instructed. "It isn't seemly for you to be frightened like a coward," he reminds the man politely. "But sit still and bid the others to sit quiet. For you do not yet know clearly what Agamemnon intends. Now he's testing the men, but soon he will smite them. Didn't we all hear what he said in council? He's hot-tempered. Let's not anger him, lest he harm his own people. For kings who are nurtured by Zeus have great passions. Agamemnon's honor comes from Zeus, and all-knowing Zeus loves him."

You see that Odysseus is following Athena's instructions, employing kindly words and reasoned argument to restrain kings and preeminent men. Athena did not specifically advise using reason; but that, of course, is her special province as the goddess of wisdom. Gently, politely, Odysseus is explaining to noblemen that a coward fears battle but a sensible man trusts the intentions of a powerful king and prudently fears his passions.

But whenever Odysseus sees some man of the *demos* (people), and finds him shouting, you notice that he does something very different. Lifting the scepter, he strikes the man with it and issues a sharp command. "Sit still without moving and heed the word of others who are better than you. You are unwarlike and completely lacking martial valor. You are never of any account in war or in council. We cannot all be kings here. The sovereignty of many is not a good thing. Let one man be ruler: one king, to whom Zeus has given the scepter and the power of judgment, so that he can make deliberations."

For men of the people, Odysseus uses not kindly, reasoned arguments but instead blows and harsh criticism. Just brute force and intimidation. And a flat assertion that there should be one king only. *If your own society is similarly hierarchical, Odysseus's treatment of eminent men one way and ordinary men another will seem perfectly comprehensible to you. But you will still notice that in his harsh treatment of the men of the* demos, *the ordinary or lowborn men, Odysseus is interpreting Athena's explicit instructions—to restrain each man with kindly words—rather freely. You might also find yourself reflecting that Agamemnon is an extremely poor poster boy for Odysseus's commendation of the one-king principle. No one seems to question how Agamemnon came to be in charge, but now maybe you are questioning it.*

But you also see that Odysseus's efforts succeed. He proceeds through the army, recalling the men to order. And now the men are rushing away from their ships and shelters and back into the assembly. The sound is like the roaring of a wave in the resounding sea when it hits the mighty shore, and the sea thunders.

All the men sit obediently in silence, except for one. Thersites, unable to restrain himself, continues shouting. This man's thoughts are disordered, the narrator explains. He always speaks rashly and improperly. He likes to quarrel with kings, likes to say whatever he thinks the other men will find funny. Bow-legged and lame, Thersites is the ugliest man among them all. His shoulders are hunched, and the hair on his pointy head is clumpy and sparse. Odysseus and Achilles hate Thersites the most, because he is always criticizing them. But now he is railing at Agamemnon. His shouting angers all of the men. Inadvertently, he directs their anger not toward Agamemnon but toward himself. But still he keeps on screaming at Agamemnon. "What do you want now?" he cries. "Your shelter is filled with the best of the plunder and the best of the women we've captured. We give you your share first, whenever we sack some town or citadel. Do you want more gold? Some other beautiful young woman for your exclusive use? It is not seemly for one who is the leader to bring the sons of the Greeks into troubles." *You understand that Thersites is thinking about the quarrel Agamemnon caused earlier by deciding to take away Achilles's prize girl and keep her for himself. Everyone witnessed this. You know that Thersites is making perfectly valid accusations. The other warriors must realize this, too.*

"Oh, you weaklings," Thersites continues, addressing the men now. "You cowards. You are women, not men. Let's sail homeward with our ships, and let's leave this man here in Troy to brood over his honor-prizes, so that he may see whether we have been helping him or not. Agamemnon has dishonored Achilles, a man better than himself by far. Seizing Achilles's prize, depriving Achilles, Agamemnon holds the girl himself. Good thing Achilles isn't very angry," Thersites continues with exaggerated sarcasm. *You and the men have all witnessed Achilles's fury. You know that he has withdrawn from the fighting and rages still against Agamemnon.* "Yes, Achilles just lets it go," Thersites persists, turning now to glare at Agamemnon. "For if he didn't, this would be the last time you treated anyone so outrageously."

Thersites keeps ranting at Agamemnon, "shepherd of the people." *The narrator's use of this standard descriptor for Agamemnon strikes you as oddly inappropriate in this context, since Agamemnon does not seem to care for the welfare of his "flock" of warriors as a shepherd would his flock of sheep.* Suddenly, Odysseus appears beside Thersites and yells at him angrily, "You are a fluid speaker, but you babble endlessly! Restrain yourself. Don't think that you, one man alone, can quarrel with kings. There is no man worse than you, of all of us who have come here together with Agamemnon below the walls of Troy."

Odysseus's eyes burn into Thersites as he continues. "Therefore, you should not harangue and reproach kings. Our homecoming is not your responsibility. We don't yet know how our efforts will turn out or whether we will make it home well or badly. But you sit here now criticizing Agamemnon, shepherd of the people, because the Greek warriors give him many prizes for success in battle. And you hurl abuses." Odysseus's tone becomes deadly. "I'll tell you something. Here's what will happen. If ever again I encounter you speaking foolishly as you are now, may my head no longer remain upon my shoulders, may I no longer be called the father of my son, if I don't strip from you your cloak and tunic which hide your nakedness, and strike you from the assembly with shameful blows, sending you weeping to the swift ships."

Not stopping at threats, Odysseus raises the scepter and strikes Thersites hard on his upper back and shoulders. Thersites just folds up. Warm tears fall from his eyes. A bloody welt from the golden scepter starts up on his back. He sits down now, frightened. Grieving, he looks around helplessly, wiping away tears from his cheeks.

But what do the other men do? They laugh, of course. They are distressed for Thersites, but still the laughter is sweet. Looking at others nearby, each man says, "Oh, indeed, Odysseus has done countless noble deeds, introducing good plans and conducting the war, but this is the best thing by far that he has done. He keeps this word-slinging scoundrel out of the assembly. Surely now the haughty passion of Thersites will not again impel him to quarrel with kings using reproachful words." That is how the men all speak, laughing.

Not long before this, just after the quarrel between the mortals Agamemnon and Achilles, you heard the singer tell of an assembly of the gods on Mount Olympus and a quarrel between the gods Zeus and Hera. How different the divine quarrel is from mortal ones! Hera hates the Trojans, and she doesn't want Zeus to grant Achilles's request and allow the Trojans to kill a

LEADERSHIP (ILIAD 1–2)   21

lot of Greeks. But Zeus just tells her to shut up. And that's it. Hera sulks, but no one cares, least of all Zeus. His power is eternal and absolute. You see that Hera can't challenge Zeus's authority in the way that Achilles or even Thersites challenges Agamemnon's. The divine assembly ends with the gods feasting happily together, and Hera and Zeus going to bed together. There's laughter, too, in the divine assembly as in the human one, and it's similarly unkind. The gods laugh at the limping god Hephaestus as he bustles about among them. But no one seems to mind. Not even Hephaestus.

It's late, and the singer must be tired, because he stops now. Perhaps you've heard this tale before, of Odysseus taking charge for a time during the siege of Troy, ordering the Greek warriors back into assembly, and then silencing the outspoken Thersites. You've likely known for a long time the events stemming from the decisions of all of these men. Hearing this piece of an often-told tale this evening, you feel as if you have dipped briefly into a great river that has long been flowing and will continue to flow steadily for eternity.

You probably know that the quarrel between Achilles and Agamemnon will cause terrible suffering for the Greeks. You can't understand what Agamemnon thought he might achieve by "testing" his warriors and misrepresenting the dream he had from Zeus. If he expected the men to show a superhuman commitment to continuing the siege, their courage undiminished even though they must now fight Trojans without Achilles's help, then Agamemnon was sadly mistaken. Brought back to order by Odysseus, the Greeks will remain and fight. But without their best warrior to defend them, many Greeks will be killed by the Trojans, as Achilles wished. He wanted Agamemnon and all of the Greeks to realize what a mistake it was to dishonor him, but one of the slain Greeks will be Achilles's best friend. That's not an outcome Achilles would have wanted.

The warriors seem happy to watch Odysseus silence the loud-mouthed, low-born Thersites. But like you, the epic's audience, they surely know that everything Thersites is saying is true. Agamemnon does seem impulsive, selfish, and reckless, as Thersites claims. You probably know that the Greeks will eventually destroy Troy and recover Helen, but many will die in the process and many more will die afterward during their homeward voyage. Even the leading men will fare badly: Achilles will die during the siege. Odysseus will wander and suffer for a decade afterward. Agamemnon will make it home to his own kingdom, only to be murdered *immediately by a man who has seduced his wife and usurped royal power while Agamemnon was away fighting at Troy. By honoring men like Achilles, Odysseus, and Agamemnon and allowing them to make decisions for them, by laughing at the one man willing to speak the truth, these warriors do not seem to be acting in their own best interests. But what else would you imagine they could do?*

POOR PRIORITIES AND
COUNTERPRODUCTIVE COMPETITION

In these early scenes from the *Iliad*, the characters remain oblivious to the problem, but the audience sees it clearly: the *Iliad* depicts a community with a power structure and a set of priorities that simply do not function to the benefit of anyone. Even the chief men of this warrior society, by adhering to its principles, end up hurting themselves and the people over whom they rule.[1]

The *Iliad* enables the audience to judge the characters' statements and actions more objectively than the characters themselves can. Consisting of third-person narrative interspersed with statements and speeches of various characters (young, old, male, female, mortal, and divine), the epic gives its audience, ancient or modern, a broader perspective than the characters within the tale have. Unlike the audience, Greek warriors do not see the scenes within the city of Troy, and Trojans do not see the scenes within the Greek encampment. No mortal characters are privy to the scenes among the gods on Olympus. Access to all of these scenes permits the audience to see that the human characters' priorities and behaviors produce deadly conflicts and provide inadequate tools for resolving them.[2]

Set in the tenth year of the Trojan War, the *Iliad* focuses on other conflicts within that larger confrontation. The quarrel between Agamemnon and Achilles launches the story, and the quarrel's devastating consequences will play out as the epic proceeds. The opening scenes begin to suggest that the central problem is not simply Agamemnon or Achilles as individuals, but a hierarchical value system that pits powerful, ambitious men in competition against one another, each pursuing his own interests at the expense of, rather than for the benefit of, everyone else in the community. Such a hierarchical and destructively competitive power structure would have been as familiar to the epic's earliest audiences in archaic times (eighth to sixth centuries BCE and earlier) as it is for us in the twenty-first century CE.

Agamemnon holds nominal authority over the Greeks, but he proves inept as a leader, provoking conflict and alienating his army's best fighter. Achilles feels wronged, but his decision to opt out of the war will bring harm to his own people. Odysseus forcibly restores order, but he applies his methods unfairly, and his behavior is harsh and even thuggish at times. He brutally silences a man who everyone knows is speaking the truth. The characters within the epic find Thersites's behavior objectionable and ignore the truth of his words, but the external audience of the epic sees clearly that Thersites speaks the truth. Viewing Agamemnon, Achilles, and Odysseus in action, we begin to wonder what constitutes "good" leadership, as no doubt Homer's earliest audiences must have wondered, too. What should the community seek in a good leader?

If a king is understood to be a god or to have been appointed by a god, this question cannot be asked. But, most crucially, the ancient Greeks never considered their kings or rulers to be divinities. They knew that even a king was fully mortal, vulnerable to injury, illness, and death. Yes, Agamemnon inherited his authority from his ancestors and, originally, from the gods. His scepter symbolizes this. But nevertheless he, like any other man, is not infallible. He is capable of great achievements and also spectacular failures, wise decisions and stupid ones, just like anyone else. And other warriors can challenge his authority, as Achilles does in attempting to prevent him from taking his prize and, subsequently, in choosing to withdraw from battle. Even the lowborn Thersites can criticize the king, though he suffers for his audacity.[3]

Instead of depicting mortal rulers as divinities, these tales expose the contrasts between divine and human political authority. The *Iliad* shows that an autocratic power structure works just fine among gods, because divinities live forever and Zeus's authority remains eternally secure. On Olympus, dissent has no adverse consequences for the gods.[4] Unlike Agamemnon's mortal power, Zeus's divine authority cannot be challenged. Hera can criticize her husband without incurring harm or creating problems for the other gods. Zeus's autocratic authority remains absolute and preserves the stability and harmony of the divine community (*Il.* 1. 533–611).[5]

By contrast, among human beings, autocratic political authority, hierarchical relationships, and the resulting competition for power and status constitute not the solution but the problem. Although not nearly as absolutely autocratic as the gods' society on Mount Olympus, the warriors' society in the mortal realm shares similar hierarchical features. A few prominent men command hundreds of others, with Agamemnon at their head. A clear divide exists between wellborn, wealthy noblemen and lowborn, ordinary fighters. We witness Odysseus's method of marshalling the Greeks back into a second assembly (after Agamemnon unintentionally motivates them to rush back to their ships): Odysseus reasons with kings and men of influence (*Il.* 2. 188–97), but he beats men of the *demos* (people; *Il.* 2. 198–206). No equal treatment or egalitarian ethos here.

These warriors' values are not egalitarian but *aristocratic*, since each warrior seeks *kratos* (power) by being *aristos* (best). All define "bestness" as successfully protecting friends and harming enemies.[6] Valuing honor and eager to avenge wrongs done them, these warriors all assume that how other people see you and feel about you matters most.[7] (Arguably, this primitive conception of identity has resurfaced in our own times as a consequence of digital social media.) The *Iliad* proceeds, however, to call into question the characters' conception of honor and their definition of deeds deserving of honor.

This society's autocratic power structure and its entrenched political and social hierarchy cause bitter conflict and terrible suffering for the human characters within the story. Despite opposition from highborn and lowborn alike, Agamemnon has the authority to do as he pleases. His decision to appropriate Achilles's prize provokes the devastating rage of his community's best warrior. Reprehensibly, no one within this tale objects to men treating women as property, but even the epic's earliest archaic and classical audiences, accustomed to objectifying and dehumanizing women, could see that Agamemnon's deep insecurity and myopic rapacity will have catastrophic consequences for the people he leads.

The warriors within the epic seek honor won in battle, the prizes that symbolize it, and the satisfactions of revenge, but as the *Iliad* proceeds, the audience will discover that these values achieve little that is constructive or desirable. Anger at the insult to his honor makes Achilles withdraw from battle. His absence from the fighting causes the death of many Greek warriors, as Achilles had wanted; but the dead also include Achilles's dearest friend. Although the *Iliad* emerged in a culture steeped in these ancient, traditional ideals of honor and vengeance, it is also already exposing the consequences of its characters' traditional certainties: deadly personal quarrels and even brutal war for stupid reasons, torrents of blood pointlessly shed, unspeakable human suffering, and inadequate leaders who care only about their own honor and not the community's welfare.[8]

Autocratic human authority not only promotes conflict among human beings, but also appears to limit human leaders' access to diverse opinions and truthful discourse. In divine assemblies, speech is perhaps free but inconsequential. Objections to Zeus's authority have no real significance and little effect on the gods. Nor does divine dissent provide Zeus with any information he might need to know. In assemblies of human warriors, by contrast, violence and intimidation limit human leaders' access to the truth.[9] The lowborn warrior, criticizing Agamemnon's greed and his insult to Achilles, accurately describes the king's offenses exactly as the epic's external audience and the warriors within the tale have witnessed them and as Achilles experienced them (*Il.* 2.212–42). Odysseus, in silencing this man with verbal abuse, threats, and blows, reminds us that powerful individuals in a fiercely competitive and hierarchical society do not generally welcome or tolerate criticism and consequently fail to benefit from it.[10]

The stories in the *Iliad* predate by many hundreds, perhaps thousands, of years the Athenians' unprecedented experiment in democratic government in the fifth century BCE. Democracy was not even a concept when tales of the Trojan War began to circulate (and we don't know when that was). And yet the *Iliad* begins by exposing the deficiencies of autocratic leadership and the destructive consequences of the ruthless pursuit of honor in a hierarchical power structure.

CRUELTY AS A MARKER OF TYRANNY AND STUPIDITY

In their treatment of Thersites, Agamemnon and Odysseus suppress accurate information but preserve their own status and authority, and the
warriors subordinate to them appear compliant and complicit. It is always
risky to speak truth to power, but this particular critic, the lowborn, loud-
mouthed, foolish Thersites, has to learn the hard way that he himself is not
in a position to criticize the king's authority. Thersites's ugliness and lack
of self-restraint indicate his physical inferiority and lower social status (*Il.*
2.216–19). In this hierarchical society, only someone as powerful as Achilles can challenge Agamemnon and get away with it, not some ugly, low-
status weakling. Odysseus preserves the hierarchy using threats and blows
to put the transgressor back in his place (*Il.* 2.270). Far from objecting
to this brutal suppression of the truth, the other warriors laugh heartily.

Such laughter at the infirmity or misery of another person or living
creature characterizes and solidifies unequal power relationships, not only
then but also now. In the divine gathering on Mount Olympus, the gods'
laughter at Hephaestus's lameness affirms Zeus' authority and reinforces
the unity of the group. Similarly, the laughter of the mortal warriors, seeing Thersites beaten, strengthens the mortal power structure. The narrator describes Thersites's physical and emotional pain and observes that the
other men are distressed for him but laugh anyway (*Il.* 2.265–70). There
is no need to assume, anachronistically, that the warriors fail to see Thersites and themselves as members of an oppressed class. No such concept
existed. The warriors' motive for laughter is age-old and simple, prompted
by discomfort, fear, or even relief that Odysseus is not beating them. As in
Homer's world, so too in ours: cruel laughter at the suffering of another
person reinforces a hierarchical political structure. Jeering bystanders, witnessing another's suffering, may experience a transitory pleasure or relief
at their own temporary safety and invulnerability. Tyrants and bullies of all
ages and kinds know that bystanders' cruel laughter affirms a bully's position at the top of the heap. In the twenty-first century as in archaic times,
underlings and sycophants feel compelled to laugh when the brutality or
cruelty of those in power demands that they do.

Juxtaposed with the heartless laughter of gods at Hephaestus's expense, however, the cruel laughter of the human beings witnessing Thersites's pain and subjugation appears thoughtless and foolish.[11] Unlike gods, all mortals are vulnerable to suffering and death, even the most powerful ones among us. The gods can laugh with impunity at the misfortune of others. Human beings can only enjoy a transitory or self-deluding feeling of security. Our circumstances can change in an instant. Even more explicitly than the *Iliad*, the *Odyssey* emphasizes the precariousness of human fortunes and the short-sightedness of cruel laughter at the suffering of another (see chapter 5). Centuries later in the Athenian democracy of the fifth century BCE, some of the tragedies and comedies began to expose the complete irrationality of laughing at another's misfortune.[12] As human beings, we are all vulnerable. That clarity, however, remains hundreds of years in the future for Homer and for the *Iliad*'s original audiences.

But already in the *Iliad*, the warriors' delight, and perhaps their sense of reassurance, in witnessing someone else being beaten and put in his place suggests a logical flaw in their thinking: the lowborn man speaks truth to power, and others subjected to and suffering from that same harmful power structure fail to recognize their own fortunes in his. (By causing Achilles to withdraw from battle, Agamemnon has made all of the Greeks terribly vulnerable to destruction by the Trojans.) The eternal power structure among the gods on Olympus provides no useful model for mortal beings and their inevitably transitory mortal relationships. Unlike inconsequential divine laughter, the warriors' laughter at another's expense, their cruel enjoyment of cruelty, appears emblematic of inadequate political leadership and uncritical, self-destructive complacency.

Emerging hundreds of years before the Athenians developed democratic political institutions, the *Iliad* nevertheless hints that the rejection of tyranny and the establishment and maintenance of a more egalitarian society entails the rejection of cruelty as entertainment. In the twenty-first century, the *Iliad* reminds us that the movement away from tyrannical violence and intimidation requires us to have the capacity to feel others' pain and to recognize the foolishness of enjoying someone else's misery.

The *Iliad* emphasizes that, for human beings, autocratic power is a *problem*. High achievers compete ruthlessly for honor, wealth, and supremacy at the expense of the community's welfare. Truth succumbs to violence and intimidation. Cruelty and bystanders' enjoyment of it constitute the emblem of tyrannical leadership and thoughtless subjection to it.

THE PRACTICAL AND MORAL LIMITS OF DIVINE INTERVENTION

In the *Iliad* and *Odyssey*, kings are not gods, but actual gods do seem to be everywhere, and it is easy to mistake them for the source of the action. The mortal characters often attribute to the gods all responsibility for events, but the narrative exposes their error, permitting the epic's external audience to view divine actions and events in the divine realm that are inaccessible to the epic's mortal characters. The gods interact with one another and with human beings, but the audience witnesses these interactions far more comprehensively and clearly than the mortal characters do. Distancing our perspective from that of the human characters within the story, the narrative persistently reminds us that the gods do not determine the course of events. The gods neither control human behavior nor set an admirable moral example for human beings to emulate. The ancient Greeks may have believed that some or even most things resulted from divine intention or fate, but the Homeric epics encouraged them to focus on those things that did not result from divine actions or fate. Unlike the characters within the epics, the audience comes to see that since many or even most things are not in human control, human beings must therefore turn their attention to human decisions, choices, words, and actions and their consequences—the very things that are within human control.[13]

Far from dictating mortal intentions or decisions, divinities often appear merely as visible manifestations of human motivation and decision-making. During the initial quarrel between Achilles and Agamemnon, Athena, goddess of strategy, reasoning, and skill, embodies or externalizes Achilles's own better judgment. Visible only to Achilles (*Il.* 1.198) and to hearers or readers of this story, Athena intervenes to prevent Achilles from killing Agamemnon (*Il.* 1.206–14). Personifying Achilles's reassessment of his own impulses, Athena advises him that killing Agamemnon is not in his own best interests, because he will gain more prizes later if he restrains his anger now. Similarly, in directly addressing Odysseus later, urging him to persuade the warriors back to the assembly (*ll.* 2.172–82), Athena embodies not only Odysseus's commitment to remaining at Troy but also his distinctive perceptiveness and persuasive abilities. Combined with the narrator's observation that Odysseus is feeling distressed, and that he's standing next to his ship but hasn't touched it (*Il.* 2.169–71), Athena's intervention externalizes this one warrior's reluctance to abandon the siege of Troy and his plan to prevent his allies from doing so. Audible only to Odysseus (and to the epic's external audience), Athena does not determine Odysseus's behavior; she simply makes his thought process visible to people hearing or reading the tale.[14]

The gods personify or externalize not only human motives and thoughts but also the requirements of "fate." For the *Iliad's* characters, the term "fate" refers to immutable constraints of the story, the enduring plot elements framing these tales for centuries. Scholars refer to these fixed narrative features as the "poetic tradition." The ancient Greeks considered them their historical tradition.[15] The Greek warriors' sudden decision to stampede toward their ships would be shocking to anyone familiar with tales of the Trojan War, as ancient Greeks undoubtedly were familiar as far back as the evidence permits us to assume. (I've certainly ruined the suspense for you, if you didn't already know that the Greeks did sack Troy and did recover Helen.) To get the story back on track, the gods must intervene at this point to prevent the Greeks from giving up and sailing home (*ll.* 2.155 ff.). In this instance, divine action might appear to play a determinative or causal role in preventing something from happening that is not in accordance with fate. But, as the ancient Greeks understood it, no tale of the Trojan War could rewrite "history." Everyone knows that Troy did fall. Agamemnon's stupidity and ineptitude cannot make that *not* happen.

In addition to embodying human thought processes and guaranteeing the plot framework, the gods also have their own agendas independent of the needs or wishes of human beings. Anyone familiar with the D'Aulaires' beautiful *Book of Greek Myths*, a children's book, may mistakenly believe that the Greek gods "could do no wrong,"[16] but this claim must entail a very perverse notion of "right" and "wrong." In fact, the powerful gods in the *Iliad* are completely antithetical to modern Judeo-Christian notions of divinity.[17] They are neither infallible nor merciful nor humane. The mortal characters do not realize—but the narrative permits us to see—that the gods' role in human affairs is by no means just. Simply as a favor to Achilles's immortal mother, Zeus agrees to allow Trojans to slaughter numerous Greek fighters (*Il.* 1. 503–30). Unlike the *Iliad*'s mortal characters, the epic's audience witnesses the gods impulsively and indiscriminately inflicting or planning to inflict destruction on groups of people, even entire cities (e.g., *Il.* 1.8–53, 1.370–85, and 4.31–67).

The *Iliad* provides no real moral justification for the gods' preferences and impulses. Hera, for example, never bothers to explain why she hates the Trojans, even when directly asked (*Il.* 4.31–33), She does not need to explain, because the tale was long familiar even to the *Iliad*'s earliest audiences: the Trojan prince Paris insulted Hera. As a young boy, roaming among the hills above Troy one day, Paris encountered, as one might, three beautiful goddesses. Asked to decide which of the three was the most beautiful, Paris selected Aphrodite, goddess of love, choosing her over Hera, Zeus's consort, and also over Athena, goddess of wisdom. This choice, called the Judgment of Paris, earned Paris Aphrodite's love, and the perpetual hatred of Hera and Athena.[18] Hera wants to destroy an entire city because one young prince just wasn't that into her.

Motivated by their own personal whims and preferences, gods in the *Iliad* do not necessarily reward the good behavior or punish the bad behavior of human beings. The connection between human action and divine consequences remains imprecise. Offending a god may reliably earn divine punishment, but even pious worship will not inevitably ensure divine favor. The characters retain confidence in the efficacy of prayer and ritual offerings to the gods, but the audience sees that even an extravagant, elaborate sacrifice advised by a seer cannot guarantee divine favor and assistance (e.g., *Il.* 6.286–311).[19]

The gods' arbitrary and sometimes vicious decisions and actions encourage the epic's external audience, ancient or modern, to realize that human beings must determine what is "good" and what is "bad" not in relation to the interests, desires, moral standards, or moral examples of all-powerful supernatural beings, but in relation to the consequences that any human decision has for themselves and for other human beings.

A MATTER OF CHOICE

Divine behavior provides a counter-model against which to measure the choices of mortal characters. The divinities act despotically, driven by their own whims, unconcerned for the welfare of those in their power and unaccountable to anyone but themselves. By showing the extent and the limits, both practical and moral, of the gods' intervention, the narrative permits the audience to judge the statements, actions, and priorities of human leaders. Gods, impervious to permanent injury and death, need fear no adverse consequences—to themselves—from their own behavior. Mortal decisions, by contrast, have grave mortal consequences. Unlike Zeus, Agamemnon cannot disregard his subordinates' opinions and desires with impunity. By mistreating Achilles and causing his withdrawal from battle, Agamemnon imperils his people and himself. Opting to wield authority as if he were, like a god, impervious to repercussions, a mortal leader appears thoughtless. Mortals who willingly acquiesce to his authority must not be thinking clearly.

Human characters blame the gods for the misery they experience, but the epic permits the audience to see that human choices are far more determinative than divine actions, and their consequences more predictable. The narrative identifies selfish, short-sighted leadership as a substantial source of human suffering.[20] Agamemnon blames Zeus for his problems, claiming, "Zeus has given troubles to me. He strikes me with fruitless strife and quarrels" (*ll.* 2.375–76). But this comes *after* we've seen that Agamemnon's own insecurity, greed, and stupidity, his arbitrary affront to Achilles's honor, is chiefly responsible for the Greeks' current difficulties.[21]

Impulsive and irresponsible, Agamemnon fails to anticipate the predictable consequences of his own bad decisions. Unilaterally, he has the bright idea to "test" the Greeks to see whether they will fight or flee home if given the choice (*ll.* 2.73–75).[22] Lying to the warriors, he misrepresents his dream, complaining, "Zeus won't let us win. Let's run away" (*ll.* 2.110–41). In consequence, the warriors immediately stampede toward their ships (*ll.* 2.142–54). For ten long years, these men have been far from their homes and families, living in rough shelters, fighting and dying in a fruitless effort to recover one stolen woman. Of course they would prefer to go home. The narrative makes it clear to the audience that Zeus did not determine or require Agamemnon's decision to "test" the Greeks' resolve. The mortal characters continue to identify the gods as the primary causal principle, but human principals make one poor decision after another, choices that to the audience appear to be entirely optional.[23]

Witnessing mortal leaders' destructive choices, the audience begins to reevaluate the characters' definitions of honor, political authority, and moral achievement. The Greek warriors within the epic never doubt their decision to punish the Trojans for their misdeeds, but the audience cannot share their certainty. The Greeks appear to have the moral high ground, if moral and high it may be called, of avenging the kidnapping of Helen and the affront to Greek honor. No one within the ancient archaic society depicted in the epic questions the men's treatment of women as property, or their confidence in the moral imperative of vengeance. But as the war continues and the death toll mounts, this story prompts the audience to consider whether Helen's beauty and the decision to avenge her theft really do justify the resulting slaughter and human suffering. Combining detailed descriptions of gruesome hand-to-hand combat with poignant, evocative similes, the narrative emphasizes the colossal waste of young lives in their prime.[24] The human characters' choices appear to promote no one's best interests.

The opening scenes of the *Iliad*, while suggesting that the alternative to established political authority is chaos, nevertheless begin to undermine the traditional ideal of autocratic political order. When a king's poor choices send his own warriors into headlong flight, a powerful man of insight and influence restores order by usurping political authority and grabbing the king's scepter, explicit symbol of hereditary power. In the process, this man articulates the argument for the traditional autocratic rule of kingship.

Restraining the men of the people from their chaotic retreat and beating them away from the ships and back into the assembly, Odysseus insists on the importance of having just one man as ruler (*Il.* 2.203-6). Let there be one ruler, yes—but who? The Greeks' current leader, Agamemnon, has certainly dropped the ball.

Despite Odysseus's explicit validation of autocratic authority and stable political hierarchy among men, both of these things prove detrimental to the human beings in this story. Agamemnon's inherited authority does not make him a good leader of men. Greedy, impulsive, insecure, and incapable of comprehending or caring about the experience of others, Agamemnon epitomizes the despot. Unlike the characters within the epic, the external audience comes to see Zeus's manner of wielding power not as a model to emulate, but as a cautionary example. The immortal Zeus has eternal, absolute control; the mortal Agamemnon does not and cannot. Unable to cope with dissent or to understand human psychology, Agamemnon cannot begin to emulate Zeus's divine authority.[25] His woefully incompetent example suggests that no mortal leader should even try.

By distinguishing the audience's perspective from that of the characters, the *Iliad* begins to cultivate the audience's capacity for moral decision-making. If the gods have their own agenda, and *human* choices and actions produce good or bad outcomes, then what should we mortals honor and strive for? How do we decide what and who is best? Agamemnon, Achilles, and even Odysseus appear unable to promote the well-being of their community. None of the three seems particularly interested in doing so. Agamemnon and Achilles pursue their own honor at the expense of others. Even Odysseus, by preventing the Greek warriors from fleeing homeward, ensures the slaughter of many by the Trojans. At the same time, we also know that the Trojans' leaders, by refusing to return Helen, are guaranteeing their own city's destruction. The behavior of these powerful men prompts the audience to consider, "What qualities do we want in a ruler or powerful leader?" "Which qualities deserve honor?" These questions initiate the rejection of tyranny, and they remain as pressing today as they were three thousand years ago.

Long before anyone had ever heard of or even thought of democracy, the *Iliad*'s opening scenes emphasized that unrestrained and unaccountable autocratic power and immutable socioeconomic hierarchies make human communities vulnerable to the whims and stupidities of their most ruthless, ambitious, and selfish members. We might feel today that we don't need the *Iliad* to point this out to us. But even a casual appraisal of the world's political trajectory in the twenty-first century suggests that we do.

CHAPTER 2

COMMUNITY [*ODYSSEY* 1-4]

Imagine yourself again in a world long before smartphones. You are enjoying another big feast. It's probably at the home of the most powerful man in the community. Maybe that's your father or your uncle. Maybe it's you. This could be a late summer evening. You are reclining comfortably on a soft rug and thick cushions, and you can smell in the air the salt tang from the sea. You have finished eating, but you are still sipping your wine, as a singer begins a new tale.

Accompanying himself on a lyre, the singer starts with a prayer to the goddess of poetic inspiration, asking her to supply the story he is about to tell. This is a story about a man who has been away from home for a very long time. None of his friends or family knows where he is or if he still lives. He fought at Troy for ten years and sacked the city. But since then he has been forced to wander for nearly ten more years. Traveling far and wide, he has seen many different communities and learned a great deal. But he has also suffered terribly on land and sea, striving to return home to Greece with his companions. Ultimately, he couldn't save his companions. They destroyed themselves by their lack of self-restraint. This one man will eventually make it back alone to his home on the island of Ithaca, the singer reassures you. But even there he will struggle and suffer greatly, because Poseidon, god of the sea, hates him.

For now, though, this man, Odysseus, remains stuck in the middle of nowhere. All of the other Greek warriors who survived the war at Troy and the arduous return voyage are already home. The goddess Calypso is keeping

Odysseus against his will on a remote island. She wants him to be her husband and to remain with her forever.

But this story doesn't begin with Odysseus. It starts with an angry complaint made by Zeus, the king of the gods. *Normally, you never overhear conversations between the gods. But the singer's tale enables you to imagine yourself present at an assembly of the gods on Olympus.* Zeus is denouncing human beings for their inability to take responsibility for their own poor choices. He considers it really shameful that human beings blame the gods for their sufferings, when the reality is that mortals bring more suffering on themselves. *Perhaps you have always assumed that the gods control everything? Apparently they do not.* As evidence, Zeus cites the example of the lover of King Agamemnon's wife. When Agamemnon returned victorious from Troy, his wife's lover murdered him. The gods had explicitly warned the murderous lover that Agamemnon's son would soon kill him in revenge. And that is precisely what happened next. Not even the gods' direct warning, Zeus laments, prevented the adulterous usurper from acting so foolishly and self-destructively.

Athena agrees with Zeus that the death of Agamemnon's killer was well-deserved. It's a cautionary lesson to any man. But Athena is troubled about Odysseus, the man stuck on Calypso's island in the middle of the ocean. Calypso keeps trying to persuade him to remain with her and forget his home. But Odysseus desperately wants to return home to Ithaca. He is eager even just to see the smoke rising above the houses. Athena insists that Odysseus is so miserable on Calypso's island that he longs to be dead. She wonders why Zeus is "so incensed" with Odysseus. *Punning on the man's name, using the verb odusaō, meaning both "to hate" and "to be hateful to," Athena makes you notice the oddness of the name Odysseus and its suggestion that the man is both a hater and an object of hate: not a straightforward role model, but a problem.* Athena now asks whether Zeus has forgotten all about Odysseus.

Of course Zeus has not forgotten. But Poseidon hates Odysseus for blinding his son the Cyclops, and is obstructing his return home. (Odysseus became stranded on Calypso's island when his ship was destroyed on the open sea.) Zeus now decides that all of the gods must ensure that Odysseus gets home. Conveniently, Poseidon happens to be away from Olympus on other business, and Zeus points out that Poseidon won't be able to contend alone against all the other gods.

Athena suggests sending the messenger-god Hermes to tell Calypso of the gods' decision. Meanwhile, she herself will go to Ithaca to motivate Odysseus's nearly-grown son to begin searching for his father. She will guide Odysseus's son to the communities of Sparta and Pylos to seek news of his father and begin to earn *kleos* (glory) for himself by having some adventures and achievements of his own. *Apparently Zeus is not simply going to order Calypso to release Odysseus and arrange for a ship to carry him home. For some reason, Athena opts to begin instead with Odysseus's son.*

It's unclear how motivating Odysseus's son to seek news of his father will accelerate Odysseus's return, but the singer proceeds to describe Athena darting down from the high peaks of Olympus. She wears golden sandals and carries the mighty bronze-tipped spear that she uses to subdue brave warriors. Traveling as fast as the wind, Athena lands at the entrance to the courtyard of Odysseus's home on the island of Ithaca. She has magically disguised herself as (or perhaps transformed herself into) Mentes, an old friend of Odysseus who lives far from Ithaca.

Athena-disguised-as-Mentes finds Odysseus's home in chaos. In his absence, many young noblemen of the community have taken over his household. Each is seeking to marry Odysseus's wife, Penelope, and they are all helping themselves unrestrainedly to Odysseus' possessions. Just now, many are playing games in the courtyard, while others recline lazily on skins of Odysseus's cattle, which they've slaughtered and eaten. Servants and slaves hurry about mixing wine, wiping tables, and cutting up meat for the suitors to consume later. (*If you truly lived in the ancient world, you would probably not consider slavery immoral or feel anger at the presence of slaves in this story, as by now in the twenty-first century you must.*)

Odysseus's son Telemachus sits unhappily among these greedy, dissolute men. You calculate that he must be about twenty, since he was born shortly before his father left for Troy. Telemachus knows that if his father were home, he would put an end to the suitors' outrageous behavior. But the suitors greatly outnumber him, and the young man doesn't have the power to make them leave. He just sits, imagining what his father might do if he returned.

Telemachus has never known his father. He must be desperately trying to piece together a coherent picture of Odysseus from the stories he has heard. Seeing Athena disguised as Mentes, Telemachus doesn't recognize the newcomer (he has never met Mentes before), but he does what he knows that a good host is supposed to do. Jumping up, he approaches the disguised goddess, indignant that a stranger has been left to stand so long at the doors. He welcomes his unexpected guest and offers generous hospitality. "Afterward," he says, "you'll tell me why you've come."

While Telemachus prepares to entertain Athena-disguised-as-Mentes, the suitors enter the house. Arrogant and insolent, they eat and drink copiously. When they begin listening to a singer whom they have forced to perform for them, Telemachus takes the opportunity to speak privately to his guest. The music masks his words, so that the suitors cannot hear.

Telemachus explains that in Odysseus's absence these lazy suitors do nothing but eat, drink, and lie around while being entertained by a singer. They are consuming Odysseus's stores of grain, wine, and livestock without permission and with impunity. Odysseus would never allow this, but he probably lies dead somewhere by now. "If he were to come home," Telemachus concludes, "these suitors would wish for nothing so much as to be nimbler on their feet. But who are you? And where are you from? What brings you to Ithaca? Are you a guest-friend of my father's?"

Athena identifies herself as Mentes, a hereditary guest-friend of Odysseus. Telemachus understands that this means that, although Mentes lives far from Ithaca, he and Odysseus have hosted one another in their homes, and their fathers and grandfathers possibly did, too. Consequently, he himself, as Odysseus's son, is Mentes's guest-friend also, as will be his and Mentes's descendants down through the generations.) Athena-as-Mentes claims to have heard that Odysseus is still alive but that he is being held captive somewhere by men who are "harsh" and "ferocious." *You notice Athena's tactful indirection. She knows exactly where Odysseus is, but she seems unwilling to tell his son that he's being detained by a beautiful goddess.* Athena-as-Mentes claims that Odysseus will return soon, since he is very ingenious. "Are you his son?" she asks Telemachus, knowing full well that he is. "You do look a lot like him."

"Well," says Telemachus, "My mother says that I am, but I don't know. No one ever knows his own origin for certain." Telemachus wishes he'd been born to some more fortunate man, a man who might have died at an old age, having remained at home living happily among his own possessions.

When Athena-as-Mentes comments on the suitors' shameful activities, Telemachus assures her that, contrary to present appearances, this house was once wealthy and irreproachable, "while that man was still at home. But now," he continues bitterly, "the gods have simply made him disappear. I wish he had died in Troy. Then he'd have won great *kleos* for himself and for his son. But as it is, the whirlwinds have carried him off ingloriously. He is gone unseen, unheard of, leaving me to suffer and grieve."

Telemachus explains that all of the *aristoi* from Ithaca and the neighboring islands are trying to get his mother, Penelope, to marry them. Penelope continues to string them all along, apparently unable to choose one, if any, to marry. (*Penelope's indecision must infuriate her son.*) Meanwhile, the suitors keep consuming Odysseus's food and wine and creating havoc in his home. The situation is terrible. You feel Telemachus's desperation.

Expressing anger and concern, Athena-as-Mentes wishes for Odysseus's speedy return. She advises Telemachus to call an assembly the following day. He must tell the suitors to return to their own homes. (*Perhaps he always felt too young to do this before.*) If Penelope wants to marry one of the suitors, she should go to her father's house and be married from there. Meanwhile, Telemachus should go in search of news of his father, visiting the aged King Nestor in Pylos and King Menelaus in Sparta. If Telemachus hears that his father still lives, he should wait one more year. But if Odysseus has died, then Telemachus will have to figure out what to do about the suitors himself.

This must be a lot for Telemachus to take in. Maybe he's hopeful, thinking his father might still be alive. But surely he's anxious, too. What if he fails at this first real attempt to do something constructive and bold? Or what if his efforts lead to his father's return and Odysseus turns out to be a disappointment? Telemachus has probably spent his whole life imagining meeting his father. It would be hard for Odysseus to meet the expectations of a son who has had nearly twenty years to create an idealized concept of his father. Worse, what if Telemachus himself proves a disappointment to his father?

Athena-as-Mentes tries to motivate Telemachus by referring to the very same story that you have recently heard the gods discussing on Olympus. Pointing out that Telemachus is no longer a child and should stop acting like one, Athena asks him, "Haven't you heard how much *kleos* Agamemnon's son won by killing his father's murderer?" *You recall that the gods viewed the adulterous murderer's death as evidence of mortals' stupidly blaming the gods for their suffering while actually bringing additional suffering on themselves. Now Athena is holding the man's killer up as a model son who avenged his father's murder. This story evidently has more than one message: Human beings shouldn't blame the gods for self-inflicted suffering, and a good son should avenge his father's death. Telemachus must be wondering whether he's up to the task. But wouldn't it be better to prevent his father's death in the first place?* "Be valiant," Athena tells Odysseus's son, "so that future generations may speak well of you." She departs suddenly. The singer narrating this tale to you says that she "flies away like a bird." *Does she vanish from sight the way a swift-flying bird might? Or does she actually transform herself into a bird? Maybe the singer himself doesn't know.* Telemachus begins to suspect that he has been visited by a divinity. He somehow feels stronger now, and more resolute.

But the singer within this story, the one entertaining the suitors in Odysseus's home, has begun to sing about events occurring after Troy fell. He describes the miserable time the Greeks had in trying to sail home after sacking the city. Athena made the return terribly difficult for them. *It seems that Troy must be very distant from Greece. You imagine terrifying storms, shipwrecks, violent skirmishes with people in distant lands, hunger, exhaustion.*

The singer's tale draws Telemachus's mother downstairs. Seeing Penelope for the first time, you are struck by her extreme beauty and her sadness. In tears, she asks the singer to sing something else. The tale of the Greeks' wretched homecoming reminds her of her absent husband and causes her terrible pain.

Telemachus sternly tells his mother to stop objecting. He insists that Zeus, not the singer, is responsible for the contents of the story. *You see that Telemachus is doing precisely what Zeus complained that mortals do: blaming the gods for human decisions and the resulting consequences. You know that the Greeks chose to sail to Troy to avenge the theft of Helen.* Telemachus further maintains that people like hearing this particular tale, and that many men died trying to return home from Troy, not just Odysseus. Telemachus orders Penelope back upstairs to her weaving work, proclaiming, "The mastery of this household is mine." That's hardly true, of course, but his command shocks Penelope. *Apparently, her son has never addressed her in this way before. It does seem that Athena's words have begun to have an effect on him.*

Now Telemachus speaks strongly to the suitors, too. At an assembly to-morrow, he says, he will tell them to return to their own homes and start consuming their own food stores and livestock instead of his. "If you insist on staying," he continues, trying to sound forceful, "I will pray to Zeus that you all die unavenged within these halls." *As threats go, this one strikes you as somewhat less than intimidating. But still, it's a start.*

Telemachus's sudden boldness surprises the suitors, but they remain un-impressed. He clearly has no control over them. By inheritance, the household is his, but he has no real power. He is trying to assert his authority, but he cannot get rid of the suitors or make them do anything. Still, he does begin to deceive the suitors, telling them that he is now certain that his father will never return. *You alone know that he is lying, that he recognized Athena and believed her.*

Early the next morning, Telemachus dresses, strapping on his sword and his beautiful sandals. Looking quite impressive—like a god, even—he announces an assembly and gathers the suitors. He enters the meeting carrying a bronze spear and accompanied by two swift dogs. The herald hands him the scepter, and Telemachus angrily explains that he has called the assembly because the suitors are destroying his household. He does not have the power to drive them out, but he begs them all to go away and leave him in peace. Enraged and in tears, he throws the scepter to the ground. *Evidently still lacking whatever it is that makes a leader authoritative and able to command respect and obedience, Telemachus does not seem likely to achieve his aim.*

And of course he does not. Instead, the suitors blame Penelope for re-fusing to choose one of them to marry. *You may be surprised to learn that this decision is Penelope's to make.* She has been stalling the suitors for more than three years, claiming that she will not make a choice until she finishes weaving a funeral shroud for Odysseus's father. The suitors have discovered that Penelope weaves during the day but unravels her weaving at night. The shroud is never finished. "As long as she keeps at this," say the suitors, "we will keep right on eating up the household."

Telemachus replies that he cannot force his mother to marry against her will. He repeats his request that the suitors return to their own homes and consume their own food and wine instead of his. "If you insist on staying," he threatens again, using the exact same words as before, "I will pray to Zeus that you all die unavenged within these halls."

At just this moment, Zeus sends an omen: two eagles swoop directly overhead, slash at each other with their claws, and then fly off to the right. A seer interprets this as a clear sign that Odysseus will return. When Odysseus first left home, this same seer had prophesied that Odysseus would return in the twentieth year. And that's now. The seer claims that Odysseus is currently planning to destroy the suitors, and that this will be disastrous for many on Ithaca—the suitors' families, you assume—unless they can figure out how to stop the suitors now. "But let the suitors also stop themselves," the seer advises, "for this is better for them." *You realize that the behavior of these so-called* aristoi *imperils them and the entire community. If Odysseus kills the suitors, their families will have to avenge the deaths of their kin. The conflict would escalate quickly. It appears that the suitors alone have the power—but not the will—to restrain themselves.*

The suitors dismiss Zeus's omen as meaningless. They speak mockingly and disrespectfully to the seer. One says he wishes the seer had died with Odysseus. He threatens the man and continues to insist that Telemachus send his mother back to her own father's house to be courted and married from there. "If Penelope keeps delaying the marriage," he says, "we suitors will continue to consume all of Telemachus's possessions."

Telemachus sees that it is hopeless. The suitors are determined. Words are useless. Telemachus now asks for a swift ship and twenty oarsmen to take him to Pylos and Sparta. He wants to find out if anyone has heard anything about Odysseus. *How powerless Telemachus is! He must ask the suitors to grant him this ship and permission for the journey.*

Suddenly, an elderly man speaks up. He is Mentor, a former companion of Odysseus. Left in charge nearly twenty years ago when Odysseus sailed for Troy, Mentor has grown old. He cannot contend with the suitors. Nevertheless, he speaks forcefully, urging them to grant Telemachus's request. "Why should any king behave with kindness and justice," he asks, "since no one now seems to remember Odysseus?" Recalling that Odysseus was gentle and kind and ruled "like a father," Mentor criticizes the *demos* for not speaking out against the suitors, even though they outnumber the suitors. *You suddenly understand that this assembly includes not only the* aristoi, *but all the men in the community. Mentor implies that the "ordinary" men have an obligation to try to use words to keep the wellborn, powerful ones among them in check.* Arrogant and obnoxious, the suitors insultingly reject Mentor's advice. No one else objects.

Walking alone on the beach afterward, Telemachus prays to Athena for help. She suddenly reappears—this time not as Odysseus's foreign guest-friend Mentes, but in the guise of Mentor. The two names do seem remarkably similar; and in both guises, manifest in human form, the goddess of strategy and cunning advises and assists Telemachus. With the help of Athena-as-Mentor, Telemachus readies a ship with provisions and select oarsmen. The suitors continue to feast and party shamelessly and to mock and insult Telemachus. They claim that he's unlikely to return from this journey. *Are they threatening him?* They joke darkly that this would make their own "labor" so much easier.

Not wanting his mother to worry, Telemachus departs without telling her. Accompanied by Athena-as-Mentor, he leaves in the middle of the night. The black ship slices through the water, running swiftly all night long, driven by a west wind sent by Athena. *You imagine Telemachus's anxiety and excitement. The sharp salt wind on his face must be a refreshing change from the stultifying air of his oppressive and chaotic home. Maybe he squares his shoulders. At last he's finally doing something.*

Arriving in Pylos the following morning, Telemachus finds the entire community on the beach performing an orderly and magnificent sacrifice to Poseidon, ritually killing animals for a feast. *You might reflect, as Telemachus must, that the suitors back home on Ithaca make no such appropriate sacrifices to the gods. They simply kill and eat Odysseus's livestock.*

Athena-as-Mentor advises Telemachus to approach King Nestor directly. Telemachus hesitates. He is young and in awe of questioning an older man, uncertain how these things are done. But, with Athena-as-Mentor leading, Telemachus approaches the king as he presides over the gathering with his sons.

The people of Pylos welcome the newcomers warmly. Nestor's son takes them by the hand and seats them comfortably at the feast. Providing ample food and wine, he urges them to make a prayer and a libation to Poseidon, since this banquet is in his honor. Nestor's son properly serves Athena-as-Mentor first, since s/he appears to be the older of the two visitors.

Only after they finish eating does Nestor ask his guests who they are and why they have come. He wonders whether they are wandering like pirates, bringing evil to others. *Surprisingly, Nestor has offered generous hospitality while still recognizing this as a possibility.*

Emboldened by Athena, Telemachus identifies himself, explaining that he seeks news of his absent father. (From other tales of the Trojan War, you may remember Nestor as an aged Greek warrior and a long-winded storyteller.) Now Nestor relates at length the suffering and losses that he and all of the Greeks endured in Troy. The *aristoi* all died there, Nestor says sadly. It would take too long to recount all the evils they suffered. *Recalling Penelope's grief at hearing tales of the Greeks' difficult homecoming, you begin to see that even for the surviving victors, as for their loved ones, the Trojan War has already become a story not of glorious conquest but of terrible suffering.*

Nestor praises Odysseus's cunning, and claims that he and Odysseus worked together, consistently agreeing in thoughts and feeling. "After we sacked Troy," he says, "Athena caused a terrible quarrel between Agamemnon and his brother Menelaus." *Nestor blames Athena, but you suspect that human choices were responsible, just as in Agamemnon's earlier quarrel with Achilles. You have heard Zeus say that human beings blame the gods but exacerbate their own suffering.* This subsequent quarrel between Agamemnon and Menelaus divided the Greeks. Nestor and his followers headed home, continuing on their journey even after some of the others turned back to rejoin Agamemnon. Nestor made it safely home to Pylos—thanks, he thinks, to a substantial sacrifice to Poseidon.

Nestor has no news of the others, but he asks Telemachus, "Surely you have heard of how Agamemnon's son avenged the murder of his father by slaying his killer?" Exactly as Athena-as-Mentes had done earlier, Nestor reminds Telemachus, "Be valiant, so that someone of the men to come may speak well of you." *This story of Agamemnon's son keeps coming up. Like Athena, Nestor considers this avenging son an admirable role model for Telemachus. You reflect that if Penelope accepts one of her suitors, as Agamemnon's wife accepted another man, then Odysseus's and Telemachus's story could easily repeat that of Agamemnon and his son. How will Odysseus manage to avoid getting killed like Agamemnon?*

Telemachus agrees that the vengeance of Agamemnon's son is a glorious example and something for singers to sing about. He prays that the gods will give him such power to take revenge on the suitors. Doubtful that Odysseus will ever return, he asks Nestor to tell him the story of Agamemnon's sad homecoming.

During King Agamemnon's long absence from Greece while he was away fighting at Troy, Nestor explains, a usurper overcame the queen's initial reluctance and finally led her, willing, to his own house. By the time Agamemnon's brother Menelaus returned home, Agamemnon's son had already avenged his father's murder at the hands of his mother's lover. "One piece of the lesson in all of this for you," Nestor informs Telemachus, "is that you shouldn't stay away from home for too long, lest the suitors consume and divide up everything and leave you with nothing." Nevertheless, Nestor urges Telemachus to visit Menelaus in Sparta. He has returned from Troy only recently, and may have heard something about Odysseus.

For the land journey from Pylos to Sparta, Nestor offers horses and a chariot. He will send his own son along as guide. Ever the generous host, Nestor insists that Telemachus and Athena-as-Mentor spend the night not on their ship but in his house, sleeping comfortably on blankets, lovely rugs, and soft cushions. Claiming to need to return to the ship, Athena-as-Mentor disappears—again, the narrator says, "like a bird." All recognize her now for a goddess, and Nestor utters a fervent prayer. He does not ask for long life, or wealth, or happiness, but for *kleos*, the glory that men bestow on one another by remembrance in epic stories. He asks the same for his children and his wife. *The narrator tells you that Athena hears his prayer, but you are hearing this story now, so you already know that she did. Nestor's kleos survives; singers are still singing of his exploits, even hundreds of years after he must have died.*

In the morning, after a comfortable night and an orderly sacrifice to Athena, organized and presided over by King Nestor, the people divide the meat properly and feast. Telemachus looks splendid, freshly bathed and wearing new clothes. Nestor orders his sons to ready the chariot and horses, and Telemachus sets off for Sparta, accompanied by Nestor's oldest son.

In Sparta, as in Pylos, order, happiness, and hospitality prevail. Once again, Telemachus arrives in the middle of a feast, a wedding feast this time. King Menelaus and his people are celebrating his daughter's marriage. A singer is singing and playing the lyre. There are dancers. Everyone is enjoying the festivities.

One of Menelaus's attendants, seeing the newcomers, goes to tell the king that two visitors have arrived. Menelaus criticizes the man for leaving guests standing by the doors for even an instant. He bids him unyoke their horses and bring the visitors in at once to be entertained.

The horses are unyoked and fed, and Telemachus and Nestor's son are brought inside Menelaus's magnificent home with its lofty roof. The halls glitter with bronze, gold, amber, silver, ivory. The two travelers, now bathed and anointed with oil and dressed in fresh clothes—each in a thick mantle and tunic—receive a hearty welcome and abundant food. "Afterward," Menelaus says, "we'll ask you who you are."

The visitors marvel at Menelaus's gleaming halls and splendid possessions, imagining that the realm of Zeus on Olympus must be like this. But Menelaus points out that no mortal could ever rival Zeus, since Zeus's halls and possessions are immortal.

Menelaus returned in the eighth year after the Greeks sacked Troy, bringing back much plunder, but like Nestor, he too considers his adventures in Troy a source of suffering for himself and for others. Perhaps this is only a backhanded way of boasting about his exploits, but Menelaus maintains, "I wish that I lived in these halls having only a third of these things and that the men were all safe, the ones who perished at that time in wide Troy, far from their homes in Greece." Menelaus says that he grieves the most for Odysseus.

He worked so hard in Troy, and all he got for his efforts was suffering. Odysseus's father, his prudent wife Penelope, and his young son Telemachus must surely be mourning for him now.

Telemachus has not identified himself, but Menelaus appears to have guessed who he is. Hearing his father's name, Telemachus begins to cry. Menelaus wonders whether to say something directly or to wait for Telemachus to speak. *Neither Menelaus nor the singer finds Telemachus's tears unmanly. In the ancient world, strong men cry without stigma. You'll soon encounter Odysseus, a formerly great warrior and king, crying miserably on Calypso's island.*

While Menelaus tries to make up his mind, Helen comes downstairs from her bedroom. *Yes, of course, Helen. The Helen. She is back in Menelaus's halls, none the worse for wear.* Astoundingly beautiful, she looks like a goddess. Helen must have been working at her weaving upstairs, for her attendants now set up a chair for her and arrange her workbasket. *You have probably heard other tales of Helen's time in Troy. As the mistress of the Trojan prince Paris, Helen remained idle, supervising her maids' work but not weaving herself. Now, back home with her husband Menelaus, she has evidently been resurrected as an admirable, industrious wife.*

Helen recognizes Telemachus instantly. "This man looks exactly like the son of Odysseus," she says. Menelaus, claiming to have seen the likeness too, is delighted to entertain Odysseus's son. He speaks at length of his friendship with Odysseus and all that he would have done for him if the gods had permitted Odysseus to return home safely.

Remembering Odysseus, everyone weeps—even Nestor's son, thinking not of Odysseus, whom he never knew, but of his own brother who died in Troy. *The grief of Nestor's son reminds you yet again that many Greeks paid a heavy price for the conquest of Troy: even people who weren't there.*

As in Pylos, this gathering includes a plentiful meal and much wine. Putting into this wine some magical Egyptian substance that causes people to forget their troubles, Helen proceeds to tell the story of how Odysseus once snuck into Troy, disguised as a beggar. Helen alone recognized him. Odysseus managed to carry much important information back to the Greek ships. Taking up the story, Menelaus tells of the trick of the Trojan horse, and Odysseus's ability to keep all the men silent while they hid inside.

The following morning, after a comfortable night on luxurious beds made up specially for Nestor's son and himself, Telemachus tells Menelaus why he has come to Sparta. He describes the chaotic, intolerable situation on Ithaca, and asks whether Menelaus knows what has happened to Odysseus.

Indignant at the suitors' behavior, Menelaus predicts their destruction by Odysseus upon his return. He relates that while returning from Troy, he encountered the immortal sea divinity Proteus, who described in detail the shameful murder of Agamemnon. Proteus urged Menelaus to hurry home, apparently to avenge his brother's murder. "For you might encounter the killer still living," Proteus told him, "or Agamemnon's son may have killed him first." *You know that Agamemnon's son did avenge his father's death. Telemachus knows this, too. King Nestor told him. But this is the fourth time you have heard this same story referred to. How is Odysseus going to avoid ending up like Agamemnon, murdered in his own home?*

After this, Menelaus continues, Proteus told him about Odysseus, who is currently being held against his will by the immortal goddess Calypso.

Abruptly, Telemachus announces that he really enjoys hearing these stories and could sit there for a year listening to Menelaus. But now he must return to his companions waiting for him back in Pylos. He suggests that Menelaus give him a nice guest-gift and send him on his way. *Telemachus seems unconvinced by Menelaus, and awkwardly dismissive in his eagerness to leave, saying essentially: "Great stories, Menelaus, and thanks for dinner, but you know we've really got to get going." Does Telemachus believe Menelaus that a goddess is detaining Odysseus against his will? The whole story seems fantastical. The sea divinity Proteus only answered Menelaus's questions after first attempting to evade capture by transforming himself sequentially into a lion, snake, leopard, boar, water, and a tree. This doesn't strike you as an entirely reliable source. Unlike Telemachus, however, you know that the part about Odysseus, at least, is true. Calypso is detaining Odysseus on her island somewhere in the middle of the ocean. But Telemachus could easily have doubts.*

While Telemachus enjoys another feast with Menelaus and his people in Sparta, the narrator returns you to the great hall of Odysseus on Ithaca, where the suitors continue their reckless partying and their unrestrained gorging on Odysseus's possessions.

The situation is worsening: the suitors are plotting to kill Telemachus on his return. They were shocked to discover that Odysseus's son, as young as he is, was able to sail to Pylos, taking the best young men of the community with him. "Best" here seems to mean that Telemachus was accompanied by other young noblemen. The suitors are now preparing to ambush and kill Telemachus when he returns and his ship reaches the straits between Ithaca and Samos, a neighboring island. *Will the suitors' plot succeed? You won't find out for quite a while.*

MORTAL POLITICAL AUTHORITY AND SELF-RESTRAINT

In 2011, when numerous despotic regimes began to collapse, many people, including influential politicians and pundits, seemed confident that democratic institutions would somehow instantly replace ousted brutal dictators and tyrants. But democracy did not, in fact, spontaneously emerge in most former dictatorships. And anyone who had read the *Odyssey* should not have been surprised. The situation on Ithaca in the absence of its king illustrates the consequences of abruptly removing an autocrat. Not democratic political order but chaos results. To avoid chaos, the *Odyssey* suggests, a human community needs some form of mortal political authority capable of establishing and maintaining order. In ignoring this warning, we have to keep relearning that lesson the hard way.

If you are looking for advice on how to eradicate tyranny and create a harmonious, successful society, you might make a note of this: Simply remove a king or a tyrant and the result will very likely be disorder and misery. For everyone. Some form of stable political authority is a necessary (though not sufficient) criterion for the creation and preservation of a desirable human community. We ourselves have only to look at recent political developments around the world for confirmation that this is so. Hindsight is 20/20, as they say, but the Greeks' political development *begins* with this insight more than two thousand years ago.

Even more remarkable, the *Odyssey* is already beginning to undermine the legitimacy of unfettered and unaccountable autocratic authority by suggesting that the powerful *have an obligation* to the people subject to their power. In the archaic world of Homer's characters and earliest audiences, "political authority" meant a king, or perhaps a small group of powerful elites, since democracy did not yet exist even as an idea. Nevertheless, the *Odyssey* defines a "good" king as a ruler who makes life better rather than worse for everyone in the community. Anyone with power, the *Odyssey* suggests, is responsible for the quality of life of everyone subject to it. Despotism in every form, whether a consequence of rule by the one, the few, or the many, fails to meet this criterion defined by the *Odyssey* from the outset as essential to admirable political authority.

Odysseus desperately wants to return *home*, and the beginning of the *Odyssey*, detailing his son's experiences and adventures, defines for us the features that make "home"—life in a human community—desirable. The opening scenes of the *Odyssey* expose, by negative example, two essential requirements for making communal life preferable to solitude: mortal political authority and self-restraint. Both are conspicuously missing from Odysseus's home while he is away. The *Odyssey* commends monarchical rule but adds a crucial refinement: *desirable* mortal authority requires that the powerful exercise self-restraint, as the noblemen seeking to marry Odysseus's wife manifestly fail to do. In the king's absence, with no one to restrain them, many of the leading young men in Ithaca (108, to be exact) are abusing their power. They have taken over the king's household and are greedily consuming his possessions, seeking to marry his wife while she stalls for time. Neither Penelope nor her son nor anyone in the community can rein in these powerful, gluttonous, destructive young men, least of all the suitors themselves. And yet, Telemachus calls these intruders the *aristoi* (best men) of the community (e.g., *Od.* 1.245 and 2.51), and the narrator calls their two greediest and most obnoxious leaders "best [*aristoi*] by far in excellence [*aretē*]" in comparison to the others (*Od.* 4.629). The father of one of these two later calls all of the suitors "best [*aristous*] by far" of the people of the entire community of Ithaca and its surrounding islands (*Od.* 24.429).

In the *Odyssey*, as in the twenty-first century, high socioeconomic status and general admiration do not by themselves guarantee responsible behavior. With no self-restraint and no one to challenge them, these *aristoi* are behaving despotically. They verbally abuse the wife and son of the absent king, and they violate all decent norms of behavior toward guests, servants, slaves, and others in the community. Heedless of any possible consequences, they are having a grand time, ravaging Odysseus's household, eating and drinking themselves into a stupor, and having sex with Odysseus's slave women. Abusing their inherited status and numerical superiority, the suitors are making life unbearable for everyone.

The suitors' greed and lack of self-restraint, toxic to everyone else's happiness, contrasts with the generosity and kindness of a good mortal ruler capable of fostering an ideal communal life. The absent king Odysseus previously ruled benevolently, presiding with fairness and kindness over a happy, thriving community. He respected his obligations to those under his authority, earning the affection and loyalty of his family, servants, slaves, and subordinates. He treated guests hospitably and made his community flourish. Even Telemachus knows that his father was a popular host (*Od.* 1.176–77) and a kindly king, governing gently "like a father" (*Od.* 2.47). In the assembly, Mentor criticizes everyone's inability to recall and reward Odysseus's just and benevolent rule. Why should any king bother to be fair and thoughtful, Mentor asks, if none of the people Odysseus ruled even bothers now to remember and honor his efforts? (*Od.* 2.230–34). Penelope, too, accuses the suitors of willful ignorance and shameful ingratitude in choosing to ignore their parents' accounts of her husband's generous and impartial authority. "Odysseus never did or said anything unjust," she says, "which is the (usual) *dikē* [custom or way] of kings who are sacred to the gods. One hates one mortal but loves another. But Odysseus never did anything wicked at all to any man."[1] By contrast, she insists, the suitors' passion and shameful deeds are manifest, and they have no gratitude for prior benefits (*Od.* 4.687–95). Despite Odysseus's nearly twenty-year absence, his family, friends, and many servants and slaves remain loyal. Everyone—except the greedy suitors, and the servants and slaves they have seduced or intimidated—longs for Odysseus's return.[2]

Not heredity, affluence, or social status, but conduct distinguishes Odysseus from the suitors. Taken together, his behavior and theirs suggest that human excellence is by no means an automatic consequence of high birth, wealth, and public admiration. Praising Odysseus's surpassing *aretē* (excellence; *Od.* 4.725), Penelope uses the same word the narrator used to describe the suitors (*Od.* 4. 629). *Aretē* seems to denote highest moral status and public esteem, but we can see that the suitors are not behaving admirably. We have not yet met Odysseus for ourselves. Will his conduct, unlike that of the suitors, corroborate his reputation for "excellence"? The question begins to suggest that the qualities of human excellence must be demonstrated, not merely inherited or asserted.

The contrast between the suitors' abuse of their power and Odysseus's prior, responsible use of his also reminds us that, unlike authority in the divine community on Olympus, mortal authority will always face the problem of political succession.[3] The chaos in Odysseus's home and the contentious assembly on Ithaca emphasize that the absolute autocratic order enforced by Zeus on Olympus provides no useful example for a mortal ruler, because it requires *permanence*. When Telemachus, visiting Sparta, admiringly likens King Menelaus's opulent halls and courtyard to the realm of Zeus, Menelaus rejects the analogy, responding, "Indeed, no one of mortals could ever contend with Zeus, for his halls and possessions are immortal (*Od.* 4.78–79). Even if Telemachus could succeed in assuming his father's authority, he will not live forever. His son would face the same challenge. And nothing guarantees that either Telemachus or his descendants could or would replicate Odysseus's restrained, just, and benevolent authority.

No human being could replicate Zeus's perpetual autocratic authority in its methods, either. Zeus remains eternally capable of compelling obedience from other gods not by debate and persuasion, but by tyrannical force and intimidation. By contrast, Telemachus cannot alone dominate the mortal assembly on Ithaca by permanent physical superiority or the threat of force. Emboldened by Athena, he makes a feeble attempt to rein in the suitors, but he lacks the ability to back up his words.

Instead of presenting Zeus's unfettered and unchallenged immortal authority as desirable or attainable, the *Odyssey* suggests that mortal power requires restraint and, even better, self-restraint. In the assembly on Ithaca, the seer recommends that everyone consider how they may restrain the suitors, since their coming destruction by Odysseus will be an evil for many in the community. The seer urges the suitors, in their own interests, to stop themselves (*Od.* 2.161–69). Mentor, too, suggests that members of the community have an obligation to condemn the suitors' abuse of power. He criticizes the *demos* (people) for remaining "speechless" and not restraining the suitors by speaking out against them, even though they outnumber the suitors (*Od.* 2.239–41). The *demos* may be physically outmatched, but both the seer and Mentor identify public condemnation as a potent and restraining moral force. By remaining silent, the members of the community, no less than the suitors, are failing to exercise their own power responsibly.[4]

The beginning of the *Odyssey* (the title meaning "the exploits of Odysseus") thus places the experiences of this one *polutropos* (complicated) man in a broader political and ethical context.[5] The *Odyssey* promises to be an adventure story about one man's travels and travails as he strives to return home following ten years of warfare in a foreign land; but as the story begins, this particular man is quite literally nowhere. The narrator claims, essentially, "Once upon a time there was an intrepid man who traveled far and wide. Here's what was happening where he wasn't." By making Odysseus as absent for us, the audience, as he is for the characters within the tale, the opening of the epic emphasizes the costs of this man's long absence for his family, friends, and community. Anyone eager today to celebrate the fall of tyrants should bear in mind that the absence of autocratic rule makes a human community vulnerable to the depredations of a powerful, unrestrained few. A desirable communal life requires much more than the mere absence of an autocrat.

Unlike divine political order, subject to Zeus's permanent and unassailable authority, mortal political order is inevitably impermanent and contentious. The absence of an accepted mortal political authority results in the complete disruption of communal life and exposes the need for human beings to exercise self-restraint. The inability of the powerful to control themselves hurts everyone. The *demos* fail to object to the behavior of the *aristoi* in their community. And the *aristoi* themselves prove incapable of self-restraint, ignoring the warning of an expert seer that unless they change their grasping and heedless ways their story will not turn out well (*Od.* 2.161–76). Persisting in their headlong rush toward self-destruction, the suitors provide an ominous model for our own twenty-first century political moment, in which the powerful lack self-restraint and the power-less are losing confidence in the ability of mortal political authority, in the form of laws and institutions, to constrain them.

MUTUAL RESPECT AND RECIPROCITY

The political vacuum on Ithaca in the king's absence exposes the need for mortal political authority and suggests that the constructive exercise of human power, whether derived from noble birth or from numerical superiority, requires self-restraint. But the first four books of the *Odyssey* also identify two additional requisites for desirable communal life: mutual respect and a defined set of reciprocal obligations observed among and between everyone in the community, powerful and weak alike.

The negative example of life without a good king on Ithaca frames two examples of life under a good ruler in Pylos and Sparta, where mutual respect and reciprocity prevail. As an admirable, beloved king, Odysseus ensured harmony and happiness within his community. He respected his obligations to his subjects, and they respected theirs to him. His absence produces disorder, conflict, and misery.[6] The suitors see no reason to moderate their behavior; they are too young to remember life in a well-ordered community. Telemachus is too young as well. By accompanying him on his travels, we discover, as he does, the harmony and happiness possible in a stable community governed by a generous king capable of promoting the welfare of everyone.

In both Pylos and Sparta, Telemachus finds kings present in their own palaces, presiding over orderly, flourishing communities. Both kings use their established authority to make their families, subjects, and guests comfortable and happy. Their people, in turn, accept their king's authority and fulfill their obligations to him. King Nestor and King Menelaus are both impeccable hosts. Telemachus arrives in each instance in the middle of a formal ceremony: a sacrifice to Poseidon in Pylos, and a wedding at Sparta (*Od.* 3.4–11 and 4.1–14). In Pylos, the king and his sons are holding an assembly and preparing a feast. Nestor invites Telemachus and his companion, Athena disguised as Mentor, to join in. He offers generous hospitality and information about Odysseus, sending Telemachus off to Sparta the next day guided by one of his own sons (*Od.* 3.31–485). The scene virtually repeats in Sparta: an orderly festival, Menelaus's people feasting, relaxing, enjoying music, dancing (*Od.* 4.1–19), lavish hospitality bestowed on the visitors (*Od.* 4.37–67). As in Pylos, the question of the guests' identities comes up only after they have eaten (*Od.* 3.65–74, 4.94–95, and 116–19). By mentioning Odysseus, Menelaus makes Telemachus cry (*Od.* 4.113–16). But just like Nestor, he is kind and generous.

We may marvel at such unstinting hospitality offered to strangers before their identity has been ascertained, but the archaic system of *xenia* (guest-friendship) exemplifies the ability of mutual respect and reciprocity to promote everyone's self-interest. In Sparta, King Menelaus makes the connection explicit: when one of his attendants wonders whether they should welcome the visitors or send them on their way, Menelaus yells at him and reminds him of the hospitality they themselves have received in times of need (*Od.* 4.25–36). Menelaus's anger may prompt us to recall Telemachus's dismay at seeing the suitors leave the visitor, Athena-disguised-as-Mentes, standing at the door (*Od.* 1.118–20).[7] Menelaus's criticism of his attendant's hesitation overtly connects hospitality with self-interest. You want to be hospitable to strangers *so that* when you are a stranger in a foreign land you, too, will receive hospitality when you need it. In archaic Greece, *xenia* was crucial to a traveler's survival. Since wealth was not easily portable, even wealthy travelers had to rely on the kindness of strangers. The system only worked if everyone knew that it was reciprocal. The fact that Zeus himself was understood to be the guarantor of the system emphasized the predictable consequences of violations.[8]

Telemachus's pleasant experiences in Pylos and Sparta underscore, by contrast, the miserable quality of life available on Ithaca. At the end of book 4, the narrative returns us to the situation on Ithaca and defines a series of oppositions: everything that makes life organized and enjoyable in Pylos and Sparta is completely lacking on Ithaca: orderly religious worship, formal sacrifices and celebrations, music, storytelling, hospitality to visitors.[9] On Ithaca the suitors' avarice, absence of decency, and lack of self-restraint make all of these elements impossible. The political situation in the surrounding community is also completely disordered. No one is in control. The king's son has to sneak away, hoping that the suitors will not notice, and they are plotting to murder him on his return. Without Odysseus and with the suitors in residence, the system of hereditary monarchy cannot function. Telemachus cannot learn firsthand from his father's example, or inherit his father's authority. He cannot ensure comfort and happiness for his people. The situation is so perverted that his very life is in danger.[10]

Again, we must remember that democracy was not yet a concept in the archaic world of Homer's characters and earliest audiences; a good monarch was the best one could hope for. But, crucially, the *Odyssey* defines a "good" monarch as one who promotes respect for reciprocal obligations among all members of the community, including himself. Pylos and Sparta exemplify the autocratic ideal of hereditary kingship. In both communities, the kings' sons can model their own behavior on their father's wise and benevolent conduct, and can expect to inherit their father's position and authority one day. Learning from their conscientious fathers, the kings' sons acquire the skills and obligations of leadership along with their biological inheritance. By fostering mutual respect and reciprocity among everyone in the community, the kings in Pylos and Sparta make life better for everyone.

While reinforcing the ideal of hereditary monarchy, the *Odyssey* nevertheless simultaneously begins to undermine it by suggesting that great power in no way ensures respect for reciprocal obligations. Unlike a good king such as Odysseus, Nestor, or Menelaus, the suitors refuse to respect their obligations to others in the community and fail to encourage others to respect theirs. Lacking any self-restraint, or even self-protective caution, this community's *aristoi* appear in no way worthy of the name. By failing to respect their obligations toward people subject to their power, they are destroying their community and also bringing destruction on themselves.

In our own times we see the powerful among us, individuals and groups large and small, failing to respect their obligations toward the powerless. The *Odyssey* reminds us that such shortsighted selfishness is neither desirable nor sustainable. Like the *demos* on Ithaca, we may feel incapable of interceding. But at the very least, the *Odyssey* cautions us against admiring or emulating such behavior. Our own definition of "best" must not condone it.

INDIVIDUAL HUMAN RESPONSIBILITY
AND ARTISTIC FREEDOM

Although the *Odyssey* depicts mortal and immortal societies consisting of kings and their subjects, it begins, surprisingly, by introducing an essential prerequisite for broad political participation: the recognition that our own decisions and actions largely determine the quality of our lives. The suitors and the people on Ithaca are each making a set of choices, as are the kings and their subjects in Pylos and Sparta. One community is in the process of imploding. The other two appear to be thriving. The contrasts between life on Ithaca on the one hand and life in Pylos and Sparta on the other derive not from divine forces but from individual human ones.

This is a profoundly anti-autocratic insight. Under a divine or human autocrat, we cede choice and responsibility to another being. By accepting responsibility for our own choices and their consequences, however, we begin to delegitimize autocratic authority and to make self-governance a real possibility.

This radical idea that individuals bear responsibility for the quality of their own lives emerged, perhaps, as a consequence of ancient Greek epic poetry's freedom from the commands or expectations of a particular autocrat or divinity. Both epics originated in a hierarchical society characterized by tribal allegiances to kings (whom we might term warlords) and stratified by birth and wealth.[11] Wealthy patrons of epic singers very likely sought to preserve their own status and authority. The archaic world knew nothing of democratic liberties, and yet neither the *Odyssey* nor the *Iliad* begins with an address to a king or to any patron, human or divine. In each, the narrator begins by asking the Muse to relate the tale, but the divine Muse serves only as a source of artistic inspiration.[12]

Rather than owing their existence and form to a single powerful individual or group, the tales comprising the *Iliad* and *Odyssey* were undoubtedly transmitted orally for centuries. Having no fixed written form for many generations, their emphases could shift over time. Oral tradition places certain constraints on the story that no epic singer can change. Odysseus cannot die during the sack of Troy, for example, nor can the Trojans win the war. Sometimes the narrative refers to such required plot elements as "fated" or "according to fate." These traditional plot elements provide a framework for the singer-poet, but they do not preclude variation of details and emphases. Within the constraints of the traditional plot elements, singers had a significant measure of creative freedom until the texts were written down in the mid-sixth century BCE, and therefore no longer continuing to change substantially.[13] Perhaps as a consequence of the texts' fluidity, as compared to the fixed status of stories that *begin* as written texts, neither the *Iliad* nor the *Odyssey* unquestioningly affirms the status quo. Whether or not the Homeric epics were the product of aristocratic intentions and aimed at aristocratic audiences, the gap between the characters' limited understanding and the audience's more comprehensive perspective begins to undermine many aristocratic principles.

Unlike political propaganda designed to promote a particular regime, or a sacred text that affirms religious truths, the ancient epics' independence from external political or religious constraints permitted these stories to challenge traditional ideals and assumptions. Instead of encouraging obedience or fatalism in the audience, the Homeric epics emphasize that human choices and actions greatly determine the quality of human experience.[14] Both epics evoke the audience's critical moral judgment. Both raise troubling questions about traditional autocratic power and its tendency to be abused. [15]

The prominence of gods in both the *Iliad* and the *Odyssey*, however, often makes modern readers mistake divinities for the source of the action. Fate, religion, and the gods all constitute a significant part of the characters' conception of their lives, but in fact the gods do not cause the substance of the events described. Instead, the words and actions of human characters drive the plot, as the *Odyssey* reveals from the outset. This is a story about a specific human being, but the first scene introduces not Odysseus but the gods in council.[16] The narrator explains that Odysseus, having lost his companions while trying to get home after sacking Troy, is being detained alone on a remote island by the goddess Calypso; but Odysseus does not appear until book 5. The epic begins instead with Zeus's complaint that mortals are responsible for their own suffering but blame the gods for it (*Od.* 1.32–34). No mortal characters within the story hear Zeus's observation;

only the other gods do—as do we, the poem's audience. Zeus is reminding us that gods are *not* solely responsible for human fortunes, that human
beings blame gods but in fact bring extra trouble on themselves. As ruler
of gods and men, Zeus would know.[17]

Zeus's insistence on the potency of individual human agency empowers
us against despots by encouraging each of us to take responsibility for our
own life and to opt for what will make it better rather than worse. Zeus's
comment suggests that as human beings we are more autonomous than we
may like to believe. The idea can be uncomfortable. We don't necessarily
like to recognize that our choices and actions have direct, and maybe even
predictable, consequences. It might be easier to cede all decision-making
to some powerful person or supernatural being, but we would have to be
confident that she or he had our best interests at heart. The *Iliad* emphasizes that the gods do not particularly care to promote the welfare of human
beings, and that mortal leaders often prioritize their own interests at the
expense of the people they rule (see chapter 1). The suitors' behavior on
Ithaca corroborates this insight. Zeus's assertion reminds us that we ourselves have greatest responsibility for our own well-being.

Only by accepting responsibility for decisions in our own lives, and by
learning to distinguish good choices from bad, can we begin to craft a desirable existence for ourselves. The *Odyssey* begins by suggesting that a "good"
homecoming and a "good" home are the product of human choices and
priorities.[18] We know in advance that Odysseus will make it home, but the
narrative turns our attention to how and why—not whether—Odysseus
will succeed, what he learns along the way, and what we can learn from
him. Odysseus, Nestor, and Menelaus choose to exercise their authority
constructively, while the suitors do not. References to Agamemnon's disastrous homecoming remind us repeatedly that human choices can determine
outcomes. Odysseus will have to choose differently if he doesn't want to
end up like Agamemnon.

The emphasis on individual human responsibility fortifies us against autocracy and autocratic abuses of power, and it also makes the principle of
hereditary kingship difficult to sustain. Like the *Iliad*, the *Odyssey* reveals
that hereditary power offers no guarantee of good leadership. In the *Iliad*,

Agamemnon's inherited authority proves destructive to himself and to the men who have agreed to accept his leadership (see chapter 1). The *Odyssey* even more explicitly undermines the aristocratic principle of automatically transferring political power from father to son. In the *Odyssey*, a son's claim to legitimate authority turns out to depend not on his father's status but on his own conduct. By birth, Telemachus ought to inherit his father's kingship, but he must first demonstrate that he possesses his father's capacity for authority. And the odds are against him since, as Athena tells him, "Few sons, you know, are equal to their fathers. More are worse, and few are better than their fathers" (*Od.* 2.276–77). Human characters persist in thinking that nobility is a product of inheritance, not conduct (e.g., Menelaus at *Od.* 4.62–64), and Telemachus may resemble his father physically, as Menelaus and Helen observe (*Od.* 4.140–50). During his travels, Telemachus does begin to display the cunning intelligence, eloquence, and thoughtfulness characteristic of his father (e.g., *Od.* 3.124–25 and 4.204–6). But if Athena is correct that few sons are as good as their fathers—and, as the goddess of wisdom, she presumably is—then a political structure based on inherited authority will harm rather than benefit the community. Athena's observation identifies the challenge that Telemachus faces in trying to equal or surpass his excellent father. But it also exposes the regressive force of nepotism, a common feature of despotic rule now as then.

Admirable political authority, the *Odyssey* reminds us, requires taking responsibility and making good choices. To acquire power over his household and restore order to his community, Telemachus cannot simply *be* the king's son; he must *do* something about the greedy, unrestrained, impulse-driven suitors. Now approaching manhood, he must begin to pursue *kleos*, the greatest goal in life, as Homer's characters believe: the glory that consists of tales of one's achievements being eternally retold in epic poetry.[19] By visiting Telemachus in disguise to get him moving, Athena embodies an otherwise invisible event: Telemachus's decision to seek news of his father and begin his own adventures. Athena does not command Telemachus. She decides to "urge [him] on" and to "place fighting strength in his thoughts," so that he can call the suitors into an assembly and "warn them to desist" (*Od.* 1.88–91). She undertakes to "send him to Sparta and sandy

Pylos for the purpose of inquiring about his father's return" and so that he can achieve his own noble *kleos* among men (*Od.* 1.93–95).[20] Pursuing his inquiries, Telemachus is not following orders but acting as a responsible, independent agent.

Artistic freedom, freedom from external religious or political authority, permitted the *Odyssey* to emphasize human responsibility for human experiences and to challenge the traditional aristocratic certainty that power can and must be automatically transferrable from father to son. Autocratic regimes do not generally foster freedom of expression in the arts, literary or otherwise, and they do not encourage independent human decision-making and individual responsibility. Preferring compliant and uncritical subjects, strongmen and despots like to control the narrative. They do not welcome stories critical of their regime. Stories produced at the behest of or in the interests of a religious or political authority leave little room for independent thought, critical moral judgment, or dissent, either for those who transmit the stories or for those who hear or read them. By encouraging only acquiescence, such stories tend to foster our susceptibility to domination by a powerful authority—for good or ill. Autocratic power structures, mortal and divine, may derive from a natural human tendency. They certainly predominate throughout human history. But in the absence of artistic freedom, tyranny flourishes. Sadly, art produced and driven by financial interests can have the same effect, since the profit motive encourages producers to pander to an audience of consumers rather than to cultivate, as the *Odyssey* begins to do, an audience of critical moral thinkers capable of taking responsibility for their own lives.

FARSIGHTED SELF-INTEREST

Irresponsible, grasping, and unaccountable political power remains prevalent in our world while benevolent and conscientious leadership remains rare, but our stories shape our priorities. They can validate greed, impulsiveness, and cruelty, or they can encourage us to value our own long-term self-interest. By providing negative and positive models of mortal authority and its consequences for communal life, the *Odyssey* encouraged the ancient Greeks to exclude tyrannical cruelty and brutality from their conception of good leadership and desirable human relationships. The ancient Greeks themselves exemplified admirable leadership perhaps infrequently in their own conduct, but at the very least their stories enable us to know it when we see it.

Stories identify and affirm a set of shared ideals, and the *Odyssey* explicitly emphasizes the capacity of storytelling to promote a harmonious and desirable community. Telemachus's visits to Pylos and Sparta demonstrate the role of storytelling for memorializing important events and impressive deeds, and for creating bonds among members of a community. Nestor, Menelaus, and Helen all find comfort in sharing tales of their experiences. In turn, Telemachus learns of the exploits of his father and others of his generation. He learns what others consider worth doing and worth valuing—that is, worth memorializing eternally. Stories guide Telemachus in developing and shaping his own priorities so as to pursue the achievements that will earn him *kleos*, the glory of eternal remembrance in poetic song. Helen's and Menelaus's tales of Odysseus emphasize the value of cleverness, deception, and self-restraint (*Od.* 4. 240–58, 269–89).[21] Nestor's and Menelaus's tales also stress the importance of exacting swift revenge in order to preserve one's inheritance (*Od.* 3.193–200, 306–16, and 4.512–47).[22] These are admirable attributes and goals in the nondemocratic world of the characters and the epic's earliest audiences.

And yet, unlike the characters within the epic, the *Odyssey*'s external audience sees that admirable ideals are already evolving. Stories of the Trojan War, substance of the *Iliad* and a great proving ground for human achievements, have already become tales of grief. This war, initiated and pursued for vengeance and restitution, now appears as a source not of magnificent satisfaction but of misery (e.g., *Od.* 3.86–87, 100, 103–17; and 4.93–103, 199–200). Far from glorifying the Greeks' victory over the Trojans, speakers in the *Odyssey* emphasize the terrible sufferings of warfare and its aftermath.

As a preamble to the story of Odysseus, the first four books of the *Odyssey* not only begin to undermine confidence in the desirability of warfare but also pose the timeless political question: What is required to make communal life desirable? For the *Odyssey*'s earliest audiences, the answer was the traditional one: a kind and generous king whom everyone respects and obeys. In the twenty-first century, we know that this is so rare that it is not realistic to desire it. And even the most perfect king does not live forever. Nothing guarantees that his successor will be equally perfect, and it is statistically most unlikely.

The *Odyssey*'s validation of ideal kingship is unsurprising, since the epic emerged hundreds of years before anyone had ever heard or thought of democracy, whereas democratic government offers *us* another model. But a crucial point for us in thinking about the process of defeating despotism is that in the absence of a powerful autocrat, democratic government does not in any way spontaneously happen. In the *Odyssey*, the absence of a legitimate, universally accepted ruler produces anarchy and chaos, not (I have to emphasize this) democracy. This suggests that we cannot assume that you just overthrow a dictator and democracy materializes as a result.

The chaos on Ithaca in the absence of its king even begins to suggest that removing the dictator may have to be not the beginning but the *end* of an orderly transformation of social values.[23] Direct democracy, decision-making by majority vote, makes the community completely dependent on the character and priorities of the majority of its citizens. If the majority of individuals in a community fail to exercise self-restraint, fail to see the need for mutual respect and reciprocity, fail to value artistic freedom, and fail to take responsibility for their own actions, then despotism will flourish regardless of who holds power and what they choose to call their regime.

Encouragingly, the *Odyssey* shows that eradicating tyranny requires no great self-sacrifice but only a clear understanding of self-interest: the ability to recognize that reciprocal, harmonious social relations make life better for everyone. In practice, true selflessness is likely to be rare. The pleasant, well-organized communities in the opening books of the *Odyssey* reveal, however, that a functioning, flourishing communal happiness does not require any extraordinary, selfless altruism. Instead, the primitive system of *xenia* epitomizes a kind of reciprocity in social life that stems from self-interest. Other reciprocal behaviors—politeness, civility, decency, respect, and even kindness, compassion, and generosity—similarly need not derive from selflessness. The model of *xenia* powerfully suggests that reciprocal, harmonious social relations can emerge from a clear understanding of self-interest.[24]

The *Odyssey*, like the *Iliad*, depicts an aristocratic society and characters with aristocratic values, but both epics hold the world of their characters up to reevaluation by the audience. The *Odyssey*, unlike the *Iliad*, concentrates not on warfare but on the requirements for human survival and communal life. What exactly do people need to survive? What sort of community makes life better rather than worse for everyone? Ideally, a fair, egalitarian government provides a structure for continually asking and answering these very questions by *peaceful* rather than violent means. Homer and his original audiences could never have conceived of democratic government, but centuries before any such idea emerged, epic tales began to pose the central questions of communal life and to develop the skills needed to address them.

The *Odyssey* begins by identifying elements required to make life in community more desirable for individuals than life in isolation. These elements include self-restraint, mutual respect for reciprocal obligations, and a general preference for order over chaos. Exemplifying the value of permitting art to flourish unconstrained by the dictates of a political or religious authority, the *Odyssey* suggests that a desirable community becomes possible if we take responsibility for our own actions and their consequences, and if we can develop a farsighted understanding of our own self-interest.

The epic cautions us, as it warned the Greeks centuries ago, to choose our leaders and role models carefully. The divine autocrat relies exclusively on violence and intimidation to produce order. The mortal leader needs better tools. The *Odyssey* reminds us that human authority has the power to promote either communal misery or communal harmony and success. Individual achievement at the expense of everyone else cannot, therefore, define a "good" human leader. This suggests that politicians, celebrities, and financially successful individuals do not deserve our respect, admiration, and emulation because they are good at promoting themselves and their own interests. They do not deserve respect for unrestrained material acquisition and ostentatious consumption. The opening scenes of the *Odyssey* insist that leaders deserve respect, admiration, and emulation for leading well—that is, for fulfilling their obligations and promoting the well-being of everyone in the community.

In contrast to the tyrannical winner-takes-all mentality often visible even in our own contemporary, so-called democratic politics, the *Odyssey* identifies political authority as *responsible* for the quality of life of everyone subject to it. No despotic abuse of power, whether autocratic, oligarchic, or popular, meets this criterion. Throughout history, the failure to define political authority as *a set of obligations toward the governed* has permitted numerous "revolutionary" or "democratic" leaders to substitute their own tyrannical rule for that of ousted tyrannical predecessors. By contrast, the *Odyssey* locates optimal order in the authority of the "best," but defines "best" to include not merely birth, wealth, military might, or even intelligence. By definition, the "best" rulers benefit not themselves alone but the community as a whole. The *Odyssey*'s portrait of communal order and happiness stands as a condemnation of all forms of tyranny. It offers both a challenge and an invitation to every human community.

CHAPTER 3

REALITY (*ODYSSEY* 5-8)

You are enjoying another evening's entertainment at the home of someone wealthy and powerful. Firelight casts flickering shadows on empty platters and baskets. Surrounded by other well-fed dinner guests, you listen as a skilled singer continues the story of the adventures of Odysseus.

The singer invites you to envision the enchanting ideal of an island paradise. Graceful trees and flourishing bushes grow right down to a gleaming beach of pale sand. You picture brightly colored birds on land and sea, thriving grapevines weighted with grape clusters, abundant freshwater springs, and lush green meadows. Even an immortal would admire and enjoy the sight of this marvelous island. An exquisite goddess dwells inside a nearby cave. Cedar smoke from her fireplace permeates the air.

It all seems perfectly idyllic, and yet . . . a solitary man sits weeping on the beach. His back to the lovely island, he stares miserably out at the barren sea.

The messenger god Hermes has just arrived from Olympus with a message from Zeus for Calypso, the goddess within the cave. Seated beside a warm fire, Calypso sings as she works at her weaving. *Although not mortal, Calypso exemplifies the perfect beauty, industry, and domesticity that any man in ancient times, and perhaps many later times, would want in a wife.*

Calypso provides Hermes with nectar and ambrosia before asking why he has come. Hermes explains that he has traveled all the way to this remote island because Zeus commanded him to do so. *You already knew this, having overheard the gods' previous assembly.* Calypso's island is so distant from any human habitations, Hermes adds, that no one would willingly traverse the unspeakably vast salt water to get here. *You realize that Hermes expresses the human perspective on the island's isolation. The distance traveled should be irrelevant to him, since a god can travel any distance in the blink of an eye. And why would a god care whether the island is far from all human habitations?*

Zeus has decided, Hermes explains, that Calypso must send on his way the man she keeps with her here, "since it is not his destiny to perish here apart from his friends; his fate is to see his friends and to reach his own grand home and his country." *Again, not news to you; both the narrator and Zeus have emphasized this repeatedly.* Hermes does not mention the man's name.

Reluctant to comply, Calypso complains that the gods always resent female goddesses having relationships with mortal men. She mentions a couple of mortal men beloved by goddesses but cruelly destroyed by divine force. "So now you gods refuse to let me keep this man, even though I saved his life," she objects bitterly, "after Zeus destroyed his swift ship when he was far out in the middle of the wine-colored sea. Then all of his other noble companions died, but the wind and a wave brought him here. And I loved and cared for him, and I thought I would make him immortal and ageless for all of his days." Calypso is really upset, but she knows that she cannot disobey Zeus. No one can. "Since it is not possible for any god to evade or to baffle the mind of Zeus," she says grudgingly, "let the man go upon the barren sea, if Zeus encourages and bids him."

Very unhappy that she must release the man, Calypso refuses to provide him with a ship. She points out that she does not have one. She will provide advice, but that is all. She goes to talk to Odysseus and finds him on the beach still weeping. His sweet life is ebbing away as he grieves for his return home. The singer explains that the divine goddess no longer pleases him. (Evidently, then, she did please him at one time.) Although he has been spending his nights with this beautiful divinity, he has done so reluctantly, at least of late, and during the day he does nothing but weep, sitting on the seashore. *From tales of the Trojan war, you remember Odysseus as a bold, confident, assertive figure, and it troubles you to see him so overwhelmed by his current situation. Where is his impressive fighting spirit now? He appears to have lost even that.*

Calypso explains that she is going to send Odysseus away, and she urges him to cut down trees and build himself a raft. She will supply food, wine, and clothes so that he can make it home.

Odysseus does not say, "Great. I'm off then. Bye." Instead, he protests. He does not believe Calypso. He thinks that she intends to trick him. Crossing the huge, treacherous expanse of the sea in a ship is difficult enough. How could it be possible in a flimsy raft? No, Odysseus refuses to go anywhere unless Calypso swears that she is not plotting some other suffering for him. Calypso admires his skepticism and gives him the oath he requires. *You believe her, since you know that she is following Zeus's command. Odysseus believes her, too, but his initial caution and skepticism do seem sensible.*

After a hearty meal, Calypso poses the crucial question: "Are you really determined to go home?" She warns Odysseus that he is destined to endure much more suffering. "If you only knew how much suffering is in store for you," she says, "you would choose to remain with me, keeping watch over this house, and you would be immortal." She knows that Odysseus longs for his own wife, but she reminds him that as a goddess she herself is, of course, far more beautiful. She points out the obvious: no mortal woman could ever rival a goddess in beauty.

Odysseus readily agrees that his mortal wife Penelope cannot match this spectacularly beautiful goddess in appearance. *You know, as he does, that Penelope will of course grow old and eventually die, while Calypso is beautiful now and forever.* But still Odysseus desperately longs to return to his own home. To achieve this, he is prepared to endure whatever he must. "I have already suffered a great deal, both in the waves and in battle" he reminds Calypso. "I'm ready to deal with anything that comes next." *Does Odysseus's answer surprise you? He is rejecting an offer of immortality. He is turning down eternal sex with a beautiful goddess in this splendid island paradise, because he prefers to go home. He would rather risk his life in an exposed raft on the open sea. Is he making a foolish choice? Would you reject an offer of this kind?*

Despite his determination to leave, Odysseus seems willing to have sex with Calypso for one more night. The following morning the goddess provides the necessary tools for raft-building. She shows Odysseus the tall trees to use, and then she returns to the cave, while you watch him artfully construct an intricate raft. This is a lengthy, complicated, detailed, and painstaking process: lots of cutting and shaping and fitting and joining. The raft, when finished, is the size of a large ship built by a skillful carpenter. It has a mast for a sail and a rudder for steering. Odysseus is evidently a talented craftsman. Calypso gives him cloth, and he makes the sails well, too. By means of levers (he must have made these also), he drags the raft down to the shining salt sea. The whole project takes him four days.

On the fifth day, Odysseus sets off. Calypso has given him food and water, and she sends a favorable breeze to help him on his way. There are no goodbyes between the man and the goddess. They exchange not a word in parting. What could either of them say? Calypso has already said she does not want Odysseus to leave. Odysseus cannot say, "I wish I didn't have to go." He has no such regrets. He rejoices as he sails away, and he never looks back.

An excellent steersman, Odysseus follows Calypso's directions, sailing and remaining awake for seventeen days straight. But on the eighteenth day, as he nears the land of the Phaeacians, Poseidon sees him. Furious because Odysseus blinded his son, the Cyclops, the great god of the sea gathers storm clouds and, suddenly it is nighttime. All the winds blow in force. The waves loom large, and Odysseus is frightened. Remembering Calypso's warning about all the suffering ahead of him, Odysseus expects to die and wishes he had died in the Trojan War instead. Dying there, he would have won *kleos*. *You realize that if he dies here and now, he will earn no* kleos *at all. A man drowning alone in the middle of the sea displays no exploits. There are no witnesses. No one will sing of his achievements ever after. Submerged, he will disappear without a trace.*

The winds blow Odysseus off the raft and break its mast. After struggling in the waves, Odysseus manages to climb back onto the raft but remains at the mercy of the winds and the currents. A kindly sea goddess advises him to abandon the raft and swim for shore. She offers him a magical *kredemnon* (headband) as protection. Odysseus responds with what you are beginning to see as characteristic skepticism. What if the sea goddess means to trick him? He decides on a compromise approach. He accepts the divinely offered headband, but he decides to stay with the raft as long as possible, knowing that once it disintegrates he will have to swim.

Poseidon continues to whip up the storm winds and the waves. Odysseus soon finds himself naked, clinging desperately to one last piece of his raft. Poseidon heads home to his own glorious halls, gloating happily.

Meanwhile, for two days a favorable wind—Athena's contrivance—impels Odysseus toward land. A huge wave nearly crushes him against jagged coastal rocks, but he has the thought—given by Athena—to cling to a rock and then swim out of the wave until he finds a safe place to go ashore, at the mouth of a river. *You appreciate that only Athena's help could explain his fortunate survival under these circumstances.*

As he crawls onto the sand, Odysseus is a mess, swollen and exhausted from having been in the sea so long. He has swallowed a lot of salt water. Still, he prudently contrives a warm, dry hiding place, heaping together dry leaves in a small spot well protected by wild olive bushes. Having ingeniously concealed himself, he gladly lies down to sleep.

The following events seem somehow vaguely familiar to you. Waking up the next morning in this new land, Odysseus encounters a beautiful young princess. She has gone to the shore with her maidservants to do the family clothes washing. *This unusually mundane activity for a princess will prove convenient for subsequent plot developments.* Odysseus first observes the girls in secret to ascertain that they are, in fact, human. Having recently encountered two goddesses, he's taking no chances. Finally emerging from his concealment in the bushes, Odysseus shields his nakedness by holding a leafy branch. Not surprisingly, his appearance terrifies the girls. *You can imagine how wild and strange he looks. He's completely naked and has been floating in the sea for days.* The girls sprint away down the beach—all except the princess, who remains facing the wild-looking stranger.

Odysseus debates with himself what to do. Should he grasp the girl by the knees and beg her for help in the customary fashion of a suppliant? This might anger her. Instead, he decides to speak while remaining at a distance. His words are clever and calculating, designed to flatter and reassure her. First, he asks whether she is a goddess or a human being. Her beauty, he says, makes it impossible to tell. He explains that he has only just survived being in the sea for twenty days, and he asks her to show him her city. He asks for clothing, too, to cover his nakedness. "In return," he says, "I hope the gods will give you all you desire." He then lists precisely the things that a young princess in such a tale as this might be expected to want: a husband, a home, a happy marriage.

Odysseus's strategy works. Observing that he seems like a man who is neither foolish nor lowborn, the princess explains that he has arrived on the island of Scheria. She is Nausicaa, and her father is king of the Phaeacians. This kingdom is very remote, and the Phaeacians are especially dear to the gods. Nausicaa recognizes her obligation to welcome all strangers and beggars. She orders her handmaids to give Odysseus food, drink, a bath, and clean clothing. Odysseus tactfully insists on bathing and dressing himself. Afterward, Athena, still watching over him, makes Odysseus look especially splendid: taller, bigger, very handsome. The princess already appears to be quite smitten, and she wishes for a husband resembling such a man as this, or even that this man himself might wish to remain on Scheria.

The princess then guides Odysseus back to her city. Prudently fearing malicious gossip, she asks him to wait outside the city and follow along a bit later, allowing her and her maids time to return home first. In listing the relevant landmarks along the route he must take, Nausicaa describes a thriving community. The Phaeacians have a lofty, turreted wall, a harbor with fully equipped ships, a public meeting place sacred to Poseidon and constructed out of stone. The princess mentions a spring and a meadow. The estate of her father, the king, has a blooming orchard. Her reference to Poseidon and her mention of a grove of black poplars belonging to Athena indicate that here, too, the gods enjoy appropriate worship. Nausicaa advises Odysseus to request aid from her mother, the queen, first of all. "If you can win her over," says the princess, "there's a good chance you'll make it home."

Following the princess's instructions, and aided by Athena, Odysseus proceeds through the city unobserved and arrives at the great halls of the king and queen. Along the way, he marvels at the harbor, ships, walls, and assembly places of the Phaeacians. Athena offers an account of the ancestry of the king and queen. The queen knows everything, according to Athena, and she resolves quarrels among men. The palace is truly spectacular: vast and grand. with threshold and walls of bronze. Silver and gold decorate the doorway. Odysseus sees figures of guard dogs crafted by the god Hephaestus, and a beautifully painted frieze. Thrones line the walls. The leading men of the community take their seats in council here, drinking and eating. The palace is lit by torches held by golden figures of young men. Phaeacian men are great sailors, and the women are superb at weaving. Extensive gardens, orchards, and vineyards surround the palace, providing abundant produce year-round. Two springs supply fresh water continually.

Entering the palace, Odysseus addresses the queen appropriately, and all goes well. The queen and king welcome him with bountiful hospitality. Odysseus describes his arrival from Calypso's island and his rejection of her offer of immortality, retelling in somewhat abbreviated form the story you have just heard from the singer who is narrating this tale to you: the raft, the storm, his days floundering in the sea and washing up on the beach, and the encounter with the princess. Odysseus approvingly mentions her prudence in asking him to follow later, rather than accompany her through town.

The king and queen are impressed. They like the look of this man. The king says they are used to meeting gods face-to-face, and that it occurs to them that Odysseus might be a god. He claims the gods visit the Phaeacians without disguise, the way they visit Cyclopes or Giants. In any case, the king and queen like the way Odysseus talks and the way he thinks. The king wishes that Odysseus would marry his daughter and be his son-in-law. He would give him a home and many possessions—but only if Odysseus wants to remain on Scheria. He would never keep anyone against his will. If Odysseus prefers to leave, the Phaeacians will prepare a ship and take him to his home the very next day. No one in the assembly objects. There is no discussion or debate. The king and queen make all decisions without any need for anyone else's input.

Happy at hearing this, Odysseus prays that Zeus give good fortune and inextinguishable glory to the king, and that he grant that he himself be able to reach his own homeland. *Odysseus seems no more tempted by the king's generous offer of marriage with the lovely princess, a home, and plentiful possessions than he was by Calypso's offer of immortality and eternal youth. He must really want to see his beloved wife and get to know his son. He must miss his parents and friends. He's responsible for the lives of so many people at home.*

The next day, the king summons an assembly of all the Phaeacians. The ship is quickly readied, and a great feast follows. At the feast, a trusty singer entertains everyone with tales of the *klea andrōn* (glorious achievements of men). He sings of Trojans and Greeks, and of the famous quarrel between Achilles and Odysseus. *You are puzzled. You remember the story of the great quarrel between Achilles and Agamemnon and its dire consequences, but this must be some other story, of a different quarrel. You do not get to hear it.*

Listening to the singer, Odysseus begins to cry, hiding his head under his cloak. *His sadness troubles you. In stories of his exploits during the Trojan War, Odysseus always seemed to meet challenges joyfully.* The Phaeacians enjoy the singer's tales very much, and only the king notices Odysseus weeping. He considerately ends the feast and the singing and leads everyone outside, where they hold competitions in boxing, wrestling, running, and other physical abilities.

Prompted by one man's hostile taunts, Odysseus competes at discus throwing, hurling the discus an astounding distance. He boasts that he excels also in archery and spear throwing (arts of war). The mood is tense. Odysseus is angry and the other men are wary.

Again the king intervenes. He soothes Odysseus by acknowledging his excellence and censuring the other man's rudeness. He admits that the Phaeacians are not good at boxing or wrestling but that they are fast runners and excellent sailors. They like feasting and music, warm baths and fresh clothing. And they are especially good at dancing.

Now there is dancing, and the singer sings another tale. This one is about the gods Ares and Aphrodite: a long story about divine adultery with a delightful, comical ending. In the house of Hephaestus, the war god Ares sleeps with Hephaestus's wife Aphrodite, goddess of love. Hephaestus crafts a trap and ensnares Ares and Aphrodite in unbreakable bonds. The other gods gather to watch, and they laugh delightedly, seeing how the slow-moving Hephaestus has outsmarted and entrapped the swift war god. Hermes observes that even so, he would like to be Ares sleeping with the beautiful Aphrodite, even in such a snare and with all the gods watching. His comment evokes more laughter among the gods. Finally, Poseidon persuades Hephaestus to release Ares. The war god heads off for Thrace (a region of Greece that you know of as wild and uncivilized), and the goddess of love returns to Cyprus, a place dear to her and distant from Thrace.

Everyone enjoys this tale, even Odysseus. *You, however, find yourself struck by how inconsequential adultery is among immortals. Not so the repercussions of adultery in tales of human affairs! Paris's theft of Helen launched the Trojan War. And the adultery of King Agamemnon's wife led directly to his murder, and then to a follow-up vengeance killing when Agamemnon's son killed his father's murderer. You know that even now, would-be adulterers, the suitors of Penelope, are plotting to murder Odysseus's son on his return to Ithaca. In contrast to the singer's lighthearted, humorous tale of divine adultery, human sexual transgressions seem far more complicated and consequential.*

After the storytelling and the dancing, the Phaeacians give Odysseus splendid guest gifts. The man who was rude earlier offers an apology now. Odysseus accepts the gifts and the apology, and wishes the man well. He has another bath, puts on another set of fresh clothes, and then exchanges tender words with the young princess. She bids Odysseus farewell and asks only that he remember her when he is home in his own land, since he's indebted to her for saving his life. Odysseus promises that if he makes it safely home, he will pray to her every day as if she were a goddess, for she did save his life.

At that evening's feast, Odysseus compliments the singer for his accuracy. The singer has sung of all that the Greeks did and experienced and suffered at Troy, as if he had been present himself, or had heard the stories from someone who was there. Odysseus asks him now to sing the tale of the wooden horse, which Odysseus once caused to be led into the citadel of Troy as a deception after first filling it with the warriors who then emerged to destroy Troy utterly.

The singer obliges, relating the tale at some length. Surprisingly, though Odysseus requested this story, it too, like the singer's previous tales of Trojans and Greeks, makes him cry. *You might have expected Odysseus to feel pleasure in hearing an account of his own cleverness and successful deception. He asked for the tale; he must have thought he would enjoy it. The deception certainly worked, and the story of his achievement is already circulating. How else could the singer know it? This is the very definition of kleos. You might also remember that Menelaus told Telemachus a version of this story. Warriors in these tales always seem to be striving for kleos, yet hearing a song of his own kleos does not make Odysseus happy.* The singer comments that the resulting battle, after the Greeks burst forth from inside the hollow horse, was most dreadful.

More surprising even than Odysseus's tears at hearing the tale of his clever trick of the Trojan horse, the narrator likens him crying to a woman weeping over the body of her husband who has received a mortal wound fighting to defend his citadel and his children. Seeing her husband convulsing and dying, the woman wails loudly and embraces him. But men behind her, striking her back and shoulders with the ends of their spears, lead her away into slavery, toil, and misery. Her cheeks are wasting away with pitiable anguish. This, the narrator tells you, is exactly how Odysseus weeps now, hearing the tale of the wooden horse. *You'd have thought that Odysseus, having succeeded in sacking Troy, would be likened to the conquering warriors in the analogy, not to their female victim. The simile leaves you feeling confused and vaguely troubled.*

As before, the king alone notices Odysseus's tears. He stops the singing; and only now, after having hosted Odysseus for so much time, does he ask his guest's name and story. As in Pylos and Sparta, this question comes not before but after the host has provided ample hospitality. The king wants to know where the stranger is from, and how he arrived in Scheria. He wants to know why his guest weeps upon hearing tales of the fate of the Greeks and of Troy. *You, too, wonder why stories of the Greeks' glorious conquest make Odysseus cry.*

CHOOSING REALITY

Supernatural and fantastical elements in the *Odyssey* help to make this story enticing and entertaining. We all enjoy a good story, and fantasies of imaginary people, places, and events can offer us escape and refreshment from the difficulties of real life. Some people find adventure stories involving supernatural elements and magical creatures most enjoyable of all, and the genres of fantasy and science fiction are extremely popular. Films, television series, and video games encourage us to enter other worlds and other "realities." Such fictions can be both delightful and educational.

In the twenty-first century, however, many of us have come to prefer fantasies, our own and those of others, to the reality of empirical, lived experience. We are at risk of becoming a species of "magical thinkers," incapable of distinguishing fantasy from reality or even wanting to. Facts can be harsh and unpleasant. Real problems and conflicts may admit no easy or even good solutions. But a preference for fantasy over reality, and an inability to distinguish the two, leads us to substitute magic for logic, and to reject empirical knowledge and practical solutions to the problems of real life. In the realm of fantasy the laws of physics do not apply. In real life, however, they do. Our unreflective embrace of fantasy may be corroding our capacity for rational thought, and preventing constructive political discourse and creative problem solving.[1]

The *Odyssey* cautions against this very real danger: that we may enjoy fantasy too much, that we may choose to substitute illusions and delusions, irrationality and magical thinking, for the challenges and possibilities of human life in the here and now. Odysseus's adventures begin with his remarkable choice of reality over fantasy. This choice initiates his return to his home, family, and kingship. This choice *permits* him to recover his political authority and to reestablish order and happiness for himself, his household, and his community. He has the opportunity, twice, to remain in a fantasy paradise, but he opts instead for the hard work of real life. We know that if he chooses otherwise, the suitors' despotic behavior will continue unchallenged, because Odysseus will never return home to stop them. Odysseus's example reminds us that a preference for fantasy over reality may be empowering the despots and would-be despots in our own times, because they are hard at work in the real world, while we are amusing ourselves in imaginary ones.

The first four books of the *Odyssey* define the components of a desirable community, while books 5 through 8 proceed to identify the human choices required to make such a society a real possibility. In the *Odyssey*'s nondemocratic world of "kings" (we'd call them warlords) and their subordinates, a successful community means a fixed hierarchy with a legitimate, respected king and obedient subjects. Despite this anti-egalitarian social and political structure, the *Odyssey*'s definition of "good" authority and "good" community excludes tyrannical behavior. In a desirable community, all members, even temporary ones (visiting strangers) respect and fulfill their reciprocal obligations toward one another. Above all, the early

REALITY (*ODYSSEY* 5–8)   77

scenes in the *Odyssey* emphasize that individuals with power have obligations toward those without power, and are responsible for the quality of life in their community. The next section of the epic, describing Odysseus's departure from Calypso's island and his arrival among the Phaeacians, identifies the essential first step toward achieving this conception of individual and communal success: the *choice* to prioritize reality over fantasy.

The *Odyssey* includes supernatural elements along with natural ones, but instead of blending fantasy with reality, the epic encourages us to see the two realms as distinct but related. Book 5 begins back in the divine realm, with the gods in council again. (This might even be the same council we witnessed at the beginning of book 1.) Odysseus, too, is in a supernatural realm, stuck on the idyllic island of the goddess Calypso, where he's been for seven long years, completely absent from the world of human beings.[2] Olympus and Calypso's island are separate from the natural world, but the narrative, by making the audience omniscient, enables us to see that events occurring in these supernatural realms have consequences for human beings in the real world. Athena explains to Zeus that Odysseus's predicament provides a terrible moral example. Odysseus was a good king, and now no one even remembers him, Athena says. His son has gone to seek information about his father, and his own life is in danger. Odysseus's suffering implies that the gods do not care about justice. If Odysseus remains with Calypso in her magical island paradise, then there can be no justice in the world. What mortal king will choose to be just, Athena wonders, if the great ruler of the gods cannot even bother to be just? (*Od.* 5.7–20). Human beings' conception of the gods on Olympus, Athena implies, influences actual human behavior. Similarly, a good ruler's detention in a fantasy paradise permits the despotic behavior of others to imperil his family and community in the real world. In other words, what happens in the world of fantasy does not remain in the world of fantasy.

Odysseus's example suggests not only that ideas about the supernatural have real-life consequences, but also that the acceptance or rejection of life in the realm of fantasy is a choice. At Athena's urging, Zeus agrees that it is time for Odysseus to leave Calypso's island and make his way home, but the goddess only releases Odysseus because *he himself wishes to go*. He's clearly unhappy on Calypso's island, sitting alone on the beach when Hermes arrives, and weeping desperately (*Od.* 5.82–84). Despite her reluctance, Calypso must obey Zeus (*Od.* 5.118–40). But before letting Odysseus set off on his raft, Calypso tries to persuade him to change his mind, warning him of the suffering that lies ahead if he declines her offer of immortality (*Od.* 5.206–7). But Odysseus prefers reality. He tells Calypso he knows that Penelope, a mortal, cannot hold a candle to her, a goddess. Even so, he longs to leave and is ready for whatever comes next (*Od.* 5.215–24). Odysseus rejects immortal life and eternal sex with a beautiful goddess, because he prefers the things that only mortal life can provide: family, community, opportunities for adventure and achievement. Even the prospect of suffering and hardship does not deter him.

Why on earth would Odysseus reject Calypso's offer and choose to leave the fantasy world and rejoin the real world of human beings? On Calypso's island, Odysseus is completely invisible to other human beings. No one knows where he is, what he is doing, or even whether he remains alive. The Greek verb *kalupto* means "to cover," "to conceal," or "to cover with dishonor." Calypso's name is the future tense in the first person singular, meaning "I will cover," "I will conceal," or "I will cover with dishonor." And that is, in fact, what Calypso has done and is offering to do to Odysseus forever. Accepting Calypso's offer would mean giving up all human relationships, all adventure and achievement, all possibility of the glory that human beings value, celebrate, and *remember*.[3]

In urging Zeus to intercede for Odysseus, Athena makes Odysseus the test case for the operation of divine justice in human affairs. Do the gods care about justice? Should we? Will justice prevail in the end? Odysseus's preference for reality over fantasy exposes a most fundamental prerequisite for creating a just and desirable community of real live individuals: the rejection of some fantasy of an ideal, immortal existence.

Odysseus's example reminds us that individual achievement and communal success can begin only if we embrace the reality of life in this world, with all of its sufferings and all of its pleasures. If Odysseus remained on Calypso's island, the suitors would continue to abuse their power at home.

Odysseus would never return to stop them. To defeat despots in reality, we must, like Odysseus, prioritize real life.

A FANTASTIC EDUCATION

Prioritizing reality does not mean abandoning fantasy altogether, because fantasy can be instructive. Struggling to leave Calypso's eternal paradise, Odysseus offers a constructive role model. The refusal to remain in the realm of fantasy, a necessary first step to achieving a successful life, initiates new challenges and opportunities. Books 5 through 8 illustrate the capacity of a fanciful tale with magical elements nevertheless to expose attitudes and skills essential to survival in the real world.

In books 5 through 8, impressive caution, determination, and ingenuity enable Odysseus to extricate himself from the idyllic world of fantasy. (Later sections of the narrative will reveal additional attributes necessary to Odysseus's ultimate survival and success.). We know that Odysseus will make it home; Zeus says that he will return with lots of treasure (*Od.* 5.41–42). But the remainder of the epic demonstrates specific abilities and habits of mind that give him the possibility of reestablishing his admirable relationships with his family and community. From book 5 onward, the epic's narrative keeps our focus on Odysseus's choices and actions.

Caution, determination, and ingenuity characterize Odysseus as he prepares to leave Calypso's island. Shrewdly, he refuses to depart unless Calypso swears that she means him no harm (*Od.* 5.177–91). His determination to return home emboldens him to brave any hardship (*Od.* 5.219–24). He painstakingly and ingeniously constructs a raft and sails. Calypso provides the tools and materials, but the craftsmanship is his alone, for the goddess departs and leaves him to it (*Od.* 5.234–42). The narrative details the construction minutely, and the resulting craft sounds like an elaborate vessel rather than a crude, simple "raft" (*Od.* 5.243–61).[4]

Caution, determination, and ingenuity equip Odysseus to reject the magical form of immortality offered by Calypso, and this in turn gives him a clearer understanding of the actual form of immortality possible in the real world. Departure from the comfort and safety of a fantasy paradise

exposes him to the terrifying peril of complete dissolution and obliteration. Fearing a solitary death by drowning, Odysseus realizes that *kleos*, the
glory eternally conferred by epic poetry, cannot occur in isolation. Great
achievements require witnesses who will judge them worth celebrating and
retelling. Watching the storm clouds gather, Odysseus envies his comrades
who died memorably and gloriously at Troy (*Od.* 5.306–12). If he drowns
alone in the middle of the ocean, he will remain unknown, anonymous.
No one will tell tales of his exploits. Odysseus's rejection of fantasy and his
struggle against oblivion reminds us that human achievements deserving of
admiration and eternal commemoration require the presence and survival
of other people. Odysseus remains certain that great achievement means
success in warfare, but we know that he is on his way to a more constructive and beneficial achievement: he will eradicate people who are abusing
their power, and he will reestablish harmony and happiness for his family
and community.

The narrative also hints symbolically at this interdependence between
individual and communal survival and achievement. Odysseus's experience
demonstrates the value of caution, determination, and ingenuity for prevailing over adversity, but his isolation from a human community makes him
especially vulnerable to complete obliteration. His own solitary effort, his
ingeniously constructed raft, protects him from drowning only temporar-
ily. Once it shatters and Odysseus finds himself adrift in the sea, a goddess
offers him a divinely protective *kredemnon* (headband, or short veil; *Od.*
5.346–47). Since the plural of this word also means "battlements of a city,"
the goddess's offer of a magically protective garment implicitly highlights
the vulnerability of an individual to destruction in the absence of the real-
life protections afforded by a citadel.[5]

Understood as a paradigm and read symbolically, a fanciful, magical fiction can have constructive benefits in the real world. The goddess's offer of
a magically protective garment as Odysseus struggles all alone for survival
reminds us that even a high achiever with Odysseus's extraordinary caution,
determination, and ingenuity needs the community in order for his *kleos*
to survive. Real immortality, this magical symbol suggests, requires other
people. That realization may be the most potent discovery of all.

CHOOSING REALITY *AGAIN*

The temptation to remain in the world of fantasy does not disappear simply because you resist it once. Odysseus's encounter with the Phaeacians offers him a second opportunity to choose between fantasy and reality. The community of the Phaeacians initially appears to be a real place, inhabited by human beings. But it is not a real place, and its inhabitants are not quite human. The entire story of Odysseus's experience on the Phaeacians' island seems like a setup. Like Odysseus, we are at risk of being taken in. That is precisely how fantasy works. But we need not fall for it.

The narrative at first draws us in, but it subsequently invites our critical assessment. The familiar, fairy-tale-like elements of this story—a destitute wanderer who is really a king, a helper intervening to aid the protagonist, a beautiful young princess, the prospect of marriage—make us anticipate a predictable and inevitable "happily ever after" ending.[6] But we also know that a match between this wanderer and this princess is impossible, because we have known from the very beginning that Odysseus will succeed in returning home to Ithaca. The tension between our expectations for this kind of story and our foreknowledge of Odysseus's return home invites us to wonder how this particular wanderer will avoid marrying the princess and remaining in her land. Odysseus will need his capacity for caution, determination, ingenuity, and more.

More, in this case, turns out to be tact and imagination. Among the Phaeacians, Odysseus combines caution and ingenuity with perceptive tact and an impressive ability to imagine the points of view of others. On first seeing the laundry-washing princess and her young attendants, Odysseus demonstrates his talent for envisioning someone else's experience. Knowing that he looks terrifying in his current state, he takes care not to alarm the princess. He flatters her, likening her to a goddess. In asking her for help, he cleverly imagines her thoughts exactly, understanding that a young princess would be thinking of marriage (*Od.* 6.180–84). The princess herself thinks that Odysseus might just be husband material. Maybe he has even cleverly put this thought in her mind. Although he is a man in his forties, Odysseus nevertheless can envision the viewpoint of a young girl.

The entire scene prompts us to consider standard fairy-tale-type questions: Will the wanderer impress the parents of the princess? Will they discover that he is really a king? Will the couple live happily ever after? But this narrative will soon direct our attention to a new, atypical, but more crucial set of questions: Will this wanderer *choose* to marry the princess? Will he *want* to live with her, happily ever after, among her people and in her land?

The life of the Phaeacians initially seems so wonderfully attractive and desirable that it may take us a while to realize that it is so perfect that it cannot possibly be real. The Phaeacians inhabit an island almost as idyllic as Calypso's. As in Pylos and Sparta, the places Odysseus's son visits in books 3 and 4, perfect order prevails among the inhabitants: a king and a queen control the palace and surrounding community. As in Pylos and Sparta, the people seem prosperous and happy. A guest receives generous hospitality. There is music and storytelling. All the requisite elements seem present. But some things are just not quite right.

Odysseus admires the Phaeacians' *agorai* (assembly places; *Od.* 7.44), but we see that these do not serve a normal function. The word *agorai* comes from the verb meaning "to gather." In the *Iliad*, Greeks and Trojans hold such gatherings for making political decisions. In assembly, Agamemnon and Achilles quarrel. In various assemblies, warriors debate and plan. The Phaeacians have such gathering spaces, too; but here they do not function as places for men to argue, plan, or resolve their differences. The Phaeacians have no need for verbal debate or conflict resolution, because their queen takes care of this for them. According to Athena, the Phaeacians' queen is unequivocally loved and respected. Intellectually, she lacks nothing, and she resolves disputes between men toward whom she is well-disposed (*Od.* 7.69–74).

In addition to possessing unnatural "gathering spaces" that do not function as places of assembly where men argue and seek to resolve conflicts, the Phaeacians also have agricultural spaces that do not function naturally: gardens and orchards that defy the laws of nature. The king's orchards, containing many types of fruit trees, produce magically all year round. The fruit never spoils and never ceases. It grows perpetually in winter and in summer. The west wind ensures that there is always ripe fruit at any given moment (*Od.* 7.117–20). The king's grapevines and vegetables also magically ripen year-round, and two springs perpetually provide water with no human effort required (*Od.* 7.121–32). We know that none of this is normal.

Most abnormally, the gods actually show themselves *openly* to the Phaeacians when they visit. At Ithaca, Pylos, and Sparta, Athena disguises herself as a mortal in order to speak to human beings. But the king of the Phaeacians explains that the gods join directly in their feasts and celebrations and do not disguise their identity, even when they meet Phaeacians individually. This is because, the king explains, "we are near to them, just like the Cyclopes and the wild races of giants" (*Od.* 7.201–6).[7] Cyclopes and giants are magical, monstrous creatures. If the Phaeacians are like them, then clearly they are not normal people.

Even that desirable, reciprocal norm of human life in the archaic world, *xenia* (guest-friendship), emphasized repeatedly in the *Odyssey*'s first four books, appears not beneficial but problematic on the island of the Phaeacians. As in Pylos and Sparta, so too on Scheria the inhabitants commendably offer generous hospitality to an unexpected and unknown arrival, but in this instance their irreproachable hospitality constitutes for their guest not a constructive benefit but a seductive risk. Although he shows Odysseus exemplary hospitality, the king would like his guest to marry his daughter and remain on the island. As before on Calypso's island, the choice belongs to Odysseus, since the king promises to convey his guest back to his home, if that is what the guest wants. But Odysseus feels no temptation to remain in this second island paradise (*Od.* 7.309–33).[8] A decision to stay and marry the princess would imperil the system of guest-friendship, because by remaining permanently Odysseus would lose the opportunity to reciprocate in Ithaca his Phaeacian hosts' hospitality, and his descendants would lose this opportunity as well. In Pylos and Sparta, the proper observation of the rules of *xenia* characterizes a harmonious community ruled by a benevolent king. Here, however, *xenia* risks preventing a good king from returning home to restore harmony and reassume his benevolent rule.[9]

Ultimately we realize that the Phaeacians are not really people at all, because they lack the most fundamental and characteristic feature of human life: struggle. The Phaeacians do not need to struggle to obtain food, because their orchards and gardens produce it magically. They also evidently have little experience of physical conflict, since their king acknowledges that they are not very good at boxing or wrestling (*Od.* 8.246). They are fast runners and great sailors, and they love dancing, music, feasts, and luxury (*Od.* 8.247–49). As a community, they also have no experience of *political* struggle. They have assemblies, but these are perfectly ordered, with the king and queen in charge and unchallenged.

We must think empirically in order to recognize that the utopian perfection of the Phaeacian community places it in the realm of fantasy. We must use knowledge derived from our own sensory experience of the world, plus logic and rational thought, to realize that the life offered to Odysseus among the Phaeacians is not a real life at all. Calypso (the name meaning "I will hide/cover") seeks to conceal Odysseus. The Phaeacians want to take him in. The Phaeacians offer Odysseus a second opportunity to abandon reality and remain in an enticing, perfect fantasy world. We ourselves get such offers all the time. Many modern fantasies, whether presented as entertainment or politics, may be similarly deceptive and seductive for us. (And the tools of modern digital technology can make them especially vivid and appealing.) To enjoy and learn from them without being subsumed or taken in, we have to scrutinize them carefully, measuring them against the evidence of our own senses, the laws of physics, the consensus of experts.

REAL STORIES FOR REAL PEOPLE

In distinguishing fantasy from reality, the *Odyssey* emphasizes the value of stories for cultivating the human capacity for imagination and empathy, crucial requirements for constructive participation in a human community. The Phaeacians provide an illuminating counter-model. Their relationship to stories further distances them from real mortal life. They have stories, just as human beings do, and they love listening to them—but stories merely *entertain* them. Stories do not move them or elevate them, because the Phaeacians cannot connect them to their own lives.[10] The Phaeacians' relationship to stories illustrates a very real risk in our own lives, too: we may enjoy stories but fail to learn from them. All stories, even escapist fantasies of immortality and happily-ever-after, or fanciful explanations for scientifically understood phenomena, can be illuminating, but only if we engage our critical faculties and examine their influence on us and on our actual experiences and relationships.

In the world of human beings in Pylos, Sparta, and Ithaca, stories provide entertainment but also offer important information and moral examples. They emphasize both great achievement and great suffering. In Pylos and Sparta, accounts of the impressive deeds of previous generations teach Telemachus a shared set of communal ideals.[11] For people in Pylos, Sparta, and Ithaca, tales of the Trojan War have already become stories of anguish and loss. Tales of Troy are stories of suffering and sorrow (e.g., *Od.* 3.102-98 and 4.81-112). Telemachus weeps hearing Menelaus's account of Odysseus (*Od.* 4.113-16). On Ithaca, Penelope cries upon hearing the singer relate the Greeks' miserable return home (*Od.* 1.325-44.).

Unlike the not-quite-real Phaeacians, human beings cannot hear stories of human suffering without being moved by them; but the Phaeacians, lacking direct personal experience of conflict, hear such stories without pain and, presumably, also without learning anything. At the Phaeacians' feast, the singer's tale of the great quarrel between Achilles and Odysseus almost sounds like a reference to the *Iliad*, but it is not a reference to the *Iliad* that we have, which depicts a disastrous quarrel between Achilles and *Agamemnon*. This alternative tale suggests that the Phaeacians have the same *kinds* of stories as the ones that circulate among human beings in the world of Ithaca, Pylos, and Sparta, but not necessarily the same ones. And hearing this tale, the Phaeacians experience only delight (*Od.* 8.91). In contrast, this same story concerns Odysseus personally and makes him cry (*Od.* 8.92 ff.). He knows firsthand the hardships of quarrels and battles. Noticing Odysseus's tears, the king quickly stops the singer, but the other Phaeacians experience no sorrow and remain oblivious to his.

None of us ever fought at Troy, of course, and many of us may have the good fortune never to experience warfare at all, but the *Odyssey* reminds us that as human beings we must recognize struggle and conflict as universal and perpetual aspects of human life. Describing Odysseus's experience listening to the Phaeacian singer relate the tale of the Trojan Horse, the narrative

evokes our imagination and our empathy. Odysseus has asked the singer
to sing the tale of this clever trick that he himself devised. After ten years
of besieging Troy, the Greeks built a huge wooden horse and hid inside
it. When the Trojans foolishly wheeled it inside their city walls, the Greeks
burst out and sacked the city. Hearing the story, Odysseus weeps. Like the
king, but unlike the other Phaeacians, we also witness Odysseus's tears.

And as Odysseus weeps, the narrator likens him to a woman whose husband and city have just fallen in warfare, explaining:

> The very famous singer sang these things, but Odysseus
> melted, and tears poured down his cheeks below his eyes.
> As a woman weeps, collapsing over her dear husband,
> who has fallen before his city and his people, warding off
> the pitiless day for his citadel and his children.
> And she, seeing him quivering and dying,
> pours herself around him and wails loudly, but the men from behind
>   her,
> striking her on the back and shoulders with their spears,
> drive her up into bondage, and to have toil and misery,
> And her cheeks waste away with most pitiable anguish.
> Thus Odysseus let fall the pitiable tear from under his brows (*Od.*
>   8.521–31).

We might expect the narrator to identify Odysseus not with the conquered
woman in the simile, but with her conquerors. In his career he has done
exactly as they do, slaughtering enemy warriors attempting to defend
their city, and enslaving their wives. But in his grief and his tears, Odysseus is not like the victors in the simile. He is like their victim: a woman
widowed, captured, and enslaved after the fall of her city. Odysseus requested this tale of his clever trick and the Greeks' conquest. The story of
the Trojan Horse details a moment of supreme accomplishment for Odysseus, when his ingenuity achieved victory and great glory for the Greeks
and for himself. But instead of feeling happy in recalling this moment of
triumph, Odysseus *weeps.*

The experience of watching Odysseus cry develops our capacity for empathy. This unexpected analogy spurs our curiosity and imagination. Does Odysseus cry at hearing this tale because he now knows that his great moment of success was only the preamble to all the suffering he has experienced since: his years of wandering, years of loneliness on Calypso's island, days of nearly drowning in the sea? Does he cry because of all he has suffered and lost? His tears invite us to put ourselves in his sandals and try to imagine his feelings and thoughts. What would it be like to be Odysseus experiencing his experiences? How can a great warrior, even one who has suffered terrible hardships, be comparable to a newly widowed, about to be enslaved woman?[12]

Neither the Phaeacians nor Odysseus hear this simile, but the narrator's analogy emphasizes for us, the epic's audience, the fragility and transience of human success and prosperity. Slavery, for ancient Greeks, was sharp and ever-present evidence of the impermanence of human fortunes. It was not ethnically or racially motivated. You did not become a slave because of your ethnic identity or the color of your skin. You could be born into slavery if your parents were enslaved, or you could become a slave if your city was captured in war. You might have been royalty before, as were the Trojan king Priam's wife, daughters, and daughters-in-law before Troy fell. You might look just like your masters, but defeat in war made you a slave. Homer's original audiences knew that being at the top of the heap today does not mean you will not find yourself at the bottom tomorrow. Odysseus's own career fully exemplifies the impermanence of fortune: once a revered and prosperous king, he is now a destitute wanderer dependent on the hospitality of strangers.

The analogy in the simile overrides the obvious distinctions between Odysseus and a captive woman. It obliterates precisely the elements of identity that might make a Greek male feel secure and safe. Odysseus is a man and a conquering warrior; but in his pitiful weeping, he exactly resembles a defeated woman who is about to be enslaved. Vulnerability to suffering, this simile suggests, makes us all equal.

The equalizing effect of this simile exemplifies the *Odyssey*'s capacity to cultivate our understanding of ourselves and of others as fully human and perpetually vulnerable. By making us omniscient and giving us critical and objective distance, the narrative permits us to compare and evaluate individuals, communities, opportunities, and choices. The Phaeacians are not fully human, and they are impervious to the effects of stories. With the exception of their king, they do not notice Odysseus's tears. They do not get to hear the narrator's simile likening the weeping Odysseus to a soon to be enslaved widow. By contrast, hearing the simile and imagining ourselves in Odysseus's situation, we can acknowledge our own vulnerability and moderate our behavior accordingly. Knowledge of the precariousness of good fortune is a potential source of empathy, self-restraint, and caution.

Unlike us, the Phaeacians are essentially like gods in their carefree reaction to all stories, even tales of terrible mortal conflicts.[13] Their unmitigated and unreflective enjoyment of an account of human conflict and suffering parallels the gods' pure pleasure at witnessing rivalry and discord between divinities. The singer's tale of adultery between Ares and Aphrodite delights everyone, even Odysseus (*Od.* 8.266ff.).[14] But we see that adultery among gods has no dire consequences and is merely a source of humor and lighthearted entertainment. The gods' choices and actions have only trivial consequences for themselves. Not so with human choices, as we've seen. The theft of Helen, for example—an egregious violation of the reciprocal system of guest friendship—resulted in the Trojan War. Similarly, Agamemnon's murder by his wife's lover, a recurrent reference point in the *Odyssey*, insistently reminds us mortals of the terrible consequences that adultery can have in human life. For human beings, stories of adultery are no laughing matter. The Phaeacians, inhabitants of a fantasy paradise, cannot learn from stories. By implication, inhabitants of the real world can and must.

The *Odyssey* constantly tests and cultivates our ability to evaluate and learn from stories. The first four books expose fundamental requirements for a human community worth having: human authority responsible for the quality of communal life, reciprocal obligations respected, opportunities for free and creative development and expression, citizens possessing self-restraint and a farsighted conception of self-interest. The next four books (5–8) show the essential first step to achieving those requirements:

the decision, the *choice*, to reject some magical fantasy of eternity and perfection and to embrace reality instead.

Soon the epic will give us another opportunity to test our ability to distinguish fact from fiction. Before returning Odysseus to his home, the Phaeacians ask his identity. (As in *Odyssey* 1–4, when *xenia* is properly observed, the question "Who are you?" only comes *after* the guest has been thoroughly welcomed and entertained.) In the next section of the *Odyssey* (books 9–12), Odysseus will tell the Phaeacians, and he will show them—and us—just exactly who he is.

Most of us do not get offers as explicit as the ones Odysseus receives from Calypso and the Phaeacians to remain in a fantasy paradise, but we all must decide whether we will focus our energies on the possibility of an eternal otherworld existence or on the struggles of life in this world. Odysseus rejects immortality and eternal sex with a beautiful goddess. He rejects, too, a fairy-tale "happily ever after" with a lovely young princess in a carefree utopia. His experiences among the Phaeacians help him begin to transition back from solitude to society, reintroducing him to the rewards and the challenges of communal life. But Odysseus prefers life as a human being in the real world of human relationships, human suffering, human striving, human failure, and human success. The first eight books of the *Odyssey* both emphasize the value of communal harmony and identify the choice to embrace reality as the necessary prerequisite for establishing it.

The preference for a harmonious communal life and the prioritization of reality over fantasy cannot alone deter or defeat tyranny, but these ideas prompt us to consider for ourselves, *as individuals*, the value of various possibilities for a communal or solitary life. The kingless chaos on Ithaca attests that political authority in some form is necessary. The thriving communities of Pylos and Sparta suggest that a benevolent, generous authority and responsible citizens are desirable. The unquestioned authority of Zeus on Olympus or the king and queen of the Phaeacians might perhaps seem to be ideal. But how many real, live human autocracies achieve that degree of stability or conflict-free contentment? (And even the most benevolent autocracy deprives individuals of autonomy.) Alternatively, complete isolation from family and friends, even in an eternal island paradise, appears completely inadequate and even pointless. No one would even know of our existence. We would perish without a trace.

Understood as a parable, Odysseus's experience with Calypso and with the Phaeacians cautions us in the twenty-first century against completely losing ourselves in our own magical belief systems and fantasy worlds. A preference for magical explanations, for feelings over facts, distances us from reality and the possibility of real-life achievements worth admiring and celebrating. Even if others share our magical explanations and enter our supernatural fictions (either in face-to-face interactions, or "virtually" via digital technology), a rejection of evidence-based reasoning causes us to sacrifice the protective benefits of an actual, three-dimensional human community. The capacity for survival turns out to include, above all, the crucial recognition that individuals cannot succeed on their own.

The *Odyssey* compels us to consider why it might be preferable to live in groups rather than all alone. It encourages us to identify the interdependent components of individual and communal success. The portrait of Odysseus enables us to recognize skills and decisions necessary for survival and happiness. The seductions and deceptions of fantasy alternatives help us to cultivate our evidence-based reasoning skills. The rejection of tyranny originates in the realization that options exist and that the choices are ours.

CHAPTER 4

DECEPTION (*ODYSSEY* 9-16)

Another evening's entertainment starts, as a singer begins to sing to you the tale that Odysseus tells the Phaeacians. The singer will then continue Odysseus's story a bit further.

The king of the Phaecians has asked Odysseus to explain how he came to this island, and why tales of the Trojan War make him cry. Did he lose a relative or close companion in the fighting? You know Odysseus sailed from Ithaca to Troy many years ago, and you've heard how he left Calypso's island and washed up on the island of the Phaeacians. But how did he get to Calypso's island? What happened to him after he left Troy? The cooking fires are subsiding into coals and ash as Odysseus begins his answer.

Odysseus begins tactfully by praising the singer whom he and the Phaeacians have been listening to all evening, the one who sang the tale of Ares and Aphrodite and the tale of the Trojan horse. "Nothing is more enjoyable than hearing an excellent singer during a marvelous communal feast," he says. "But now your heart prompts you to ask my terrible sorrows so that, grieving still more, I may suffer. First, I will tell you my name. That way, if I survive, we can be guest-friends, even though my home is very far from here.

"I am Odysseus, son of Laertes, and I am well known to everyone because of my clever tricks. My *kleos* reaches heaven. My home is on Ithaca, an island visible from afar. It has a tall, leafy mountain, and islands surround it nearby. It is a craggy place but it produces noble young men. In my view, no other land is sweeter to look upon. But the beautiful goddess Calypso detained me in a cave, wanting me for her husband. Circe, the artful goddess, also re-strained me in her halls, wanting me for her husband too. But neither could persuade me. All I wanted was to go home. Nothing is sweeter than one's own country and parents.

"But I will describe my homeward journey and the many sorrows that Zeus has given me. Carried by a wind from Troy, I first plundered the city of the Ci-conians and killed their men. Then we divided up their wives and possessions fairly. I thought we should leave quickly, but my companions—what fools they were!—were not persuaded. They stayed, got drunk, and slaughtered many sheep and cattle while the Ciconians called on their neighbors for help. These were excellent warriors, and they outnumbered us greatly. We fought all day, but as the sun went down, toward the time when oxen are unyoked from the plough, the Ciconians routed us. They killed six of my companions out of each ship, but the rest of us managed to escape.

"Afterward, we survived wind and waves and weariness for ten days be-fore arriving in the land of the Lotus Eaters. I sent men ahead on a scouting expedition, but anyone who ate the sweet lotus fruit no longer wished to re-turn to the ships, preferring to remain there forever, eating the lotus. I had to drag them back to the ships and bind them under the rowers' benches. I made the rest of the men row us away from there as quickly as they could.

"Next, we came to the land of the arrogant, lawless Cyclopes. The Cyclo-pes do not cultivate their land, because it produces food spontaneously. Cy-clopes don't need to work at all, and they completely lack *themis* (law, right, custom). They have no assembly places where men take counsel. They live in caves. Each is judge over his own wives and children, and they do not care for one another.

"Directly across from the Cyclopes' harbor, there is another island with extensive woods and many wild goats. It has magnificent potential, but it never sees hunters, shepherds, or farmers. No one ever goes there to plow or plant, because the Cyclopes have no ships—because they have no ship-builders. But that island would be perfect for planting crops and for grazing sheep and cattle. The soil is rich, and there's an excellent natural harbor and freshwater spring. We landed there in the concealment of a misty, moonless night. Pulling our ships onto the beach, we stowed the sails and went to sleep. We spent the following day hunting, eating goats, and drinking wine we'd plundered from the Ciconians.

"The next day I took my ship with a few men across to the island of the Cyclopes. I was curious to know whether Cyclopes were ferocious and unjust, or god-fearing and respectful of the obligations of *xenia*. Crossing to the Cyclopes' nearby island, we saw a large cave near the sea. A high stone wall and trees surrounded a courtyard containing many sheep and goats. We saw someone, too. He wasn't really a man. He was so gigantic. Herding his flocks all alone, he looked like a mountain.

"I left men guarding the ship and went with others to the cave. I carried a goat-leather bottle of very strong wine, thinking I might need it. The huge herdsman wasn't home, so we entered the cave. It was well stocked and well organized, with crates of cheeses, milk pails full to overflowing, and pens of lambs and baby goats. My men wanted to grab cheeses and animals, race back to the ship, and sail away immediately. Now I know that would have been wiser, but at the time I wanted to see the Cyclops and see if he'd give me guest-gifts. Sadly, he wasn't going to be a charming sight for my friends. We kindled a fire and made sacrifice. Taking cheese for ourselves, we ate. Then we waited inside the cave.

"The Cyclops finally returned from pasturing his flocks, carrying a huge pile of firewood. He tossed this down inside the cave, making a loud crash. Frightened, we scurried into a corner. We watched him drive the milking ewes and goats into the cave. He left the males outside in his fenced-in yard, then blocked the doorway with an immense door-stone, a thing bigger than twenty-two wagons could have carried. He milked the sheep and goats and placed their young beneath them. He put some milk in baskets to make cheese. He kept the rest to drink.

"Only then did he see us. 'Guest-friends, who are you?' he demanded. 'Where do you come from? Are you buccaneers, sailing the seas to cause trouble for strangers?' His monstrous voice boomed inside the cave, terrifying us.

"But I spoke up bravely. I told him we were Greeks returning home after sacking Troy. I explained that winds had blown us off course, and that we wanted him to give us appropriate guest-gifts. I reminded him that Zeus guarantees the obligations of guest-friendship and punishes anyone who doesn't fulfill them.

"But he said that Cyclopes don't care about Zeus or any gods. They claim to be better than the gods, and don't fear them. He asked where we'd left our ship, but I didn't fall for that. I told him that Poseidon had destroyed it on the sea.

"Leaping up, the Cyclops grabbed two of my companions and killed them as if they were puppies, bashing their heads to the ground. He cut them into pieces, preparing his meal. Then he ate like a fierce mountain lion, leaving nothing behind. We could only cry out in horror and pray to Zeus.

"After eating the men and drinking much milk, the Cyclops fell asleep. Sneaking up, I drew my sword to kill him. Then I remembered the huge door-stone. If I'd killed him, we would all have died in that cave. We could never have moved that immense stone. So, grieving, we waited for morning.

"The next day, after milking his sheep and goats, the Cyclops killed and ate another two men. Before leaving to shepherd his flocks on the hills, he pushed the vast door-stone back in place. We remained trapped.

"But I had an idea. Inside the cave there was a great shaft of green olive wood, as big as the mast of a cargo-ship. I cut off a large piece of this and told my men to scrape it smooth. Then I gave it a sharp point and brought this to a glow in the blazing fire. Hiding this olive-wood spike, we waited until evening.

"Returning with his flocks, the Cyclops brought all of the animals inside, not just the ones he milked. I don't know why. Maybe some god ordered him to do it. He replaced the big stone in the doorway, milked his sheep and goats, and again killed and ate two more men.

"Now I ventured to offer him a drink of wine, saying I'd brought it especially for him. He drank the wine, liked it immensely, and demanded more. He asked my name so that he could give me a guest-gift. I kept giving him more wine and said my name was Outis (No one). He replied that as his guest-gift to me, he would eat 'No one' last, after his companions. He seemed to think he was being funny. Soon, though, he fell asleep, lying on his back, vomiting up bits of man-meat mixed with wine. It was disgusting.

"I quickly heated up the point of the olive-wood spike, shoving it into the coals of the fire. I spoke encouragingly to my companions so none would back out of the plan in fear. And when the spike was hot, we drove it deep into the Cyclops's eye, drilling it in exactly as a ship's carpenter drills a hole in a wooden beam. The eyelid and eye socket sizzled as they burned. The sound and the steam reminded me of the way a bronzeworker hardens a great axe or adze by dipping it in cold water.

"Shrieking in pain, the Cyclops yanked the spike out of his eye. It was covered in blood. He called out to other Cyclopes inhabiting caves on the windy ridges. Hearing him shouting, they came from every direction, demanding to know why he was making such noise and keeping them all awake. 'Surely no one is stealing your flocks, are they? No one is killing you by treachery or by force, are they?'

"And he yelled back, 'Oh, my friends, Outis (No one) is killing me by treachery or by force.'

"This certainly bewildered them! The other Cyclopes responded, 'Well, if indeed you are alone and no one is overpowering you, then you must accept that the illness comes from Zeus and you can't escape it.' They departed, advising him to pray to Poseidon, his father. And I laughed out loud at the success of my clever device.

"The Cyclops was in terrible pain, but we remained trapped. He pushed the great stone out of the doorway and sat down on the threshold, waiting to catch us in case we were stupid enough to try to sneak past.

"I quickly devised a plan. Using pliant twigs to tie the biggest rams together in threes, I tied one of my men onto the middle ram of each set. I clung to the fleece underneath the belly of one really big ram, while we waited for the long night to pass.

"In the morning, we went out through the cave doorway with the flocks. The Cyclops touched the sheep as they passed but completely missed my men and me. Outside, I released my ram and untied my companions. We raced for our ship, herding the sheep ahead. Loading them on board, we climbed in and rowed away as fast as possible.

"When we were still just within shouting distance of land, I had to gloat. Calling out to the Cyclops, I said the gods had made him pay for eating his guests. In response, he tore off the peak of a mountain and threw it at my ship. It missed, landing in front of the prow, but the resulting wave pushed us back onto shore. We pushed off and rowed away again. When we were nearly beyond voice range, I began to call to him again, but my companions

begged me to shut up. They were afraid that the Cyclops might throw something else and have better aim this time.

"But I had to tell the Cyclops who I was. 'Cyclops,' I taunted, 'If anyone
asks how you lost your eye, tell him Odysseus blinded you. I'm famous for
sacking cities. Laertes is my father, and I'm from Ithaca.'

"He called me a nobody and a weakling, and said his father Poseidon
would heal his eye.

"I yelled back that I wished I'd killed him. That's when he cursed me. He
called to his father Poseidon, asking him to prevent my homecoming. But if
it was my fortune to return home, then he prayed that Poseidon ensure that I
arrive in terrible shape, having lost my companions, and that I find suffering
at home. He threw another, bigger stone at us but missed again.

"After escaping the Cyclops, we rejoined our other companions and continued on. Still grieving for the companions we'd lost, we landed on the floating
island of Aeolus, immortal master of the winds. Aeolus gave me a leather sack
containing every wind, so that none could blow us off course. He released the
west wind to push us straight along toward home. But our story wasn't going
to finish this way, because we destroyed ourselves by our own foolishness.

"Ten days of sailing brought us in sight of home. But then I fell asleep. I
was exhausted from steering the whole time. My companions assumed that
the bag Aeolus had given me contained silver and gold. They untied the sack,
and the winds rushed out. The men screamed as the storm winds snatched
them up and out into the sea. I expected to die. But I endured and waited,
lying hidden in the ship. The winds blew us back to Aeolus's island. But he
wouldn't help us again, convinced now that the gods hated me.

"Sailing for another week, we reached the land of the Laestrygonians. I held
my ship near the harbor's edge and sent men to see what they could learn
about the Laestrygonians. There were thousands of these gigantic creatures.
They ate some of my men and hurled huge rocks at the ships. I got my ship
away quickly, but the other ships were destroyed. Sailing on, we grieved for
our lost companions, though we were happy to have avoided death ourselves.

"We arrived next on the island of the terrible goddess Circe, daughter of
the sun god. I could see smoke rising from her great halls, and I sent half of
my men to investigate. I remained behind with others at the ship. The wolves

in Circe's courtyard greeted my men like dogs seeing their master. The men could hear the goddess singing as she worked at her weaving.

"Circe welcomed my companions and gave them food and drink. But she mixed drugs into the food, which changed the men into pigs. They kept their human minds, as before, but she kept them in pigpens and fed them pig food. Only one man returned to tell what had happened. This man hadn't entered Circe's house with the others because he'd suspected some deception.

"I immediately went to rescue my men. Along the way, I met the messenger god Hermes. He was disguised as a young man. He gave me a drug to counteract Circe's drugs and told me what to do. Following his instructions, I consumed the food and drink that Circe gave me, but it had no effect. When she tried to herd me into the pigpen, I rushed at her madly with my sword. She recognized me as Odysseus because Hermes had told her I would come to her one day.

"Circe wanted to sleep with me, but I first made her swear that she wasn't planning to do me harm. I slept with her then in a luxurious bed prepared by her divine attendants. But when Circe saw that I was unhappy, she released my men and turned them back into human beings. I returned to the ship for my other companions, and Circe hosted us all magnificently for a year.

"When the year had passed, my companions insisted that it was time to return home. Circe said I could leave, but that I would have to go to the underworld before I could get home. The prospect devastated me. No one has ever reached the underworld by ship. But Circe gave me precise instructions, which I followed carefully.

"In the underworld, I saw and spoke to the spirits of the dead. From the spirit of the seer Teiresias, I learned that Poseidon hated me and was preventing my homecoming because I'd blinded his son. Teiresias said I would be able to return home if I chose to restrain my passion and the passion of my companions. Warning me not to eat the cattle of the sun god, he said I'd eventually return home all alone and find my home in terrible turmoil, with men courting my wife and taking my things. But he assured me that I would defeat and punish these suitors.

"The spirit of my mother came to me next. I hadn't known she'd died. She told me that Penelope remained faithful to me, and that Telemachus was administering my lands. She said that my father still lived and longed for me terribly. I tried to embrace her, but my arms encircled nothing. She explained that when mortals die, the spirit leaves the body and flutters away like a dream.

"I also spoke with many spirits of other famous women, whose stories you've probably heard. But there were so many I honestly couldn't tell you all their names. The night isn't long enough. And I really do need to sleep now."

Odysseus's tale has captivated his listeners. The Phaeacian king and queen ask him to stay the night while they ready the ship to take him home and prepare gifts for him. Odysseus says he would willingly remain an entire year if necessary, if they give him many things, since that's far better than returning emptyhanded.

Praising Odysseus as a vivid and credible storyteller, the king says that none of his people thinks Odysseus is lying or telling made-up stories "from which no one might see or know anything." *You wonder whether this is true. Do you believe Odysseus?* The king urges him to continue his tale.

"Well, if you insist," says Odysseus, "I'll tell you what happened to the men who survived the Trojan war but were destroyed, when they arrived home, by the will of that evil woman." *In a second, you'll realize he means King Agamemnon's wife Clytemnestra.*

"In the underworld I saw the spirit of Agamemnon," Odysseus explains, "and it made me cry to see him. He said that upon his return, his wife's lover, with her help, murdered him and his companions just as if he were an ox and his men were pigs slaughtered for a feast. His wife, Clytemnestra, also killed Cassandra, a daughter of Priam, king of Troy." *Again, the same story that Zeus, Athena, Nestor, and Menelaus all mentioned. Now you're getting Agamemnon's perspective.* "Agamemnon's spirit insisted that there's nothing worse than a disloyal wife," Odysseus continues. "I agreed. Look at all the trouble Helen caused! Agamemnon's spirit warned me to be cautious when I returned home, since women are so untrustworthy.

"The spirit of Achilles was very surprised to see me in the underworld, where the unseen dead dwell, the phantoms of toiling mortals. I tried to cheer him by reminding him that when he was alive we honored him as if he were a god, and that now he rules over the dead.

"But Achilles dismissed my effort to console him. He said he'd rather be a poor servant to a completely destitute man than ruler of the dead in the underworld. He really hated being dead.

"Achilles asked for news of his father and son. About his father I knew nothing, but I told him that his son behaved nobly at Troy in council and in battle, sailing toward home afterward with honor and his fair share of plunder. This pleased Achilles very much.

"All the other spirits approached me, except the great Greek warrior Ajax. He was still furious over the decision made at Troy about Achilles's immortal armor. After Achilles died, the Trojans judged that I and not Ajax should have Achilles's armor. Now Ajax's spirit refused to talk to me. Even dead, he wouldn't subdue his anger. He strode away without saying a word.

"I also saw many other spirits, including Hercules, who told me of his sufferings and his own successful journey to the underworld and back. I wanted to see more of the great men of the generations before mine, but I became frightened and returned to my ship, ordering my companions to row away fast.

"We remained with Circe another day and night. She told me how to get past the enchanting, immortal Sirens. Everyone wants to hear their singing but then, entranced and unable to leave the Sirens' meadow, wastes away from starvation. Circe told me to have my companions block their ears with soft wax and tie me to the mast so that I could listen as we sailed by without being permanently captivated and unable to leave. Circe also told me how to get safely past the Clashing Rocks; the monstrous, man-eating Scylla with her six necks and six terrible heads; and the horrible whirlpool Charybdis. Circe warned me not to touch the sheep or cattle on the island of the sun god. Otherwise, I wouldn't make it home.

"I followed Circe's instructions, and everything happened as she said. Hearing the Sirens' song was the most enthralling experience. They know the entire history of men, including all the events at Troy and before. No one ever before had heard their song and survived. I wanted to remain listening forever, but my companions obeyed my prior command not to untie me, and we sailed on past.

"Our passage between Scylla and Charybdis was horrifying, and I had to work hard to keep my companions' spirits up. Scylla gobbled up six of my men. That was the worst thing I ever saw. The men shrieked and stretched out their hands to me as Scylla gulped them down.

"I tried to convince my companions not to land on the island of the sun god, but they were so hungry and weary that they wouldn't listen. I warned them not to kill and eat the sun god's sheep or cattle, and they swore they wouldn't. But we were stuck there for a month, the south wind blew continuously, and our food and wine ran out. One day, while I slept, my companions killed and ate the cattle.

"Calypso told me afterward that the sun god Helios found out, and Zeus decided to destroy my ship and companions. When we left the sun god's island a week later and were out in the middle of the sea, storm winds and Zeus's thunderbolts and lightning blasts shattered our ship, hurling my men into the water. They never made it home.

"I managed to tie the keel to the mast and floated along on that through the storm. The winds blew me back through Scylla and Charybdis. I clung to an overhanging olive branch for a long time, while Charybdis submerged my keel and mast before finally belching them out again.

"On the tenth day afterward, the gods drew me near Calypso's island. I have already told how I got here from there. I hate to tell a story twice when it's been told clearly already."

Odysseus stops speaking. The king of the Phaeacians assures Odysseus that he thinks he will make it home, and he bids his people to be generous in providing gifts. They load and ready the ship, and everyone returns to the palace for another feast.

You realize that Odysseus never explained why tales of the Trojan War make him cry. He, Nestor, Menelaus, and others like them consider warfare the most admirable activity for men, but they all find remembering wartime events painful. This does not make them question their priorities, but it might make you question them. How admirable or desirable are experiences that are miserable in the recalling?

In contrast, Odysseus seems to enjoy retelling his post-Troy adventures: his time with Circe, his trip to the underworld, his encounters with the Cyclops and other monsters. He's evidently proud of his own endurance, ingenuity, and cleverness. His story seems so plausible. Or does it? Presumably you've never encountered such monsters. Or talked to the dead.

The narrator now resumes speaking, and events move quickly. On the Phaeacians' ship, Odysseus falls asleep. Deposited still asleep on Ithaca along with a great pile of gifts, Odysseus awakens with no idea where he is. Athena has cast mist over everything. Suddenly a young shepherd appears. The narrator tells you that this is Athena in disguise. The "shepherd" tells Odysseus that he's on Ithaca. Cautious and apparently unconvinced, Odysseus proceeds to lie, claiming that he's heard of Ithaca but has never seen it. He fabricates a long tale, maintaining that he's from Crete, that he killed a man in a quarrel over possessions taken when Troy fell, and that he suffered a long, arduous sea voyage but was finally deposited here by some Phoenicians.

You recognize Odysseus' lengthy explanation as resembling the truth but also entirely false. So, of course, does Athena. Athena knows that Odysseus is lying, and his deceptiveness delights her. She identifies herself to him, and she praises his caution and cleverness. Clearing the mists so that he can see Ithaca for himself, Athena describes the situation inside Odysseus's home and the suitors' plot to ambush Telemachus. She helps Odysseus plan his return and revenge, and she disguises him as an old beggar so that no one will recognize him.

Athena goes to find Telemachus, who is still in Sparta, while Odysseus sets off inland through the woods toward home. He arrives first at the shelter of one of his slaves, an elderly swineherd who has faithfully been tending Odysseus's pigs during his master's long absence. The old man welcomes the disguised Odysseus warmly without recognizing him. He offers his guest ample food and wine, and he laments the absence of his kindly, beloved master, explaining that he sailed to Troy but hasn't returned. The swineherd criticizes the suitors who have commandeered Odysseus's home and are feasting unrestrainedly on Odysseus's livestock.

Despite the swineherd's evident faithfulness and unhappiness, Odysseus continues to conceal his identity. He assures the old man that Odysseus is on his way home, but the swineherd doesn't believe him. He knows that beggars often tell falsehoods to ingratiate themselves with their hosts. He doesn't believe that his master will ever return, but like Odysseus's wife, father, and son, he hopes he will. The swineherd praises Telemachus, telling his guest where he's gone and why. Eventually, he asks his guest to identify himself.

Once again, Odysseus spins a long, lying tale. This one is really lengthy. Again he says he's from Crete. But this time he's the illegitimate son of a wealthy man, disinherited by his father's legitimate children. He brags extensively about his own impressive talent for warfare and the numerous successful raiding expeditions he led. He went to Troy with the Cretan force and returned home after sacking the city, but stayed only a month before leaving for another expedition against Egypt. In Egypt his good luck failed. Lacking caution and self-restraint, his men attacked immediately, without reconnoitering first. They were routed and killed, but he himself was spared and given hospitality by the Egyptian king. After seven years he was deceived by a treacherous Phoenician man who hosted him for a year but then planned to sell him into slavery in Libya. Shipwrecked on the voyage to Libya, the "beggar" claims, he floated on the mast and landed in Thesprotia. He was nearly enslaved there, too, but he escaped and hid. The gods brought him here to the shelter of a sensible man. The "beggar" insists that the Thesprotians told him that Odysseus was definitely on his way home.

Such a long, convoluted tale! So many details, so like the truth but not quite. The swineherd can't think why the beggar would lie to him. (*Does he suspect that this is Odysseus?*) He doesn't believe that his master is on his way home. He has been deceived by liars before, and he won't be conned. Still, he continues to provide generous hospitality.

Odysseus continues to lie to him, telling another long tale about an ambush that he and Odysseus led at Troy. Odysseus is trying to convince the swineherd to give him a warm cloak by describing the generosity of another warrior toward him on this particular nighttime ambush. (*You see that Odysseus is a relentless swindler.*) The swineherd has no extra clothing to provide, but he makes his guest a warm, comfortable bed, and promises that Telemachus will give him new clothes when he returns.

Meanwhile, Athena urges Telemachus to make his way homeward from Sparta, and she advises him on how to avoid the suitors' ambush.

While Telemachus heads for home, Odysseus learns from the swineherd that his father, Laertes, remains alive, grieving terribly for his absent son and for his wife, who has died of grief, missing her son. Hearing this, the "beggar" remains in character, shedding not a tear. Preserving his disguise, Odysseus also listens attentively as the swineherd tells how he became Odysseus's slave. He was the son of a king in Syria, but he was kidnapped as a child by Phoenicians and sold to Laertes. *Like Odysseus's false tales of near enslavement, the swineherd's story reminds you how easily human fortunes can change.*

The following morning, Telemachus arrives safely in the harbor of Ithaca and walks to the swineherd's shelter. The swineherd's dogs greet him joyfully. Evidently the young man is familiar and beloved here. The swineherd welcomes his young master with tears in his eyes, as happy and relieved as if he were greeting his own long-absent son. Odysseus remains silent. *You can only imagine his emotions as he gazes on his nearly adult son, whom he last saw as an infant.* The swineherd informs Telemachus that the suitors continue to abuse their power while Penelope still endures miserable nights and tearful days.

The swineherd introduces Odysseus as his guest from Crete, and Telemachus expresses sadness that he can't host the man properly in his home. Condemning the suitors' behavior, the "beggar" wishes that he were younger or that Odysseus had a son. He listens attentively as Telemachus, naming his father, grandfather, and great-grandfather, explains that he's an only child with no brothers to help him in his father's absence. Outnumbered, he can't hold out much longer. Telemachus commands the swineherd to notify his mother of her son's return. The swineherd also wants to tell Laertes, but Telemachus orders him to tell his mother to send a secret message to the grieving old man later.

When the swineherd departs, Athena suddenly appears in the guise of a tall, beautiful woman. Visible only to Odysseus, she tells him that it's time to identify himself to Telemachus, and she miraculously transforms him back into a strong man in his prime. To his astounded son, Odysseus abruptly announces, "I am your father." Telemachus's initial skepticism lasts but a moment. He takes his father at his word. Odysseus explains (truthfully, you know) that Phaeacians deposited him on Ithaca and gave him abundant gifts, now hidden in a nearby cave. *Like his father, Telemachus doesn't show his emotions. Is he impressed with the man he's meeting essentially for the first time? Does he feel happy? Relieved? Anxious? Like his father, he never lets on.*

The reunion is brief. Father and son must determine how to defeat the far too numerous suitors. Assuring Telemachus that he has Athena and Zeus on his side, Odysseus instructs his son to return to the house and behave normally, but to gather up every weapon in secret and lock them all away in the storeroom, leaving only two swords, two spears, and two shields for himself and his father. He must let no one know of his father's return. Not even Penelope. Odysseus will follow afterward in his beggar's disguise.

While the suitors return from their failed ambush, arguing over whether to make another attempt to kill Telemachus, Athena transforms Odysseus, still in the swineherd's shelter, back into an elderly, decrepit beggar. The swineherd, returning, informs his guests that he believes the suitors' ship has returned. Unperceived by the swineherd, father and son share a look and a confident smile. *To you, their plan seems sketchy at best.*

DISTINGUISHING FACTS FROM FALSEHOODS

This section of the *Odyssey* fortifies us against the deceptions of a consummate con artist. The tyrant or would-be tyrant requires gullible subjects unwilling or unable to fact check his assertions, no matter how outlandish they may be. The successful tyrant excels at spreading numerous and contradictory falsehoods, so as to destroy the very concept of truth.[1] Tales narrated by Odysseus in the *Odyssey*, however, evoke our skepticism and cultivate our empiricism because we have other evidence against which to measure them. The longest one, told by Odysseus to the Phaeacians, contains many supernatural elements. Later, back on Ithaca, Odysseus offers various accounts of his own identity that contradict facts previously established by the narrator. In order to follow the *Odyssey*'s twists and turns and appreciate Odysseus's cleverness, we ourselves must strive to distinguish the truth from the lies.

Imaginary and fantastic stories can be pleasurable and educational, this section of the *Odyssey* suggests, but only if we recognize a distinction between fact and fiction.[2] We've seen that Odysseus cannot begin to recover his identity and restore order in his home and community until he rejects a fantasy existence of immortality and unending sex and, shortly afterward, a fairy-tale life of effortless prosperity and eternal happiness. By choosing to reject an imaginary, supernatural existence, Odysseus makes real life in a desirable human society an actual possibility. But "real life," our own included, inevitably incorporates stories of all kinds, and these can be both delightful and instructive. Odysseus's description of his own adventures, while perhaps the most lively and entertaining section of the *Odyssey*, also strains our credulity. The narrator of the *Odyssey* never vouches for the authenticity of Odysseus's account. Our only evidence for the genuineness of these adventures is that Odysseus says that they occurred. [3]

Unlike many works of fiction, the *Odyssey* does not ask or permit us to suspend disbelief. We cannot fully enjoy adventure stories like the Harry Potter series, for example, or movies like the *Star Wars*, *Avengers*, *Hunger Games*, *Spiderman*, or *Iron Man* series, if we insist on thinking, "Oh, that's impossible. That could never happen." To appreciate such stories we must immerse ourselves in the world of the narrative and refrain from asking awkward questions. To enjoy the *Odyssey*, however, we must continuously strive to disentangle the true from the false. If we unquestioningly accept everything we are told, we miss not only the cleverness but the whole point.

Odysseus's tales caution us against mindless credulity. His exciting and—let's be honest—implausible narrative includes numerous supernatural characters and events. No other sections of the poem, related by the *Odyssey*'s third-person narrator, contain so many fantastical elements and magical creatures. Odysseus describes not only a gigantic one-eyed Cyclops and a ram big enough to carry a man (*Od.* 9), but also a bag containing all of the winds (*Od.* 10); an interlude with the divinity Circe, who turns men into pigs and back again (*Od.* 10); a visit to the underworld (*Od.* 11); and encounters with the mesmerizing Sirens and the horrific monsters Scylla and Charybdis (*Od.* 12).[4] This abundance of supernatural features, concentrated in Odysseus's account, must prompt hearers or readers of the epic to wonder whether his stories are true or false. Do we believe him? Should we?

Odysseus's narrative, so extraordinary for its fantasy elements, encourages our skepticism. Odysseus is a compelling storyteller, and the Phaeacians

seem to accept his artful tale as true. But in the middle of his guest's account of visiting the underworld, the Phaeacian king makes a point of assuring Odysseus that everyone believes his tales.[5] The king says that none
of the Phaeacians think that he's lying or telling fabricated stories "from
which no one might see or know anything" (*Od.* 11.363–66). It is as if the
king were saying, "We believe you, Odysseus, but there's thousands that
wouldn't." This explicitly puts us on the alert—if a tale of a journey to the
underworld hasn't already. The king's insistence that no one thinks Odysseus is lying recalls us to our responsibility as listeners to distinguish fact
from fiction. By suggesting that a "false" story is one that teaches nothing,
the king reminds us to measure every story against our own empirical experience. Unlike the Phaeacians and other characters hearing Odysseus's
deceptive tales later in the narrative, we have other evidence against which
to measure Odysseus's claims.[6] Lies teach nothing, the Phaeacian king suggests, but fiction can be instructive. In order to "see or know"—that is, to
learn anything from Odysseus' tales—we have to be able to distinguish the
facts from the fabrications.

Only once we fully prioritize reality can we learn from stories without
being deceived or misled by them. We don't know whether any of the tales
in the *Iliad* or *Odyssey* are factually true or historically accurate. But until
prose writers in the fifth century BCE asserted that the ancient tales were
too distant in time to be verifiable, the ancient Greeks did not really begin
to differentiate *muthos* (myth) from "history" (the word derives from the
Greek *historiē*, meaning an inquiry into the facts so as to make an informed
evaluation). The Greek historians Herodotus and Thucydides opted to
narrate contemporary or near-contemporary events, drawing primarily on
their own experience or other eyewitness accounts.[7] Prior to this, Greeks
of the archaic period, as the Phaeacian king's interruption suggests, distinguished not "history" from "myth," but truth from falsehood in narrative
storytelling.

Whether we distinguish history from myth or truth from falsehood, we
all need stories. The early scenes in the *Odyssey*'s "real world" of Ithaca, Pylos,
and Sparta include storytelling as an essential source of education and a
necessary means of preserving and ordering life in a healthy community. On

chaotic Ithaca, the singer's tales merely provide cover for a secret conversation between Telemachus and Athena-disguised-as-Mentes (*Od.* 1.153–57.). But in the thriving, harmonious communities of Pylos and Sparta, stories preserve the memory of impressive deeds and offer examples of choices and actions to avoid or to emulate (e.g., *Od.* 3.102–200; 3.253–328; 4.78–112; 4.235–89; 4.347–587). The stories of Nestor, Menelaus, and Helen preserve and transmit the values of the community to members of present and future generations.[8]

Stories can educate us and connect us to one another, but the *Odyssey* suggests that the distinction between "true" and "false" matters, and that recognizing the distinction is our responsibility. When Telemachus visits Sparta, King Menelaus describes in detail his own encounter with the supernatural shape-shifting Proteus, the old man of the sea (*Od.* 4.384–570). Menelaus claims that when he and his men tried to capture Proteus, the god transformed himself into a lion, a snake, a leopard, and a boar, and then into water and then a tree (*Od.* 4.455–58). This story seems no more plausible than Odysseus's visit to the underworld, and the *Odyssey*'s narrator similarly never attests to its authenticity. Menelaus's hearers within the epic—his wife, guests, and obedient subjects—do not question the presence of supernatural elements in their king's story. Such credulity befits subordinates in an autocratic community such as Menelaus's Sparta. As king, Menelaus can expect to be believed. No one says, "Wait a minute, hold on a sec . . . how did . . . ?"

Like Menelaus, twenty-first-century autocrats and would-be autocrats rely on others' inability or unwillingness to question the truth of their stories and pronouncements, but the *Odyssey* encourages skepticism in its external audience, the hearers or readers of the epic. Odysseus's tales of his own adventures invite us to doubt his reliability as a narrator. Prodded by the Phaeacian king's interruption, we may begin to compare this story (and every story) to our own experience of the world. When Odysseus narrates, the *Odyssey* becomes substantially less realistic and more fantastic. Even after the epic's third-person narrator resumes the account of Odysseus's adventures in book 13, Odysseus continues to tell many other tales during the second half of the *Odyssey*. We discover that if we do not attempt to sift the facts from the falsehoods, the truth from the tricks, we cannot begin to comprehend Odysseus's talents or to learn from his story. Odysseus's tales remind us that the facts do matter. Matching wits with Odysseus, we develop the skills to fortify ourselves against modern autocrats who bombard us with fictions, even contradictory fictions, so as to eradicate the very concept of objective fact.

EVALUATING THE AUTHORITATIVE SPEAKER

Nothing thwarts a would-be tyrant more than an audience of perceptive individuals capable of assessing a speaker's self-aggrandizing claims and recognizing his harmful use of clever rhetoric. Defense against the falsehoods of any authoritative storyteller requires us to be astute critical thinkers capable of evaluating evidence and judging for ourselves. Odysseus prides himself on his own curiosity, ingenuity, and verbal abilities, but his own tales suggest that these attributes are all double-edged. His account of his own adventures consistently demands our skepticism and empiricism, crucial protections against mindless subjection to a tyrant's deceptions.

Odysseus is a superb wordsmith, and he thinks very highly of himself, but by measuring his words against his actions, we develop our ability to come to our own conclusions. Odysseus himself indirectly warns us not to be mindlessly credulous, by repeatedly emphasizing his own talent for craftiness and deception as he narrates his lengthy tale to the Phaeacians. Listening to him speak, we begin to see that he will do whatever it takes to survive, and that he celebrates his own curiosity, ingenuity, resourcefulness, and endurance. But it is up to us to decide whether we consider all of this admirable. Odysseus's story of blinding the Cyclops explains why Poseidon hates him, and it also exposes the dual potential of Odysseus's nature: he is ingenious, yes, but he lacks restraint. He has foresight and determination, but he is an opportunist, and his greed and curiosity get him—and others—into trouble.

A compelling speaker knows how to flatter his audience, and Odysseus artfully presents the land of the Cyclopes as a symmetrical perversion of the orderly, idyllic community of the Phaeacians.[9] The Phaeacians have effortless material abundance and luxury, plus permanent and unchallenged (and therefore not fully human) political order. The Cyclopes have a supernatural abundance of food, too, but no political order whatsoever. Odysseus says that the Cyclopes do not need to work because their land produces food spontaneously. But he also says that they have no laws or political institutions of any kind. They have no *themis* (law, right, custom), no assembly places, and no king. They live separately in caves, and each Cyclops acts as judge for his own children and wives. The Cyclopes do not care for one another (*Od.* 9.106–15).[10]

Odysseus may be shaping his account to flatter his immediate audience, the Phaeacians, but he is also exposing an important political insight. Any audience—ancient or modern—will observe the poor quality of life available to the Cyclopes in the absence of political and social order. Individuals in the politically stable society of the Phaeacians enjoy numerous features of a thriving community: not only abundant food supplies but also a harbor, a splendid palace with a beloved king and queen, assemblies, communal feasts, sporting competitions, stories, song, dance. The Cyclopes live isolated in caves.

In emphasizing the value of political order and the bleak existence possible without it, Odysseus also encourages his audience's critical judgement, because his interpretation and corroborating evidence appear inadequate. Odysseus connects the Cyclopes' lack of social and political organization to their lack of ordinary human creativity and industry, but his own account does not support this assessment. Explaining that the Cyclopes have no need to work, Odysseus criticizes their lack of technology, but this turns out to be not quite true. Odysseus faults the Cyclopes for lacking the imaginative ability to exploit the natural resources of the island just outside their own harbor. (By implication, he also celebrates his own entrepreneurial spirit.) He sneers at their technological backwardness, noting that they have no ships and so cannot develop the nearby island's resources (*Od.* 9.125–36). We see, however, that the Cyclopes do have the technology to make cheese, and that the Cyclops Polyphemos is very industrious in herding and milking his animals and manufacturing cheese (*Od.* 9.233–49). Despite Odysseus's claims, lack of technology cannot account for the Cyclopes' lack of political order.

Disdaining the Cyclopes' lack of technology, and showing unmitigated
confidence in all human contrivance, Odysseus inadvertently cautions us
against such indiscriminate enthusiasm for technology. The *Odyssey* as a
whole encourages the audience to recognize the ambivalent force of human
invention; technology solves problems but also creates new ones. Ingenuity and technological skill enable Odysseus to blind the Cyclops and escape
from his cave. Odysseus uses analogies to woodworking and metalworking
to describe driving the massive olive-wood spike into the Cyclops's eye (*Od.*
9.382–86 and 389–93). But the blinding incurs a god's hatred. Similarly,
Odysseus's ability to construct a raft singlehandedly out of natural materials enables him to leave Calypso's island (*Od.* 5.234–61). But this also puts
his life at risk on the open sea. His ingenious trick with the wooden horse
enables the Greeks to sack Troy, but it also causes suffering not only for
Trojans but also for Greeks: the subsequent battle is especially horrible (*Od.*
8.519–20). Odysseus criticizes the Cyclopes for their lack of shipbuilders,
but shipbuilding produced the Trojan War and terrible misery for Trojans
and Greeks, both during the war and after. Without ships, the Trojan prince
Paris could never have sailed to Greece in the first place, nor could the Greeks
have sailed to Troy to avenge the theft of Helen.[11] Odysseus's unmitigated
enthusiasm for human technology characterizes him as unscrupulously ambitious and enterprising, but a ship or a raft, like a smartphone, tablet, or
social media platform, is only as good or life-enhancing as its user. Odysseus's adventures and the entire Trojan War itself suggest that technology
is neither good nor bad per se; it all depends on how it is used.

Odysseus's confident assertions about the Cyclopes and himself cultivate
our ability to resist a speaker's value judgements and instead sharpen our
own. Like technology, human skills and personality traits can be double-
edged. Curiosity is, of course, a spur to creativity and invention, but it has
risks. Odysseus prides himself unequivocally on his curiosity and ingenuity,
while we see that these traits, along with acquisitiveness, also get him into
trouble. On the island of the Cyclopes, curiosity and greed imperil Odysseus and his companions and cause the deaths of six men. Finding the cave
of the absent Cyclops filled with milk, cheeses, lambs, and goats, Odysseus
wants to see the Cyclops and discover whether he will provide guest-gifts

(*Od.* 9.224–29). As he narrates the tale to the Phaeacians, Odysseus real-izes that plundering the cave and departing swiftly, as his companions ad-vised, would have been preferable (*Od.* 9.224–30). But in the moment of finding the cave, his curiosity and greed defeat caution.[12]

Odysseus takes pride in his own curiosity, but we see that it also leads him to violate the norms of civilized behavior. Walking in and helping themselves to the Cyclops's possessions in his absence, Odysseus and his companions replicate the suitors' behavior in Odysseus's home on Ithaca. In a host's absence, you are not supposed to enter his home and help your-self. Under the reciprocal system of *xenia*, you may expect a warm and generous welcome, but whether or not the host opts to offer this remains entirely up to him.

Instead of exemplifying admirable curiosity, this episode shows that an absence of self-control perverts a normally useful reciprocal process, since lack of restraint on one side produces an even more egregious lack of restraint on the other. Odysseus's violation of the guest's responsibili-ties causes the Cyclops's spectacular violation of the host's responsibilities. Seeing Odysseus and his men inside his cave, the Cyclops immediately asks who they are and what they are doing. That's not how *xenia* works. For ex-ample, in Pylos and Sparta and on the island of the Phaeacians, all models of traditional social order, the host reserves that question for *after* he has entertained his guests generously. But by the time the Cyclops sees Odys-seus and his men, they have already helped themselves to what they wanted. Like the suitors on Ithaca, they have precluded the possibility of the host fulfilling his responsibilities under *xenia*. The Cyclops violates the rules of *xenia* most egregiously, preventing his guests' departure and eating some of them. He begins by addressing Odysseus and his men as *xeinoi* (guest-friends; *Od.* 9.252), reminding them—and us—of their obligations under *xenia*. But we see that the system, ordinarily so beneficial to both guests and hosts, is here completely not operating.

Extricating himself from this nearly disastrous situation, Odysseus dem-onstrates the ambivalent potential of human speech to do good or cause harm. In this encounter, Odysseus's supreme ingenuity takes the form of wordplay. Telling the Cyclops that his name is *Outis* (No one), he prevents the Cyclops from identifying his attacker to the other Cyclopes.[13] As he describes the scene to the Phaeacians, Odysseus delights in his own manipulative artistry, but he demonstrates in addition a self-destructive lack of verbal restraint. By his own account, he incurs Poseidon's anger by blinding the god's son, but the god's anger becomes Odysseus's problem only because he can't resist bragging about the blinding afterward. Having escaped with his remaining companions, but unable to leave well enough alone, Odysseus insists on mocking and taunting the Cyclops (*Od.* 9.473–79). The Cyclops responds by hurling the summit of a mountain at the ship, nearly destroying Odysseus and his men (*Od.* 9.481–86). Nevertheless, and despite his companions' protests, Odysseus still wants full credit for the blinding, and he gratuitously announces his name, his father's name, and his home (*Od.* 9.502–5).[14] Odysseus's *words*, not merely his actions, evoke the Cyclops's curse and Poseidon's decision to obstruct Odysseus's return home.

Odysseus's use of language in his encounter with the Cyclops invites us to assess both the benefits and the risks of this potent human invention. Odysseus is a talented storyteller, but what exactly does that mean? Someone who entertains? Someone who seeks to profit from his listeners' credulity? Or someone who cultivates listeners' skepticism and capacity for rational deliberation? Just like technology or ingenuity of any kind, a talent for verbal communication can help or harm individuals and communities. Odysseus's deception of the Cyclops shows that the clever use of language can promote survival. Epic tales themselves provide a verbal form of immortality by memorializing *klea andrōn* (the glorious achievements of men).[15] But Odysseus's gratuitous, shortsighted self-promotion, his need to boast to the Cyclops of his own "achievement," imperils his homecoming and ultimately destroys all of his remaining companions. Although such an impulse to boast might seem unremarkable in a victorious Homeric warrior in the heat of conflict, Odysseus's example here cautions against the misuse of language and an unrestrained, unreflective appetite for *kleos* (glory; the singular of *klea*). Both of these things can imperil a speaker and those who accept his authority.

A functioning egalitarian community must resolve disputes using words, not swords. But Odysseus's tales, and especially his encounter with the Cyclops, remind us that words have great power and must be interpreted and used with caution. (What if the Cyclops had responded, "Outis?! What kind of a name is *that*? I think you're trying to trick me." What if Odysseus had restrained his boastful impulse afterward to tell the Cyclops his real name?) If we prefer not to be duped like the Cyclops, unquestioningly accepting as factually true the unverified and sometimes unverifiable pronouncements of others, then we need to be more discerning and more capable of measuring a story logically against objective evidence. If we don't want to harm ourselves, like Odysseus, by our own unrestrained use of language, then we must, equally, think before we speak. We must develop the capacity to evaluate authoritative speech, including our own.

EVALUATING OUR OPTIONS

Such thoughtful discernment requires effort, however, and the despot or would-be despot offers to relieve us of the burden of all deliberation. "Believe me," says the despot. "I'll tell you what's fake and what's true, what's bad and what's good. My judgments are the only ones that matter." Uncritical acceptance of authoritative pronouncements diminishes our capacity for rational thought, making us easy dupes. By cultivating our skepticism and empiricism, however, Odysseus's account of his own adventures empowers us to identify and evaluate our options for ourselves.

Contact with Odysseus develops our ability to assess the claims of an authoritative speaker. Odysseus gleefully encourages us to admire his extreme cleverness and resilience, and often his self-restraint, but we begin to recognize that he lacks restraint in his desire for self-promotion. It certainly would have been more prudent not to boast of his identity to the Cyclops. And his entire narrative sounds more than a bit self-aggrandizing, despite his emphasis on his own unique self-restraint. (He stresses, for example, his companions' failure to resist slaughtering the sun god's cattle while he alone refrains from eating and survives.) Odysseus ends his tale with his arrival on Calypso's island, because he has earlier told his audience, the Phaeacians, how he came from Calypso's island to theirs (*Od.* 7.240–86). But he can't resist praising his own storytelling ability—concluding, with self-satisfaction, "I hate to tell a story twice when it has been told clearly already" (*Od.*12.453).

Odysseus's tales encourage the audience not only to assess the consequences of cleverness and self-promotion, but also to measure real-life decisions against an imagined post-death existence. Lacking any empirical evidence of life after death, we cannot prove one conception more valid than another, but our vision of an afterlife shapes our values and our choices in real life. Describing the underworld, Odysseus reveals that there is no real life after death. The underworld is neither a heavenly paradise nor an agonizing hell. It is, instead, nonlife. Odysseus identifies existence in the underworld as the complete antithesis of everything that makes human life meaningful, pleasant, and desirable.[16]

Emphasizing the complete undesirability of existence in the underworld, Odysseus implicitly celebrates his own achievements and invites us to pursue our own. His visit to the underworld, fantastic as it seems, validates both his unique capacity for survival in the real world of human beings and his unequivocal rejection of magical offers of immortality. We now realize that Odysseus had already visited the underworld, had already seen how miserable it is to be dead, when he turned down Calypso's offer of immortality and eternal sex and the Phaeacians' offer of happily-ever-after in paradise. Knowing full well the misery of death, Odysseus nevertheless rejected the possibility of some eternally happy fantasy existence, preferring instead the experiences, relationships, and achievements of mortal life. His description of the underworld encourages us, too, to abandon an enticing ideal of a desirable afterlife if we seek to construct an admirable life in this world.

Commending his own choices, Odysseus elevates his achievements over those of Achilles, protagonist of the *Iliad*. In the *Iliad*, Achilles prioritizes vengeance over survival, accepting an early death as long as he can kill his friend's killer. In the *Odyssey*, by contrast, Odysseus consistently prioritizes survival and possesses the skills to preserve his life. Encountering the morose spirit of Achilles in the underworld, Odysseus tries to cheer him, reminding him of the great honors he received from the Greeks during his life and urging him to take comfort in thinking of the power he holds now over the dead (*Od.* 11.482–86). Odysseus insists, in effect: "You wanted great honor and you got it, didn't you? And now you're a big shot down here, right?" But Achilles claims that it's better to be the poorest of the poor on earth, a servant to a man with no property and no authority, than to rule over all of the dead (*Od.* 11.488–91). By emphasizing the complete undesirability of existence after death (even the great Achilles thinks it's terrible to be dead!), Odysseus devalues the warrior's traditional willingness to die for the honor of immortal *kleos,* and he glorifies instead his own unique talent for survival. [17]

Odysseus invites us to admire his own achievements over those of Achilles, but his comparison permits us to judge for ourselves. Achilles values his principles more than his own survival, whereas Odysseus prioritizes survival and the challenges of real life. Both alternatives are available to each of us. Like Achilles, we can opt to do what we deem right regardless of the risks of danger or death. (But now, having met Achilles in the underworld, the choice to emulate him includes the knowledge that death is no picnic.) Alternatively, like Odysseus we can strive to do everything necessary to survive. Which of these two approaches is the more admirable? Well, it depends on the circumstances.

The authoritative storyteller wants us to accept his definition of admirable behavior, but we remain free to choose. In reality, the rejection of tyranny requires every individual to cultivate the capacities of an Achilles *and* the capacities of an Odysseus. To resist the depredations of a despot, we must, like Achilles, be willing to take risks and even at times to sacrifice in order to uphold our principles. At the same time, like Odysseus we must be ingenious and flexible when circumstances require it. We must share both Achilles's determination to do whatever is necessary and Odysseus's determination to do whatever is necessary *to survive.*

Above all, we must choose worthy goals. Achilles chooses revenge over survival, but he discovers that vengeance escalates interminably, harms his community, and fails to soothe his own grief. Ultimately, he experiences empathy as a more constructive alternative.[18] If we admire Achilles today and seek to emulate his courage and integrity, we must opt to defend not vengeance but values worth dying for. Odysseus prefers real life to a fantasy existence of immortality, eternal sex, and fairy-tale happily-ever-after. He undermines any imagined ideal of a post-death paradise. If we admire Odysseus and seek to emulate his ingenuity and versatility, we must determine to uphold values worth living for, values essential to individual and group survival and success: reciprocal values such as responsibility, generosity, kindness, compassion, freedom, and tolerance.

RECOGNIZING THE TRUTH ABOUT LYING

By refusing to let the audience suspend disbelief, and instead encouraging logical deductions from empirical evidence, the *Odyssey* fortifies us against the tyranny of those who would divorce truth from real, lived, perceptible experience. Encouraged by the *Odyssey* to measure a speaker's statements against his actions and other evidence, we empower ourselves against authoritative but deceptive pronouncements.

The effort to match wits with Odysseus cultivates our critical reasoning skills.[19] Odysseus's tales remind us that lies can be instructive as long as we perceive them as lies. Over time, the ancient Greeks' interest in distinguishing fact from fiction helped them to reject the tyrant's unilateral, unassailable claim to truth and to move toward rational debate and reality-based group decision-making. Eventually they devised broader forms of political participation, including direct democracy. But long before anyone had conceived of democratic government or egalitarian social relationships, the *Odyssey* began to suggest that individual and communal survival and success require the capacity to distinguish truth from falsehood. Unless the powerless possess the desire and the skill to identify deceptive claims as falsehoods, the powerful easily conceal their abuse of power behind any disguise they choose.

The *Odyssey* calls our attention to the distinction between truth and falsehood, but it also presents lying as an admirable survival skill and truth telling as a marker of stupidity.[20] In the hierarchical, nondemocratic world of the *Odyssey*'s characters, deception and lying prove vital to an autocrat's survival. Lacking Odysseus's talent for deception, Agamemnon expects to recover his own kingship just by showing up. He promptly falls prey to the treachery of his wife and her lover. By contrast, Odysseus proceeds cautiously, concealing his true identity and spinning numerous lies.[21]

The repeatedly evoked contrast between Agamemnon's failure and Odysseus's impending success reveals that unequal or abusive power relationships *promote* lying as a survival skill. The currently powerful, like Agamemnon's wife Clytemnestra and her lover, or the suitors on Ithaca, use deception in the service of their own narrowly conceived self-interest. (Clytemnestra covertly betrays her husband. The suitors secretly plot to murder Telemachus.) Similarly, the currently weak, like the returning Odysseus, must rely on deception in order to succeed. In consequence, the gullible, like Agamemnon and the suitors, become pawns, susceptible to the self-interested manipulations of ingenious, authoritative storytellers.

By now, of course, unlike the *Odyssey*'s characters and earliest audiences, we know that models of political organization other than autocracy exist, and that a cultural admiration for lying undermines those other options. In the twenty-first century we know all too well that dishonesty completely corrupts civic relationships. Lies can benefit one individual or group at the expense of others, but they also prove toxic to the functioning of democratic institutions, and to citizens' necessary confidence in the functioning of those institutions.[22]

Having emerged in times that had never seen or heard of democracy, the *Odyssey* nevertheless invites us to consider the benefits and costs of lying in the "real world" of Homer's mortal characters. Although the third-person narration resumes in book 13, Odysseus continues to tell many false tales throughout the second half of the epic. His lies result from caution and skepticism. They reveal truths about himself, and they please a goddess, but they also exacerbate the suffering of human characters, including even his own family and friends.

We can find humor and dramatic irony in Odysseus's first encounter with Athena on Ithaca. Unlike him, we know that he is actually addressing Athena. And we also know that Athena knows exactly who he is. She pretends not to recognize Odysseus, but she informs him that he is on Ithaca. Although delighted at this news, Odysseus fails to recognize either his island or the goddess. Caution and skepticism prevent him from responding, "Oh, that's great. It's good to be home." Instead, he launches into a lengthy, completely fabricated story, claiming that he's from Crete and has heard of Ithaca but has never been there. Like any good liar, Odysseus knows to add abundant details to make his story believable; he says he was exiled from Crete after murdering a man in a dispute over plunder taken from Troy, then later transported to Ithaca by Phoenicians (not Phaeacians; *Od.* 13.221–86). His lies and his talent for lying please Athena and earn her love. The goddess remains safely immune to his deceit because, being a goddess, she knows what is true and what is not. She cheerfully identifies herself to Odysseus and praises his natural talent for cunning and deception, claiming that it is most like her own (*Od.* 13.287–301).[23] The joke is on Odysseus, and we are in on it.

But maybe the joke is on us, because Odysseus's lies paradoxically reveal the truth about him: he is a liar. Lies and deception constitute essential components of his capacity for survival. Admiringly, Athena insists, "Not even in your own land are you about to leave off from your deceptive and deceitful *muthōn* (tales), which are *philoi* (dear) to you *pedothen* (in your very heart, or literally "from the ground"; *Od.* 13.294–95.) Fundamentally a con artist, Odysseus could never fall prey to one, because he requires the confirmation of his own senses. Even after Athena identifies herself, Odysseus fears that she may be trying to trick him, and he refuses to believe her assurance that he is actually on Ithaca until he can see the island for himself (*Od.* 13.324–28).

Like the goddess, and unlike the *Odyssey*'s mortal characters, the audience can appreciate that lying both conceals and exposes Odysseus's true identity. His aliases, for example, which offer verbal puzzles for us to solve, similarly encapsulate the truth. Identifying himself to the Cyclops as *Outis* (No One), he expresses an essential truth, since he's currently wandering in a fantasy realm: he's no one, he does not exist, in the world of human beings. No human being within the *Odyssey*'s "real world" knows of his survival. In the same way, Odysseus is simultaneously *mē tis* (not anyone) and *mētis* (craft/cunning).[24] Later, his long years of wandering ended, Odysseus will test his own father by claiming to be from Alybas (or "Wanderville"—so it's kind of true) and identifying himself as Epēritos, a fake name evoking *eperizō*, meaning "to contend or strive against," or *eris* (strife), implying "man of strife"—both possibilities actually offering fairly accurate descriptions of Odysseus (*Od.* 24.302–14).[25]

Odysseus's wordplay and lies arm him against others' deception, and they please a goddess, but they have adverse consequences for other human beings, including not only his enemies but also people who care about him. At no cost to herself, Athena enjoys his fundamentally deceptive character, but his lies subsequently prolong the suffering of his most faithful slave, the elderly swineherd. Athena herself vouches for the loyalty of this devoted old man (*Od.* 13.405–6), but Odysseus nevertheless tests it. He could relieve the old man's suffering immediately by telling the truth. Instead, he spins lies. The narrator tells us that the swineherd has continued to take care of Odysseus's possessions (*Od.* 14.3–4), and the man grieves unceasingly for Odysseus (e.g., *Od.* 14.39–44), devotedly tending his absent master's pigs. Without recognizing the newly returned Odysseus, the swineherd entertains him respectfully and hospitably. But Odysseus persists in deceiving him, again claiming to be from Crete. He says that he fought bravely in Troy but suffered terribly afterward in Egypt. He says he's had word of Odysseus, and that Odysseus is on his way home (*Od.* 14.192–359).[26] The swineherd turns out to share his master's need for empirical proof, remaining skeptical and refusing to believe Odysseus's story (*Od.* 14.361–89). Odysseus could end the old man's misery and uncertainty immediately, but his caution requires deception.[27]

Odysseus's caution and deceptiveness similarly prolong the pain of his own son. When Telemachus arrives at the swineherd's shelter, having returned from his own travels, Odysseus watches the swineherd rise to greet him.[28] At this point the narrative includes a remarkable simile likening the swineherd greeting Telemachus to a father welcoming his beloved only son, who has returned home after a ten-year absence, and kissing his son as if the son had escaped from death (*Od.* 16.14–21).[29] This simile encourages us to imagine the emotions that *Odysseus* must be feeling. But it *substitutes* for a reunion between Odysseus and Telemachus that might occur right now. Such a reunion would ease Telemachus's distress immediately. And it might gratify the audience. But it would not be very suspenseful, and it might be risky for Odysseus.

Not only caution and the story's dramatic requirements but also empiricism prompts Odysseus to extend, by lying, the anguish of his family. He must first learn his son's character and the nature of the current situation in his own home. Telemachus immediately proves cautious and resourceful like his father. Prevented by circumstances from behaving properly as a host (*Od.* 16.69–89), he sends the swineherd to tell his mother that he has returned safely (*Od.* 16.130–31). But like his father, he remains willing to protract his grandfather's suffering. The old man has been grieving terribly for his absent son, and even more acutely since Telemachus departed (*Od.* 16.138–45). But only at the swineherd's suggestion does Telemachus agree to inform his grandfather of his own return, and he orders the swineherd to have Penelope notify the old man secretly later, well aware that he is prolonging the old man's misery (*Od.* 16.147–53). Odysseus's father will not learn of his son's return for quite some time.

Beyond extending his family's suffering, Odysseus's lies exemplify the *Odyssey*'s great challenge to unthinking trust in the surface meaning of an authoritative con artist's statements. Odysseus has the power to compel his son's belief, but our belief he must earn. His reunion with his son demonstrates the authority of a father's words. After the swineherd leaves, Athena prompts Odysseus to identify himself to Telemachus. It's a weird moment. Odysseus says, essentially, "I'm your dad. I'm home." Telemachus, exhibiting caution and skepticism akin to that of his father, responds, "No, you're not. That's not possible." This seems a reasonable response, given that Telemachus has never known his father. But then Odysseus simply asserts his parental authority, ending the conversation by claiming, in effect, "I am your father because I say so"—or, more literally, "As far as you are concerned, yet another Odysseus will not come here, but I am such a sort as he" (*Od.* 16.204–5). It's an ambiguous statement worthy of this deeply ambiguous man.

This scene emphasizes for the epic's audience the value of objective facts and the necessity for logical deduction. Lacking empirical proof or access to DNA testing, Telemachus must accept Odysseus's claim on faith.[30] His initial skepticism does suggest that he is his father's son, but he himself recognizes that no one can ever really know his own origins for certain, as he observes initially when Athena asks about his paternity (*Od.* 1.215–16).[31] Unlike Telemachus, however, we do not have to accept Odysseus's identity on faith, since the narrative has repeatedly affirmed it. Even so, Odysseus's conduct, not his assertions, must demonstrate whether he really is the admirable husband, father, and king he once was. He's twenty years older than when he left for Troy. Does he still have the capacity and the desire to regain and maintain his benevolent authority over his home and community? What will that require?

In addition to reminding us that authoritative pronouncements cannot establish truth in the absence of objective facts, this exchange between Telemachus and Odysseus suggests that a father's absolute authority to compel his son's unquestioning belief and trust without evidence offers no desirable political model. Odysseus's capacity for deception will help him to regain his autocratic authority, but it does not guarantee that he will rule justly or wisely. Like a father, the tyrant requires us to assume his paternal benevolence on faith. His ability to compel our credulity and trust by violence, intimidation, or sheer force of personality perpetuates his power, preserves our subordination, and infantilizes us. By now, in the twenty-first century, we know well that autocratic rule, lacking constraints and accountability, is never reliably benevolent or life-enhancing for those subject to it.

The *Odyssey*'s validation of lying as a vital survival skill in an autocratic society implicitly cautions us against admiring or succumbing to authoritative falsehoods. In the nondemocratic world depicted in the *Odyssey*, lies and deception will enable one autocrat to survive and to reestablish his benevolent political authority. Knowing nothing of democracy, Homer's original archaic audiences will have accepted this as a desirable outcome. But by presenting lying as necessary to the autocrat's survival, the *Odyssey* reminds *us* that lying perpetuates inequality and makes everyone vulnerable to the abuse of power.

Although the *Odyssey* encourages us to differentiate reality from fantasy and truth from falsehood, the process does not come naturally to us and demands hard work, whereas credulity permits us to get on with daily life.[32] Modern digital technology often thwarts our efforts, since it can blur the line between fact and fiction (as in "virtual reality" and "reality TV"). But failure to distinguish fact from fiction deprives us of the capacity to learn from experience. Failure to distinguish fact from fiction cripples our creative energies, limiting our desire and ability to discover accurate explanations and constructive solutions in the real world. An inability or unwillingness to differentiate truth from lies empowers the unscrupulous and the corrupt. Accepting or rejecting others' claims, or asserting our own, without evidence—or, worse, despite evidence—makes us easy prey for dictators and despots. By divorcing truth from verification, we signal a willingness to accept their pronouncements without question. Abandoning the need for verification, we also forfeit the possibility of persuading others. Not fact-based discussion and debate but violence, intimidation, and perhaps bribery become everyone's only tools for handling disagreements. "Democracy" becomes merely a costume worn by tyrants.

The *Odyssey* suggests that the distinction between "true" and "false" isn't merely a matter of opinion. Truth must be objectively verifiable. "False" and "fake" can't simply mean, "I don't like your claim" or "I believe otherwise." Tyrants need us to accept false stories from which we can learn nothing except subservience. They need us to deny the reality of our own experience. They need us to accept, as George Orwell has it, their proclamation that "two and two are five." Contact with Odysseus teaches us to respond: "Really? Prove it."

CHAPTER 5

SUCCESS (*ODYSSEY* 17–24)

Again you sit comfortably in someone's prosperous home, having enjoyed a good dinner and abundant wine. A singer begins to sing the concluding part of Odysseus's adventures. This could be the same singer as on previous nights. Or a different one. It doesn't matter. You expect the story to be the same, no matter who sings it. Now the ending begins:

The swineherd and a ragged old beggar proceed along a dusty track toward the home of Odysseus. The beggar leans on a curved stick. A battered leather satchel hangs from his stooped shoulders. Only you and Telemachus know that this defeated-looking man is Odysseus.

Soon, a goatherd driving some long-eared goats overtakes the two men. The goats belong to Odysseus, but they are to be dinner for the suitors. Knowing where the two old men are heading, the goatherd yells at the swineherd for bringing a beggar to the feast. He mocks the disguised Odysseus as lazy, gluttonous, and useless. Passing Odysseus on the narrow path, he kicks him hard.

Odysseus wants to bash the man with his stick and smash his head to the ground, but he remains silent and does nothing. The loyal swineherd prays for the return of his master Odysseus and the punishment of this disloyal, disrespectful goatherd, who serves the suitors and helps them consume Odysseus's property. In response, the goatherd threatens to kidnap the swineherd one day and sell him into slavery abroad. Confident that Odysseus is dead, he prays for Odysseus's son's death also. Then he walks on.

Approaching the home of Odysseus, the two old men hear music and a bard singing. They smell food from the suitors' feast. The grand house has a large courtyard with strong, beautifully built double doors. *You imagine Odysseus' eagerness to be home at last after twenty long, difficult years. But he does not rush inside. He knows he must be careful.*

While Odysseus considers his options and talks quietly with the swineherd, an old, frail dog lying on a nearby manure pile raises his head. Obviously uncared for, the dog is filthy and covered with ticks. But he has recognized Odysseus. Folding back his ears, he wags his tail. This is Odysseus's own special hunting dog, Argus, once a superb, swift tracker, but now feeble and mistreated in his master's long absence. Odysseus recognizes the dog but conceals his tears from the swineherd; he cannot greet his dog without risking revealing his identity. *You imagine his pain at being unable to acknowledge and caress his faithful dog.* Passing on into the house, the swineherd notes the servants' neglect of Odysseus's once splendid and loyal dog, observing, "Slaves don't do what they're supposed to do when their master isn't around to make them." The loyal Argus, having seen and recognized his beloved master, closes his eyes and dies.

When Odysseus in his beggar's disguise enters the house, Telemachus offers him food, but the suitors treat him with callous brutality. Asked for food, they insult him. One throws a footstool, striking him on the shoulder. Odysseus must be seething, but he keeps his temper. He reproaches the suitors, insisting ominously that if the gods and the Furies, the spirits of vengeance, care at all about beggars, the man who threw the footstool will die before he ever marries. His words increase the man's anger, but the other suitors begin to think that striking the beggar was a mistake. "What if he is a god in disguise?" they wonder.

Learning of the incident, Penelope is upset. She calls the swineherd upstairs to her room, and he reports all that the beggar has told him. "He's an amazing storyteller," the swineherd says. "He's like the most enchanting, divinely inspired singer. He tells me that Odysseus is nearby and is bringing home many valuable things."

Penelope wants to hear this directly from the "beggar" himself, and she sends for him via the swineherd. But Odysseus thinks it safer to wait until sundown. Darkness will permit them to speak in private. Penelope approves of the stranger's prudence.

Later that evening, another beggar objects to Odysseus's presence on his begging turf. Insulting, and unaware that he is accosting Odysseus in his own home, this resentful old man threatens to force Odysseus out of the house. Odysseus tries to avoid fighting, but the other beggar is relentlessly offensive. The suitors laugh, enjoying the confrontation between these two destitute, desperate men. Urging on the fight, they set a prize of food for the winner. Before fighting, Odysseus prudently makes the suitors swear they won't assist his opponent. He then beats the other beggar to a bloody pulp. The suitors laugh heartily, enjoying this brutal, cruel spectacle.

One suitor, giving Odysseus the promised prize, seems slightly nicer and more generous than the others. He speaks respectfully to Odysseus and wishes him good health and prosperity. Odysseus replies, "You seem sensible. So I'll tell you something. Of everything that breathes and creeps upon the earth, a human being is the most frail and insignificant. At his peak of vigor and excellence, a human being never expects to suffer any evil in the future. But when the bad times come, you must bear them. Look at me. I was once wealthy and successful. But I behaved stupidly and did many irresponsible things, giving in to my violent impulses. That's why you should always be thinking about what's lawful, customary, and right. I see how you suitors are treating the wife and possessions of this man, Odysseus," he continues. "I know he's nearby. I hope you never have to face him. Once he comes home, it will be bloody."

The man returns to the other side of the room, saddened by Odysseus's warning. He can see what is coming, but he can do nothing about it.

Now Athena gives Penelope the idea to come downstairs and show herself to the suitors, to increase their desire for her and also to seem more honorable to Odysseus and Telemachus. Penelope worries that the many years of grief have ravaged her once beautiful appearance, but while she sleeps, Athena restores her beauty, making her look especially tall and attractive.

Downstairs, Penelope stands beside a pillar of the well-made roof. *You get the implicit analogy: like the pillar, she's the mainstay of this house, preserving its integrity in Odysseus's absence by her steadfast loyalty and refusal to remarry.* She criticizes her son for allowing the suitors to insult the stranger. Telemachus accepts her rebuke, but he can do nothing.

The suitors praise Penelope's beauty, but she responds sadly that she lost her beauty when Odysseus left for Troy. His return would enhance her *kleos*, but now she is distressed. When he left, Odysseus told her to care for the household and his parents. If he failed to return, and he thought this not unlikely, she should remarry when Telemachus reached manhood. Thought of remarriage dismays her, but the current situation is unbearable. "In former times," Penelope continues, "suitors used to bring splendid gifts. They didn't just come and consume someone else's property."

Pleased, Odysseus admires Penelope's ability to conceal her real purposes while charming the suitors and trying to get gifts from them.

The suitors do assemble some gifts for Penelope, but they and the slave women continue to treat Odysseus disrespectfully. The young female slaves have been sleeping with the suitors, and one of them yells at Odysseus for remaining in the house. When Odysseus threatens to tell Telemachus, the women become frightened and hurry away.

Another suitor calls Odysseus bald, lazy, and gluttonous. Odysseus retorts that he could defeat the other man in farm work or in battle. Cursing this "beggar's" fearless audacity, the suitor throws another footstool. He misses Odysseus, hitting a luckless wine pourer instead. The pitcher clangs to the ground as the man falls heavily, groaning.

The suitors complain that this new "beggar" is ruining their pleasure, but Telemachus surprises everyone by shouting harshly. "You must be out of your minds! You've feasted and drunk our wine. Go home and go to sleep." But then he seems to lose his nerve. "When you feel like it, that is," he adds. "I'm not chasing anyone away."

Startled by Telemachus's sudden boldness, the suitors take another drink, pour a libation to the gods, and depart at last for their own homes. Odysseus and Telemachus proceed to gather every helmet, shield, and spear in the house and lock them in a storeroom.

When Telemachus goes upstairs to sleep, the offensive female slave yells at Odysseus again and threatens to throw a torch at him. Odysseus wonders why she hates him. "Fortune is unpredictable," he warns her. "I was once rich, prosperous, and generous to beggars. Your mistress may come to hate you, you know, or Odysseus may return. Even if he doesn't, Telemachus is growing up." Like the suitor earlier, the young slave woman fails to heed Odysseus' sensible warning.

Overhearing the exchange, Penelope scolds her slave. She has returned downstairs and now asks the "beggar" his identity and origins. *Will Odysseus finally end her grief, uncertainty, and loneliness?*

Praising Penelope's impeccable behavior, Odysseus claims that her *kleos* reaches wide heaven. He likens her to an admirable king, whose lands and people flourish under his excellent rule and leadership. *Odysseus's analogy surprises you: Ithaca at this moment is no such thriving community. How strange, too, that he likens a woman to a powerful king.* Odysseus begs Penelope not to ask his identity, for the story makes him much too sad.

Instead, Penelope tells her own poignant story, detailing her sorrow at losing her husband and her beauty, her grief and longing for Odysseus, her wish for his return, and the increase that would mean for her own *kleos*. *Like men in this story, Penelope seems very preoccupied with her posthumous reputation.* She describes her suffering at the suitors' atrocious behavior, her weaving trick, and her maidservants' betrayal. Her parents and son are urging her to remarry. Frustrated and desperate, she again asks the "beggar" his identity. *Surely Odysseus will tell her now?*

"Since you keep asking," he says, "I will tell you." And he launches into the story of being from Crete and having hosted Odysseus there once. *He's such a convincing liar. The many details of his long-winded story sound just like the truth.*

But his tale makes Penelope weep. Crying, she resembles a snow-capped mountain as the snows melt in spring and the water, flowing down, floods the rivers. Penelope cries for her lost husband, but he sits before her. Watching her cry, Odysseus pities her but keeps his gaze steady. Unlike Penelope, he holds his emotions in check and conceals his own tears. *Is this admirable willpower? Or is there something relentlessly callous about this man?*

Regaining self-control, Penelope asks the "beggar" for proof. What was Odysseus wearing when he hosted him, as he claims, long ago in Crete? "Well, it's been a long time," Odysseus says evasively. "But I'll tell you how he appeared to me." And he proceeds to describe Odysseus's clothing exactly.

Penelope cries again, certain now that her guest hosted Odysseus as he claims. She offers to make him her own guest-friend, and he assures her that Odysseus is nearby. "He has lost his companions," Odysseus explains, "but he'll return soon, bringing many splendid things."

Penelope remains skeptical, believing Odysseus dead. She offers the "beggar" a bath, clean clothes, a comfortable bed. Tomorrow, clean and properly attired, he can join the feasting.

Odysseus refuses the bath and bed, saying he prefers to remain as he is. But he agrees to have his feet washed by an old, reliable slave woman. Washing Odysseus's feet, the old woman recognizes a scar on his leg and instantly knows the "beggar's" true identity. She'd noticed, even before, his resemblance to Odysseus. *Why did Penelope miss this? Or did she? Will the old woman reveal Odysseus's identity?*

First, the narrator tells you the story of the scar and also the origin of Odysseus's odd name. As a young man, Odysseus was wounded by the tusk of a wild boar while visiting his mother's father. This grandfather had named Odysseus at birth. An apparently cranky, sour man, this grandfather disliked Ithaca and assumed others did, too. So he'd named his baby grandson after that feeling of dislike, devising his name from the verb "to be hateful," meaning both "to be full of hate" and "to be hated." *Like the scar, this strange, inauspicious name marks Odysseus clearly. It appears to have been prophetic: Odysseus has already caused much misery for others and for himself. You know he's going to cause more.*

Startled at recognizing the scar, the old woman drops Odysseus' foot, overturning the washbasin. Weeping, trying to embrace Odysseus, she turns to Penelope, about to tell her the truth. But Odysseus reacts quickly. He grips the old woman's neck and threatens to kill her if she breathes his secret to a soul. "What are you doing?" he hisses. "You nursed me when I was a baby. Are you trying to kill me now?" Odysseus shows impressive command of his emotions. And he seems ruthless. The woman speaks not a word.

Later, talking again with Odysseus, Penelope recounts her grief and solitary sleepless nights. She wonders whether to remain loyal to her husband or to choose one suitor and remarry, as Telemachus urges. In her indecision, she likens herself to the nightingale mourning her own son, whom she herself killed. (*Penelope is alluding to a gruesome ancient tale of tyrannical atrocity:*

A king raped his wife's sister, then cut out her tongue to ensure her silence. The woman managed to tell her sister by depicting the assault in a woven cloth. The sisters took vengeance by killing the king's son and feeding his body to the unwitting father. The king, the queen, and the queen's sister were subsequently transformed into birds, the queen into a nightingale. Like the queen in this horrible tale, Penelope doesn't know whether her husband has betrayed her during his long absence. You know he's had affairs with goddesses but not with any mortal women. Penelope has no idea.

Penelope tells her guest about a recent dream: A great eagle swooped down and killed her twenty beloved geese. The eagle told her, "This is not a dream. It's real. This will happen. The geese are the suitors. Before, I was an eagle, but now I'm your husband. I will destroy them all." Waking, Penelope saw her geese eating grain about the house as before. *She seems to find reassurance in this. Is she ambivalent about the suitors? Do these young noblemen make her feel attractive and admired? She must feel very lonely in Odysseus's absence.* Odysseus assures Penelope that the dream's meaning is clear, but she remains unconvinced.

Penelope abruptly decides to set a contest for the suitors. She will marry whoever shoots an arrow through a line of twelve axes. Odysseus could do this from a great distance. The "stranger" approves the plan, and Penelope returns to her room and cries herself to sleep. *Penelope's motive in setting the contest remains unclear. Has she given up hoping for Odysseus's return? Or has she recognized Odysseus and devised a way to get a lethal weapon into his hands? Did Odysseus subtly signal his identity to her? Is she just tired of waiting?*

Odysseus lies on a bed of blankets in the courtyard outside his own house. Anger and a desire for revenge keep him awake. Seeing the disloyal slave women leaving the great hall to go sleep with the suitors, Odysseus wants to leap up and kill them. But he controls himself, telling himself to wait and endure. All alone, he plans his revenge.

The next day, an oxherd drives in cattle for the day's feasting. Assured by the disguised Odysseus that Odysseus will soon return and kill the suitors, the oxherd responds, "I certainly hope so. I'd dearly like to help him do it."

During the feast, the suitors continue to insult Odysseus. One throws an ox hoof, which Odysseus dodges easily. His reflexes remain sharp, apparently, despite his hardships and the twenty-year interval. The goatherd who kicked Odysseus on the path the previous day insults him again. Odysseus stays silent. Telemachus again surprises everyone by openly criticizing the suitors, but he clearly can't control them or even the slaves in his own home.

Having listened outside the door of the great hall, Penelope goes to an immense, beautifully built storeroom high at the top of the house and removes an enormous bow and quiver, guest-gifts from a friend Odysseus met years ago. Outrageously, this same man was later killed by Hercules while a guest in Hercules's home. *This anecdote makes you wonder whether it is ever right to kill a guest in your own home. Could it be correct under any circumstances?*

Taking the bow and quiver, Penelope stands again beside the post supporting the roof and addresses the suitors. "You've been eating and drinking everything in this house, and none of it belongs to you. You want me to marry one of you? Well, here is a contest for you. I will marry whoever can string this bow and shoot an arrow through a line of twelve axes."

Each suitor hopes to succeed. Telemachus says he'll try also, to prove himself worthy of his father's possessions and authority. Then his mother could stay in the house and not remarry. *You appreciate his cunning; he knows his father is already present.* Telemachus sets up the axes and tries three times to string the bow. He might have succeeded on a fourth attempt, but Odysseus signals, with a jerk of his head, not to try again.

While each suitor tries and fails to string the bow, Odysseus takes the loyal swineherd and oxherd outside. "What would you do if Odysseus were to appear right now?" he asks them. "Would you help him? Or would you support the suitors?" Both men immediately pray to Zeus for Odysseus's return. They convince Odysseus of their loyalty and sincerity.

"Well, I am home," Odysseus announces. "I've returned after twenty years. And I see that you two alone of my slaves have remained faithful." He shows his scar to prove his identity and promises them tremendous rewards, if he succeeds in defeating the suitors.

Meanwhile, the last suitor fails to string the bow. All are ashamed. Odysseus used to string this bow easily. The suitors decide they'll try again tomorrow, and they resume drinking. Outraged at the "beggar's" request to try the bow, one of the suitors warns Odysseus, "Look, we're tolerating you. Are you drunk? Do you think we'll put up with you if you string the bow? We'll kidnap you and sell you to some king we know, a destroyer of men. Just shut up and drink your wine."

Despite Penelope's assurance that the beggar can't intend to marry her, the suitors fear the shame they'd incur if this lowly, destitute man succeeds where they have failed. They've already behaved so shamefully, she responds, that they really shouldn't worry about incurring more shame now. She offers a reward—clothing, a spear, and a sword—if the beggar strings the bow. But Telemachus tells his mother sharply, "Go back to your weaving. See that your servants do their work, too. Let us men worry about the bow. Especially me. I'm in charge here."

Telemachus's blunt assertion of his authority over the situation shocks his mother. She withdraws to her room and cries herself to sleep.

The suitors object, but the swineherd gives Odysseus the bow. Odysseus tells the one loyal female slave to lock the doors of the house from outside. Once he takes up the bow, everyone sees instantly that he knows how to handle it. He strings it easily, expertly, the way a singer strings a lyre. Then he plucks the bowstring, as if plucking a lyre, and it makes a clear, piercing sound, like the note of a swallow.

The suitors' high spirits plummet. Zeus signals approval with a loud thunderclap, and Odysseus, still seated, bends the great bow and shoots an arrow clear through the line of axes.

Horrible carnage follows. Odysseus sends a shaft through the gullet of a suitor who is carelessly lifting a costly, two-handled cup to his lips. Blood spurts from the man's nostrils, as he falls backward, knocking over a table and sending its contents flying. "You never thought I'd come home, did you?" Odysseus coldly asks the defenseless suitors. "You've been plundering my home. Now you will all die."

The suitors try to flee, but the doors are locked. "You've killed the man responsible," one suitor insists. "He was in charge. He did it all. He planned to kill your son. But we'll give you back your things. We'll pay you back. As much as you want."

Odysseus is unappeasable. "Nothing you could give me could stop me from killing you, not everything you own plus everything you could get from elsewhere." Odysseus's desire for revenge exceeds any possible material compensation.

The suitors rush at Odysseus with swords, thinking to push past him and get outside. If they can alert the townspeople, they may be able to overpower Odysseus. But they have no chance. Odysseus shoots an arrow through the chest of one, and Telemachus stabs his spear through the back of another. Odysseus's arrows fly, and each downs a suitor, while Telemachus races to the storeroom for more spears and armor.

The treacherous goatherd manages to get some weapons and shields from the storeroom for the suitors. (Telemachus has accidentally left a door open.) When the goatherd returns for more, Telemachus and the swineherd catch him. Odysseus orders them to bind him and suspend him painfully from the rafters. They mock the goatherd as they leave him hanging in agony.

Odysseus, Telemachus, and the two loyal slaves continue to block the doorway. Spears hurled at them by the suitors miss their targets because Athena deflects them, but Odysseus and his supporters always hit their marks. They kill every suitor, even one who grabs Odysseus by the knees and protests his innocence. "I never did anything wrong," the suitor insists. "I was always trying to restrain the other suitors. Where is your gratitude for that?"

"You're in my house," Odysseus responds. "You must have hoped I'd remain absent so you could have my wife." The man is still speaking as Odysseus slices his head from his shoulders. There is blood everywhere. *You imagine the splayed bodies, jagged wounds, lifeless faces.* The suitors all lie dead, like fish caught in a net and heaped on a sandy beach. Odysseus and Telemachus have spared the singer and the herald. Both served the suitors only under compulsion.

The old slave woman, summoned by Telemachus, begins to shout in triumph, seeing the dead suitors, and seeing Odysseus covered in blood, like a lion who has just eaten an ox. But Odysseus silences her. "It's not naturally right or divinely sanctioned to boast over slain men," he says. "These men are responsible for their own destruction." Odysseus orders the old woman to have the slave women stack the bodies in the courtyard and clean up the mess. He tells Telemachus, the swineherd, and the oxherd to kill the disloyal slave women afterward. *You might wonder what options these slave-women had. They certainly didn't have as much choice as the suitors did.*

Telemachus fashions a cruel, horrible death for these slaves. His father has told him to slit their throats, but Telemachus thinks that's too painless. Instead, he strings them up by their necks like birds. He and the two loyal slaves mutilate the insulting goatherd most viciously before killing him, too.

Meanwhile, the loyal old slave woman, laughing, rushes upstairs to tell Penelope. "Your beloved husband is home!" she cries. "He has killed all of the suitors. Come see for yourself!"

"You're mocking me," Penelope says in disbelief. "You're lucky you're so old. If you were any other of my serving women, I'd punish you for this."

"No, it's true," the old woman persists. "He's here. It's that beggar that everyone was mocking. Telemachus knew, but he kept his father's secret so that he could get his revenge."

Penelope leaps up excitedly, weeping as she hugs her servant. "Tell me everything! What happened?" The woman says she only heard the battle. She hid in a storeroom until Telemachus came for her. Then she saw Odysseus surrounded by the great pile of corpses. "You'd have been delighted to see him standing there all covered in blood like a lion," she assures Penelope.

"No, no," says Penelope, shaking her head. "Stop exulting. It isn't true. Maybe some god or other has murdered the suitors. But Odysseus is dead. He'll never return."

"Can you be so faithless?" the old servant wonders. "It's him. I saw his scar myself last night when I washed his feet. That scar from the boar years ago. I'm certain. I wanted to tell you right away, but he threatened to kill me." Still unconvinced, Penelope must see for herself.

Downstairs, Penelope sits silently opposite Odysseus. "What's wrong with you?" Telemachus demands. "How can you be so hard-hearted? Any other woman would go right up and talk to her husband who has been absent so long."

"I don't know what to say," Penelope replies. "I'm not even sure it's him." She stares at the stranger, adding cryptically, "If it is him, we have other ways of knowing each other. Secret things that only we two know."

Odysseus smiles. He's confident that Penelope will soon understand. "But we must make plans," he tells his son. "We would risk being the victims of vengeance if we had killed just one man in the community. Usually a murderer must flee into exile. But we've killed all of this community's *aristoi* young men. We must consider how we will prevail." *Odysseus knows that the suitors' families and friends will seek revenge. This political problem takes precedence. How will the conflict not escalate into all-out war, with Odysseus, Telemachus, and their few loyal supporters vastly outnumbered by the suitors' enraged kin?*

Telemachus hands the problem back to his father, saying, "You're best at figuring out this kind of thing. We'll do whatever you say."

Odysseus immediately devises an elaborate deception, a pretended celebration to fool the townspeople into believing that the suitors remain alive and are still partying within the house. Now he has a bath and gets splendid new clothes, and Athena enhances his appearance. Only then does he reproach Penelope for refusing to recognize him. No other woman would be so hard-hearted and stubborn, he insists.

But Penelope fears making a disastrous, irrevocable mistake. Can this man possibly be her husband? He's twenty years older than the Odysseus she knew. The stakes are very high. If this man's an imposter, Penelope's loyalty will have been for nothing. Lack of caution now could ruin everything for herself, her son, and her husband—if by chance Odysseus ever did return.

Seeing Penelope's resistance, Odysseus asks the old maidservant to make up a bed for him in the main hall. But Penelope tells the woman to take Odysseus's own bed from inside the bedroom and make it up outside for the stranger.

"Who has moved my bed?" Odysseus shouts angrily. "No one could move it! Even a god would have difficulty! I built that bed myself, solid and strong. I built the whole house around the thick trunk of an olive tree, making that the bedpost and the foundation of the house." *His detailed description of his construction process makes you recall the raft he crafted on Calypso's island.* "That bed is fixed and immovable," he says. "unless someone cut under the stump."

This convinces Penelope, since no one except she, Odysseus, and one servant has ever seen the bed. *This seems implausible, but you see that the*

details of this bed and Penelope's trick—or was it a test?—unite and define this
couple. Uniquely similar in their ingenuity and constancy, they are, like the olive-
tree bedpost, enduringly alive and fundamental to the stability of their home and
all who depend upon it.

"I was always afraid of being like Helen," Penelope explains, excusing her previous caution and bringing Odysseus's story full circle, back to the cause of the Trojan War and the beginning of all the suffering. "There are always people who plot to take advantage of you. Even Helen wouldn't have fallen for a stranger if she'd known how it would all turn out. But I believe you now, because no one else could have known about our bed."

Weeping, Penelope embraces Odysseus in ecstatic relief. She's like a ship-wrecked swimmer who has finally reached dry land. *The analogy surprises you,* *since Odysseus, not Penelope, was the one literally shipwrecked, but the compari-* *son emphasizes the fundamental similarities between her suffering and his during* *his long absence.* At last, Odysseus weeps too.

In bed, after delighting themselves in lovemaking, Penelope and Odysseus delight themselves in telling each other their stories. *Using the same verb to* *describe the enjoyment of sex and the enjoyment of stories, the narrator suggests* *that both activities are intensely pleasurable and potentially procreative. You won-* *der about the "offspring" of this long tale itself. What is it producing or creating?*

The story cannot end here, because the political problem remains. Odysseus is home, reunited with his wife and son, and his house is no longer in turmoil. But he has yet to regain his political authority and restore peace, prosperity, and happiness to his community. A huge pile of dead men remains inside his courtyard and a vast number of potential avengers await outside.

The following morning, Odysseus and his son, heavily armed, head for the country, where Odysseus's father, Laertes, lives.

As you wonder how Odysseus and his few supporters will manage to prevail over the hundreds who will seek to avenge the suitors' deaths, the narrator describes the descent of the suitors' spirits to the underworld. There, the spirit of Achilles sees the spirit of Agamemnon and exclaims in surprise, "You were so prosperous and powerful. We all thought you'd be especially fortunate." Evidently knowing of Agamemnon's murder by his wife's lover, Achilles continues, "If you had died at Troy, the Greeks would have made a huge funeral mound for you, and you'd have achieved great *kleos* for your child also. But as it is, your death is most pitiable."

"You were so lucky," Agamemnon's spirit responds. He describes the Greeks' fight to recover Achilles's corpse, their grief, and the elaborate funeral and funeral games they held. Burying his ashes in a jar with the ashes of his dearest friend, they built a huge funeral mound, visible from afar by men now and in the future. "You are dead," Agamemnon concludes sadly, "but you still have your *kleos*. Everyone will always remember your great achievements. My own situation is entirely different. Zeus planned for me to be killed at home by my wife and her lover." *Agamemnon takes no responsibility for his actions, but you reflect that his story might have ended differently if he had been cautious, like Odysseus, or if Clytemnestra had been loyal and clever, like Penelope.*

Now the suitors arrive in the underworld, and the spirit of Agamemnon recognizes one of them as a guest friend. "How did you all die?" He asks. "Were you shipwrecked?"

"We wanted to marry Odysseus's wife," the suitor explains. "She wouldn't choose, and she planned to kill us." He describes Penelope's weaving trick. *He says nothing about consuming Odysseus's food and wine uninvited. He also somehow fails to mention the suitors' plot to murder Telemachus.* "But Odysseus returned," the suitor says. "He conspired with his son and his swineherd. He showed up disguised as an old beggar, and we didn't recognize him. We mistreated him, but he just took it. Then he and his son hid our weapons. He made his wife set the contest of the bow." *You recall that this contest was actually Penelope's idea.* "None of us could string the bow, but Odysseus strung it easily and began killing us. Some god must have helped him, because we couldn't escape and we all died." *Like Agamemnon, this suitor takes no responsibility for his own behavior and its consequences.* "Our bodies lie unburied still," he explains. "Our own people don't yet know we're dead."

The spirit of Agamemnon praises Odysseus for his good fortune in having an excellent, thoughtful wife. Penelope's *kleos* never will perish. "Not like my wife, the murderer of her own husband," he adds sourly. "She makes all women look bad." *That's his takeaway from the suitor's story. Like the suitors, he's incapable of reevaluating his own choices.*

SUCCESS (*ODYSSEY* 17–24)   137

Meanwhile, at his father's house, Odysseus remains cautious to the point of cruelty. Seeing his father working alone in a field, Odysseus feels great sadness for the frail, wretched old man, but he doesn't rush to identify himself and relieve his father's anguish. Instead, he wonders whether to test him. As before, caution conquers compassion. "You look like a good worker," Odysseus says, "but you're in a very sorry state. Who's your master? Someone told me this is Ithaca, but I don't believe it. I once entertained a man from Ithaca. He said he was the son of Laertes. I gave him many gifts." Carefully listing each item, Odysseus seems terribly unkind.

Weeping, Laertes answers despairingly, "Yes, this is Ithaca. But violent, out-of-control men hold it. Your guest-gifts were wasted. My son isn't home and can't reciprocate your hospitality. He must have died. We don't know whether on land or sea. He's had no funeral. But when did you host him? Who are you, and where are you from? How did you get here?"

Surely Odysseus will finally tell his father the truth? No, again he lies, claiming to be from Alybas, a made-up place name evoking *alaomai* (to wander), so it sounds to you like "Wanderville." Claiming that his father was named Apheidas ("Bountiful") and his grandfather Polypēmōn ("Baneful"), Odysseus says he's called Eperitos. *This too, sounds almost right, like "Striving man," or maybe "Chosen man." The name sums up Odysseus's experience as the Greek warrior most distinguished by struggle and suffering. His wordplay reminds you of the trick he played on the Cyclops. But now he's deceiving his own father.* The old man falls forward, moaning loudly in his grief. He pours mud down over his grey head.

At last, even the coldly calculating Odysseus yields—from compassion? Or has his father passed his test? "It's me, father!" he cries, embracing the old man. "I'm home at last. I have killed the suitors and avenged the evil they did to us."

Again you see the family likeness, because it's Laertes's turn to be skeptical. "You say you're my son," he says. "Prove it." At this, Odysseus shows him the scar from the boar tusk. *Odysseus's failure to use this "proof" on Penelope suggests that their reunion required instead an explicit sign of their enduring intimacy and the centrality of that intimacy to their household's survival. The scar wouldn't have meant anything to Telemachus, an infant when his father left.*

But why didn't Odysseus show it at once to his father? Does he enjoy toying with people? Odysseus also adds a tale about himself as a small boy, accompanying his father in the orchard.

Convinced, Laertes delightedly embraces his son. But the suitors' would-be avengers remain the most pressing concern for this newly reunited father and son.

Back in town, the singer and the seer try to dissuade the suitors' enraged kin from seeking vengeance. Certain that Odysseus had divine support, they insist that the suitors were in the wrong and that their families and friends, ignoring good advice, failed to make their sons stop their evil behavior. They persuade some of the would-be avengers, but more than half arm for battle.

This cannot possibly end well for Odysseus, his family, and his community. It can only impossibly end well.

Abruptly, you are back on Olympus hearing gods converse. "What do you intend?" Athena asks Zeus. "Will you let these men kill one another, or will you make them friends?"

"You know I always intended for Odysseus to return and take revenge on the suitors," Zeus says. "Now they can all be friends. Let them have wealth and peace, as before." *This seems implausible and contrived. But, of course, since Athena values vengeance, as the Odyssey's characters all do, only her fortuitous intervention could enable them to survive and enjoy happiness.*

Disguised again as Mentor, Athena joins Odysseus and his few supporters as they prepare for battle. Odysseus urges his son to distinguish himself in the coming fight, so as to win *kleos.* Both father and grandfather rejoice at Telemachus's readiness to fight bravely.

With Athena's help, Laertes kills the first attacker, spearing him through his helmet. Odysseus, his son, and their few loyal companions are going to kill every one of their enemies.

Suddenly Athena's voice booms above the fray. "Restrain yourselves from the grievous battle!" she cries. Calling them all "men of Ithaca," she reminds them (*and you*) of their membership in the same community. "Stop fighting," she shouts, "so that as soon as possible you may be parted without bloodshed." Hearing Athena's voice, the terrified attackers flee.

But Odysseus lunges in pursuit, like a great eagle swooping after his prey. Athena must address him individually. "Restrain yourself, Odysseus. Leave off from this strife of battle that levels all alike, lest Zeus become angry with you."

Odysseus instantly obeys, rejoicing in his heart. He seems as happy to stop fighting as he was to continue. Still disguised as Mentor, Athena sets pledges for both sides to swear to. She has brought the conflict to a peaceful resolution. *How else could this story end so? Could these men have developed superhuman good sense and self-restraint? Perhaps Athena embodies their better judgment. Could you have restrained yourself in such a situation? Why would you?*

SURVIVAL SKILLS FOR EVERYONE

This ancient tale of one king's survival and successful return presents autocratic (and hereditary) political authority as the ideal form of political order, but at the same time, it also introduces the profoundly egalitarian idea that skills crucial for survival and success are accessible not only to a male warrior-king but, in fact, to anyone. By now in the twenty-first century, hereditary autocratic authority constitutes just one of many political options, but in the world of the *Odyssey*'s characters and earliest audiences, the stability and welfare not only of the king and his family but of the entire community completely depends on the return of the benevolent king. In the concluding books of the *Odyssey*, Odysseus's distinctive ingenuity, skepticism, empiricism, and self-restraint achieve success, preserving his life and enabling him to destroy the lawless, abusive suitors. But the epic presents these four attributes as neither the guaranteed product of noble birth nor as skills exclusive to Odysseus. The wellborn suitors lack them entirely, while other characters possess all or some of them. We observe ingenuity, skepticism, empiricism, and self-restraint not only in Odysseus's father, son, and loyal slaves, but also and most especially in Odysseus's wife. Despite the *Odyssey*'s origins in a hierarchical, aristocratic, male-dominated culture accustomed to treating women as property and prizes, the epic nevertheless begins to suggest that the skills required for success are not necessarily derived from noble birth nor limited to men. Crucial to anyone's survival, these abilities appear also available to the old and the young, to the enslaved as well as the free, and to women no less than men.

Maybe the notion that a set of skills or talents could be equally accessible to all seems obvious to you. Maybe not. The idea is fundamental to
any conception of egalitarian human relationships. The *Odyssey*'s characters fail to perceive the radical implications of the epic's commendation of
these particular abilities. But by suggesting that anyone could potentially
excel in them, and that noble birth is no guarantee that someone will, the
Odyssey poses a direct challenge to power structures based on birth, wealth,
race, religion, or gender. To reject such narrowly based or exclusive power
structures, we must recognize that human identity depends on what individuals opt to say and do. It's a matter not of DNA or circumstances but
of conduct. Undeniably, Homer's audiences in archaic times, and also later,
failed to take this ball and run with it. But the *Odyssey* put it into play. It's
only a beginning, but it is a beginning.

In Odysseus's world as in ours, the abuse of power frequently correlates
with the objectification, subjugation, and mistreatment of women. In the
stratified power structure of the *Odyssey*'s characters, men view women as
emblems of male achievement and honor. Male competition for a woman
provides a defining theme and plot element, as the suitors compete to marry
Penelope so that they can take over Odysseus's home and possessions. Odysseus's absence itself results from male competition for a woman, since the
Greeks sailed to Troy in order to recover the stolen Helen.[1] Repellent as the
idea is to modern liberal sensibilities, the suitors' sexual intercourse with
Odysseus's female slaves typifies their commandeering of all of his property.[2]
Sadly, in the twenty-first century, the concept of the "trophy wife" has not
entirely disappeared, and some people persist in viewing women as markers of male honor or status.

Characters within the epic tend to see women as objects rather than as
thinking, feeling human beings, but the narrative begins to undermine this
perspective. Several mortal women in the *Odyssey* possess considerably more
individuality and autonomy than hierarchical, male-dominated cultures
often permit. Helen, now back in Sparta, seems a kind, self-assured, and
discerning hostess and a skilled storyteller (e.g., *Od.* 4.120–46, 219–64).[3]
The queen of the Phaeacians seems wise, considerate, authoritative, and ju-
dicious (e.g., *Od.* 6.303–15 and 7.64–77). On Ithaca, the loyal old slave

woman instantly recognizes Odysseus by the scar on his leg, despite his
twenty-year absence (*Od.* 19.392).[4] Her continued allegiance to Odysseus
shows that a female slave can be as constant and reliable as a loyal male
slave like the swineherd or oxherd. The *Odyssey* particularly emphasizes
Penelope's humanity and individuality by detailing her experience and revealing her perspective on events. She regularly speaks and even describes
her own interior life, including her dream, for example (*Od.* 19.535–53).[5]

As an autonomous, thinking being, Penelope embodies traditional ideals
of wifely loyalty and constancy, but she also shares her husband's capacity
for ingenuity, skepticism, empiricism, and, to an extent, self-restraint. Ingenuity specifically characterizes both Odysseus and Penelope and gives them
some control over their circumstances. Craftiness helps Odysseus during his
adventures, and his trick on the Cyclops epitomizes his capacity for clever
deception. Similarly, ingenuity enables Penelope to postpone choosing a
new husband for three years. She tricks the suitors by claiming that she
must first finish weaving a shroud for her father-in-law. Weaving during the
day, she secretly unravels her work at night, avoiding remarriage until the
suitors discover her deception (*Od.* 2.93–110, 19.137–56, 24.126–48).[6]

Penelope's clever ingenuity gives Odysseus pleasure and affirms the in-
timate connection between this husband and wife. He enjoys hearing her
criticize the suitors for consuming another man's property and failing to
bring her gifts (*Od.* 18.277–80). It's unclear how he knows that Penelope
is deliberately misleading the suitors (*Od.* 18.281–83), but his confidence
that he can deduce her intentions as the suitors cannot implies that she
shares his talent for cleverness.[7]

Penelope shows both ingenuity and some limited autonomy in setting
the contest of the bow and promising herself as the prize (*Od.* 21.73–77).
Telemachus affirms her traditional status as an object for male competition, informing the suitors that the prize is a woman unique among Greek
women (*Od.* 21.106–7). But in initiating this contest with herself as the
prize, Penelope oversteps the limited role of objectified prize object, making herself both prize and game maker.[8]

In her ingenuity and her attempts to control her situation, Penelope,
like Odysseus, prioritizes empirical knowledge, deriving understanding from

direct sensory experience. Immediately after expressing joyous relief at her son's return from his travels, Penelope asks what he has seen (*Od.* 17.44). Her question directly associates Telemachus's travels with Odysseus's adventures, since the narrative begins by explaining that Odysseus *iden* (saw)[9] many cities of men and came to know their thoughts (*Od.* 1.1–3). This verb in the perfect tense means both "I have seen" and, therefore, "I know," and the desire *to see and know* motivates Odysseus throughout his travels. The verb itself, connecting "seeing" with "knowing," encapsulates the essence of empiricism.

The need for empirical knowledge makes both Odysseus and Penelope skeptical. Both prefer firsthand certainty to others' verbal assurances. Odysseus initially refuses to believe Athena's claim that he has awakened on Ithaca. He must see for himself (*Od.* 13.324–55). Similarly, Penelope refuses to believe the "stranger's" assurances that Odysseus will return (*Od.* 19.313). Later she refuses to accept her slave woman's claim that Odysseus *has* returned and killed the suitors (*Od.* 23.11). Despite hearing that the "stranger" has Odysseus's distinctive scar (*Od.* 23.74) and seeing the suitors lying dead (*Od.* 23.83–84), Penelope remains uncertain that this man is indeed Odysseus (*Od.* 23.92–94), and she tests him using secret information known only to herself and her husband (*Od.* 23.109–10). By telling her slave to move the bed, which she and Odysseus both know cannot be moved, Penelope cleverly provokes Odysseus into providing clear evidence of his identity (*Od.* 23.175–206). She finally accepts that he is who he says he is, "since," as she says, "you have related very plain signs" (*Od.* 23.225).[10]

Penelope's ingenuity, skepticism, and empiricism reveal her great similarity to her husband, and Odysseus himself emphasizes the parallel in a surprising simile. Still disguised as a beggar, he likens Penelope to a good and pious king who governs well over many prosperous people and preserves justice. Because of his good government, the lands and flocks are fertile, the sea is full of fish, and the populace is thriving (*Od.* 19.107–14). This analogy recalls the quality of life in Pylos under king Nestor and in Sparta under king Menelaus, the two flourishing societies that Telemachus visits (*Od.* 3 and 4). The description of peaceful order and prosperity also recalls the reign of Odysseus before he sailed to Troy. It underscores the total absence of such desirable elements on Ithaca during his absence.

But most remarkably, in this simile Odysseus equates *a woman* with a faultless and good king. Insisting that Penelope's *kleos* reaches wide heaven (*Od.* 19.108), Odysseus uses a phrase almost identical to the one he uses to introduce himself and his tale of his own adventures. He announces to the Phaeacians, "I am Odysseus, son of Laertes, and I am a care to all men because of my stratagems. My *kleos* reaches heaven" (*Od.* 9.19–20). *Kleos*, the glory that human beings confer on one another, is the highest communal acknowledgement of *male* achievement. Odysseus attributes to Penelope, a woman, *kleos* just like his own.[11]

This fundamental equation of male and female *kleos* consists, perhaps, in the equal vulnerability of husband and wife to suffering, and in their equal capacity for endurance. A second simile, containing another startling gender reversal, reinforces the equation. At the reunion of wife and husband, when Penelope finally yields to his persuasion, Odysseus begins to weep. As Odysseus embraces his wife, the narrator explains,

> Thus she spoke. And she aroused in him still more the yearning for lamentation.
> And he wept, holding his beloved, careful, and knowing wife.
> As when land appears welcome to ones who are swimming
> —men whose well-made ship Poseidon has shattered on the sea—
> and the ship has been driven by the wind and a towering wave,
> and just a few men, swimming, have managed to flee toward land out of the grey salt water,
> and much sea brine has covered over their bodies,
> and, joyful, they step upon the land, having fled the evil.
> So, then, was her husband welcome to her as she gazed upon him (*Od.* 23.231–39).

Wait . . . what? *He* is as welcome to *her* as land is to shipwrecked sailors? But *he* was shipwrecked and nearly drowned. Shouldn't the analogy assert that *she* is as welcome to *him* as land is to a shipwrecked sailor? Beginning as Odysseus weeps and holds Penelope in his arms, this lengthy simile initially seems to describe his experience but describes hers instead. Like a shipwrecked sailor floundering in the sea, Penelope has endured on Ithaca adversity equivalent to her husband's hardship during his adventures.[12]

By individualizing Penelope and equating her character and experience with that of Odysseus, the *Odyssey* permits the audience to see Penelope as a specific human being rather than an unfeeling, unthinking, undifferentiated object. But it is a mistake to interpret Penelope's example anachronistically and project onto her story any modern, liberal, democratic ideas about the inherent equality of women and men.[13]

For the *Odyssey*'s characters and original ancient audiences, Penelope's uniquely admirable example primarily illuminates the roles of the *men* in her life. Her status marks Telemachus's transition from childhood to manhood. Initially, her limited control over her situation manifests her son's immaturity and powerlessness, as Telemachus complains that Penelope cannot reject the suitors outright but also cannot eject them from the house (*Od.* 1.249–51). Later, after Penelope has set the archery contest, Telemachus signals newfound maturity and authority by ordering Penelope back inside to resume weaving and supervising her maidservants, and insisting that the men will take care of the bow and that he himself is in charge (*Od.* 21.350–53).[14] By claiming exclusive power over the bow and the household and exercising control over his mother, Telemachus shows that he has begun to achieve a man's status and responsibilities.[15]

The portrait of Penelope defines not only her son but also her husband, since her talents mirror Odysseus's and emphasize his distinctive capacity to possess such a uniquely virtuous wife. Agamemnon lacked such a faithful wife. In his absence she took a lover, who murdered him on his return from Troy (e.g., *Od.* 24.192–202). Similarly, Helen's husband, Menelaus, lacked a wife with Penelope's caution and perceptiveness. Penelope fully appreciates this contrast. Having finally acknowledged the "stranger" as her long-lost husband, she explains that she always feared being taken advantage of by someone, as Helen was. Even Helen, Penelope insists, would not have had sex with a foreigner if she had anticipated the consequences (*Od.* 23.215–21). Penelope's career exemplifies the power that a story can have over an astute listener's life, because knowledge of Helen's story and the desire to avoid replicating Helen's example make Penelope more prudent. But the contrast between Penelope's loyalty and foresight and the deficiencies of Clytemnestra and Helen emphasizes, above all, Odysseus's extraordinary ability to merit and receive such virtuous fidelity.[16]

The *Odyssey*'s idealized portrait of Penelope also has a self-mocking dimension that cautions against importing modern liberal attitudes toward male and female equality into this ancient tale. In the underworld, Agamemnon insists that Penelope sets a glorious example for women to emulate,[17] but in contrasting herself with Helen, Penelope implies that if Helen had possessed adequate skepticism, foresight, and self-restraint, then the Trojan War would never have happened. This is ironic and even humorous: if every woman were just like Penelope, then the events of the *Iliad* and *Odyssey* would never have occurred. Men like Achilles and Odysseus would have no opportunities to win *kleos*. Epic poets like Homer would have no great deeds to narrate and celebrate. Yes, Penelope sets a glorious example. Her *kleos* establishes the female ideal; but if women were to actually attain it, Penelope reminds us, men would have none. The *Odyssey* thus presents female *kleos* as the reflection of male *kleos* but also as a threat to it.

Men in ancient Greece may have wanted their wives to emulate Penelope, but her example did not lead them to consider women their intellectual, moral, or political equals either while tales of Odysseus were first coalescing into the *Odyssey* (eighth to sixth centuries BCE) or in the classical period that followed. In democratic Athens of the fifth century BCE, women had *less* autonomy and authority than they appear to have had hundreds of years before in the world the *Odyssey* depicts. Living secluded lives and unable to vote or own property, they never fully came of age and remained under male authority, like children or slaves.[18]

The *Odyssey*'s portrait of Penelope actually supports Athenian men's determination in the fifth century BCE to keep women under male control. Male authority appears necessary if women are deemed not less intelligent than men but less capable of controlling their emotions. Penelope's inability to refrain from weeping contrasts with Odysseus's extreme self-control. Both Odysseus and Penelope weep frequently throughout the *Odyssey*, but

Odysseus only weeps if tears will not imperil his survival. On Ithaca he shows impressive self-restraint, concealing emotions that might expose his identity prematurely. The narrative makes the contrast explicit: Penelope weeps upon hearing Odysseus's lying tales, whereas watching her, Odysseus feels like weeping but restrains himself (*Od.* 19.204–12). He resists weeping until the suitors are dead and a display of emotions will no longer endanger him (*Od.* 23.231–40).[19] In their ability to control their emotions, Odysseus and Penelope are *not* alike.

Although today we might opt to see in Odysseus and Penelope an implicit equation between male and female nature, experience, and achievement, the *Odyssey*'s ancient audiences are unlikely to have done so. Even now, many people devalue women's individual subjective experience and deny women equality with men. Such misogyny accompanies and promotes tyranny, since the abuse of power requires, by definition, a willingness to view other human beings as objects, as means to the ends of the one or ones with power.

And yet, despite its origins in an autocratic, male-dominated culture, the *Odyssey* began, thousands of years ago, to equate the experiences of a particular man and his wife. The epic hints at the possibility of and necessity for both men and women to value and cultivate ingenuity, skepticism, empiricism, and self-restraint. Despite his impressive talents, Odysseus cannot succeed in destroying the grasping, obnoxious, self-indulgent suitors unless Penelope shares most of his skills. By equating the suffering and the achievement of husband and wife, the epic begins to suggest that the defeat of tyranny is a team effort and not the work of men alone.[20]

EMPIRICISM REVISITED: VENGEANCE AS A PROBLEM, NOT A SOLUTION

Abuses of power stem from the desire and the ability to treat other human beings as objects. Objectified as prizes or emblems of male achievement, women become sources of conflict and catalysts for acts of revenge, not only in the archaic world of the *Odyssey*'s characters and earliest audiences but even today, at times, in some cultures and subcultures worldwide.[21] The dehumanization of specific people or groups corrodes egalitarian political processes and permits a single individual or a self-selected few to obtain and preserve unchecked and unaccountable power. People eager to acquire and abuse power actively promote misogyny and other forms of prejudice. By whipping up anger, fear, and resentment, despots endorse violence against dehumanized others as a supremely admirable moral obligation.[22]

Dictators and strongmen encourage us not only to objectify and dehumanize others but also to mistake vengeance for justice. Although the *Odyssey* validates the equation of vengeance with justice, it nevertheless also begins to undermine it, presenting vengeance as a source of greater conflict. The characters within the hierarchical authoritarian society depicted in the epic often treat women as material objects and equate revenge with justice, but the narrative shows the audience that revenge inevitably produces reciprocal, often escalating, violent revenge.[23]

The *Odyssey*'s characters, divine as well as mortal, consider revenge necessary and good. All remain convinced that for Odysseus's story to have a just and happy ending, he must return and take revenge on the suitors. The gods unequivocally approve of vengeance and deem it justice. Initial discussion among the gods on Olympus raises the question of whether the gods care about justice. The answer depends on what happens to Odysseus. Athena accuses Zeus of not caring about Odysseus (*Od.* 1.59–62) and therefore not caring about whether human beings are just. She wonders why a mortal king should try to be just if the gods are not just to Odysseus (*Od.* 5.7–12). Zeus promises that Odysseus will get home (*Od.* 1.77), and he sets things in motion so that Odysseus can return and take vengeance on the suitors (*Od.* 5.24). For the gods, Odysseus's return and successful revenge will demonstrate that the gods do care about justice and that they do make sure that justice prevails among human beings.

Like the gods, the *Odyssey*'s mortal characters also never doubt the justice of Odysseus's revenge. Odysseus denounces the suitors' *hybris* (violent arrogance) and *biē* (force; *Od.* 17.565).[24] Penelope considers their behavior most extreme, "for not ever do any mortal men, being outrageous [*hybrizontes*], so contrive wicked deeds" (*Od.* 17.587–88). Odysseus identifies the destruction of the suitors as work that is "necessary" for him to do (*Od.* 22.377). The loyal slave woman laughs delightedly as she reports to

Penelope that Odysseus has returned and killed the suitors (*Od.* 23.1). She assures Penelope that she too would have enjoyed seeing Odysseus covered in blood like a lion (*Od.* 23.47–48). She reminds Penelope (and us) that Odysseus's revenge is exactly what Penelope prayed for (*Od.* 23.54–57, 17.494). Although Penelope still does not believe Odysseus responsible, she feels certain that the suitors got what they deserved, because, she says, "They did not honor any mortal, whether lowborn or noble, and therefore they suffered evil because of their own wickedness" (*Od.* 23.65–67).

The narrative as a whole seems to corroborate the conviction of the *Odyssey*'s characters that the suitors' destruction comes as the direct, logical, and just consequence of their own wrongdoing. The epic's narrator presents the suitors' misdeeds in meticulous detail, describing their outrageous behavior not only during Odysseus's absence but also upon his return. The suitors not only violate the rules of *xenia* (guest-friendship) by occupying Odysseus's home uninvited, partying endlessly, and consuming his provisions, cattle, sheep, and wine; they also verbally and physically abuse the disguised Odysseus when he tests them by begging (*Od.* 17.360–64). One criticizes the swineherd for bringing this "beggar" to the feast, and he threatens Odysseus with a footstool (*Od.* 17.409, 458). Another throws an ox hoof at him (*Od.* 20. 299). The suitors even propose abducting and selling their "guest" in Sicily (*Od.* 20.382). One threatens Odysseus with destruction if he strings the bow (*Od.* 21.305). Among the suitors' crimes, Odysseus includes their attempts to kill him and Telemachus (*Od.* 22.264).

Undeniably, the suitors behave atrociously, but Odysseus's reaction might seem excessive. He kills one suitor when the man is not attacking him, but is about to take a drink and is defenseless (*Od.* 22.9). This man is the most aggressive and violent of the suitors, it's true, but Odysseus slays him like a hunter killing an unsuspecting animal, not like a warrior battling a human enemy. Odysseus kills another suitor who is begging for his life and claiming that he tried to stop the others' outrageous behavior (*Od.* 22.312). Earlier, the narrator has remarked that this man does disapprove of the suitors' behavior (*Od.* 21.146). Odysseus kills him anyway (*Od.* 22.312–29).

To modern sensibilities, capital punishment for theft, threats, and extreme rudeness may appear very harsh, but the *Odyssey* suggests that the suitors deserve their punishment because they freely chose to act as they did. Odysseus spares the singer and herald, accepting that they served the suitors only under compulsion (*Od.* 22.344–58).[25] In contrast, Odysseus murders the suitor who disapproved of what the others were doing but was complicit anyway. That suitor had a choice and made the wrong one.

The suitors' moral transgressions derive from an intellectual deficiency. Unable to think logically, they fail to interpret stories and to understand analogies. Unlike Penelope, perceiving in Helen's story a warning for herself, the suitors fail to heed the "beggar's" explicit warnings. The man murdered while about to take a drink is one of the two suitors called by the narrator *aristoi* (best) of the suitors (*Od.* 4.629). He is also their apparent leader. But he lacks the intellectual capacity to interpret the story that Odysseus pointedly offers. In his beggar's disguise, Odysseus explains that he himself was previously prosperous. He spins a long, lying tale about an expedition to Egypt. The story's point is the implicit general analogy: *Anyone* could be in my shoes and go from wealth to destitution. The details are relevant, too. Odysseus says that on this fictional expedition to Egypt he sent his men to investigate and report back, but that instead they plundered the Egyptians and provoked a violent response, getting themselves killed or enslaved. Failing to connect the story's details to his own life, the suitor misses the point completely: that good fortune may be impermanent, and gratuitous greed backfires catastrophically. He orders Odysseus away from his table and threatens him (*Od.* 17.419–45).

The suitors' intellectual failure also includes a lack of empiricism. Foreseeing the coming slaughter, the seer cautions the suitors to heed the evidence of their senses, insisting that he himself can see and hear and consequently understands what is coming. Therefore, he will not linger to witness it. The seer recognizes that the suitors lack the sense to flee (*Od.* 20.365–70). In claiming that the suitors are "behaving outrageously" (*hybrizontes*), and that they "are contriving wicked deeds," the seer directly echoes Penelope's previous accusations (*Od.* 20.370 and 17.588). But the suitors ignore this warning, just as they ignore Odysseus's warning, and they continue their outrageous behavior.

By detailing the suitors' transgressions and emphasizing their moral and intellectual failings, the *Odyssey* implies that they deserve the punishment that Odysseus inflicts, and the narrative evokes little sympathy for them. Although their gory deaths recall battle scenes in the *Iliad*, the descriptions conspicuously lack the poignant details or emotional similes that in the *Iliad* evoke sympathy for the slain.[26] One simile actually does the reverse, dehumanizing the dead suitors by likening them to fish caught in a net and dragged out onto the sand (*Od.* 22.383–89). Fishing, a useful survival technique, provides food; the analogy reinforces the necessity or utility of slaughtering the suitors, but it invites no sympathy for them. [27]

Though offensive to modern convictions, the narrative also suggests that the disloyal slaves deserve to be tortured and killed for freely chosen misdeeds. Compelled, like the singer and the herald, to serve the suitors, other slaves nevertheless and despite their servitude, have some limited control over their own choices. The goatherd's transgressions appear egregious and gratuitous: unprovoked, he verbally abuses, threatens, and kicks the disguised Odysseus (*Od.* 17.215–235; 20.178).

Though we in the twenty-first century must recognize the twelve disloyal slave women as victims of sexual assault, the epic depicts some of their offensive behavior toward Odysseus and his family as freely chosen. These women undoubtedly have far less freedom of choice than do the male singer and herald, but Odysseus doesn't care whether they slept with the suitors willingly or unwillingly. Making no effort to determine this, he refuses the loyal old slave woman's offer to identify the relevant slaves (*Od.* 19.497), but in the end he accepts her assessment (*Od.* 22.421–25). Presumably, all of the slave women were under equal compulsion by the suitors, and Odysseus gives them no opportunity to plead their own case. Like the goatherd, however, the slave woman Melantho gratuitously scolds and threatens Odysseus without provocation (*Od.* 18.327 and 19.65).[28] The careless neglect of Odysseus's faithful dog exemplifies, as the swineherd observes, the slave women's active but thoughtless disregard for *all* of their responsibilities in their master's absence (*Od.* 17.311–21).[29]

By depicting the slaves' disloyalty and abusive behavior as a choice, the narrative presents their torture and murder as deserved and fully consistent

with the archaic conception of justice as revenge. Odysseus's successful return and resumption of his authority requires their destruction. And Odysseus orders only the *killing* of the goatherd and the disloyal slave women
(*Od.* 22.172 and 440–45); *Telemachus* chooses to kill them in particularly
painful and horrible ways (*Od.* 22.187–200 and 461–76). Odysseus condemns the slave women to die for their sexual betrayal, but Telemachus
emphasizes their freely chosen crimes, which he experienced firsthand. He
devises painful deaths for them, first because they abused Penelope and
himself, and only second because they slept with the suitors (*Od.* 22.462).
Their unprovoked verbal abuse shows that the slave women did in fact have
some choice in how they behaved.[30]

Portraying Odysseus's violent anger as just and constructive, the *Odyssey* reminds us that motives matter, but methods and results count for
more.[31] Anger can sometimes promote a necessary and productive response
to injustice, but it tends to distort judgment, and it often achieves counterproductive results. In the twenty-first century, anger and the desire for
violent revenge continue to devastate communities and states worldwide.
By contrast, Odysseus's restrained, proportionate attack appears to restore
his legitimate and benevolent political authority.[32] Except that it doesn't.
Odysseus's revenge provokes in the suitors' families the desire for reciprocal vengeance. The supernatural intervention of Athena resolves everything
for the *Odyssey*'s characters, but nothing for the audience.[33] The epic's unsatisfying ending emphasizes instead for the audience that violent revenge
poses a lethal threat to civil society.

In the power vacuum created on Ithaca by the king's absence, no individual established sole authority. Chaos and predation reigned. Odysseus's
revenge destroys one set of abusers of power but cannot restore order or
communal harmony. Though gratifying and admirable to Odysseus's supporters within the epic (and no doubt to many in the poem's audience even
today, as in earlier times), Odysseus's vengeance instead promotes greater
violence and disruption.

The *Odyssey* encourages its audience to find satisfaction in Odysseus's
success, but it also reminds us that vengeance is not a solution but a problem. We know that Odysseus is a good king. The use of violent force to

overthrow oppressors, however, offers no guarantee of responsible leadership. In a society such as that of Odysseus, lacking a reliable, honest police force and judicial system—a shortcoming sadly not uncommon still today—violent revenge appears the correct and necessary response to verbal and physical assault. Odysseus, the returning homeowner and king, has no other options for defeating the rapacious and abusive suitors. Even today, anger frequently prompts well-meaning people to accept violence as the appropriate response to violence and verbal abuse. But if we, like the *Odyssey*'s characters, mistake vengeance for justice, then we condone the tyrannical use of force, violence that is exercised without recourse to judicial process. In a civil society, a society governed by the rule of law, victims of tyrannical abuse must have recourse to reliable legal protections. Otherwise, as history has shown repeatedly, one abuse of power will most likely yield to another.

SELF-RESTRAINT AS SELF-INTEREST

The *Odyssey*'s characters view murderous revenge as the only way for Odysseus to succeed in restoring order and harmony, but the epic cautions that retaliatory violence will likely escalate and become interminable. The *Odyssey* reveals the practical problem of vengeance, as the suitors' bereaved relatives gather to avenge the killings of their loved ones. Athena, goddess of strategy, intelligence, cunning, and craft, must intervene to prevent violent revenge from destroying the entire community. By implication, the wisdom of Athena, the wisdom to resist the passion for violent revenge, could prevent our own violent conflicts from escalating. It's not about turning the other cheek. It's about understanding our own self-interest.

The *Odyssey* shows that vengeance escalates because avengers generally seek to get even—and then some. For the enraged avenger, the addition of cruelty helps, so extreme cruelty often accompanies revenge. Avengers view the *enjoyment* of cruelty as a nice perk of the process. They may consider the addition of jeering and sarcastic mockery emotionally satisfying, as when Telemachus and the swineherd torture the goatherd and then jeer as they leave him to suffer (*Od.* 22.195–99). Impelled by their "enraged passion," they later mutilate him horribly (*Od.* 22.474–77). Similarly, the loyal oxherd vaunts as he kills the suitor who threw the ox hoof at Odysseus, and he claims sarcastically to be giving this suitor a "guest-gift" in exchange for the ox hoof he "gave" Odysseus (*Od.* 22.287–91). In our world, as in that of Odysseus, cruelty and the enjoyment of cruelty, while often accompanying a lack of adequate judicial alternatives to violent revenge, expose a primitive, shortsighted mindset.

The desire to inflict greater harm in retaliation is not fully rational, since nothing can undo the initial offense. Emotional distress, not rational calculation, drives the urge not to match but to exceed the original harm. Consequently, material compensation cannot satisfy. Facing the murderous Odysseus, one terrified suitor agrees that "wicked things" have been done to Odysseus. Although he accepts no personal responsibility, claiming that it was all another suitor's fault (*Od.* 22.45), this man offers reparations (*Od.* 22.55). But Odysseus rejects any possible amount of material compensation (*Od.* 22.61–65). Certain that not even an infinite amount of material recompense could ever equal the original injury, Odysseus recognizes that the need for revenge destroys the possibility of *any* rational equations.[34]

The *Odyssey* goes further in exposing the irrationality inherent in the desire for revenge. Despite the characters' approval of vengeance, Odysseus's own insight that human fortunes are precarious and variable makes equating revenge with justice deeply illogical. Odysseus explicitly warns the suitors about the variability of fortune (*Od.* 18.130–50). Human beings are subject to the fortunes Zeus bestows. Prosperity and power are insecure and unstable. A man may be at the top one minute and at the bottom the next. "That's why you should always be thinking about what is lawful and customary and right," argues Odysseus (*Od.* 18.141).[35] He warns the slave women, too, about the precariousness of prosperity (*Od.* 19.74).

The variability of human fortunes makes vengeance logically problematic, because one man's vengeance only provokes another's: one day you will be the avenger, the next day the victim. Odysseus, of all men, should understand this. His very name identifies giving and getting suffering as reciprocal processes. *Odussomai* combines "to be incensed with" and "to be incensed at," "to hate" and "to be hated" (*Od.* 19.407–9)—like the English "hateful," meaning both "hating" and "hated."[36] Awareness of the reciprocal nature of hatred and the instability of human fortunes may explain why Odysseus does not gloat over the dead suitors and stops the old slave woman's triumphant cry, telling her, "It is not *hosiē* [naturally right, or divinely sanctioned]to boast over men who have been killed" (*Od.* 22.412). Odysseus never loses touch with reality, and he remains fully rational as he exacts his revenge. However, the knowledge that human fortunes are variable and that hatred is reciprocal makes the *audience* begin to suspect that equating vengeance with justice is not entirely logical.

And the end of the *Odyssey* shows that vengeance fails to resolve the political problem, since the suitors' surviving relatives seek to exact vengeance of their own. Odysseus accurately predicts that the suitors' kinsmen will come to avenge their deaths (*Od.* 23.117–22). Only supernatural intervention prevents the vast bloodshed of a full-blown battle (*Od.* 24.482–86). The *Iliad* shows that vengeance killings prompt reciprocal killings and that vengeance does not even satisfy the individual avenger; Achilles's grief and wrath escalate as he murders and mutilates.[37] But the *Odyssey* goes further in exposing vengeance as a practical political problem: vengeance threatens communities precisely because it is an inherently never-ending and ever-escalating process.

In the hierarchical world of Homer's characters, with equality and democracy as yet unimagined, the best option is a benevolent king, such as Odysseus was before he left for Troy. Viewing women not as individuals valued in their own right, but as markers of male status and achievement, men in the *Odyssey* unquestioningly accept women's subjugation to men. The theft, or attempted theft of women produces vengeance and bloodshed.[38] Lacking a reliable police force or judicial system (also not yet even concepts), Odysseus can succeed only by deceiving and then slaughtering his enemies. His lies and violent revenge expose his enemies' lack of self-restraint and their disastrous inability to draw logical deductions from empirical evidence. The *Odyssey*'s characters approve uncritically of vengeance and celebrate its successful accomplishment, but the narrative prompts the audience to reconsider.

The *Odyssey* suggests that ingenuity, skepticism, empiricism, and self-restraint can permit an admirable ruler and his supporters to defeat a much larger group of rapacious, violent, and shortsighted adversaries. At the same time, however, the epic undermines the equation of vengeance with justice. The equation proves illogical on the individual level, since human fortunes are inherently variable, and it proves nonsensical on the social level, since vengeance is reciprocal, escalating, and interminable. While violence destroys one set of abusers of power, it offers no guarantee of prudent and benevolent leadership, political harmony, or prosperity in the future. Not violence but instead the farsighted wisdom of self-restraint, symbolized by Athena's intervention, proves vital to individual and communal survival and success.[39]

CHAPTER 6

JUSTICE (AESCHYLUS'S *ORESTEIA*)

Sitting in Athens with thousands of others, you gaze upon the gates of Agamemnon's palace long ago and far away in Argos. You are at the theater, about to see the story of Orestes. Everyone has always admired and praised Agamemnon's son. Killing his father's killer, Orestes got revenge, earned glory, and set a shining example for every son to follow.

King Agamemnon, glorious conqueror of Troy, belatedly discovered upon returning home to Argos in Greece that his wife had betrayed him during his long absence. The queen's lover, Aegisthus—Agamemnon's own first cousin!—plotted to kill the returning king, and took him by surprise. Having stationed a watchman to notify him immediately of the king's return, Aegisthus prepared an ambush. He pretended to hold a festival, and welcomed Agamemnon to his home. He entertained the king hospitably and slaughtered him in mid-meal, like an ox at his manger. He killed Agamemnon's companions, too, as if they were pigs for some feast. The queen helped her lover. She also murdered Agamemnon's war prize, Cassandra, a princess of Troy. This daughter of King Priam died most pitiably, screaming as she fell upon Agamemnon's dying body.

This was no magnificent, glorious battle. This was just sad, shameful slaughter: sprawled bodies and puddles of blood all mixed among wine bowls and overturned platters of food. Aegisthus ruled Argos for seven years afterward, until Agamemnon's son Orestes, returning from Athens, killed him. Orestes earned eternal glory, and Aegisthus paid for ignoring the gods' warning not to seduce the queen or kill the king.

This happened long ago in Argos. Your grandfather and great grandfather knew this story, as did the many generations before them. But somehow Orestes's story is just beginning.

A man lies prone upon the palace rooftop. Deeply unhappy, this watchman has been lying on the palace roof every night for a year, ordered by Queen Clytemnestra to watch for torch fires signaling the fall of Troy. *In the often-told tale of Agamemnon's sad homecoming, the watchman has always seemed a mere plot device, but now, hearing his complaints, you begin to imagine his experience as he lies uncomfortably night after night through cold and rain, trying to stay awake. You've always heard that the usurper Aegisthus commanded the watchman to warn him of the king's imminent return. But now you learn that the queen herself cleverly devised this system of torch signals to relay the news from Troy well in advance of Agamemnon's arrival. She, not her lover, seems to be in charge.*

Suddenly, the watchman sees the first signal fire. Ecstatic, he hurries to tell the queen. As he departs, he describes the situation inside the palace—sort of. Unable to speak freely, he only hints cryptically that all is not well. If you know what he means, then you know what he means.

A chorus of elderly men of Argos emerges from the palace and begins to sing and dance. Ten years ago, the chorus sings, Agamemnon and his brother Menelaus led a great army to Troy in pursuit of Justice. They planned bloodshed in recompense for a stolen woman and a guest's violation of the hospitality guaranteed by Zeus. *You realize the chorus is referring to Helen's abduction by the Trojan prince Paris.* Both anxious and hopeful, the chorus members proceed to metaphors and riddles. They sing of armor, spears, eagles, omens, and powerful "child-avenging" *menis* (rage). *You might recall that Achilles's menis nearly destroyed the Greeks at Troy, but what is this "child-avenging" rage? What child? What vengeance? Orestes's story, as you'll see, includes many murdered children and many acts of vengeance.* Praying to Zeus, who gave human beings the capacity to learn from experience, the chorus explains that suffering alone produces knowledge. *You find this thought terrible, but also hopeful. At least knowledge is possible.*

The chorus tells a dreadful tale. The Greek fleet, gathered for the attack against Troy, could not set sail. Battering headwinds, sent by the goddess

Artemis, detained the ships at the Greek port of Aulis for endless days. The men were starving, their ships rotting. A seer explained that to appease the goddess, Agamemnon must sacrifice his own daughter—or let his men and allies starve to death in Aulis. Facing these two horrible options, the king and his brother wept copiously, striking the earth with their staffs. *You've always known what Agamemnon chose, but as the chorus recounts these events, you see that once he chose, he did not agonize over his terrible decision. Proceeding methodically, without reconsidering, Agamemnon murdered one girl—his own daughter! —in order to launch a massive expedition to recover another girl.*

The chorus describes the sacrifice in painful detail. Agamemnon's young daughter understood it all. She begged her father to spare her, but he killed her as if she were a sacrificial goat. He had her mouth gagged, lest her cries bring a curse on his household. As she was lifted above the sacrificial altar, her yellow robes swirled about her. Agamemnon's men assisted, despite his daughter's imploring looks. Gagged, she could not speak, but with her eyes she tried to remind the men of how she used to sing and entertain them at feasts in her father's halls.

The chorus refrains from describing the death blow, but you know the rest. With Artemis appeased in this ghastly way, favorable winds began to blow, and the Greeks sailed for Troy. The chorus does not relate the events at Troy or on the Greeks' return journey afterward. They only insist enigmatically that justice is coming down on some people so that they learn by suffering. Whom do they mean? The Trojans? The Greeks who died at Troy or after, on the way home? Or does the chorus hint at justice and suffering—and knowledge—still to come?)

Now Queen Clytemnestra emerges from the palace. Addressing her obsequiously, the chorus asks if she has any news. "Yes I have," she answers smugly. "Troy has fallen. The Greeks captured the city last night." Exultant, Clytemnestra is also very pleased with her clever system of signal fires. The chorus is skeptical. How could she know of Troy's fall so soon? Troy is far away. No messenger could possibly reach Argos in less than a day. But Clytemnestra confidently insists that her husband himself has sent her the news from Troy.

Clytemnestra pictures the grim scene in Troy at this very moment: cries and chaos, women weeping over the bodies of their men, orphaned children sobbing for parents they will never see again. The Greek victors must hunt for food, but they can at least sleep under the shelter of captured homes without needing to keep a watch. *Clytemnestra's dismal description prevents you from imagining the Greeks' victory as anything especially desirable or glorious.*

"If they only show respect for the gods," Clytemnestra continues ominously, "and refrain from plundering sacred temples, they might make it home safely." *From ancient tales, you know that the victorious Greeks succumbed to passion and greed instead, plundering and ruining the gods' shrines in Troy. The gods destroyed most of the Greeks, therefore, as they sailed homeward. Clytemnestra's warning reminds you that winners have choices. Victory requires self-control. The Greeks' lack of restraint in victory was shortsighted and short-lived.* But there's more. "Even if the Greeks avoid incurring the gods' anger," Clytemnestra says, "suffering may still come from ones who are dead. Or some unexpected troubles might come." *The coming troubles are not unexpected by you; you know what's in store for Agamemnon.*

As Clytemnestra reenters the palace, the chorus thanks Zeus for the Greek victory. The chorus members' tone remains surprisingly gloomy, however, not celebratory. They recall punishments inflicted for ancestors' misdeeds. They sing of *peitho* (persuasion) and *atē* (ruinous folly), which made Paris violate his obligations under *xenia* and steal the wife of his host. They describe pain at the hearth and mourning in the home of every Greek who sailed to Troy. They mention funeral urns holding the ashes of dead warriors. They describe a general feeling of bitterness that so many died for the sake of someone else's woman. Fearing the avenging Furies, since every misdeed brings a reciprocal penalty and every victor may be vanquished, the chorus makes the Greek victory seem not glorious but menacing—if in fact the Greeks have won. The chorus members still suspect that Clytemnestra's certainty is merely wishful thinking.

But a herald arriving from Troy confirms the queen's report. The Greeks have indeed sacked Troy. *This herald's prompt, convenient arrival makes you realize that time is malleable in the theater. Much time passed while the chorus was singing. Just go with it.* The herald is thrilled to have come safely home. He never thought he would make it. Troy lies in ruins, its temples flattened. *You recognize that this is exactly what Clytemnestra warned against.* Agamemnon has punished Paris and all his people for Paris's theft of Helen.

Though part of the conquering force, the herald does not exult in the victory. Instead, he describes the hardships of the Greek invaders: wretched nights on hard ground, bedbugs, scanty food, rain, cold, bitter winter snows, sweltering summer heat. He'd prefer not to talk about it. Why retell the tale? It was bad enough to live through it once. *The herald's attitude surprises you. You've heard tales of the Greeks' glorious exploits in Troy and after told and retold ever since you can remember. How can the herald think there's no point in retelling these stories?*

Unlike the herald, Clytemnestra is jubilant. She wishes that her husband may come home to a wife who is just as faithful as when he left. *You appreciate the chilling irony of her words.*

The herald now describes the terrible storm that destroyed most of the Greeks as they sailed from Troy. Ships crashed against each other in swirling water and driving winds. "Afterward, in the bright light of dawn," he says, "we saw the Aegean blossoming with Greek corpses and pieces of their wrecked ships." *"Blossoming" strikes you as a perverse descriptor for a horrible scene of carnage.* The herald's own ship miraculously survived the storm. "With any luck," he concludes, "Agamemnon's brother Menelaus has made it home, too."

The chorus blames Helen for it all. The chorus members describe a man rearing and nurturing a baby lion in his halls. The small cub is cute and loving, but once full-grown it turns on the household and kills everyone. *This dark tale evokes many analogies. Helen, for one: Menelaus brought her home as his wife, but she betrayed him and caused the death of many Greeks. Paris, for another: he was born in Troy, but grew up to bring destruction on his own city. You think of Clytemnestra, now poised to welcome her husband to his own home. She's up to no good. The powerful image of the once-cuddly cub turned vicious killer will stay with you as Orestes's story unfolds. The lion described by the chorus simply does what lions do, following its natural instincts with no effort at self-restraint. As an analogy for the human characters, however, this lion makes you wonder whether human beings have other options—and, if so, how these might be implemented.*

While the chorus sings and you ponder such questions, much time passes. The victorious Agamemnon has returned from Troy, bringing his war prize, the young Trojan princess Cassandra. The chorus greets Agamemnon eagerly. Unlike the herald, the king is triumphant. "I accomplished *dikē* [justice]!" he proclaims proudly. "We punished the Trojans for their theft of Helen. We destroyed their city completely. We achieved vengeance! A flesh-eating lion overleaping the ramparts licked up an abundance of tyrannical blood!" *This last adjective makes you think of this king's despotic murder of his own child, and perhaps also the general tendency of tyrants to cause bloodshed.* Agamemnon is certain that *nike* (victory) accompanied him on this venture. He hopes that she always will.

Following the herald's depressing account and the ominous choral songs, Agamemnon's self-satisfaction and moral certainty seems impressively short-sighted. You know what awaits this exultant king. His boastful reference to a "flesh-eating lion" reminds you of the lion cub that grows up to destroy its nurturers. You may think, too, of the Greeks' deceptive Trojan Horse, mentioned often in ancient tales. Like the lion cub in the choral song, the Trojan Horse seemed appealing and benign. Welcomed into the city, though, it proved to contain Greek warriors who burst forth to kill Trojans and devastate Troy. You know that the destructive chain of events continued, as the Greeks themselves fared badly after sacking the city.

Before Agamemnon can enter the palace, Clytemnestra emerges. She greets her long-absent husband coolly, to say the least, failing even to acknowledge him at first. She addresses the chorus and describes her own experience during the ten-year war, waiting for news, sifting rumors, suffering at each discouraging report. On first mentioning Agamemnon, Clytemnestra calls him merely "this man," insisting that he could not possibly have been wounded as many times as she heard he had. Her suffering was so extreme, she says, that she nearly chose to kill herself more than once. This is why, she explains, now finally addressing Agamemnon, she sent their son Orestes away to be cared for by friends. It was unsafe for him here at home. The people were so unruly.

You marvel at Clytemnestra's self-absorption. And her explanation for Orestes's absence seems suspicious. Was she trying to protect Orestes, or herself and her lover from Orestes? Now, belatedly, Clytemnestra expresses joy at seeing her husband home, safe at last. She supplies a rapid-fire series of extravagant metaphors, claiming that Agamemnon "is the dog guarding the farmyard, the mast's forestay that saves the ship, the tall, straight pillar supporting the high roof, a father's only child, a clear spring to a thirsty traveler, land appearing to sailors who have lost all hope." *She's definitely overdoing it more than a bit.*

Even worse, welcoming Agamemnon into the palace, Clytemnestra doesn't want him to step on the ground. She orders dark red tapestries to be spread before him, "so that *dikē* may lead him home," she says. "And, as for everything else," she continues cryptically, "the power of thought, being victorious, will justly establish all that has been decreed with the gods' will." *Her highflown language is incomprehensible, but like Agamemnon, she's utterly confident in her own understanding of what* dikē *(justice) and* nikē *(victory) mean.*

The situation is very awkward. Eastern despots are known to trample on beautifully embroidered fabrics rather than set their royal feet on the hard ground. But such behavior is inappropriate for Greek kings, and Agamemnon at first objects strenuously. He criticizes his wife for her long-winded speech and for greeting him abjectly, like a woman or a barbarian. *Clearly this marriage has issues. Unlike Odysseus and Penelope, this husband and wife neither respect nor admire nor understand one another.* Agamemnon flatly refuses to walk on the carpets. That might be fitting for gods, he says, but it is sure to bring down envy and destruction on a man.

"Wouldn't Priam, king of Troy, have walked on such woven splendors if he had defeated you?" Clytemnestra asks.

"Of course," Agamemnon agrees. He's aware that, unlike Greeks, many Eastern peoples deemed their kings gods.

"So why do you hesitate?" Clytemnestra persists. "What are you afraid of? If others envy you, isn't that good?"

This contest of wills appalls and fascinates you. You know that Agamemnon should not yield to Clytemnestra's persuasion. You know, as he does, that his walking on these woven tapestries like an Eastern tyrant is a very bad idea. But you also get the feeling that he sort of wants to. Eventually, of course, Agamemnon gives in. He knows that it is wrong and inauspicious to trample these beautiful tapestries—and he does it anyway.

Agamemnon disappears into the palace, and Clytemnestra orders the Trojan princess Cassandra inside too, but the girl does not move. *Does she not understand? Does she even speak Greek? She was silent the whole time that Agamemnon, Clytemnestra, and the chorus were talking.* Finally, Cassandra opens her mouth, but instead of words, she repeatedly shrieks a ritual cry to Apollo: "*Otototoi popoi da!*" and the god's name.

You might remember Cassandra from ancient tales. Cursed for rejecting Apollo's sexual advances, she can foretell the future, but the god made sure that no one would comprehend or believe her. As is absolutely the case now. Cassandra seems to know all about Agamemnon's family—past, present, and future. But her words are riddling, ambiguous, and incomprehensible to everyone present. She speaks of a "god-hating abode" that is "conscious of many troubles" involving "murders of kin." She bewails the "man-slaughtering and blood-sprinkled ground." She claims to trust "these witnesses and these whelps (or maybe "cubs") bewailing murders (or maybe "sacrifices") and roasted flesh consumed by the father (or maybe "on the father's side"). *It's all completely baffling.*

Suddenly, Cassandra recoils at some new horror. She is describing something. Someone doing something to someone right now. You cannot follow, and neither can the chorus. A net of death. Something happening in the bath. "The sharer of his bed shares in the responsibility for his death," Cassandra exclaims.

The chorus cannot comprehend. They know something bad is happening, and they wonder if Cassandra is evoking avenging Furies, but her prophecy seems nonsensical. They think Cassandra is out of her mind. They recall the nightingale, grieving incessantly after killing her own son in revenge against his father. *You may remember Penelope's reference to this ancient tale of reciprocal atrocities. This nightingale seems to be an emblem of utterly perverted family relationships, but like the chorus you can't understand Cassandra's meaning.*

Cassandra grieves for Paris, for Troy, for the uselessness of her father, Priam's, religious observances. She foresees her own death. "I'm done with prophecies," she exclaims suddenly. "The avenging Furies inhabit this house. They sing of the *atē* [ruinous folly] that began it all. And they spit upon the one who tramples the hostile bed of his brother." *What does she mean?* She turns to the chorus. "You be my witness. I know the ancient misdeeds of this house!"

Cassandra shrinks at her own terrible visions: the murdered children whose father tasted their pitiable flesh. She sees an avenging lion in the bed (*there's that lion again*), and the mistress of the house on guard against her master's return. "The one who led the ships, the destroyer of Troy, does not perceive the dog's pretense of affection!" she cries. "She's going to kill him. The female slays the male. She's like a double-ended serpent or rock-dwelling Scylla, that great bane to sailors. I don't care if you believe me," she concludes. "It will all come true."

The chorus begins to understand. "I can get part of it," they say. "I shudder at your mention of Thyestes's feast of his own children's flesh. I can't track the rest of it, though." *You may not remember Thyestes. Don't worry; it will all become clear.*

"You're going to see the violent death of Agamemnon," Cassandra says bluntly. But even this direct statement eludes the chorus. They pray that she is wrong. "You're praying," she tells them. "But the killing is their concern." The chorus members still fail to understand. They want to know "what man" is preparing this distress.

Suddenly, Cassandra screams. She feels on fire. A two-footed lioness, she says, will kill her. "As one prepares a cup of poison, she mixes in retribution for me, too. While sharpening her sword for the man, she boasts that my murder is vengeance for him bringing me here." Facing her own death bravely, Cassandra knows that she will not die unavenged. "Another avenger will come!" she predicts, "a mother-slaying son, to avenge his father. He is a wanderer and an exile now." *She must mean Agamemnon's son, Orestes.* "But he will put the finishing touches on this *atē* [ruinous folly] that is destroying kin." Knowing that her time is up and that there's no escape, Cassandra heads toward the palace gates. The chorus members marvel at her calm fortitude. They consider her courage in the face of death to be glorious. *Maybe you agree—or just find it sad.*

As Cassandra enters the palace, you hear a horrible cry from within. "Oh! I've been hit a fatal blow!" The chorus members silence one another and wonder who has spoken. You recognize Agamemnon's voice: "Oh! I've been hit a second time!"

The chorus cannot help him. No one can help him now. Frantically debating what to do, the chorus members can agree on nothing. Words are useless. They want to know clearly what has happened to Atreus's son. *When Agamemnon first arrived, the chorus members wondered whether to call him* "king," "conqueror of Troy," or "offspring of Atreus." Now, hearing him dying a violent death, they have chosen the third option, the title identifying him not with his own deeds but with his father's.

Suddenly the palace gates swing open. Standing beside the corpses of Agamemnon and Cassandra, Clytemnestra congratulates herself for killing her husband. She is not ashamed to say that earlier she had cleverly said things that were opportune but untrue. She refers to an ancient quarrel, and the long time she had for plotting. She tangled Agamemnon inescapably in some garments, like a fish in a fishing net. She struck her husband twice, and he cried out twice as he collapsed. "After he fell, I struck him a third time," Clytemnestra boasts, "as a gift vowed to Zeus under the ground, preserver of the dead." Not caring what the chorus thinks, Clytemnestra considers her accomplishment "more than just."

Clytemnestra's unfeeling analogy of Agamemnon to a dead fish might remind you of the unsympathetic simile that the narrator used for the suitors killed by Odysseus. Her reference to Zeus as the god under the ground and guardian of the dead shocks and appalls you. Zeus is the great god of Olympus high above the earth, who guarantees oaths and the obligations of xenia. Hades, not Zeus, is god of the dead below. Clytemnestra seems horribly perverted in her values. She likens Agamemnon's spurting blood to the fall of spring dew. She equates death with birth, claiming that she delighted in this shower of blood as much as crops enjoy the Zeus-given buds bursting in springtime.

When the chorus members criticize Clytemnestra for the murders and threaten to banish her, she accuses them of having a double standard. "When Agamemnon killed my child, as if she were a sacrificial animal, where were you then? Why didn't you punish him with banishment?" She cries in fury. Her words bristling with double-meanings, she swears by *dikē* (justice) and insists that her husband and Cassandra "have not accomplished unavenged (or "dishonorable") things." Cassandra's murder, she says, "brought an additional delicacy to the luxury (or "wantonness") of my bed." Clytemnestra is gleeful and unrepentant.

You'd never really thought of Clytemnestra as a bereaved mother avenging her child's murder. You never thought much about her at all, except as the antithesis of the loyal, steadfast Penelope. In ancient stories, not Clytemnestra but her lover kills Agamemnon. And yet, whether or not Agamemnon deserved to die, you fail to see how Cassandra did. Is Clytemnestra's murder of one girl to avenge the murder of another really more just than Agamemnon's murder of one girl to avenge the theft of another? Neither murder seems just. Both murders seem depraved.

Appalled by Clytemnestra, the chorus members wish for death. Again, they blame Helen for the bloodshed in Troy and now here in Argos. They weep for Agamemnon and predict the coming of his avenger, who "will render *dike* for the blood of eaten children." The chorus must mean the story that both they and Cassandra mentioned earlier: the children of Thyestes, roasted and fed to their own father by his brother Atreus, father of Agamemnon. Atreus was retaliating against his brother for sleeping with his wife. *"The blood of eaten children" also reminds you of Agamemnon's daughter—sacrificed like the animals the Greeks ritually sacrificed, cooked, and ate—and of Cassandra, another innocent young victim. The chorus predicts another avenger, so the succession of retaliatory murders will continue. How is one "more just" than another?*

But Clytemnestra insists that she has repaid Agamemnon in kind for murdering his own daughter. "Having suffered what he deserved, let him not boast of his achievements in Hades," she proclaims. *In ancient tales of the underworld, you've heard the spirit of Agamemnon lamenting his own inglorious death and contrasting it with Achilles's glorious one. He certainly was not boasting. Clytemnestra would be pleased. You are not sure she deserves to be.*

The chorus predicts more trouble, since "justice is sharpening itself for another deed of harm, on other whetstones of fate (or "other provocations to rage.)" Who is left now, the chorus wonders, to bury and mourn Agamemnon? Certainly his widow cannot do it.

Clytemnestra claims sarcastically that the spirit of Agamemnon's dead daughter will be there to greet him and embrace him in the underworld.

The chorus members view the dreadful chain of retributive murders as inevitable. They see only "reproach countering reproach." Each new avenger pays in his turn, and "it is difficult to judge." Moreover, "Action brings suffering, as long as Zeus remains on his throne." The members of the household are "accursed," and "the race has been welded to *atē* [ruinous folly]." Clytemnestra says that she would be quite happy to have this be the end of it. *No doubt. Every avenger would be content to let the violence cease with his or her own act of vengeance.*

But the violence will not end here, because Clytemnestra's lover suddenly appears, exultantly addressing "the kindly, justice-bearing light of day." *You had almost forgotten about Aegisthus. Ancient stories always blamed him for seducing the queen and killing the king.* Now, belatedly, he claims credit for the whole plot and its success. He delights in Agamemnon's death and proclaims that the gods have now avenged the crime of Agamemnon's father, Atreus.

Aegisthus, Clytemnestra's lover, is the surviving (youngest) son of Thyestes, the man who was fed his older children by his own brother, Agamemnon's father. (Aegisthus and Agamemnon are first cousins.) Atreus drove his brother out of Argos when the two fought over the kingship. Upon Thyestes's return, Atreus killed, dismembered, cooked, and fed the man's own children to him. *Aegisthus's meticulous description now practically provides you with the recipe.*

Aegisthus has been planning revenge for a long time. "I myself, justly, am the plotter of this murder," he boasts. "Atreus drove my father and me out—I was only a baby. But when I grew up, the divinity *Dikē* led me back again. I contrived this whole plan." *You saw Clytemnestra in action, so you find it difficult to agree that Aegisthus did it all, as he claims.* "Having seen this man ensnared in the nets of Justice," Aegisthus continues, "I wouldn't even mind dying right now." Like Agamemnon and Clytemnestra, Aegisthus is certain that justice equals vengeance.

The chorus members dare to criticize Aegisthus for his vaunting, and for the murder. At the moment of *dikē*, they say, he won't be able to ward off the people's curses and the stones they will throw. Aegisthus responds as any tyrant would, threatening the chorus with fetters, blows, and starvation unless they keep silent. *You begin to notice that the silencing of verbal dissent by force and intimidation appears central to tyrannical power.* The chorus members boldly continue to accuse Aegisthus of tyranny, treachery, and cowardice. He lacked the courage to kill Agamemnon himself, they say. They wish that Orestes would return and kill both Aegisthus and Clytemnestra.

The chorus prepares to fight Aegisthus's supporters, But Clytemnestra intervenes. "No," she says. "There has been enough bloodshed." She claims that she and Aegisthus accomplished "what was necessary," and she wishes this to be the end of it. The chorus and Aegisthus continue to sling accusations back and forth, but Clytemnestra urges her lover to ignore the "trifling yelpings" of the chorus. "Ruling together," she announces confidently, "you and I will set this house upright." *You know that they will not.*

And now, as you watch, a second play begins. Two young men approach the tomb of Agamemnon: Orestes has returned from exile, with his friend Pylades, to avenge his father's shameful murder. Orestes's older sister Electra emerges from the palace, accompanied by a chorus of slave women. The two young men hide behind bushes and watch the women mourn the dead king. The chorus women sing of the misery and ruin of a once great house. They know that more bloodshed is coming. Electra prays that the gods bring her brother home from exile to take revenge on their father's killers, now living in degenerate luxury in the palace. Treated like a slave by her own mother the queen, Electra seeks vengeance, as justice for the dead and victory for herself and her brother.

Orestes steps out from hiding and identifies himself to his surprised and delighted sister. Apollo has commanded Orestes to avenge his father's death. Grief for his father and the loss of his inheritance impel him as well. He also wants to free the city of Argos from the usurpers' tyranny and to regain his rightful kingly authority.

The chorus agrees, insisting that "*dike* clamors greatly for what is owed, blood for blood. Death shouts for an avenging Fury." The chorus women are keen to exult over a newly slain man and woman.

Lamenting their own helplessness and dishonor, brother and sister pray for assistance from their father's spirit. Electra likens her mother to "a savage-minded wolf." Fanning the fury of these new avengers, the chorus observes, "Just so you know: the queen mutilated your father's corpse before burying it."

Orestes devises a deceptive plan. Treachery has destroyed his father. Treachery will destroy his father's destroyers. He and his friend will gain entrance to the palace by pretending to be foreign travelers. Once inside, Orestes will kill Aegisthus.

The ensuing exchange borders on comedy: a knock at the palace door, a bewildered queen. Who is this guest-friend? Failing to recognize her now adult son, Clytemnestra offers hospitality, including hot baths. *Her offer is grotesquely ironic, since she murdered Agamemnon in the bath!*

Orestes, in disguise, pretends not to recognize his mother. He has a message for the rulers of Argos: a man he met on the road told him that Orestes is dead, but maybe that's of no interest to her? Uttering appropriate words of grief (*you doubt her sincerity*), Clytemnestra sends an elderly slave woman to summon her lover with his armed attendants.

Treacherously, the chorus women intervene. Encountering the elderly slave woman, they alter her message: she is to tell their hated master to come alone, unguarded.

Unaccompanied, Aegisthus hurries into the palace, eager to learn whether the story of Orestes's death is true. You hear his death cries emanating from inside the palace.

Now it's Clytemnestra's turn. Her grief at the death of her lover seems real. So does her terror at seeing Orestes with his bloody sword. "You aren't going to kill me, are you?" she pleads. "I'm your mother. I nursed you when you were a baby."

The young man hesitates. He turns to his friend. "What am I to do, Pylades?"

"Do what Apollo told you to do," Pylades replies sternly. These are his only words in the play.

Angry recriminations between mother and son follow, but the outcome is never in doubt. "By killing my father, you killed yourself!" Orestes screams finally, as he and Pylades shove the defenseless queen into the palace.

The chorus sings exultantly of justice. And now Orestes stands over the corpses of his mother and her lover. He glories in his own achievement, and he condemns his mother's wickedness.

But something is wrong. Orestes's mind no longer seems under his control. His thoughts are disjointed. Something is plaguing him. "Ah! Ah!" he shouts in horror. He claims to see monstrous females, swarming with snakes. These must be his mother's avenging spirits. He has justly exacted vengeance, but he knows that he has incurred pollution for killing his own mother. He must flee into exile. Flailing wildly at nothing you can see, Orestes rushes offstage.

Praying for Orestes, the chorus identifies this as third in a series of "wretched miseries," suffered first by the father tricked into eating his own children, next by the king murdered in his bath, and now third by this man. Did he come as a savior or as a destroyer? Where will it all finish?

The third play begins in the temple of Apollo at Delphi. A bloodstained man kneels at the altar, seeking purification. His sword drips with blood. Monstrous female creatures surround him, black-robed, nauseating, gore dripping from their eyes. These are the Furies, the bloodthirsty, implacable spirits of vengeance. Snakes, sprouting from their heads, writhe and hiss. *You know that you are at the theater, but your horror is real.*

The god Apollo—*in person!*—promises eternal support to the desperate Orestes. Apollo has put the Furies to sleep for now, but he tells the young man to flee to Athens, city of Athena, and to beg the goddess for her judgment. Orestes departs, and Clytemnestra's ghost rouses the Furies to pursue him. Apollo chases the disgusting, primitive, bloodthirsty creatures from his temple, insisting that their brutal atrocities belong not in his sacred abode but in the cave of a blood-gulping lion. He flatly rejects the Furies' retort that he himself invited them in by commanding Orestes to kill his own mother.

Orestes, still plagued by his mother's avenging spirits, now appears before the temple of Athena on the Athenian Acropolis. (*Geography, like time, is malleable in the theater.*) He begs for Athena's final *dikē* (justice). The Furies explain that they must avenge murders of blood kin. Orestes counters that he avenged his father's murder and followed Apollo's command.

Recognizing that this conflict is too difficult for any one individual, even a goddess, to resolve, Athena convenes a *dikē* (jury trial). This will be a permanent institution for the city. Commanding a trumpeter to signal the start of the trial, Athena gazes directly at the audience. *Is she giving you, the theatergoers, the role of jurors in this trial of vengeance and matricide?*

Orestes and the Furies make their case. Apollo testifies on Orestes's behalf, certain that the murder of a king by his treacherous wife is a far more consequential crime than matricide. But the Furies counter that by killing his mother, Orestes has spilled his own blood and incurred eternal pollution.

Athena instructs the people of Athens to cast their votes in accordance with their own opinion. *She means you! Do you vote that Orestes is guilty, or not guilty?* Athena asserts that this legal procedure for murder cases, now used for the first time, has been established for all time, so that reverence and fear will prevent injustice and protect the people of Athens forever.

The Furies threaten dire consequences for the land unless they obtain *dikē* (justice). They and Apollo exchange vicious accusations. But the votes are evenly split, and Athena casts the deciding vote in favor of acquittal. Androgynous goddess that she is—born not from a mother, but directly from Zeus's head—Athena subordinates the interests of the murdered murderous mother and her avenging female spirits to the interests of the male defendant and his male patron god.

Orestes rejoices. The Furies, predictably, are furious. Enraged at having been dishonored and humiliated, they call for *dikē* and threaten vengeance. Claiming that they will poison and blight the entire land, the Furies continue to understand *dike* as "justice as vengeance," though Athena is assigning the word a new meaning: "jury trial."

Gradually, painstakingly, tactfully, Athena persuades the Furies to reconsider. Assuring them that they have not been dishonored, she promises them an exalted place in the city, enthroned near their own altar and reverenced by all of the citizens.

The Furies continue to rage, but Athena remains respectful and persistent. She reminds them that they will receive even greater honor if they make the city of Athens prosper. She insists that they have not been defeated, and she pledges to make them powerful for all time. The Furies will have victory forever, if they transform themselves into fertility goddesses.

And they do! Such is the force of Athena's rational persuasion. The Erinyes (Furies) transform into Eumenides (Well-Minded Ones). They agree to make Athens prosper, but they will retain their monstrous forms and vengeful power. Dwelling beneath the city, they remain free to erupt at any time they choose.

The play concludes in a grand torchlit procession. Cries of triumph fill the air. *You feel relief and anxiety in equal measures. Who or what has triumphed, exactly?*

REDEFINING JUSTICE: REPURPOSING AN ANCIENT TALE

The age-old equation of revenge with justice perpetually plagued ancient Greek society, just as retributive killings and tribal or gang vengeance still menace twenty-first-century societies. The principle of "an eye for an eye" may suit an individual's anger and sense of fairness, but it destroys individuals, families, and communities. As murder follows murder in Aeschylus's dramatization of the story of Orestes, killers and killed all remain certain that revenge equals justice. Each side assumes that it has justice on its side, and that because its opponents are wrong, it must be right. In the *Oresteia* as in life, conflict and carnage ensue.

We know, as Aeschylus and his contemporaries did, that there's an alternative. The Athenian lawgiver Solon established the trial by jury in 595–594 BCE, nearly a century before the advent of democratic government. But this solution was still controversial and divisive when Aeschylus produced the *Oresteia* in 458 BCE. Even today, the short-term satisfactions of vengeance continue to appeal to many people. A good legal procedure is fine, but it only works if everyone understands that it is necessary, that it is better than violent retaliation to violent crime, and that it operates fairly.

But how do you convert the traditional certainty that vengeance equals justice into a new understanding of justice as a communal legal procedure? Even after you have institutions in place, how do you get everyone to accept judicial outcomes whether they like them or not? You need a good story. And the Greeks had plenty. From the late sixth throughout the fifth century BCE, Athenian tragic plays reenacted, with revised details and emphases, ancient tales long familiar from epic poetry. New versions of old tales sparked reassessment and debate. Athenian tragedies helped to expose the destructiveness of the traditional tribal goals of helping friends, harming enemies, and pursuing vengeance. They promoted new ideals more conducive to preserving civil society and democratic institutions.

Although ancient Greeks were often suspicious of change (their word for "new," *neos*, also meant "unexpected, strange, evil"),[1] Aeschylus's *Oresteia* directly challenges the traditional view, emphasized in the *Odyssey*, that Orestes's vengeance on his father's murderer is morally correct and unquestionably admirable. Produced exactly a half century after the establishment of democratic government in 508 BCE, and nearly a century and a half after Solon instituted jury trials, this trilogy traces the causes and consequences of a series of reciprocal vengeance killings. The first two plays (*Agamemnon* and *Libation Bearers*) emphasize the escalating violence. The third play (*Eumenides*) validates the jury trial as an imperfect but preferable alternative.[2]

Hundreds of years before Aeschylus produced the *Oresteia,* the *Iliad* and *Odyssey* began to question the usefulness of vengeance, but both epics nevertheless present revenge as fully compatible with and necessary to good social order. The *Odyssey* especially implies that revenge can be essential, constructive, and admirable. Odysseus's successful homecoming and his vengeance on the suitors marks the accomplishment of Zeus's justice.[3] Agamemnon's homecoming is notably less successful, but the *Odyssey*'s characters insist that his son Orestes admirably and justly avenges his father's death by killing the murderer. The *Odyssey* says nothing about Orestes killing his mother Clytemnestra as well. Gods and mortals in the epic all view Orestes as a dutiful, exemplary son. His vengeance is morally unproblematic and thoroughly praiseworthy.[4]

While the *Odyssey* presents Agamemnon's murder as an unambiguous injustice and commends Orestes's act of vengeance, the *Oresteia* shows instead that the traditional definition of "justice" as "vengeance" constitutes a problem—for everyone. By changing crucial details, Aeschylus undermines the *Odyssey*'s unquestioning admiration for Orestes. In Aeschylus's retelling, Orestes achieves nothing glorious or praiseworthy by avenging his father's death. He merely adds another horrible murder to a long history of crimes committed by numerous members of a deeply problematic family.[5]

The *Oresteia* exposes the devastating consequences of retributive violence, as each violent act in this new version of the tale derives from and produces others. The *Agamemnon* traces the sequence of reciprocal violence back to Agamemnon's father's murder of his own nephews to punish their father for adultery with his (Agamemnon's father's) wife. Clytemnestra kills Agamemnon to avenge his sacrifice of their daughter. By making Clytemnestra herself—*not* her lover, as Homer has it—murder Agamemnon, Aeschylus undermines the *Odyssey*'s portrait of Orestes as a dutiful son; avenging his father's death requires Orestes to kill his own mother. In the

Libation Bearers, vengeance motivates Orestes and his sister to kill Clytemnestra and Aegisthus. Orestes is following Apollo's command. But instead of restoring order, as Homer implies, this act of revenge, a son's murder of his own mother, transfers the conflict from the human to the divine realm, since no human avengers remain. In the *Eumenides*, Apollo's support for Orestes's vengeance enrages the Furies, ancient goddesses who avenge murders of blood kin. They demand Orestes's blood in return. The solution to this unending, ever-escalating conflict requires a complete transformation of the ancient definitions of justice and victory.[6]

The transformation requires the substitution of verbal debate for physical conflict. The traditional definition of success as violent conquest imperiled the survival of civil society in fifth-century BCE Athens, just as it threatens civilization in our own times. For the ancient Greeks as for us, warfare and violence remained constants in storytelling and in reality. The *Iliad* and *Odyssey* suggest that competition for honor, material possessions, and women inevitably causes violence, suffering, and death. Physical competition defines a hierarchical culture. How else do you know who is best? (Enthusiasm for competition also led the ancient Greeks to invent the Olympic Games.) But physical conflict similarly defines tyranny, as tyrants use physical force and intimidation to suppress the expression of ideas and opinions. In contrast, free, open, nonviolent competition between ideas and opinions defines a functioning civil society. Emphasizing the destructiveness of violent competition, the *Oresteia* promotes the radical idea that, unlike physical conflict, competition between interests and opinions does not inevitably have to produce war, suffering, and death. It could instead be constructive.[7]

Tragedy was a novel, uniquely Athenian poetic genre, but in essence it wasn't altogether new.[8] The *Oresteia*, like all Athenian tragedies, develops ideas already discernible centuries before in the *Iliad* and *Odyssey*: human life is finite, death is the end, the afterlife holds no pleasure, and the gods and fate do not especially care about human beings.[9] Homeric epic tales focus on human choices, actions, and suffering. They connect foresight, self-restraint, and compassion with human survival and success. Tragedy similarly depicts human beings confronting challenging predicaments, facing difficult choices, and exhibiting behavior to emulate or condemn. Like the epics, tragedies present multiple perspectives and show the consequences of human choices. Asking, "What am I to do?" (*L.B.* 899), Orestes ponders the question central to every tragedy, as it is central to every human decision. (Often, lacking good options, we must choose the least bad.) Like the epics, tragedies encourage the audience to reexamine ancient certainties about what is valuable or admirable in human life.

Emerging around 534 BCE, perhaps a generation before the Athenians began their democratic experiment, Athenian tragedy was a form of "political" theater. But this was not theater of protest in the modern sense, since the performances were state-sponsored and a vital part of mainstream Athenian civic life. Addressing the community as a whole, the Athenian tragic competitions, like democratic government itself, trusted in the ability of every individual citizen to judge—to choose which play should win first prize, to assess moral conflicts within the plays, and to evaluate the same moral issues when making domestic and foreign policy decisions.[10]

Reworking traditional material, new tragic versions of old, familiar tales exposed the logical consequences of ancient moral certainties.[11] Aeschylus's reinterpretation of the ancient tale of Orestes encouraged Athenians to question the self-destructive definition of "justice" as "vengeance," and to embrace a new definition of "justice" as the rule of law and the trial by jury. This reassessment is as vital for us today as it was for Aeschylus's original audience, since the primitive equation of justice with revenge, whenever and wherever it resurfaces, imperils the rule of law and destroys communities.

The *Oresteia*'s validation of opinions and words over axes and swords never implies that all opinions and ideas are equally valid. Mining ancient tales for moral lessons, the ancient tragedians, like the archaic epic poets, never suggest that all decisions and values are equally admirable or desirable. Competition remains the vital principle. In the *Eumenides*, opponents assert their claims, and the citizens judge them on their merits. Few things are more dangerous to a democratic society and more favorable to despotism than an inability or unwillingness to judge the facts on their merits. The refusal to engage in the competition of moral claims, an approach termed "values relativism," is lethal to the survival of democracy.[12] Democratic government promises all citizens equality before the law, but to prevent tyrannical abuses of power, democracy must incorporate the essentially hierarchical principle that some choices and priorities are better than others. Some ideas and opinions really are preferable, but only the free and open exchange of ideas enables us to choose wisely *and to keep on choosing wisely.*

Aeschylus's retelling strips Homer's story of its traditional moral lesson and shows instead that vengeance accomplishes nothing desirable. The *Oresteia* demonstrates that the definition of justice as retaliation (or, more accurately, as retaliation plus interest) does not resolve conflicts but perpetuates them, resulting in more violence and more killing. In the twenty-first century, some of us may already recognize vengeance as a universal toxin, but this insight is not usually obvious to those who mistake vengeance for justice. Aeschylus makes it obvious.

THE DANGERS OF BINARY THINKING

Like Aeschylus's contemporaries and all human beings, we are prone to define right as the opposite of wrong. The complete and total wrongness of our opponents' views affirms our conviction of the rightness of our own. Our opponents, in turn, find validation for their own moral convictions in the utter depravity of ours. Aeschylus, however, alerts us to the possibility that we may both be wrong. Objectivity enables us to reassess. Like Aeschylus's original audience, we have no personal stake in this particular conflict and can view it without passion or partisanship.[13] The *Odyssey* permits little doubt that Agamemnon's murder was wrong and Orestes's vengeance was right, but Aeschylus makes us reconsider whether any of the acts of revenge in this story can be judged morally right or just.[14]

Each avenger claims to act justly, but Aeschylus prevents us from easily taking sides. The *Odyssey* evokes sympathy for Agamemnon, glorious conqueror of Troy, shamefully murdered by a cowardly usurper, but the *Agamemnon* calls that sympathy into question. The traditional tale emphasizes Agamemnon's victory and his deliberate but necessary sacrifice of his daughter to launch his expedition, but Aeschylus shifts our attention away from the acts attributed to Agamemnon by necessity (i.e., by poetic tradition) and toward his tyrannical behavior as depicted in the play.

Aeschylus cannot rewrite the past as the Greeks understood it; Agamemnon did sacrifice his daughter, and he did sack Troy.[15] But the play exposes Agamemnon's despotic character: once he opts to kill his own daughter rather than let his army starve, he fails to agonize afterward, as any decent, humane person must.[16] Detailing the horrible scene as the murdered girl experiences it, the chorus evokes sympathy for her suffering (*Ag.* 228–47). Agamemnon decides quickly, acts ruthlessly, and remains unmoved by his daughter's pleas. Fearing that she may utter a curse, he has her gagged (*Ag.* 235–37). Without attributing to Aeschylus and his original audience a twenty-first-century aversion to misogyny and violence toward women, we can note, as Aeschylus's contemporaries surely did, the symbolic association of monstrous, tyrannical cruelty with gagged speech. Regardless of the audience's sensitivity to the plight of women in a male-dominated society, by depriving his daughter of the power of speech, Agamemnon exemplifies for us, as no doubt for Aeschylus's contemporaries, the ability of the tyrant to silence protest.[17]

Undermining traditional admiration for the great Greek conqueror of Troy, Aeschylus's portrait of Agamemnon connects ostentatious material self-aggrandizement directly to degeneracy and self-destruction. The *Iliad* depicts Agamemnon as hot-tempered, self-serving, and shortsighted. The *Odyssey* presents him as the antithesis of Odysseus, an object lesson in how *not* to return home after a long absence. But Aeschylus *shows* exactly how Agamemnon's own ambition, vanity, and moral deficiency precipitate his death. In contrast to the herald's grim account of the Greek victory (*Ag.* 503–680), Agamemnon proudly boasts that he exacted justice from Priam's city (*Ag.* 812–13). But his sacrifice of his daughter, and his actions on his return all undercut his assertion. The chorus implicitly criticizes a father's tyrannical slaughter of his own child, but Agamemnon himself invites our condemnation of his lack of foresight and absence of impulse control. He graphically exhibits reckless arrogance, behavior understood by the Greeks to guarantee self-destruction.[18] Entering the palace while treading upon beautiful tapestries, Agamemnon strides grandly and confidently toward his own death.[19] He knows that trampling the tapestries constitutes the sort of arrogant display characteristic of Eastern tyrants (*Ag.* 935–36). He knows that it violates *aidōs* (a sense of shame or honor; *Ag.* 948–49), but he does it anyway—and, as before, he fails to agonize over a consequential decision. Today, like Agamemnon, authoritarian rulers and wealthy, powerful individuals often extravagantly flaunt their numerous possessions and excessive consumption. Agamemnon's myopic egotism and its consequences, however, suggest that grandiose vanity and lack of self-restraint are not admirable but self-defeating.

The play encourages little admiration for this autocrat, but it also does not commend his murderer. Clytemnestra claims moral justification for killing Agamemnon, but Aeschylus makes it difficult to agree with her. She insists that she spread the tapestries for Agamemnon, "in order that justice may lead him into his unhoped-for home" (*Ag.* 911). But when she rejoices after the murder and identifies the third and fatal blow as "a votive favor (or debt of gratitude) to Zeus," Clytemnestra perversely calls Zeus "god of the underworld" (*Ag.* 1385–87). She likens her joy in the showering of Agamemnon's blood to the joy of nature in springtime (*Ag.* 1390–92).[20] The analogy echoes the herald's grotesque claim that the Aegean "blossomed" with dead bodies after storms wrecked the Greeks' ships as they headed home after sacking Troy (*Ag.* 659). Just as the herald's gruesome account undermines the glories of war and conquest, Clytemnestra's inverted imagery, signaling her perversion and corruption, invalidates her claim that justice and the gods are on her side.

In addition to the perversity of her assertions, Clytemnestra, no less than Agamemnon, exhibits a tyrant's myopic self-confidence. Like any despot, ancient or modern, she feels free to disregard public opinion. Certain that only her own opinion matters, she calls her own right hand a "worker of justice" and does not care whether the chorus praises or blames her (*Ag.* 1403–6). *She* accuses the *chorus* of injustice for condemning her murder of Agamemnon, but not his murder of their daughter (*Ag.* 1412–21), and she swears by "the justice accomplished for my child" (1432).

Even as she rejects the judgment of the chorus, Clytemnestra evokes the judgment of the audience.[21] Like the husband she loathes, Clytemnestra kills a completely innocent victim. She even claims that she gets added enjoyment from killing Cassandra (*Ag.* 1446–47). The chorus continues to lament Agamemnon's death by treachery (*Ag.* 1489–96, 1513–20) while Clytemnestra insists that Agamemnon deservedly suffered for killing his daughter (*Ag.* 1525–29). But what justifies Cassandra's murder? If Agamemnon's murder of one innocent girl is wrong, how is Clytemnestra's murder of another any less so? We may sympathize with Clytemnestra as a bereaved mother,[22] but the play's conclusion does not permit us to identify her revenge as justice.

While the *Odyssey* puts Orestes clearly in the right, the *Agamemnon* compels the audience to evaluate the merits of each character's claims. Even to an audience in the fifth-century BCE accustomed to male dominance, Agamemnon's death no longer appears a simple wrong rectifiable by a son's vengeance. Every character in the play, and in the rest of the trilogy as well, repeatedly calls his own actions *dikē* (just or right),[23] but the *Agamemnon* ends without validating one claim over another.[24]

The play's conclusion emphasizes instead the continuation of conflict. Certain that he has avenged Agamemnon's father's act of killing his own nephews and feeding them to their father, who also happens to be Aegisthus's father (*Ag.* 1577–1602), Aegisthus calls himself the "just [*dikaios*] plotter" of the murder (*Ag.* 1604). Having seen Agamemnon "in the nets of *dikē*," he says, he would think it fine even to die now (*Ag.* 1610–11). We appreciate the irony; in the next play, he will. The chorus believes that Orestes may return (*Ag.* 1667), but the play ends with Clytemnestra confidently telling Aegisthus to ignore the chorus. Together she and he will now manage the household well (*Ag.* 1672–73). Her misplaced certainty borders on the comical.

The characters in the *Agamemnon* learn nothing from their own terrible tale, but the audience can. Early on, the chorus explains that Zeus established the experience of suffering as the source of learning (*Ag.* 174–78).[25] This idea is the essence of empiricism. Not divine revelation, faith, or magic but actual human experience, especially painful experience, produces knowledge. Aeschylus's story of a ruthless, self-aggrandizing, and overconfident autocrat and his enraged, treacherous wife warns against the polarized thinking that assumes that if one side in a dispute is wrong and unjust, then the opposing side must be right and just. In reality, in a passionate dispute—particularly a violent one—it is far more likely that both sides are wrong. Nevertheless, each side probably contains a grain of truth or a facet of justice.[26]

Bitter partisan divisions and violent political conflict, not uncommon wherever and whenever human beings congregate, expose a human tendency to assume that because one side in a dispute appears deeply wrong then the other side must be right. The *Agamemnon* challenges us to reconsider this binary fallacy, and to explore better options.

BETTER OPTIONS: PERSUASION, JUSTICE, AND VICTORY FOR ALL

The human capacity for verbal persuasion enables a zero-sum conception of justice and victory to evolve. Justice defined as "I'm right and you're wrong" creates constant conflict. Victory understood as "I win; you lose" promotes inevitable suffering, because inevitably, someone loses. The *Oresteia*, however, promotes the radical suggestion that justice and victory could benefit everyone.

The second play of the trilogy, the *Libation Bearers,* continues to emphasize that justice-as-retaliation perpetuates violence and perverts family relationships. The characters continue to accept the traditional definition of justice as vengeance,[27] but as Orestes and his sister conspire together and murder their mother and her lover, the audience sees that vengeance makes kin fear kin (*L.B.* 234), destroys family life (e.g., *L.B.* 49–50, 338–39), and replaces family affection with savagery (e.g., *L.B.* 421–22). It makes children hate their mother (e.g., *L.B.* 101 and 189–91) and a mother hate her children (e.g., *L.B.* 737–40, 992–93). The play ends with another two dead bodies, those of Clytemnestra and Aegisthus, and again the certainty that the conflict continues (*L.B.* 1065–76).[28]

Undeniably, the human characters are behaving like beasts. The chorus members in this play, unlike in the first, are fully complicit in the vengeance plot, and they celebrate the two new murders as a triumph of justice. But they also evoke that ominous lion image again (*L.B.* 935–41). A motif frequently repeated throughout the trilogy, the lion exemplifies the natural violence of human beings as predatory mammals. The third play, however, the *Eumenides*, emphasizes the constructive potential of the uniquely human capacity, not shared with lions, for articulate, persuasive speech.[29]

As the *Eumenides* begins, the reciprocal murders in the first two plays have produced conflict not only among mortals but also in the supernatural realm. The Olympian god Apollo commends the justice of Orestes's killing of his mother, but Clytemnestra's avenging Furies, powerful primal goddesses who avenge murders of blood relatives, are demanding Orestes's blood as just recompense (*Eum.* 261–75). Apollo accuses these hideous, bestial creatures of brutality and injustice (*Eum.* 185–95, 221–23). They have pursued Orestes from Argos to Athens.[30]

To resolve the conflict, the play enacts a jury trial, offering the audience the opportunity to judge the merits of the case.[31]Apollo fails to see any similarity between the bloody retribution that the Furies crave and the retaliatory murder that he himself ordered Orestes to commit (*Eum.* 202–3), but he knows that Athena must decide the case (*Eum.* 224).[32] Athena, however, recognizes that no individual can make this decision, not even she herself, since, as she explains, "The matter is a rather great thing, if any mortal supposes to judge this. Nor is it even *themis* [lawful, customary, or right] for me to distribute justice for hot-blooded murder" (*Eum.* 470–72). Instead, Athena convenes an assembly and has the herald blow a trumpet blast (*Eum.* 566–69). No other surviving tragedy includes a trumpet blast, but a trumpet always signaled the start of a new play in the theater. By connecting the audience's experience as theatergoers to the story being enacted, the trumpet *in* the play, signaling the beginning of the trial, incorporates the audience into the action as participants in a new kind of *dikē* (justice), the word now meaning a trial by jury.[33]

The process requires the free speech that is impossible under tyranny. In the *Agamemnon*, despotic suppression of verbal dissent punctuates the escalating violence. As the play begins, the night watchman laments the lack of free speech in Argos, claiming that he cannot reveal details of the city's current political situation because an ox has stepped on his tongue (*Ag.* 36–37).[34] (This sounds marginally less funny in Greek.) Agamemnon gagged his daughter at her sacrifice in order to silence her pleas or her curse (*Ag.* 235–37). As the play concludes, Aegisthus threatens to "yoke with a heavy bit" anyone who fails to obey him (*Ag.* 1639–40).

The *Agamemnon* associates the suppression of speech, by violence or intimidation, with tyranny and with inevitable, interminable, ever-escalating conflict, but the *Eumenides* extols freedom of speech and the constructive potential of verbal persuasion. Adversaries are free to argue their cause (e.g., *Eum.* 436–42 and 470–89). And when the legal procedure alone proves inadequate to resolve the conflict, Athena's persuasion makes the Furies willing to accept the verdict (e.g., *Eum.* 793–807, 823–36, 881–925, 968–75).

Persuasion initially seems unlikely to prevail. Athena says in advance that she herself will vote for Orestes, so he will be acquitted even if the jury is deadlocked (*Eum.* 734–41).[35] But by casting the deciding vote for acquittal (*Eum.* 752–53), Athena enrages the Furies. They view the verdict as entirely unjust, and they threaten violent revenge on Athens and its citizens (*Eum.* 778–92). The Furies' reaction accords with their essential nature; Apollo associates them with bloodthirsty bestial violence, insisting that they ought "to dwell in the cave of a blood-drinking lion" (*Eum.* 193–94).

The *Oresteia*'s recurring insistence on the innate violence of lions highlights, by comparison, the human capacity for articulate speech, a crucial attribute distinguishing us from ravening beasts. Centuries earlier, animal imagery in the *Iliad* and *Odyssey*, by likening human beings to animals, began to emphasize the contrasts between them. The *Iliad* frequently presents warriors as analogous to lions (e.g., *Il.* 11.112–21, 547–56; 17.657–54). But in the heat of battle, Menelaus points out that leopards, lions, and wild boars do not vaunt in victory (*Il.* 17.19–23).[36] Similarly, in the *Odyssey*, after Odysseus kills the suitors, the narrator likens him to a blood-covered lion who has killed and eaten an ox (*Od.* 22.401–6), but Odysseus himself immediately criticizes the old slave woman for vaunting over the dead (*Od.* 22.407–12). The epics suggest that warriors *can* act like wild beasts but that unlike wild beasts, they do not always have to. The *Oresteia* makes this even more explicit. Unlike lions, we have other options.

The substitution of a jury trial for a vengeance killing involves the substitution of debate and persuasive speech for physical violence. In the *Odyssey*, Odysseus's persuasive lies cause great suffering to other people, not only his enemies but also his closest kin. But his lying skills also help him to survive and regain his home, family, and kingship. The *Oresteia* also shows this dual potential of persuasive speech.[37] Clytemnestra treacherously uses deception and persuasion to ensnare and destroy Agamemnon. She manipulates him into parading into the palace like the Greek conception of an Eastern tyrant. Playing on his weakness, she convinces him to participate in his own destruction. Similarly, in the *Libation Bearers*, the chorus calls on "treacherous persuasion" to assist Orestes in murder (*L.B.* 726–27). At the end of the *Eumenides*, however, Athena uses persuasion constructively, urging the Furies to "be persuaded" by her and not to be upset by the trial's outcome. "You have not been conquered," she reassures them. "The equal vote has come out truly, and not with dishonor for you" (*Eum.* 794–96). She promises these spirits of bloody vengeance that "with all justice [*pandikos*]" they will hold honored, "bright-throned altars" in a just (*endikou*) land and be worshipped by Athens' citizens (*Eum.* 804–7). Countering their threat to destroy Athens by blight and illness with a promise of perpetual honor, Athena makes the Furies see that it is *in their interest* to yield (*Eum.* 808–36). Athena's persuasive arguments begin to transform the Furies from violent, destructive forces into protective fertility goddesses willing to accept Zeus' authority and to foster and protect Athens and the Athenians.

In the end, persuasive speech permits the struggle between ideas and opinions to produce progress. The Furies accept Athena's offer, promising to remain in Athens and use their powers constructively (*Eum.* 916 ff.). Delighted, Athena asserts that she is glad that the goddess Peitho (Persuasion) watched over her tongue and mouth as she confronted the Furies' fierce refusal. She explains that "Zeus, guardian of popular assemblies, and our dispute over good things bring victory always" (*Eum.* 968–75). True victory turns out to mean not the triumph of one side at the other's expense, but a peaceful resolution benefiting everyone.[38]

Athena embodies the spirit of Odysseus, the spirit of Athens, that extraordinary human capacity for ingenuity and survival, but her intervention also emphasizes the fragile, provisional nature of the legal process. Athena casts the deciding vote and persuades the Furies to accept the verdict. She establishes a permanent court in Athens for murder trials, with jurors sworn in by oath (*Eum.* 482–84, 684–90).[39] But persuasion alone is not sufficient, since Athena insists that fear will continue to play a crucial role in promoting respect for law and preventing injustice, anarchy, and tyranny (*Eum.* 690–710). The spirits of revenge remain in the city, and they are still terrifying, still able to compel compliance through dread. The Furies have agreed to use their powers constructively, but they retain their destructive potential.[40]

The resolution in the play remains provisional, precarious, and unsatisfying—but preferable to the alternative. The jury fails to arrive at a decision, and Orestes goes unpunished for murdering his own mother. Justice defined as vengeance, however, produces escalating violence and destroys families and communities, as the trilogy demonstrates. Instead of order, vengeance creates chaos. While the strong emotional appeal of vengeance persists even in our own times, a jury trial rests on the recognition that not even torture or capital punishment can undo an act of bloodshed or fully satisfy a victim's rage. This recognition is progress. The community's goal cannot be to satisfy the victim, whether an injured or murdered person or his devastated kin. Satisfying the victim is not possible. Family and friends may be passionate for revenge, but even they in calmer moments know that vengeance will not restore a loved one or undo an injury. Despite its shortcomings, a legal process better serves the interests of the community as a whole.

The *Oresteia* challenges the primitive, traditional desire for vengeance and validates a legal procedure for addressing it. At the same time, the trilogy promotes the ability of individuals of any time and place to judge and evaluate empirical evidence. In a democracy, this is not simply a right; it is also a tremendous, even daunting, obligation. It is far easier to allow others to decide for you, and tyrants are happy to relieve you of the necessity of thinking for yourself. If your conception of right and wrong is completely inflexible, predetermined by autocratic pronouncements or by tradition, then you never need to think at all. You never need to develop your ability to evaluate the facts, consider logical consequences, and devise solutions when two values conflict. Tyranny demands unthinking agreement, compelled by violence or intimidation. Democracy, by contrast, recognizes verbal disagreement as vital to the benefit of all. The *Oresteia* suggests that a jury trial, a publicly judged verbal contest, although imperfect and unsatisfying, can prevent reciprocal vengeance killings from devastating families and communities. A conflict between verbal arguments can promote progress. Real victory must mean that everyone wins.

In the twenty-first century, we must recognize "equality before the law" as an as yet unrealized aspiration. Too often race, socioeconomic status, or gender influence law enforcement and judicial outcomes. Aeschylus knew that, regardless of the institutions and procedures available, the spirit of vengeance remains powerful and capable of erupting at any time. We know that inequitable policing and judicial unfairness make that primitive reversion more likely. Unequal application of the law provokes righteous anger and justifiably undermines faith in the legal system. The *Oresteia* presents the trial by jury as a healthier alternative to vengeance killings. Our great challenge is to make that vision a reality.

CONFLICT (SOPHOCLES'S *ANTIGONE*)

You are at the theater in Athens. At the same time, you are gazing upon the gates of the palace of Thebes. Antigone's story is about to begin. You know Antigone as the product of shocking incest, the daughter of Oedipus and his own mother. Oedipus killed his father and married his mother, but the truth came out at once. His mother-wife hanged herself, while Oedipus continued to rule in Thebes. (Despite the apparent brevity of their marriage, Oedipus and his mother-wife had four children together.) When Oedipus eventually died, the Thebans honored him with a great funeral and burial mound. Afterward, Oedipus's two sons killed each other, fighting over the kingship of Thebes. Oedipus's two young daughters remained to mourn their brothers' deaths.

This all happened long ago, but also, somehow, just now. The sons of Oedipus have just fought and died. Sophocles's play is beginning, and Antigone and her sister, Ismene, are emerging from the palace.

"Do you know what Zeus is accomplishing for us both even after all of our father's troubles?" Antigone asks her sister. "You and I have already suffered everything that is painful and dishonorable. But now the whole city says that the general has made a new proclamation. Have you heard anything? Are you completely oblivious to the troubles coming against your own people from enemies?" Antigone sounds confident and aggressive.

"No story has come to me since our brothers died on the same day by each other's hand," Ismene admits timidly.

"I knew it," snaps Antigone. "That's why I sent you outside the palace gates, so that you alone might hear."

"Hear what?" Ismene asks apprehensively. "You seem to be brooding over something."

"Well, hasn't Creon dishonored our brother Polynices? He has decided that our brother Eteocles is worthy of burial, but he proclaimed to all the citizens that Polynices is to be left unburied, a sweet treasure for birds to feed on. He forbids even mourning. That's what they say good Creon has proclaimed," Antigone continues sarcastically. "And he has promised death to anyone who disobeys. He is coming to tell us himself. Soon you will show whether you are noble or cowardly."

Ismene's voice quavers. "How can I be of any use in such troubles?"

"Consider whether you will work with me or not," Antigone responds crisply. She is planning to bury her brother, despite the king's proclamation.

Shocked, Ismene fears the dismal death awaiting them if they transgress the decree and authority of the ones in power. "We have to keep in mind that we are women," she urges. "We are not meant by nature to fight against men. We are ruled by ones who are stronger than we are, and we have to obey, even in situations still worse than these." *Ismene sounds weak and defeatist. But what chance could two young girls have against a king's royal authority?*

"I wouldn't order you to help, and I wouldn't want your help even if you offered," Antigone snarls. "But I will bury him. I consider it a noble thing to die doing this. Having violated human laws to do something holy, I will lie with him in death, loving him and loved by him. I must please the ones below for a longer time than the ones here," she explains, evidently valuing her relationships with the dead over her relationships with the living. "But you go ahead and keep on dishonoring the gods' ordinances," she continues coldly.

Knowing that she herself cannot oppose the citizens, Ismene fears for her sister and begs her to conceal her plan. That, she can help Antigone do.

This enrages Antigone. "Shout it out!" she screams. "You will be far more hateful keeping silent, if you don't proclaim these things to all." Ismene criticizes Antigone's passion, but Antigone retorts, "I know that I am pleasing those whom it is most necessary for me to please."

"You love things that aren't possible." says Ismene.

"Well, then," Antigone responds flatly, "when I no longer have the strength, I'll have stopped." *Her resolve seems remarkable. She has no doubts or fears. Her sister's rational objections have no effect—except to make her despise Ismene.*

A chorus of elderly Theban men now enter, singing in praise of victory. "With Zeus's aid," they announce triumphantly, "the Thebans defeated their attackers massed at the seven gates. The two brothers, having the same parents and strength and hatred, achieved a common death."

King Creon arrives, and the chorus wonders why he sent for them. "Men," Creon begins, "the gods who have long tossed this city on the rolling sea have set its affairs back upright." Continuing in this grand and authoritative tone, he praises the chorus for reverencing the throne and power of Laius, and then Laius's son Oedipus, and for remaining loyal to Oedipus's sons after Oedipus died. "But now," Creon explains, "since they have killed each other, I as next of kin hold all power and the throne." *Creon is the brother of Oedipus's mother-wife. He tries to sound calm and kingly, but he is evidently thrilled. And nervous.* "I know it's a big job," Creon continues. "It's impossible to know a man's spirit, thoughts, and judgment until he's an experienced ruler, but I have always considered the very worst the man who, out of fear, fails to make the best plans for guiding the city straight. Anyone who values a friend more than his own country—well, I say this man is nowhere. Let Zeus know it: I would never be silent seeing the citizens in danger, and I would never consider any man a friend if he is hostile to this land. The land keeps us safe. We make friends by sailing on a prosperous land. By such precepts, I will make this city great."

Creon's metaphor of the city and the land as a ship seems overdone, but you get his point: Our "friends" are our fellow citizens. Anyone hostile to our land is no friend at all. For this reason, Creon has determined to bury with all honors the brother who died defending the city, and he has forbidden burial to the one who died attacking it. The chorus accepts Creon's definition of "friend" as someone "well-minded" toward the city, and his definition of "enemy" as anyone hostile to it. *The definition somehow seems inadequate to you.* The chorus insists that no one would disobey the king's command, since "there is no one so foolish that he loves to die."

And yet, impossibly, someone has violated the king's ban. A guard arrives to announce that dust has been scattered on the traitor's corpse. Someone administered token but adequate funeral rites. The guard, terrified of being blamed, fears even to tell Creon. No one saw who did it. And there was no sign of any beast or dogs having torn the body.

When the chorus members wonder whether the gods might be responsible, Creon becomes enraged. "You ancient, mindless fools! What you say is unendurable. The gods favor this corpse? They honored and buried him as one who had done them a service? The man who came to destroy their temples and the offerings dedicated to them? The man who came to shatter their land and their laws?" The king's fury escalates. "Do you see gods honoring evil men? It's impossible." Convinced that his enemies in the city have secretly bribed someone, Creon threatens that they will pay the penalty "if Zeus has power still, Zeus whom I revere." Creon will punish the guards with a fate worse than death if they don't discover the man who performed the burial. He seems certain that the guards themselves were bribed.

As Creon reenters the palace, the guard flees in terror, thanking the gods for having preserved his life. Now the chorus members step forward. "There are many terrible, wondrous, and strange things [*deina*]," they sing, "and nothing more terrible, wondrous, and strange [*deinoteron*] than a human being." They list amazing human accomplishments: seafaring, agriculture, hunting, fishing, turning up the soil with horse-drawn plows. "With his ingenious inventions," they say, man conquers all other creatures. "He has taught himself language, and thought like the wind, and the feelings of social life, and how to provide shelter from bad weather. He is never without resources in approaching the future. From death alone will he not devise an escape, but he has contrived escapes from unconquerable diseases." *The chorus makes all human achievement sound very impressive.*

But now they continue more ominously. "Having ingenuity that is clever, arts and crafts beyond all expectations, a human being creeps at one time to evil, at another to good. Fulfilling the laws of the land and the justice of the gods, he is highest in his city. But whoever associates with what is not noble or good has no city. Let no one who would do such things ever be beside my hearth or have thoughts equal to mine." *The chorus members evidently revere the immense creative power of human beings, but they also recognize its ambivalent potential.*)

Suddenly, here is Antigone, dragged forward by the guard who earlier fled in terror. Creon conveniently reappears. The guards have caught Antigone, this young girl, in the act of arranging the burial, re-dusting the corpse that the guards had swept clean, crowning the dead man with three ritual libations. Exultant at having captured Antigone, and caring only for his own safety, the guard never questions whether she or Creon is right. *But you do begin to consider this question.*

Creon at first cannot believe that Antigone has violated his decree, but she denies nothing. She knowingly violated the king's proclamation. It did not come from Zeus or from Dikē (the goddess Justice), and Antigone insists on abiding by the gods' ancient traditions, unwritten, secure, and everlasting. Creon's ban, a mortal's proclamation, has no power to flout divinely ordained customs requiring the burial of family members. For Antigone, the thought of dying holds no pain. Pain would have resulted from failure to bury her brother.

Furious, Creon denounces Antigone for her *hybris* (reckless, self-destructive violence, arrogance, or insolence). He considers her transgression of the laws a direct affront to his masculinity. "Indeed I am not a man, and she is a man," he exclaims, "if this victory will be hers with impunity." He does not care that she's his niece. He will punish her and her sister both.

Creon calls Antigone's act an evil crime; she calls it *kleos*. For her, there's no glory greater than burying her own brother. Everyone in the city would agree, she says, if fear did not silence them. She denounces tyranny for its capacity to do and say whatever it wants.

"You alone of all these Thebans here see this," Creon responds dismissively.

"Oh, they see it, too," Antigone retorts. "But because of you, they keep their tongues in check."

When Creon points out that Antigone is honoring an ungodly man, Antigone insists that death desires the laws to be equal. Creon counters that the good, useful man and the wicked, cowardly man do not obtain an equal lot.

"Who knows whether these things are without guilt down below?" Antigone asks.

But Creon remains certain. "An enemy is never a friend, not even when he has died," he proclaims. When Antigone claims that her nature is not to hate but to love, Creon angrily tells her to go love the dead ones down below. "A woman will never rule me while I'm alive," he snarls.

Arriving at this moment, Ismene claims that she helped in the burial and wants to die alongside her sister. Antigone rejects her angrily, saying that she does not love a sister who shows her love by words alone. "You chose to live," she reminds Ismene, "I chose to die."

Creon considers them both out of their minds. He is determined to kill Antigone, even though she is engaged to his own son, Haemon. He will execute Ismene, too, for good measure. "These women must be constrained," he orders the guards, "not let loose without restraint."

Praising Zeus's everlasting, supreme power, the chorus sees destruction coming: "The god leads toward ruinous folly the thoughts of any man who considers evil to be noble. That man avoids ruinous folly for the shortest time." *Their phrasing is convoluted, but their meaning is clear: it's shortsighted to mistake evil for good.*

The king's son Haemon arrives, and Creon wonders whether he has come to rage at his father for condemning Antigone. Or does he still consider his father a friend in all that he does?

The conversation starts well. "I'm yours, Father," Haemon begins respectfully. "And you set me straight by having good, useful judgments which I will obey." No marriage, he says, will be worth more to him than his father's noble guidance.

This pleases Creon immensely. Haemon is exactly the sort of obedient offspring a man prays to produce. In Creon's view, this dutiful son constitutes evidence of his father's talent for governing, because "any man who is good and useful in arranging his family affairs is also manifestly just in the city." Demanding obedience is the key, since "the man appointed by the city must be obeyed, both as to his small and just commands and even ones that are the opposite." *Is he suggesting that citizens must obey even commands that are large and unjust?* "There is no greater evil than anarchy," Creon continues. "Therefore, we must defend order and not in any way be beaten by a woman."

But now Haemon begins—still respectfully, still tactfully—to push back against his father's certainty. He would never be the one to say that his father isn't speaking correctly. Of course Creon naturally doesn't concern himself with the actions or criticisms of others. To the average person, the very sight of Creon is *deinon* (terrible, wondrous, and strange). *You recognize the singular form of* deina, *the "terrible, wondrous, and strange" natural phenomena and human capacities that the chorus celebrated earlier.* But Haemon hears what is being said in the shadows. The city grieves for this young girl, saying that of all women, she least deserves to die terribly for the glorious deeds she has done. Burying her own brother, not allowing him to be eaten by dogs and birds—doesn't she deserve golden honor? That's what everyone is saying secretly, and the rumor is spreading.

Haemon insists that he values his father's success above all. He urges his father to be open to good advice: "Anyone who thinks that he alone has the capacity for thought, eloquence, or reason, well, these men, once unfolded, are seen to be empty." There's nothing shameful, he explains, in learning new things. Trees that can bend survive storms, he points out. Whoever guides a ship and doesn't loosen the sheet when it is necessary overturns his ship. Haemon urges his father to yield, and to stop being angry. He admits that he himself is young, but even an old person can't be right all the time, and can learn from someone who speaks well.

The chorus members agree. They think that both men can learn from one another. But Creon reacts with astonishing and terrifying fury. "So at our age we will be taught to understand nature by a man of his age?" he asks. Does Haemon advise him to honor people who produce disorder? Hasn't Antigone been seized with just such a sickness?

Haemon manages to keep his voice calm. He points out that all the citizens are on his side.

Creon retorts that he is in charge, not the people. He rules exclusively in his own interest, he confidently asserts, since the city belongs to its ruler and to no one else.

Haemon now begins to lose control, too. Criticizing his father for sounding childish, he exclaims, "A city that belongs to one man is not a city!"

Haemon's statement is incomprehensible to King Creon. "Isn't the city thought to belong to the one who rules it?" he demands.

"Alone, you would rule nobly over a deserted land," Haemon sneers, but he continues to insist that he only wants to prevent his father from committing an injustice.

Disparaging his son as a woman's slave, Creon remains furious that his son dares to criticize his father's knowledge of justice and his confidence in his own authority. Haemon argues that Creon is dishonoring the gods and is thereby endangering himself, along with his son and his son's fiancée.

Creon proceeds to denounce his son as a polluted character. Deaf to Haemon's arguments, Creon screams, "You will never marry this woman while she is living!"

"She will die, then," Haemon acknowledges. "And by dying she will kill someone else." *Whom does Haemon intend to kill? His father? Himself?*

"How dare you threaten me!" Creon shouts. *He hasn't bothered to consider the ambiguities of his son's statement.*

"I'm not threatening you, just telling you my decision!" Haemon is shouting now, too. He condemns his father's inability to listen, and he insists that he is not thinking well.

The king responds with monstrous ferocity. "You know what?" he says. "You can watch her die." He orders Antigone to be brought forward so that Haemon can be present at her death.

"Don't expect me to watch her die," Haemon announces. "And you will never see me again. Go ahead and rave on among whoever of your friends [*philoi*] are willing." And Haemon storms out. *You know that* philoi *means not only political allies but also blood relatives. Creon's willingness to sacrifice family obligations to political allegiances troubles you. The king's elderly advisors recognize the denial of burial to a traitor as traditional custom, but your sense of dread increases. Surely family connections and responsibilities cannot be so callously ignored?*

Creon appears not to care that his son has left him. He is determined to kill both young women, but at a single question from the chorus, he quickly exempts Ismene. Antigone, however, he will bury alive, in a remote, rocky cave. To prevent the city from being tainted by the murder, he will leave her a little food. "Let her pray there to Hades, god of the dead," he rants. "That is the only god she worships. Doubtless, by asking, she will manage not to die. Or at any rate she will learn—but late—that it's monstrous work to reverence death."

Has Haemon's judgment been distorted by his love for Antigone? The chorus now sings a brief ode to Eros, the divine spirit of love, lust, and passion. Eros ranges everywhere. No immortal or mortal can escape it. It drives its possessor mad. It twists the unjust thoughts of the just toward outrage. Eros caused this conflict between blood kin. Victory goes to desire, inspired by the eyes of the happy bride, desire enthroned among the mighty laws. "The unconquerable goddess Aphrodite is just toying with us," the chorus members sing sadly. They cannot help weeping for Antigone. *Despite the high-flown language of the chorus, you recognize that Antigone and Haemon are victims of Eros, victims of their own passions. As is Creon.*

"Look at me, citizens of my paternal land!" Antigone shouts. "I'm traveling my last road, beholding the light of the sun for the last time." She reminds everyone that she is going to die without ever having been a bride. She will be the bride of Acheron, god of the river in the underworld.

The chorus members claimed to weep for Antigone, but they now seem quite unsympathetic. "You go, therefore, without glory or praise," they tell her, "struck neither by illness nor the sword. You are a law unto yourself. You alone of mortals go down alive to Hades." Dismissing Antigone's analogy of herself to the mythical Niobe, turned to stone by grief, the chorus points out that Niobe was an immortal, observing: "And yet the dying like to hear that they have a fate like the gods."

Antigone feels that the chorus members are mocking her. Why can't they wait until she's dead to insult her? She says farewell to Thebes and its fountains and groves. Wretched, she sees herself as a resident alien among neither mortals nor corpses, at home among neither the living nor the dead.

"You went to the extreme of boldness," says the chorus. "O child, you tripped up against the high altar of Justice. You are paying the penalty for some paternal conflict."

Antigone laments the fate of her father, her ancestral race, her incestuous parents. Cursed, unmarried, she is going to live as a resident alien among her dead relatives.

"A certain reverence is creditable," the chorus admits. "But power cannot be transgressed. Your self-chosen passion destroyed you."

Antigone knows that she goes to her death unwept, unwed, friendless. But now Creon interrupts her lament. He is sure that no one would ever stop bewailing their own death, if that were necessary to stave off dying. Impatiently, he orders the guards to take Antigone away as quickly as possible and to entomb her alive. Certain of his own unstained purity, he claims that Antigone "*sterēsetai* [will be deprived of, or will deprive herself of] her right to dwell here above." *You note that Creon has opted for phrasing that absolves him of any responsibility.*

In a wrenching, but strange, speech, Antigone addresses her tomb, her bridal chamber, the deep-dug, ever-guarded dwelling where she will go to join her dead kin. She knows that she will be *philē* (dear) to her father, mother, and brothers for the care she took of them after they died. If she had had children or a husband and they had died, she never would have buried them against the will of the citizens. She could have had another husband and more children. But with her parents dead, her brother is irreplaceable. By such a *nomos* (law, custom, or tradition), she honored her brother. But Creon, she says, saw this as committing error and daring to do *deina* (terrible, wondrous, or strange things). *You again recall* deina *as the subject of the chorus's first song.* Denied marriage and children, abandoned by *philoi* (friends, blood relatives, loved ones), on whom of the gods, she asks, can she call? By showing reverence, she has acquired a charge of impiety. Well, if the gods approve of what's being done to her now, then by suffering, she will know that she has done wrong. But if in fact these men are the ones doing wrong, then may they suffer exactly what they are doing unjustly to her. *She remains passionate and indomitable.*

Creon orders the guards to make haste, threatening to punish them for their slowness, and Antigone utters her final protest. "O citadel and ancient gods of the land of my fathers. Behold, Leaders of Thebes, the last remaining woman of the royal family." (*She appears to have forgotten about her sister.*)

"Behold what I am suffering—and at the hands of what sort of men—I, who reverenced what was due reverence!" Then she's gone.

As if to transform Antigone's dreadful fate into something familiar, the chorus describes the suffering of other mythical figures. *Their analogies fail to diminish your unease at witnessing Antigone's horrible fate. Time passes while the chorus sings.*

The blind prophet Teiresias appears. Creon has always followed his advice before, and now Teiresias has had dire new signs. "The city is sick because of your decision," he tells Creon. "Birds and dogs have filled the altars and hearths with the flesh of the ill-fated, wretched son of Oedipus." Apparently, they've been feeding on the traitor's unburied corpse. "The gods are rejecting sacrificial offerings and prayers. Having feasted on the blood of a slain man, the birds do not shriek forth well-omened cries. Reminding Creon that everyone makes mistakes, Teiresias urges him to reconsider. "Stubbornness incurs the charge of stupidity," he insists. "What valor is there in killing a dead man?"

But Creon rejects this advice, accusing Teiresias and all prophets of greed. Teiresias accuses all tyrants of the same. They hurl insults at one another. Creon refuses to budge.

Teiresias makes a terrible prediction: In exchange for having entombed a live girl, Creon will soon give back a corpse for a corpse. And it will be a child of his own. Creon has also deprived a dead man of his proper rites. The avenging Furies will ensnare Creon in these same evils. "You think I've been bribed?" Teiresias demands. "Wait and see. You won't escape." Calling to his slave to lead him, the blind seer turns and slowly walks away.

The chorus believes Teiresias. The seer has never been wrong before. Creon now believes him, too, but he is uncertain how to proceed. Suddenly, this once confident king turns to the chorus of old men and asks them what he should do.

"Release the girl," they reply without hesitation. "And bury the man who's lying unburied. Do it as quickly as possible."

It's a difficult decision for Creon, but he makes it. He rushes off, ordering his attendants to take up axes and to hurry. He now fears that the best thing is to complete one's life while obeying established laws (*nomoi*).

The chorus calls on Dionysus, god of the theater and of the festival you are attending, in which this play is being performed. Surely Dionysus will protect Thebes, where he is honored above all, since his mortal mother was the daughter of Thebes's ancient king.

No such luck. A messenger arrives with dreadful news. Haemon has killed himself, raging against the murder his father committed. Teiresias's prophecy has come true. The queen, Haemon's mother, emerges from the palace having heard a rumor of her son's death. The messenger relates the sad sequence of events: accompanying their king, Creon's servants washed, purified, and cremated the corpse of the traitor Polynices, and then buried the ashes in a lofty funeral mound of Theban soil. Next, they proceeded to the cave to release Antigone. (*You note with surprise that Creon did not quite follow the chorus members' advice; they advised him to release the girl and bury the dead man. He opted to bury the corpse before going to free the girl.*) As Creon and his men approached the cave, they could hear Haemon bewailing Antigone's death. She had hanged herself. Creon entered the chamber, and Haemon stabbed at him with his sword. He missed his father but then, in fury, thrust the sword into his own ribs. The messenger concludes that the greatest evil for mortals is *aboulia* (ill counsel, or thoughtlessness).

Having heard this awful tale, the queen silently returns to the palace, and Creon arrives, carrying his son's lifeless body. *You hardly recognize this broken, grieving, self-recriminating father as the confident, domineering autocrat you last saw.*)

Creon recognizes the errors of his own "ill-planning thoughts," and the chorus comments—somewhat unnecessarily, it seems—that Creon seems to see justice too late. Creon blames a god, not himself, as the cause of what he refers to as his own "wild and savage paths," and therefore of his own suffering. *But you see that he's in agony.*

And there's more suffering to come. The messenger tells Creon that his wife, like his son, has died by a self-inflicted stab wound. "Ah!" Creon cries. "You have killed a dead man over again." This second loss utterly overwhelms him. At last, he takes full responsibility. "I killed you," he moans. "It's true." He commands his attendants, "Lead me away as quickly as possible, I who don't exist." Realizing that without his family he is nothing, Creon prays to die.

The chorus members assure him that it will happen. But for now, they say, "There is no release from misfortune for mortals."

THE PERILS OF POLARIZATION: REPURPOSING
ANOTHER ANCIENT TALE

The specific point of contention in the *Antigone*, the question of who deserves burial, may seem unfamiliar to us, but the nature of the argument, the moral certainty and fury of the two opponents, is not. Disputes in the twenty-first century can be as heated, apparently irreconcilable, and mutually destructive as the confrontation depicted in this play. Even in nominally "democratic" societies, not only serious political conflicts but also simple differences of opinion often seem rigidly partisan, polarized, and counterproductive. Even if you are meeting Creon and Antigone for the first time in Sophocles's powerful and disturbing play, you are not unacquainted with them. They are ancient, and they are us.

Twenty-five hundred years ago, as the Athenians were making their unprecedented transition away from a hereditary, tribal, hierarchical power structure and adjusting to their new democratic political institutions, Sophocles transformed the tale of Antigone into an object lesson in how *not* to resolve conflicts. In his version of the story, Antigone and Creon collide and self-destruct. Antigone learns nothing. Creon learns only too late. They cannot be helped. But maybe it's not too late for us.

As Aeschylus did in the *Oresteia*, Sophocles in the *Antigone* (c. 443 BCE) transports ancient mythical characters forward into his contemporary Athens. For centuries, archaic epic tales of Oedipus and his mother-wife had circulated widely, but Sophocles and other Athenian playwrights made these people—and their children—walk and talk in "modern" times. Like the *Iliad* and *Odyssey*, Athenian tragedies emphasize human choices and their consequences, and the characters provide examples of decisions and actions to emulate and to avoid. Perhaps each of us is capable of learning from our own mistakes, but like the *Iliad* and *Odyssey*, fifth-century BCE Athenian tragedies offer us, as they offered contemporary Athenians, something even better: the opportunity to learn from *other* people's mistakes.

The *Antigone* is the first of three surviving plays by Sophocles about the family of Oedipus, king of Thebes,[1] but Antigone's father Oedipus was already famous, and apparently admired (yes, *admired*!) for centuries, long before even the *Odyssey* was composed. The *Odyssey* assumes that Oedipus's story is well known. It and other surviving archaic references mention the incest of Oedipus and his mother-wife, and her suicide upon learning the truth, but these references suggest that Oedipus continued to rule Thebes even after the facts were known and that he died in battle, honored by the Thebans with a big funeral and prominent burial mound.[2] In other words, yes, Oedipus's marital situation was a little unusual, but there is no indication in these archaic references that this was a problem for Oedipus. It was awkward for his mother-wife, certainly, and she opted for suicide. But Oedipus lived on happily in Thebes and died wealthy and celebrated.

Many centuries later, however, as the Athenians were designing and conducting their comparatively short-lived experiment in radical, direct democracy (508–322 BCE),[3] Athenian tragedies mined this admittedly atypical royal family for universal lessons about human conduct and relationships. Extended archaic accounts of Oedipus and his family have not survived, nor have earlier tragic versions, but we can be certain that other versions existed, and that Sophocles had no qualms about altering them, since he revised traditional details about Oedipus and possibly invented the story of Antigone altogether.[4] In the confrontation between Antigone and Creon, Sophocles explores the great challenge that every human community faces: What do we do when we disagree?

The title character, Antigone, is the daughter of the famous Oedipus (also, of course, his sister, but that is a different story). As the play begins, her two brothers (who are also her uncles and nephews—and each other's—but again, let's not go there) have just killed one another fighting over the throne of Thebes. One died defending Thebes, the other died attacking it, having marshaled an army from a neighboring citizen-community. The newly installed king of Thebes, Antigone's uncle Creon (technically also her great-uncle, but this is no easy family tree to draw), has declared a noble funeral for the defending brother, but he has decreed that the body of the attacking brother, the traitor, be left unburied for birds and dogs to ravage.[5] In a nutshell: Antigone buries her brother anyway. Caught in the act, she confesses immediately, and Creon condemns her to be walled up alive in a cave. He soon relents and goes to release her. But by the time he arrives, she has already hanged herself. Antigone's fiancé, who is also Creon's son, kills himself, too. And Creon's wife does the same. The loss of his son and wife devastates Creon, and he ultimately acknowledges his responsibility for their destruction. No one wins.

No creative problem solving on offer here, just absolute certainties.[6] Without identifying any specific religious prohibition, Creon appears to fear offending the gods of the citizen-community by burying a traitor within the precincts of Thebes. Antigone believes that not burying the body at all will offend the gods of the underworld, who uphold the bonds connecting blood kin. To Sophocles's contemporaries, although these claims conflict, each has merit. But Creon and Antigone are each so certain of their own exclusive correctness that neither can see any validity in the other's viewpoint. Neither Creon nor Antigone can incorporate new information or accept good advice. Neither ever considers the possibility of exploring discussion, compromise, or a creative solution.

As an ancient tale adapted to a new political moment, the *Antigone* exposes a problem that remains as pressing today as it was in the fifth century BCE: Our allegiances to our families or to other subgroups within the larger civic community (friends, or people with the same interests, beliefs, or political views) often conflict with our obligations to one another as fellow citizens, or even as fellow human beings regardless of citizenship.[7] The consequences, now as then, can be catastrophic. The *Antigone* emphasizes that it is neither morally right nor possible to ignore your obligations to your relatives, your clan, your tribe. But at the same time, the play also shows that ancient, traditional loyalties to kin or tribe challenge and even threaten the impartial allegiances to fellow citizens and fellow human beings that democratic political order requires.

SECTARIAN SUICIDE: BLOOD TIES VERSUS POLITICAL TIES

We may aspire to love our neighbor as ourselves, but in practice that is very difficult to do. We naturally tend to feel greater affection for family and friends than for strangers or even fellow citizens. Our obligations to the people nearest and dearest to us not infrequently conflict with our obligations to others. By featuring the question of what to do with the body of a traitor, the *Antigone* portrays a direct clash between family loyalties and civic loyalties.[8] Antigone values family loyalties exclusively; she is determined to defy Creon's ban on burying her brother, since it violates the ancient obligation to bury family members properly. Creon, by contrast, values civic loyalties exclusively, insisting that divine law requires a traitor to remain unburied, food for birds and dogs. Antigone ignores the fact that her brother betrayed her city. Creon ignores the fact that the "traitor" is also his nephew (also his grandnephew, but OK, I'll stop. The point is that he's Creon's blood relative, as is Antigone herself). Antigone provides no exemplary model of tribal allegiances, nor does Creon provide one of civic allegiances. Instead, their intransigence shows us precisely how not to proceed.

History suggests that neither the kinship group nor the larger community can thrive if the members of either fail to respect their obligations as members of the other. To completely abandon your obligations to your family or kin, that permanent type of friends, violates something deeply human. Fascist and totalitarian societies have tried—and continue to try, with spectacular cruelty and horrific results—to obliterate family ties and to substitute exclusively civic obligations between fellow citizens or "comrades." Conversely, communities dominated by divisive tribal allegiances or ruthless political factions often devolve into continuous, devastating violence.[9] Societies in which either conception of identity triumphs at the expense of the other tend to become kleptocracies, thugocracies, or some combination of the two.

Despite ample cautionary evidence, both historical and contemporary, our own partisan and political identities often appear to be as rigid and exclusive as those of Antigone and Creon. Like Antigone, we may think "family first," and restrict our sense of obligation to our own family, disregarding any responsibilities toward others beyond our family group. Alternatively, like Creon, we may dismiss as unpatriotic or traitorous anyone who does not share our political convictions. We may sometimes conflate the categories of "family member" and "like-minded fellow citizen," but we tend to prefer and foster our connections with people who share our views—whether family members or others—and to devalue and despise people who do not.

We may have few opportunities and little desire to converse with people outside our own inherited or chosen groupings. We may hate others who do not see things the way we do. We may even come to consider people unlike ourselves less than human, and deserving of death.

The *Antigone* depicts exactly this kind of rigidly polarized confrontation as a conflict between the tribal obligations of a traditional hierarchical society and the civic obligations newly arising in a democratic polity. In the play, the dispute centers on the double meaning of *philos:* "dear one, relative, friend." Antigone uses the word exclusively to mean blood relatives. Creon uses it exclusively to mean friends defined as political allies.[10] In archaic times, your *philoi* were your "nearest and dearest," the people essential to your survival. Before democratic government existed, your *philoi*, clan, and community were one and the same. In a traditional hierarchical society such as those depicted in the *Iliad* and *Odyssey*, the highest goal of the high achiever is to "help *philoi* [friends] and harm enemies."[11] But this concept of obligations becomes problematic in a democratic citizen-community that incorporates more than one clan, tribe, party, or faction. In the play, Antigone retains the primitive conviction that friendships and enmities are permanent categories, incapable of shifting or adapting. She knows that family members remain family. Creon, however, restricts *philos* to mean "loyal and like-minded member of my citizen-community." For him, an enemy is anyone who does not see things exactly as he does. Completely lacking not only compassion but also forethought, Creon persists in claiming that "the enemy is not ever a friend [*philos*], not even whenever he dies" (*Ant.* 522). Antigone fails to comprehend Creon's definition of friendship, retorting, "I was born not to join in hatred but *sumphilein* [to join in love/friendship]" (*Ant.* 523).

Defining *philos* exclusively as "family member," Antigone ignores any obligation to fellow citizens. She tells her sister that she will bury her brother no matter what. Certain that this is the noble and holy thing to do, she's confident that "I will lie with him in death, loving him and loved by him [literally, a dear one with a dear one (*philē/philou*)], having committed the crime of doing holy things, since I must please the ones below for a longer time than the ones here. For I will lie there always" (*Ant.* 71–76).

Embracing death and an imagined eternity, Antigone considers nothing more important than the divinely sanctioned kinship bond.

Taking the other extreme, Creon defines *philos* exclusively by the *polis* (citizen-community), ignoring natural affections and obligations between family members. Creon identifies *philoi* as one's fellow citizens, and only those who place the city's needs before anything else. Creon rejects "anyone who values a friend [*philos*] more than his own country," insisting that he would never "set as a friend [*philos*] to myself a man who is hostile to the land, knowing [i.e., as I do] that the land is the one who keeps us safe. We make friends [*philous*] by sailing on a prosperous land. By such precepts [*nomoi:* laws, customs, or traditions], I will make this city great" (*Ant.* 182–91). In this chilling notion of friendship determined solely by political relationships, Creon anticipates fascism by hundreds of years.[12]

If Antigone values her dead relatives too much, Creon values his live ones too little. She claims that only family ties matter, but she appears to prefer dead relatives to live ones. He claims that only the bonds of citizenship matter, and he considers family ties irrelevant. (Theirs certainly is a peculiar family.) Both Antigone and Creon are correct—just not exclusively so. Family relationships matter, but so do civic ones. Eventually recognizing his mistake, Creon still can't get it right. He hastens to bury the corpse before going to rescue the live girl. By then, of course, it's too late: Antigone has hanged herself. As the play ends, Creon and Antigone have together destroyed both their family and their city, having eradicated its political order. With the devastation of the royal family, including the death of Creon's son, the heir to the throne, the city faces chaos.

Unfortunately, the *Antigone*'s emphasis on the devastating conflict between family loyalties and civic loyalties can be difficult for modern readers to perceive, especially if they read the play in translation. The *Antigone* is frequently misinterpreted as a dramatization of the revolt of the individual against the overwhelming power of the state. This misunderstanding derives not from the play itself, but from the anachronistic projection of modern certainties onto it. Knowledge of totalitarianism, fascism, the Second World War, and numerous more recent events tends to create not unreasonable anxiety about the vulnerability of the individual to tyrannical state control.[13] But Sophocles and his Athenian contemporaries in the mid-fifth century BCE had the opposite anxiety. For them the *polis* as a community of citizens (the concept of a "state" did not yet exist) was both necessary and fragile. The ancient *polis* offered individuals protection from foreign enemies, wild beasts, starvation, and exposure, but it was always vulnerable to destruction from these same forces. Ancient Greeks did not distrust the *polis*. They embraced it as essential to their survival.[14] In the play, Antigone does not reject the authority of the state or assert the rights of the individual against state control. She challenges only the validity of Creon's one decree.[15] Determined to fulfill her obligations to her family, she rejects Creon's definition of his ban as a *nomos* (law, custom, or tradition). She dismisses the ban on burying her brother as merely a *kerugma* (proclamation), distinguishing it from actual *nomoi* (plural of *nomos*) to which she does feel bound (*Ant.* 447–61).[16]

It is equally easy to misread this play as a confrontation between religious convictions and secular political authority. But this, too, is to project onto Sophocles's play a twenty-first-century preoccupation. Disputes over the role or limits of religion in political and social life figure prominently in our world, so we are likely to look for this conflict and to see it wherever we look. But this play has no such dispute, because both Creon and Antigone have religious as well as political motives.[17]

Both Creon and Antigone seek to obey and honor the gods—just not the same gods. Acting as a responsible ruler, Creon wants to protect his people from divine punishment. He believes that burying a traitor on home ground would offend the gods of the *polis* and bring divine wrath down on Thebes. Having discovered that the corpse has been lightly buried, Creon angrily rejects the chorus's suggestion that gods might have done it, that the gods might have desired to honor a traitor who intended to destroy their temples, land, and laws. "Do you see gods honoring evil men?" he demands. "It's impossible" (*Ant.* 280–89). Threatening the chorus members if they fail to discover the culprits or whoever bribed them, Creon invokes Zeus, claiming to speak under oath, "If Zeus still has respect from me" (*Ant.* 304).

Like Creon, Antigone also seeks to please the gods, but unlike Creon she means the gods of the dead. She argues that Zeus did not make the proclamation to ban her brother's burial,[18] "Nor did Justice, who dwells with the gods below, establish such laws, customs, traditions [*nomous*]" (*Ant.* 450–51). When Creon tries to distinguish the rights of the one who died defending the land from the one who died intending to destroy it (*Ant.* 518), Antigone responds, "Nevertheless, Hades, at any rate, desires these laws,customs, traditions [*nomous*]" (*Ant.* 519). She rejects Creon's claim that the "evil man" and the "useful man" don't deserve the same honors, saying, "Who knows if these things are guiltless/pure/undefiled [*euagē*] below?" (*Ant.* 520–21).

Neither Creon nor Antigone constitutes a constructive role model. The collision between Creon's rejection of the family in favor of civic loyalties and Antigone's "family first" certainty and disregard for civic loyalties destroys everything: family, city, and the relevant individuals. Ignoring obligations to family members, Creon suffers the devastating loss of his own wife and son. He reverses essential priorities, refusing to bury a dead man but burying the man's sister alive. Preserving crucial values, Antigone nevertheless also reverses essential priorities, valuing dead relatives, who in life seem to have cared little for one another, over live fellow citizens, and caring more for a dead brother than for a live sister.[19]

Although Antigone and Creon both contribute to the debacle, some audiences today, influenced by modern feminist and humanist ideals, may glorify Antigone as a woman standing up to a heartless man in a society that is brutally unfair to women. But such modern approval for Antigone is both anachronistic and misguided. Any ancient endorsement for Antigone would have been *in spite* of the fact that she is a woman.[20] And she achieves no admirable results. We cannot forget, as Sophocles's fifth-century Athenian audience surely could not, that Antigone is not merely *self*-destructive. Instead of providing a positive role model, she reminds us, now as then, that some ancient values must be preserved, but also that even people with valid claims can be destructive if they are not scrupulous about their methods.[21]

Sophocles's contemporaries, citizens of democratic Athens in the midfifth century BCE, found themselves simultaneously members of traditional kinship groups and members of a democratic *polis* consisting of numerous kinship groupings and ten official tribes. To preserve the *polis*, they had to discover nonviolent methods for negotiating conflicts between families or tribes. Ancient Greek initially made no distinction between "family member" and "political ally." Your *philoi*, on whom your survival depended, were necessarily both. But Sophocles produced the *Antigone* at a time when the political community had become larger than a single family or tribe, a time when tribal allegiances and civic allegiances might come into conflict. Citizenship was still defined by the father's status, but at the same time the maintenance of democratic political order, then as now, required defining individuals not by who their fathers were, but by what they themselves did and said. Creon and Antigone belong to the same family *and* the same political community. By their words and actions, they destroy both. In the twenty-first century, equipped with the finest modern technology, we are at risk of replicating their ancient story.

THE TYRANNICAL MIND

In depicting the conflict between allegiance to family and allegiance to fellow citizens, Sophocles dramatizes how *not* to go about resolving disputes. Differences between Creon and Antigone loom large: he's a man, she's a young girl. He holds power, she has none. He rules Thebes because of his noble birth, she's the product of monstrous incest. And yet, despite these manifest asymmetries of gender and power, Creon and Antigone think and act alike. Both are so certain of their own moral correctness that they are incapable of letting anything else in. They cannot listen to others or think creatively. They can only assert. They cannot *reason*. Both appear tyrannical in their self-absorption, hot temper, inability to tolerate criticism, and imperviousness to reasoned argument.[22] Sadly, these despotic attributes remain all too prevalent and familiar to us in the twenty-first century.

Creon and Antigone have noble intentions. He seeks the city's interest, and she her family's. But Creon reduces the city's interests to his own, and Antigone seems to care less for her family than for herself. Creon blatantly exclaims to his son, "Is it necessary for me to rule over this land for someone other than myself?" (*Ant.* 736). Antigone is equally self-centered, telling her sister, "I wouldn't want your help even if you offered. But I will bury him. I consider it noble thing to die doing it. . . . I will lie with him in death, loving him and loved by him" (*Ant.* 69–74). The consequences for her sister matter to Antigone not at all.

In their self-absorption, both Creon and Antigone have very short fuses. Creon erupts at his son's respectful, well-intentioned advice, snarling, "So at our age we will be taught to understand nature by a man of his age?" (*Ant.* 726). The chorus observes Creon's quickness to anger and the severity of his mind (*Ant.* 766–67). Antigone has a similarly explosive temper. She screams at her sister for offering to help conceal her plans, deeming her silence "far more hateful" than if she were to expose Antigone's intentions (*Ant.* 86–87). To her sister's observation that it isn't fitting to pursue things that are impossible (*Ant.* 92), Antigone retorts, "If you say these things, you will be hated by me" (*Ant.* 93). Antigone's quickly kindled rage toward her sister belies, of course, her assertion that "I was born not to join in hatred but to join in love/friendship [*sumphilein*]" (*Ant.* 523).

Creon and Antigone both also exhibit a despotic imperviousness to the opinions of others and a dictatorial rejection of logical argument.[23] Creon's desire to protect his citizens might seem admirable initially, but he exposes his tyrannical nature by rejecting his son's wise counsel. He refuses to reconsider his confidence in his own judgment, even when his son explains that "Learning many things and not straining too much is not shameful for a man, even if someone is a wise man" (*Ant.* 705–11). Creon furiously dismisses his son's rational suggestion that he should consider public opinion, responding, "And will the city tell me the things that it is necessary for me to command?" (*Ant.* 734). Antigone similarly fails to recognize constructive, rational advice. She asserts a truth that Creon ignores at great cost to himself and to everyone else, but she rejects her sister rather than accept her practical insight that "doing things that are excessive/futile makes no sense" (*Ant.* 67–68). She ignores Ismene's accurate observation that "you love things that aren't possible" (*Ant.* 90).[24] Antigone's persistent confidence in her own ability to accomplish the impossible, her conviction that as a young girl alone she can succeed in defying a king's decree, defies logic.

Both Creon and Antigone reject wise counsel not out of rational disagreement, but as a consequence of confidence in their own understanding of supernatural forces. Their confrontation over allegiance to fellow citizens versus loyalty to family members derives from their opposing convictions about the desires of supernatural beings. Creon is certain that he knows what the "gods above" desire. Antigone is equally certain that she knows what "the gods below" desire. Lacking any empirical evidence, neither has any grounds for certainty. Although the play affirms that human misdeeds can incur divinely sent consequences, the conflicting claims of Creon and Antigone can be neither proved nor disproved. Whether or not you find validity in both claims about divine will, as Sophocles's contemporaries undoubtedly did, the conflict between Creon and Antigone exposes the absence of any mechanism for determining moral truth or correctness when a dispute concerns the supernatural.

At the same time, the play reminds us that the tyrannical mindset has dire consequences in the real world of human beings. The ideological certainty of Creon and Antigone, their inability to take in new information, and their inability to compromise completely blind them to the obvious practical solution to their conflict. If burial of a traitor within the city limits will offend the gods of Thebes, the gods Creon honors, but failure to bury him at all will offend the gods of the underworld, the gods Antigone honors, why not bury the body beyond the city limits? That compromise—certainly obvious to an ancient audience—would offend no one's religious sensibilities. It is a measure of the rigidity and inadequacy of both protagonists' positions that this solution never even comes up in the play.[25]

Our own twenty-first-century conflicts amply corroborate the dangers of the tyrannical mindset manifest in this play. Throughout the world, ethnic, religious, class, or party loyalties and subgroup certainties often obstruct civil discourse, preclude constructive debate, and prevent creative solutions to national and global problems. Inherited or chosen allegiances, whether they recognize or ignore geographic boundaries, can prohibit the formation of civic loyalties and produce vicious sectarian violence. The *Antigone* suggests that civic allegiances can never supplant but must somehow accommodate and incorporate ethnic, religious, and other factional identities.[26]

In modern political disputes, however, we, like Creon and Antigone, frequently exhibit the tyrant's self-absorption, ideological rigidity, quickness to anger, and rejection of facts and reasoned argument. Despots dismiss all opinions except their own as unpatriotic or traitorous. Like Creon, scarcely able to get information from the terrified guard (*Ant.* 223–77, 315–26), they routinely receive misinformation and bad advice, because subordinates fear incurring their anger. With an autocrat or a small ruling minority in charge, the identities of "friends" and "enemies" typically remain fixed, largely predetermined by religion, geography, ethnicity, wealth, heredity, or some combination or variation of these components. Even under so-called democratic regimes, rigid conceptions of our own identities and responsibilities can make us equally self-involved, furiously intolerant, and impervious to rational thought.

In democratic politics, however, conducted—at least in theory—among political equals, political alignments can and must sometimes shift, as allies on some issues may become opponents on others, and adversaries must sometimes become allies.[27] The *Antigone* emphasizes the vital necessity for rational debate and creative problem solving, the two elements most patently absent in the devastating confrontation between Creon and Antigone. Twenty-first-century conflicts are potentially even more devastating, given the tremendous power of modern technology, but reasoned argument is often as conspicuously lacking. We have forgotten that opposing viewpoints are the heartbeat of democratic politics. Only by reasoned argument between diverse ideas and opinions will we be able to identify and implement the most constructive and beneficial solutions to the complex challenges facing our communities, nations, and planet.

Like Sophocles's original audience in the fifth century BCE, we have no personal or partisan stake in the conflict between Creon and Antigone. Their choices do not directly affect our own circumstances. Consequently, we can judge their values and methods more objectively. In our own times, decades of confident certainties have brought us to a similarly self-destructive impasse, as we squander tools that the ancient Greeks devised for us without themselves ever having fully implemented them: self-restraint, empirical deduction, logical debate, and democratic political institutions and negotiations. Divided not merely on questions of politics and morality but, more disastrously, on questions of reality and fantasy, truth and falsehood,[28] we scarcely speak to those who disagree with us. "What's that you say? I can't hear you!" we shout at our opponents. We do not converse. Like Creon, we may accept only the like-minded as fellow citizens. Like Antigone, we may be in love with the purity of our own beliefs without regard for the live individuals they may harm. Like Creon and Antigone, we refuse to accept that our certainties may be blinding us to better ideas and solutions.

In the late sixth century BCE, the Athenians transitioned away from tribalism and autocracy, and toward civil society and democracy. Today, by contrast, our own partisan divisions are hardening, with animosities between groups intensifying. Our confident and often unfounded or misguided certainties are driving us back toward the ancient, traditional, more primitive and exclusive tribal conception of identity. The experience of Creon and Antigone in the play shows us the likely consequence of this regression.

THE DOUBLE EDGE OF HUMAN INVENTION

In its portrait of the tyrannical mindset, the *Antigone* exposes not only the autocrat's dangerous capacity to abuse power but also the dangers of unrestrained political power per se. During the fifteen years or so separating the *Oresteia* (458 BCE) and the *Antigone* (c. 443 BCE), the Athenians removed all remaining institutionalized conservative checks on their democracy. For more than half a century (since the reforms of Cleisthenes in 508 BCE), Athens had been governed by direct democracy, a direct vote on all political decisions by all male citizens in the *Ekklesia* (Assembly). Though women, foreigners, and slaves, like children, were always excluded from political participation, institutional reforms during the late 460s and after made the government still more radically democratic. Conservative opposition remained, but by 443 BCE conservatives lacked organization and leadership, and the community's most radically democratic elements tended to prevail. [29] Democratic government, by enlisting the judging abilities of every voter, gives each one power to use either destructively or constructively. Unchallenged and unaccountable political power, whether held by an individual or by a group, whether legal or illegal—as we know, and as the Athenians came to know—has terrifying potential. The *Antigone* seems to warn against the tyrannical potential of any form of unlimited and unaccountable power, even (by implication) direct democracy in the absence of a substantive conservative check on its authority.[30] Without protections against abuse of power, a direct-majority voting process becomes indistinguishable from mob rule.[31]

The *Antigone* cautions us against unreflective confidence in unfettered majority rule, but its warning goes further, suggesting that *all* human power, including but not limited to democratic political institutions, can do good or do harm.[32] In the twenty-first century we tend to embrace new technology with the reckless and confident certainty of an Antigone or a Creon, with no thought of potentially negative consequences—until, like Creon, after the fact. But the play reminds us that human inventions are no more and no less than powerful tools. Whether or not they will be used constructively depends on what we value.

The *Antigone*'s First Choral Ode (*Ant.* 332–83) emphasizes the ambivalent potential of all human striving and accomplishment. The first three quarters of the ode celebrate remarkable human technological achievements. The chorus extols the unique creative ability of human beings to master their environment, claiming, "There are many terrible/wondrous/strange things [*deina*] (332), and nothing more terrible/wondrous/strange [*deinoteron*] (333) than a human being."[33] The chorus praises the inventive technology of "very thoughtful man" (348), listing sailing, navigation, plowing, hunting, fishing, and domestication of animals. "With his clever inventions" (349), they explain, man conquers all other creatures (334–52). The chorus especially cites the inventions of language, political organization, and architecture, since man "has taught himself language, and thought like the wind, and the feelings of social life" (355–56), as well as how to provide shelter from bad weather (354–60).

The chorus celebrates the extraordinary human capacity for ingenuity and invention, while also recognizing one absolute boundary: human ingenuity can conquer everything but death. The chorus insists that man is "all-resourceful. He's never without resources in approaching the future" (360–61). But then the chorus acknowledges the one crucial limit, conceding, "From Hades alone will he not devise escape for himself, but he has contrived escapes from incurable diseases" (361–64).

This one limit really is the game changer. Because we are mortal, we are vulnerable and need one another—our *philoi*, the *polis*—for survival. The chorus realizes that the greatest technological ingenuity will not ensure the survival and success of the individual or the *polis* unless human achievements also incorporate law and justice. No longer sounding optimistic or self-congratulatory, the chorus concludes the ode apprehensively: "Having ingenuity that is clever, arts and crafts [*technas*] (366) beyond all expectations, he creeps at one time to evil, at another to good. Fulfilling the laws [*nomous*] (368) of the land and the justice of the gods, he is highest in his city [*hupsipolis*] (370). But whoever associates with what is not noble or good has no city [*apolis*] (370). Let no one who would do such things ever be beside my hearth or have thoughts equal to mine" (365–75).[34]

Sophocles's *Antigone* does not depict individuals using power and the tools at their disposal responsibly in accordance with both relative standards of justice ("the laws of the land") and absolute standards of justice ("the justice of the gods"). Instead, the play provides a warning. Reject opposing views, embrace violence—behave, in short, exactly like a tyrant—and you will achieve only destruction. Inflexible, ill-considered, unprovable, and unfalsifiable convictions pose a dire threat to individual and communal survival. The *Antigone* highlights by negative example the most essential feature of democratic government, much more essential even than democracy's structural elements such as elections, judicial procedures, and term limits: the requirement to keep discussions open, respectful, and constructive.[35]

The *Antigone*'s First Choral Ode suggests, and the play as a whole affirms, that all human inventions and techniques for exercising control have both good and bad potential. How we use science, technology, political science, and even the institutions of democratic government depends entirely on the nature of our values and aspirations. Our most powerful tool is language itself, and the *Antigone* corroborates, by negative example, the *Oresteia*'s suggestion that nonviolent verbal conflict permits the best ideas and the best parts of ideas to combine to develop new and better strategies.

Oddly, our certainties frequently conflict even when our interests align. We all need protection from natural disasters, violent attack, and disease. We all require economic opportunities and secure, rewarding jobs, as well as safe air, water, and food. Our survival requires sustainable, nontoxic solutions and nonviolent methods for addressing disputes when our convictions collide. Many solutions will be technological, but the will, effort, and resources to discover them, and the willingness to implement them equitably, will not come from science, technology, engineering, and mathematics. Those disciplines can discover ingenious techniques, but not how, why, or whether to exploit them. Similarly, our laws and policies cannot alone protect us from ourselves. Not our technologies but our attitudes and behaviors determine the nature of our society and the quality of our lives in it.

If, unlike Creon and Antigone, we could control our tempers and critique our own convictions, we could collaborate constructively, as Creon and Antigone so spectacularly fail to do. Consumed by their own self-righteous anger and moral certainty, Antigone and Creon never even consider the obvious solution of burying the traitor outside the city limits. Their example suggests that creative solutions to our own problems may be similarly obvious, if only we allow ourselves to see them. If, unlike Creon and Antigone, we could talk *with* one another rather than *at* one another, we might be astonished at what we could discover. Our survival requires that we all get creative *together*.

THE ART OF SELF-GOVERNANCE

Recall Odysseus again in his beggar's disguise. He's dressed in rags, but there is nothing abject in his gaze. He stares straight at a reckless, insolent suitor. "You seem sensible," Odysseus tells the man. "So I will tell you something. Of everything that breathes and creeps upon the earth, a human being is the most frail and insignificant. At his peak of vigor and excellence, a human being never thinks he'll suffer anything bad in the future. But when the bad times come, you must bear them. Look at me. I was once wealthy and successful. But I behaved stupidly and did many irresponsible things, giving in to my violent impulses. That's why you should always be thinking about what's lawful and customary and right."

THE POWER TO RESIST

Tyrants strive to make us feel powerless to oppose their depredations, but Homer, Aeschylus, and Sophocles remind us that we are not powerless. The *Iliad, Odyssey, Oresteia,* and *Antigone* identify human beings as accountable for the consequences of human choices and actions. These stories remind us that we are responsible for our own survival and success, and that the abuse of power is self-defeating. Centuries before anyone had ever conceived of democratic government, ancient Greek epic poetry began to cultivate the skills required to combat tyranny. Hundreds, perhaps thousands of years later, long after tales of the Trojan War and Odysseus first began to circulate, Athenian tragic playwrights reinterpreted these and other ancient stories for recently democratic Athens in the late sixth and entire fifth century BCE. Athenian tragedies continued to shape contemporary attitudes and to reveal motives and methods for the rejection of tyranny. Twenty-first-century tyranny is merely the latest iteration of an age-old pestilence. The *Iliad*, *Odyssey*, *Oresteia*, and *Antigone* can help to inoculate us against it.

History suggests that human communities are extremely susceptible to tyranny. We find safety in groups, and we tend to defer to their most certain and forceful members. Most of us prefer to get on with our daily lives, happy to assume that we have ceded responsibility for our security and prosperity to powerful leaders who have our best interests at heart. Tragically, this is rarely the case. In practice, unrestrained and unaccountable power attracts self-serving egotists eager to advance their own interests at the expense of everyone else.

Whether they are ideologues, sociopaths, psychopaths, or merely opportunists, such individuals will not be able to see their own behavior as problematic. But even the most ruthless egotists cannot succeed without attendants, sycophants, and enablers to approve and implement their agendas. Consequently, con artists, mobsters, strongmen, dictators, and demagogues are all supremely skilled at transforming others into their attendants, sycophants, and enablers.

But Homer, Aeschylus, and Sophocles give us the power to resist. By engaging our critical faculties, they cultivate our capacity to pursue our own best interests both as individuals and as members of various groups, ethnic, religious, and civic. The *Iliad*, *Odyssey*, *Oresteia*, and *Antigone* urge us to take responsibility for our own decisions, to behave not as subjects or dupes of a self-centered, self-serving leader, but as sentient individuals able to assess facts, value diverse viewpoints, and resolve complex problems creatively.

Both the *Iliad* and the *Odyssey* depict and commend a thoroughly undemocratic society, but nevertheless both epics begin to cultivate in the audience that most essential of democratic capacities: the ability to judge for ourselves. Transmitted orally over centuries, Homeric epic tales owed no allegiance to a particular autocrat or divinity. They remained free, therefore, to challenge traditional power structures and ancient ideals of human conduct and accomplishment. Eventually coalescing in the eighth century BCE and subsequently written down in the sixth century BCE, the *Iliad* and *Odyssey* gave the audience a broader perspective than their characters have. The broader perspective enabled even the epics' earliest audiences not only to judge the characters' words, actions, and priorities, but also to reassess their own. Far from merely affirming traditional values or even simply providing mindless distraction, both epics invite the audience to critique and even reject the characters' confidence in divine agency and their unmitigated enthusiasm for violent revenge, convictions that audience members may themselves share. When mortal characters in the tales do things that turn out badly, they often claim, "A god made me do it," while the audience can recognize the characters' own poor choices as the cause. The characters identify revenge with justice, but vengeance proves problematic in both epics.

Centuries later, Athenian tragedies went even further in developing citizens' logical reasoning and compassionate moral judgment. Performed publicly at an annual religious festival honoring Dionysus, Athenian tragic plays made individual and communal self-criticism and reassessment a central, institutionalized feature of democratic political life. The ancient Greeks had been telling themselves the "same" stories for centuries, but the stories did not stay the same. By changing details and emphases, the new tragic versions of familiar archaic tales gradually helped the Athenians to relinquish hierarchical, tribal ideals and to embrace more egalitarian, civic identities and values. Both the *Iliad* and the *Odyssey* expose vengeance as inadequate and difficult to rein in, but neither work directly denounces the traditional view of revenge as necessary and just. Characters in both epics understand success as a zero-sum game: victory requires an enemy's defeat. By contrast, Aeschylus's *Oresteia* (458 BCE) encouraged contemporary Athenians to distinguish justice from vengeance and to redefine victory as a win for all concerned. Homer's characters consider good and bad, friend and foe, to be permanent, absolute categories, but Sophocles's *Antigone* (c. 443 BCE) suggests that these distinctions are not always so clear-cut. Addressing the problem of political conflict, this play exposes the self-destructiveness of an inflexible, partisan political identity. The *Antigone* offered citizens of democratic Athens a powerful warning against the perils of polarization.

Over many centuries, epic and tragic retellings of Greek myths addressed the problem of tyranny and posited moral values and habits of mind antithetical to abusive political authority. Influenced by these stories, some Greek citizen-communities, most notably Athens in the fifth century BCE, gradually began to develop democratic political institutions while still retaining numerous checks on simple majority rule. By the mid-fifth century BCE, Athenians had removed many of these conservative counterbalancing elements and had devised a radical, direct democracy. Though still excluding women, foreigners, and slaves from political participation, the system included representative bodies selected by lot, as well as ten generals chosen annually by election. A direct vote of all citizens, as in modern referenda, determined nearly all of the most consequential political decisions.

Ironically, though democratic government emerged as a consequence of the Greeks' rejection of autocratic authority, direct democracy itself perhaps prevented the Athenians from living up to the ideals and implementing the methods commended in their own epic and tragic tales. The Homeric epics and Athenian tragedies condemned tyrannical behavior in all its forms, and they gradually fostered the development of democratic political ideals and institutions. Greek tragedies also criticized the potential of democratic decision making to validate abuses of power and even to perpetrate atrocities. Despite these warnings, the majority of Athenian citizens sometimes appear to have failed to recognize the monstrous potential of *ochlocracy* ("mob-ocracy"). The Athenian system evolved over the decades, becoming significantly more moderate after 403 BCE. But during their democratic experiment, and like many or even most democracies throughout history, the Athenians continued to keep slaves, treat women like property, and violently subjugate other citizen-communities.

By ignoring the ancient Greeks or by unquestioningly assuming their cultural and political superiority, we risk repeating their mistakes. The Athenians' example cautions us in the twenty-first century against limiting our conception of democracy to "one person, one vote" and failing to recognize voting as merely one (albeit crucial) element of good governance. Modern liberal democracy is distinguishable from direct democracy or populism to the extent that it includes institutional features such as the rule of law, freedom of speech, a free press, term limits, a strong, independent judiciary and legislature, *and nonviolent regime change*. With the exception of a free press, Athenians in the mid-fifth century BCE had many such protections against tyranny, including one-year term limits and lottery selection for all offices but the generalships, juror selection by lottery, and public scrutiny of officeholders before and after their terms of service. Despite these protections and the ideals cultivated by their epics and tragedies, the Athenians sometimes failed to avoid misusing direct majority rule. As we now know, a direct majority vote can undermine institutional protections against the abuses of authoritarianism and populism, and it can trample the rights of individuals. Even when institutional protections remain, they are themselves also vulnerable to tyrannical abuse, and most especially vulnerable if majority sentiment allows.

The Athenians' experience suggests that attitudes, even more than institutions, determine the quality of life in any society. Just as the values and character of an autocrat determine the nature of an authoritarian regime, the values and character of the majority of voters determine the nature of a democratic regime, even a democratic constitutional republic. Modern liberal democracy requires *respect* for the rule of law, *trust* in the necessity of freedom of speech, and the *willingness* to protect minority interests. Democratic institutions offer necessary protections, but a majority vote, by definition, merely reflects the intellect and character of the majority of voters. It's a mirror without any illumination. If citizens are not rational, logical, empathetic critical thinkers, then a majority vote may promote the most unscrupulous and self-serving leaders and the most shortsighted and destructive policies.

While democratic voting remains a necessary feature of egalitarian government, it is not sufficient in and of itself to prevent despotic abuses of power. A prevalent misunderstanding of "democracy" in the twenty-first century as nothing more or less than decisions made by the majority in a direct popular vote turns politicians into panderers and demagogues, rather than admirable leaders capable of providing constructive insight and guidance. If a majority of citizens in any community fails to grasp the crucial value *to their own interests* of the aspirations and strategies affirmed by the Homeric epics and Athenian tragedies, then direct democratic voting may produce and legitimize tyranny. We can recognize this phenomenon today in the popularly elected "dictators for life" who are gaining power in modern states in increasing numbers.

Opponents of democratically elected authoritarian rulers regularly clamor for "more democracy," but "more democracy" is precisely the mechanism empowering those same authoritarian rulers. In turn, authoritarian dictators often claim, with no small degree of cynicism, that they embody "the popular will." The concept of the "popular will" enshrines *ochlocracy* ("mob-ocracy"). At most, the phrase is a proxy for popular rage. The "popular will" is a con artist's self-serving fiction; any populace consists of many and diverse individual wills. The public interest, however, is real, and mob rule never serves it.

Forewarned by the ancient Athenians' example, the Framers of the US Constitution sought to counterbalance democratic elements with some conservative checks on majoritarian voting and to exclude "the popular will" from political decision making. The Framers were well educated in Greek history and literature, and surviving sources from the Athenian democracy (508–322 BCE), almost without exception, disparage democratic government. The sole exception is a single speech attributed to the Athenian general and statesman Pericles (c. 495–429 BCE) by the Greek historian Thucydides (c. 460–400 BCE). But this speech, known as the "Funeral Oration" (*Thuc.* 2.34–46), occurs in a narrative context that undermines its unbounded praise for democracy. In his *History of the Peloponnesian War*, Thucydides depicts Athenian democratic decision making as largely irrational, impulsive, and self-destructive, initially capable of submitting to the guidance of a wise statesman (Pericles), but ultimately vulnerable to the depredations of self-serving demagogues. While Thucydides's critique itself attests to the Athenian system's openness to criticism, Socrates's fate (399 BCE) suggests that such openness had its limits. Forewarned by the Athenians' example, and by Thucydides (admittedly not an unbiased observer, having been himself exiled from Athens in consequence of a military defeat), the Framers crafted not a direct democracy but a constitutional republic with elements of representative democracy.

Tragically, twenty-first century technology provides opportunities, unimaginable to the Framers, to subvert institutional protections against authoritarian or populist tyranny. Freedom of speech constitutes the core democratic freedom, our greatest shield against abuses of power, but it is itself subject to abuse. Social media today amplify both the positive and negative potential of free speech. Open access constructively permits broad social and intellectual exchange, but it also exacerbates extremist distortions of reality. Lies and disinformation circulate unimpeded. So-called mainstream media, valuing profits above their responsibility to inform, promise to give equal time to "both sides" of an issue. They thereby successfully reduce complex, multifaceted problems to simplistic binaries, and equate falsehoods with facts. Their and our blind acceptance of unfounded or demonstrably false claims makes us easy prey for tyrants or turns us into tyrants ourselves.

Widely circulated and amplified by modern digital technology, misinformation distorts debate while censorship prevents it. Though they permit the open exchange of opinions, social media also enable extremist groups of every type to engage in vigilante-style silencing of unpopular opinions. Falsehoods go unchallenged, and the violence threatened online often slops over into real life. Censorship, and the intimidation and violence accompanying it, undermines the free, open, reasoned exchange of ideas vital to combating tyranny. The answer to unpopular, even hateful, speech is not less speech but more speech. Violence and intimidation, the tactics of fascism and totalitarianism, silence dissent and speed us toward tyrannical authoritarianism or mob rule.

Falsehoods, direct threats, and incitements to violence are difficult if not impossible to deter on social media or even mainstream news sources, but critical discernment and an aversion to the abusive, vigilante-style bullying power afforded by social media can be taught. Homer, Aeschylus, and Sophocles teach us to value evidence and expertise. They remind us that words have consequences, and that discernment is our responsibility. Homeric epics and Greek tragedies not only fortify us against liars, magical thinkers, and thugs but also encourage us to beware of becoming liars, magical thinkers, and thugs ourselves.

The ancient Greeks' invitation to critical self-reflection can empower us in the twenty-first century to avoid sliding or falling into authoritarianism, totalitarian populism, or combinations thereof. Homer, Aeschylus, and Sophocles identify and endorse essential strategies for opposing tyrannical inclinations not only in others but also in ourselves. Over centuries, ancient Greek epic and tragic poetry challenged the Greeks' traditional enthusiasm for violence and introduced more constructive habits of mind. Within Athens, for nearly two centuries, nonviolent democratic decision-making largely prevailed. Performances of Greek myths in Athenian tragic plays continued to expose the costs of tyrannical brutality and cruelty—not merely to victims but also, and especially, to perpetrators. Athenian tragedies even called into question the Athenians' own violent aggression and xenophobia. The ancient Greeks never lived up to the ideals of humanity, equality, and justice that their own stories introduced, but their failure does not mean that we can afford to give up on these ideals ourselves.

GOVERNING OURSELVES

Examined critically, stories can cultivate our capacity for self-government. Tyrants require their subjects simply to accept what they are told without question. Tyrannical authority discourages critical reflection and discussion, and encourages the substitution of unverified and often unverifiable opinions for objective, verifiable facts. Tyrants survive by spreading doubts so as to destroy the very concept of truth. Tyrannical power insists that reality is what the one or ones in power say it is. The rejection of tyranny requires us to ask instead, "Does the evidence support this story?" and "Does this storyteller's behavior accord with what he or she is telling me?" Self-government requires the active, respectful exchange of ideas and the careful examination of diverse arguments on their merits.

It may be in our nature as human beings to associate in groups, but it does not appear to be natural for us to associate *equitably* in groups. Aristotle (384–322 BCE) famously claimed that "the human being is by nature a political animal [*politikon zōon*]" (*Politics* 1.1253a). Since the ancient

Greeks called a community of fellow citizens a *polis*, Aristotle's claim identifies the essential human need to live not alone but among other human beings. In practice, however, whatever the requirements, constraints, or criteria for success in any community, some individuals will have the necessary abilities, skills, resources, and opportunities to attain power under those conditions more than others. Innate and environmental differences naturally create hierarchical, not egalitarian, relationships within and between groups.

Because the ambition for power and the success in obtaining it varies with individual tastes, talents, and circumstances, the rule of law serves to protect us from ourselves. John Adams famously claimed that in drafting the US Constitution he sought to create a "government of laws, not of men." In such a system, no one—theoretically, at least—is above the law. But the creation and preservation of a system based on the rule of law requires more than defined laws. It requires citizens capable of appreciating the value of the rule of law and possessing the skills or habits of mind necessary for its implementation. Law is a human construct, but it runs counter to a natural human tendency to prefer passion to reason and impulsiveness to self-restraint. Respect for a rule-based system requires the farsighted capacity to accept the rule of law, even at times when the immediate outcome does not benefit or even harms us individually. Since a rule-based system may also be grossly unfair and inhumane, self-interest demands commitment to orderly, lawful, equitable methods for changing the laws when they fail to serve the public interest.

Such farsighted self-interest derives not from law but from social attitudes and education. Our social norms greatly influence our individual capacity for self-government and our standards in judging power well used or ill used. You cannot legislate the empathy that permits Achilles to share a moment of grief with the father of his most hated and now dead enemy (*Il.* 24). You cannot legislate the elements of the craft of Odysseus: foresight, self-restraint, empirical deduction, rational deliberation, ingenuity, mutual respect, and reciprocity. We develop these qualities if our society produces and circulates stories demonstrating their immense utility. We strive to attain them if others in our community exhibit them and commend them in us. Despite the great multitude of laws in the twenty-first century, these crucial requisites for survival and prosperity seem in short supply and sadly undervalued.

The survival skills and values introduced by Homer, Aeschylus, and Sophocles require cultural validation in the form not only of narratives that we create for ourselves and share, but also of discerning attitudes toward those narratives. Regardless of the structure of political institutions, tyrannical behavior will prevail unless citizens learn to examine all stories judiciously. We must be capable of learning from stories without being deceived by them. But not all stories are equally constructive. An egalitarian society requires stories encouraging us to recognize that our individual self-interest aligns with the public interest and that we cannot succeed individually at the expense of everyone else.

To survive as political animals, we need narratives cultivating our ability to distinguish fiction from fact, prioritize reality, and learn from experience. The narratives of Homer, Aeschylus, and Sophocles prompt us to take responsibility for our own actions, to consider our own long-term self-interest, and to exercise self-restraint. They expose the inadequacy of revenge and the costs of dehumanizing or demonizing fellow citizens and foreign enemies. They encourage us to respect our obligations to one another and to welcome empiricism and constructive, compassionate, reasoned argument. The *Iliad, Odyssey, Oresteia*, and *Antigone* all suggest that to survive as political animals, we must move creatively beyond rigidly polarized alternatives, rejecting tribalism, violence, and mob rule. Homer, Aeschylus, and Sophocles expose the tyrannical potential of a closed mind and fortify us against the deceptions of real-world con artists. They remind us that the powerful are responsible for advancing the interests of those subject to their authority. They empower us to choose leaders who will not sacrifice the welfare of the community to their own shortsighted greed.

Real life is often a harsh teacher, but stories provide a painless way to learn from the experiences of other people. Homer, Aeschylus, and Sophocles offer us the opportunity to learn before it's too late. The *Odyssey*'s suitors, for example, are kleptocrats of the most straightforward variety, the ancient version of a phenomenon sadly all too familiar in the twenty-first century. Relying on their martial might and numerical superiority, the suitors use violence and intimidation to bully others, appropriate others' property, and silence criticism. Their story cautions against admiring, imitating, or assisting such people. But in the *Odyssey*'s portrait of the suitors, we might equally recognize ourselves. The suitors' abuse of their power, their deafness to dissent or cautionary advice, their greed, overconfidence, and careless indifference to the impending consequences of their actions mirror our own twenty-first-century hedonism, overconsumption, and overdevelopment, and our reckless disregard for sociopolitical inequities and looming political, social, economic, and environmental catastrophe.

Similarly, the *Antigone* cautions us today against the dangers of treating political opponents as enemies or criminals. Of the characters in these stories, Creon most recognizably epitomizes the tyrant. His rallying cry, "By such precepts [*nomoi*] I will make this city great" (*Ant.* 191), predates by more than two thousand years Hitler's identical promise to Germany and the devastation it brought to Europe, much of the rest of the world, and Germany itself. Creon's example demonstrates that the tyrant mistakes vicious, exclusive, intolerant nationalism for patriotism and leaves only ruin in his wake.

The *Antigone* also reminds us that our interests align even as our certainties collide. Regardless of our gender or ethnicity, whether we are rich or poor, Republican or Democrat, social Darwinist or social liberal, ardent industrialist or passionate environmentalist, we inhabit this planet together. If we fail to recognize our shared vulnerability to disaster, we forfeit any possibility of creative, constructive, peaceful, mutually beneficial solutions. Sophocles's cautionary tale of Antigone and Creon reminds us that in every conflict our certainties may be blinding us to better ideas.

Like Antigone and Creon, we may be fond of our own anger. Anger can provoke a constructive response to injustice, and it may bolster our confidence in the justice of our own convictions, but the *Iliad, Odyssey, Oresteia,* and *Antigone* emphasize that violence invites violence, and brutality breeds brutality. The opponents of civil society would like nothing better. If we don't want to further their aims, then we need to become wiser about our own self-interest. The narratives of Homer, Aeschylus, and Sophocles can help us to resist the seductions of violence, think clearly, and find cleverer solutions.

Violence may sometimes be necessary to defend places and values that we hold dear, but it must never be extrajudicial or opportunistic. In the famous battle of Marathon (490 BCE), the Greeks, though greatly outnumbered, successfully defended themselves and the Athenians' eighteen-year-old democracy against invasion by a Persian tyrant who sought revenge and was eager to subjugate Greece. For democracy to endure in the twenty-first century, force may similarly be necessary at times to preserve the rule of law, but it must always be a last resort, carefully calibrated and proportionate. Despots never worry about such criteria. Unlike legitimate, restrained defensive force, the use of aggressive retaliatory violence feeds the specious argument that "all sides" in a dispute are morally equivalent. Self-defense may at times require force, but aggressive reciprocal violence empowers bullies and thugs of all political persuasions. And it creates chaos and misery for everyone else.

The tyrant will always be a problem, but the tyrant is never *the* problem. The problem is the millions who fall for his falsehoods, elevate him to power, and implement or ignore his atrocities. As individuals and members of communities, we will always be vulnerable to violence, intimidation, and oppression, the cultural arts of the cave man. Dictators and would-be dictators will always try to exploit human communities and modern technologies for their own advantage at the expense of other people. By promoting a cult based on his own personality, the tyrant makes his supporters mindlessly accept as worthy goals of domestic and foreign policy his ruthless pursuit of his own interests. Tyrants triumph if we thoughtlessly worship them and mistake their lies for truth.

The compulsive, remorseless, pathological liar is probably incorrigible, but we ourselves empower the tyrant when we fail to recognize that he or she is lying to us. All narratives—fact or fiction, political speech, news story, advertisement, video, novel, play, movie, or TV show—shape our convictions, desires, and behaviors whether we are aware of it or not. The *Iliad, Odyssey, Oresteia,* and *Antigone* remind us to ask ourselves continually, "Who is telling me this? What is his or her agenda? Whom does it benefit? Whom does it harm? Do the facts support these claims?" Only then will we be able to select and honor leaders motivated not by their own material greed or thirst for power and adulation but by a sincere desire to advance the welfare of the community.

Today's extremists would have us believe either that the individual's needs must be subordinate to the needs of the group, or that the individual's needs must take priority over the needs of the group. The *Iliad*, *Odyssey*, *Oresteia*, and *Antigone*, however, suggest otherwise. The tales presented in these epics and tragedies commend neither the subordination nor the prioritization of either the individual or the group. They acknowledge instead that the needs of the individual and the needs of the group will often be in tension, frequently even in conflict, with one another. At the same time, they demonstrate that the interests of the individual and the community can and must align. These stories emphasize that individuals need the community in order to flourish, and also that the community's survival and success requires its promotion of individual achievement and prosperity.

Homer, Aeschylus, and Sophocles remind us that we cannot succeed as individuals unless we can all succeed together. Their stories cultivate the necessary emotional and intellectual tools. To survive and thrive, we must develop the capacity to choose constructively between political leaders and recommended courses of action. We need the ability to assess empirical evidence and engage in rational, productive discussions. We must become informed, discerning, participatory citizens capable of respecting the humanity of political opponents and even enemies. We must be able to distinguish democratic constitutional liberalism from mob rule. Fortified by ancient Greek tales against the tyrannical forces of today, we can learn to govern ourselves.

Acknowledgments

I am incalculably grateful to family and friends for their constant, cheerful support and their immense tolerance for unsolicited observations beginning, "You know, in ancient Greek myths, . . ." My daughters Erica and Ariela read and commented tirelessly on numerous drafts of this project, providing brilliant insights and editorial advice as well as generous and enthusiastic encouragement. Without their assistance, this book could never have emerged. My gratitude to my husband Eduardo remains boundless and inexpressible. I am immeasurably grateful for Eduardo's wisdom, humor, and kindness, and for his willingness to accompany me as I stumble on awkwardly with one foot in the ancient world and one foot in ours.

Sarah Lawrence College continues to provide a nurturing environment for academic inquiry. I am especially thankful for a course-release grant in the spring of 2019, which gave me the time to complete this project. I am indebted to the many dedicated, generous colleagues at Sarah Lawrence and elsewhere for their determination to keep alive and thriving the study of the humanities in general and Classics in particular. I am deeply grateful to April Mosolino for being my close friend and ally in the trenches, and for introducing me to my brilliant and talented agent Jennifer Lyons. April made me feel that this book was a possibility, and Jennifer made it a reality. I am also most grateful to Erica Wetter and the expert readers and editorial staff at Stanford University Press for believing in this project and shepherding it attentively to completion. Their keen insight and hard work have greatly improved the book.

This book owes its existence to the primitive spirits of ignorance, avarice, and animosity perpetually plaguing our species. Today, with twenty-first-century technology at their disposal, these noxious forces seek to undermine our most humane impulses and validate our most monstrous ones. They threaten to reduce modern social and political relationships to the primitive interactions operative between violent bullies and their helpless victims. Centuries of ancient Greek epic and tragic poetry remind us that we can and must do better.

Notes

INTRODUCTION

1. The *tyrannos* (tyrant) seized autocratic political authority over a citizen community by force. Some ancient Greek tyrants ruled wisely and exercised self-restraint. Others exhibited extreme greed and cruelty. Since the latter vastly outnumbered the former, the words *tyrannos* and *tyrannis* (tyranny) gained increasingly negative associations. The English "despotism" derives from the ancient Greek *despotēs* (master of slaves), a ruler of a household with absolute power over slaves. By the mid–fifth century BCE, the distinction between *tyrannos*, an unrestrained and usually abusive political ruler, and *despotēs*, a master of a household and slaves, had begun to blur somewhat. E.g., in Aeschylus's *Libation Bearers* (458 BCE), Electra considers free men essentially indistinguishable from slaves, if abusive tyrants rule the entire citizen community (*L.B.* 103–4).

2. Abuses of power can take various forms, and precise distinctions may be difficult to draw. See Ryan's lucid discussion of modern Marxism, fascism, and dictatorship (2012, 911–47). Ryan observes, for example, that although the Allied powers sought to defend "liberal democracy" against "fascism," Stalin's brutality and use of genocide preceded and rivaled Hitler's (941). Albright distinguishes the modern "dictator," who may fear the populace, from the modern fascist leader, "who expects the crowd to have his back" (2018, 12); but arguably, some ancient Greek *tyranneis* (tyrants)" fit the former description, others the latter. Warning that the movement toward fascism usually proceeds gradually (229–30) and appears to be gaining momentum today, Albright defines a fascist as "someone who claims to speak for a whole nation or group, is utterly unconcerned with the rights of others, and is willing to use violence and whatever other means are necessary to achieve the goal she or he might have" (245–47). Snyder explains that fascism today, as in the 1920s and 1930s, "serves oligarchs as a catalyst for transitions away from public discussion and towards political fiction; away from meaningful voting and towards fake democracy; away from the rule of law and towards personalist regimes"

(2018, 16). These elements all provide identifying markers of tyranny. Levitsky and Ziblatt meticulously detail the warning signs and steps leading toward the demise of democracy (2018).

3. On the Greeks' development of the rule of law, see especially Ostwald 1986. Kurke 1998, 156 (citing Morris 1996) considers the Athenian democracy part of a broader Panhellenic process. Raaflaub discusses the Greeks' innovations in political theory and practice (2015) and their emphasis on human responsibility for the well-being of both the individual and the community (2016). Cartledge argues that democracy was a specifically Greek phenomenon, and he rejects the view that the Roman Republic was a type of democracy (2016, 247–63).

4. *Autokratia* (autocracy)" combines *autos* (self/same) with *kratos* (power), *aristokratia* (aristocracy) combines *aristoi* (best men) with *kratos* (power), and *demokratia* (democracy) combines *demos* (the people) with *kratos* (power). See Ober 2017, 18–33.

5. The Greeks also coined *monarchia* (monarchy; *monos* [one man] plus *archē* [sovereignty/dominion]), *oligarchia* "oligarchy" (*oligoi* [the few] plus *archē*), and the antithesis of *demokratia* (democracy), namely *ochlocratia* (*ochlos* [mob] plus *kratos* [power]). For ancient Greek attitudes toward tyranny, see especially Podlecki 1966; McGlew 1993; Raaflaub 2003; Lewis 2009; Luraghi 2015 and 2018; and Panou and Schadee 2018, 1–10. Raaflaub discusses the ancient Greeks' development of arbitration and legislation in response to "elite abuses, social and economic crisis, civil strife, and tyranny" (2016, 134).

Fearing the tyrannical potential of democracy and the danger of its devolving into mob rule, the Framers of the US Constitution adopted not the Athenians' political model of radical direct (not representative) democracy, but the Romans' *Res publica* (Republic: literally, "the public business"), a hybrid of rule by one man (president; or, in the Roman Republic, two consuls), rule by the few (senate), and rule by the many (direct popular vote). The Framers also strengthened checks and balances between the three elements. Samons discusses the Founders' concerns about the mob potential of the "popular will" and their effort to exclude from governing "the people in their collective capacity" (2004, 1–17). See also Wood 1972; Richard 1994 and 2009; Melton 2013, 79–88; Cartledge 2016, 283–305; and Hale 2017.

6. For the role of myth in both reflecting and shaping Greek culture and identity, see especially Pozzi and Wickersham 1991; Meier 1993; Redfield 1994, 69–98; Nagy 1996, 130; Kurke 1998, 156; Csapo 2005, 9; Graf 2011; and Martin 2016, 5–6. From its inception, tragedy was arguably part of a broad Panhellenic process (e.g., Stewart 2017). Good introductions to Greek mythology include Dowden and Livingstone 2011, Edmunds 2014, and Martin 2016.

7. Edmunds contends that Homer is not a political thinker (1989), but many other scholars disagree. See especially Raaflaub 1989 and 2000. Seaford identifies the *Iliad*'s role in the movement away from monarchy and in the historical evolution of ideals of reciprocity (1994, 191–234). Hammer insists that Homeric epic "is engaged in critical reflection and that this reflection is political in nature" (2002, 5 and *passim*), despite the fact that the *polis* (defined by Raaflaub as "citizen-community," 2015, 10–15) did not yet exist. Hammer argues persuasively that deeming Homer "pre-political" "creates a perplexing situation in which institutions are political, but the pre-institutional activity of forming these institutions is not" (25; Hammer also provides extensive bibliography, 1–14, 19–48). Ahrensdorf presents Homer as an educator and an exemplar of "a noble and humane rationalism" (2014, 24 and *passim*).

J. H. Finley identifies myth as a "vehicle" for political thought in Attic tragedy (1967, 1–13), and Meier argues that the Athenians' fear of their own capacity for tyranny "haunts tragedies from the 450s onwards" (1993, 133). Raaflaub maintains that concern for the tyrannical potential of the Athenian democracy itself led the Athenians in the late fifth century to enact legislation placing some limits on the power of the people (2015, 20 and nn60–61).

8. Hanson identifies a relationship between democracy and warfare (Hanson 2001), and Raaflaub discusses the persistent, endemic militarism of fifth-century Athenian culture despite questions raised, e.g., by works of Euripides and Aristophanes (2001). Thucydides's *History of the Peloponnesian War* details Greek bellicosity but also implicitly censures Athenian atrocities, such as the massacres at Mytilene in 427 BCE (Thuc. 3.50), at Scione in 421 BCE (Thuc. 5.32), and at Melos in 416 BCE (Thuc. 5.85–113, 116). (Following the capitulation of Mytilene, the Athenians revised their initial decision to execute the entire population, and the figure of one thousand males murdered has been questioned; but the Athenians executed numerous men without trial and enslaved many women and children.) See Kagan's comprehensive analysis (1969, 1974, 1981, 1987).

9. Excellent introductions to fifth-century Athens and Athenian democracy include Kagan 1991, Davies 1993, and Raaflaub 1998. For analyses of the development of the *polis* and ancient democracy, see Forrest 1966; M. I. Finley 1973; Dunn 1979, 1992, 2005a, and 2005b; Ostwald 1986; Ober 1989, 1996, 2008, and 2015, esp. 157–75; Hansen 1991, 1992, and 1996; Rahe 1992; Euben et al. 1994; Ober and Hedrick 1996; Robinson 1997; Arnason and Murphy 2001; Raaflaub 2004 and 2015; Raaflaub and Ober 2007; J. M. Hall 2007; Meier 2012; Arnason, Raaflaub, and Wagner 2013; and Rosivach 2014. For the history and function of the Athenian democracy, see especially Hignett 1952; Jones 1986; Stockton 1990; Ober 1996 and 2008; Rhodes 2004; Samons 2004, 19–40; Osborne 2010; and Cartledge 2016, 91–122.

10. On women in ancient Greece and in Greek myth, see Pomeroy 1975; H. P. Foley 1978, 1981a, 1981b, and 2005; Lefkowitz 1986; Felson-Rubin 1987; Just 1989; Zeitlin 1990 and 1996; Easterling 1991; Fantham et al. 1994; S. Blundell 1995; Katz 1999; Felson and Slatkin 2004; Fabre-Serris and Keith 2015; Edmunds 2016; and Canevaro 2018.

On ancient Greek slavery, see M. I. Finley 1968, 1980, and 1987; Garlan 1988; Osborne 2010, 85–103; and Hunt 2018. Sadly, the ancient Greeks were neither the first nor the last people to objectify and enslave other people. Unlike slavery in the United States, however, ancient Greek slavery was not based on race. Everyone was equally vulnerable. Even royal birth could not prevent enslavement if the community was conquered in war. The existence of slavery, reprehensible as the practice was and is, serves as an argument in ancient Greek epic and tragic poetry for treating people in one's power well. The tables might turn, and a former master or ruler could become a slave.

For the relationship between Athenian democratic ideology and imperialism, see Knox 1957; E. Hall 1989; Raaflaub 1994 and 1997, esp. 58–61; Rosenbloom 1995; Samons 2004, 100–142; and Osborne 2010, 306–22. Foster examines Thucydides's view of Athenian imperialism as distinct from the speeches and actions that he attributes to Pericles (2010).

11. Ober argues that, remarkably, unlike the pattern typical for complex societies, in Athens during the classical period the elites did not rule (1989 and 2017). Cartledge examines the controversial question of whether to identify the Athenian system as a democracy beginning with the reforms of Cleisthenes (508 BCE) or not until Ephialtes's reforms in the late 460s (2016, 72–75). Cartledge also discusses the number of citizens (109–11). On Athenian citizenship, see also Blok 2017, Dmitriev 2018, and Kasimis 2018.

12. E.g., see DuBois 2001 and 2010 vs. Hanson and Heath 1998, Hanson, Heath, and Thornton 2000, and Bloxham 2018. See also Hanink 2017. Zuckerberg cautions against the misappropriation of classical texts by online communities seeking to advance a "patriarchal and white supremacist ideology" (2018). She also expresses concern that opponents of this agenda "tacitly cede this point," accepting "that the study of ancient literature perpetuates white male supremacy" and disagreeing "only on the question of whether that is a consequence that should be celebrated" (187). Zuckerberg laudably commends instead discussion of ancient sources "that is free of elitism and neither uncritically admiring nor rashly dismissive" (189). Assessing the "culture wars" of the 1980s and 1990s, Adler similarly observes that both sides collaborated in minimizing the importance of studying the classics (2016, 214). He urges classicists to welcome a more inclusive methodological approach, "since the heterogeneous nature of the field is among its core strengths" (4).

13. E.g., Osborne rightly criticizes Athenian democracy for accompanying "an Athenian way of life which we would judge illiberal, culturally chauvinist and narrowly restrictive." He suggests that we "stop taking cover behind 'democracy' as a term at which only cheering is allowed, and instead ask seriously how we might attain the political openness (and cultural achievement) of Athens while taking pride in a society that is heterogeneous and determinedly open" (2010, 37).

14. Similarly, Albright argues that the failure of the United States to live up to its own standards of human rights does not justify rejecting those standards or abdicating the responsibility to uphold them (2018, 214).

15. Evidence suggests that the *Iliad* and the *Odyssey*, the epic tales that we attribute to "Homer," developed orally over millennia. Nagy identifies "Homer" as the name for the Greek epic tradition rather than an individual (1996, 20–22) and argues for continuity of the Homeric epic tradition from the eleventh century to the fifth century BCE (2010, 3–28). Martin terms Homeric epic poetry "a multi-generational art form" (2016, 31).

On the narrative tradition concerning the life of Homer, see Nagy 2010, 29–58; and Graziosi 2016, 7–56. Graziosi finds no evidence for "a single original audience, or historical context, or specific political agenda in support of which the Homeric poems must have been composed" (37).

For biographical information about the tragedians, see Herington 1986, 15–31; Mitchell-Boyask 2009, 11–18; Lefkowitz 2012; and Swift 2016, 14–24.

16. Regarding myth as a source of moral examples, see, e.g., Redfield 1994, 20–29; Livingstone 2011; and Raaflaub 2012, 474, 488, and n44.

17. On the origins and processes of Homeric epic poetry, see Lord 1960, 1991, 1995; Kirk 1976; Nagy 1979, 1996, 2002, 2007, 52–82, and 2010; Cairns 2001b, 1–56; Fowler 2004; Beck 2005, 273–75; Dué and Ebbott 2010, 4–29; Gonzalez 2013; Ready 2015; and Finkelberg 2018. Nagy emphasizes the centrality of Athens in the transmission of both the *Iliad* and the *Odyssey* (2002, 9–35).

The *Iliad*'s various stories probably coalesced during the eighth century BCE, the *Odyssey*'s stories perhaps a half century later. Neither was written down until the sixth century BCE. Regarding arguments for a seventh-century BCE date for the *Odyssey*, see Cook 1995 vs. Osborne 1996, 159. Nagy emphasizes a gradual movement toward "text fixation" as a consequence of epic performances and "Panhellenic proliferation" preceding the production of written texts (1979, 7–9, 41, and *passim*). For diverse views of the "Peisistratean recension," a theory regarding the first written texts of the *Iliad* and *Odyssey*, see Thalmann 1998, 301–2 and n65.

Oral composition and transmission of archaic stories enabled details and emphases to change over time. For Homer's adaptation of earlier tales, see, for example, Peradotto 1990. Peradotto argues that "the *Odyssey* shows a highly developed

234 NOTES TO INTRODUCTION

awareness of the poet's sense of his own power to control and to tinker with the 'material' given to him by his tradition" (1990, 31). See also Reece 1993; Felson 1994, 10; Marks 2003; S. Richardson 2006; and Haller 2013. Lord identifies the singer of epic poetry as no "mere carrier of the tradition but a creative artist making the tradition" (1995, 13). Similarly, Martin identifies flexibility and innovation as features of oral performance (2016, 31).

Nagy, however, rejects the conception of Homeric myth as "a matter of personal invention" (1996, 114). See also West's challenge to "oral theory" and his resurrection of the "analysts'" approach (2011). Others have speculated that the same poet composed the *Iliad* as a young man and the *Odyssey* as an old man. West argues for written composition of the *Iliad* and *Odyssey* by two different individuals (2017), but this remains a minority opinion. Discussions of the controversy include Page 1959, 222–25; Austin 1975, 70; Nagy 1996, 114; Halliwell 2011, 56; and Austin 2011. Friedrich argues that the *Iliad* and *Odyssey* were composed by a literate poet drawing on the oral tradition (2019). Pointing out that our written version of the *Iliad* must be later than some oral version or versions of the *Odyssey*, Porter argues convincingly that each epic provides a backdrop for the other, with knowledge of one influencing audiences' reactions to the other (2019).

We cannot know who "Homer" was. We can only consider the effect of the works as we have them. The *Iliad* may appear more "youthful" in examining the causes and consequences of passionate anger and vengeance, whereas the *Odyssey*, though it includes the vengeance theme, may appear more "adult" in affirming the value of endurance, reasoning, and self-restraint.

18. On the definition, origin, context, role, and performance of tragedy, see especially Winkler and Zeitlin 1990, Cartledge 1997, Easterling 1997, Sourvinou-Inwood 2003, E. Hall 2010, Scodel 2010, and Rehm 2017.

Athenian tragedy derived from and influenced Athenian cultural attitudes, adapting ancient myths and conflating past and present. Knox identifies "tragic myth" as "a people's vision of its own past, with all that such a vision implies for social and moral problems and attitudes in its present" (1979, 23; and, similarly, Euben 1990, 50–52). Meier explains that the tragedies make the ancient stories "present and familiar" and at the same time "problematic," as they were "filtered through the experience and needs of a new age, pervaded by the demands for reason and justice, the tensions and responsibilities of the citizenry" (1993, 125). Goldhill identifies the *paideusis* (educational function) of tragedy "in the retelling of the myths of the past for the democratic *polis*" (2000, 48). But cf. Rhodes, who argues for a close connection between drama and the *polis* rather than between drama and democracy (2003). Sommerstein maintains that by the fifth century BCE, myth was already "a powerful instrument of education and socialization" (2010, 117).

19. Contrasting ancient and modern conceptions of democracy, Ryan identifies two views: democracy as "a matter of character of a whole society" versus democracy as "a set of arrangements for answering the question 'who is to rule?'" (2012, 946). Samons emphasizes the harmful consequences of the modern reductive understanding of democracy as little more than a voting process (2004, 68–71), observing that this conception makes "the character of that electorate and not the particular form of government" the determinative factor (71). Ryan notes that both Tocqueville and Mill "feared that democracy might trump liberalism" (2012, 947).

20. On Homeric values, see especially Adkins 1960, 1971, 1987; Havelock 1978; van Wees 1992; Donlan 1999; and Raaflaub 2016. Lacking much historical information for the society Homer depicts, scholars refer to the period as the Dark Ages (Donlan 1985, Dickinson 2006). Redfield identifies "epic distance" between the world of the characters and that of Homer's earliest audiences (1994, 30–36), but Raaflaub finds substantial intersections between the two, such that "the old and the new overlapped and coexisted" (1993, 44–45). Some scholars emphasize the powerlessness of the people within assemblies in the epics (e.g., M. I. Finley 1954, 80; Andreyev 1991; and Thalmann 1998, esp. 243–71). Others find a more complex interaction between leaders and people (e.g., Ober 1996 and 1998, Raaflaub 1997 and 1998, and Hammer 2002).

21. See Ahrensdorf 2014 versus Redfield 1994, 101–2. Ahrensdorf explains that Homer affirms the mortal characters' confidence in divine justice and then "proceeds to challenge this conventional piety (33–37). Rabel, however, identifies an "ironic distance" between the characters' views and the narrator's "radical critique of life lived in accordance with traditional views of heroism," which is also distinct from "what the poet wishes to communicate" (1997, 21–31). But cf. de Jong's argument that the pursuit of *kleos* (glory) motivates the poet as much as it motivates the characters within the epics (2006).

22. For imitation and allusions to earlier poetry in the tragedies of Aeschylus, Sophocles, and Euripides, see especially Garner 1990. Rinon identifies the "tragic pattern" in the *Iliad* that anticipates Attic tragedy (2008). On the flexibility of Greek myth and its limits, see, e.g., Graf 1993, Woodard 2007, Alaux 2011, and Torrance 2013.

For diverse views of the didactic function of tragedy, see Herington 1985, 67–71, and 1986, 110; Podlecki 1986, 82–86; Euben 1990, 50–58; Meier 1993, 51–61; Thomas 1995; Zeitlin 1996, 72–79; Kurke 1998; Sourvinou-Inwood 2003; Boedeker and Raaflaub 2005; Carter 2007; Barker 2009, 268–70; Goldhill and Hall 2009; Mastronarde 2010, 20–28; Osborne 2010, 368–418; Gregory 2012, 515, 529–30; and Raaflaub 2012.

236 NOTES TO INTRODUCTION

As to whether tragedy "endorses," "constructs," or "questions" "Athenian civic ideology," see especially Saïd 1998, 281–84. Some scholars maintain that tragedy reinforced aristocratic privilege in Athens, but others argue that the genre in general questions democratic values and encourages critical reflection. For diverse views, see Vickers 1973, 157; Goldhill 1986, 1990, 2000, and 2009; Vernant and Vidal-Naquet 1988; Euben 1990, 18, 35–36, and *passim*; Meier 1993, 42–48; Boegehold and Scafuro 1994; Griffith 1995, esp. 63n3 and 109n143; Foley 1996; Cairns 2005 and 2016; Carter 2007, 36–63; Rabinowitz 2008; Barker 2009, esp. 268–75; Grethlein 2010, 74–104; Mastronarde 2010, 15–21; and Burian 2011.

Goldhill views tragedy's questioning as being in conflict with fifth-century Athenian democratic ideology (e.g., 1990, 124–29, and 2000, 35, 46), but many scholars disagree, deeming the questioning of democratic values central to democratic ideology and emphasizing tragedy's educational role (e.g., Euben 1990, 35, 51–59, and 94; Carter 2007, 1–8, 19, 143–60, and passim; Barker 2009, 1–19 and n36, 278, 368, 372; and Cartledge 2016, 129). Ober identifies "the symbiosis of democracy and criticism" (1996, 142–43), and Grethlein observes that tragedy is "a genre better suited to raising questions and opening up tensions than providing clear cut answers" (2010, 83). For the composition and diversity of fifth-century audiences and the variety of responses, see Roselli 2011 and Cairns 2016, 44–54.

23. On the power of stories to shape cultural attitudes, see, for example, Peradotto 1990, 27–31; Nussbaum 1997, 9–11 and 85–107, and 2010, esp. 95–120; Goldhill 2004; and Martin 2016, 12–22 and 40–41. Nussbaum 1997 and 2010 provided significant inspiration for this book as well as my previous one, *Enraged: Why Violent Times Need Ancient Greek Myths* (Anhalt 2017). Nussbaum 1986 greatly influenced my discussion of Aeschylus's *Oresteia* and Sophocles's *Antigone* in this book.

24. On the inability of constitutional rules alone to protect democracy, see especially Levitsky and Ziblatt 2018, 97–117. Similarly, Albright identifies the historical pattern of fascists exploiting democratic institutions in order to gain power and then, once in power, proceeding to destroy those very institutions (2018, 83, 234, 237, and *passim*). Albright also notes the perverted use of the nominally "democratic tool" of the plebiscite "to spread and validate a falsehood" in Hungary today as in Nazi Germany (184–85).

25. Albright defines an "illiberal democracy" as one "centered on the supposed needs of the community rather than the inalienable rights of the individual. It is democratic because it respects the will of the majority; illiberal because it disregards the concerns of minorities" (2018, 172). Homeric epics and Athenian tragedies provide an antidote, exposing tensions between communal needs and individual needs but also emphasizing their interdependence and the costs of prioritizing either over the other.

CHAPTER 1

1. As in Anhalt 2017, I avoid the words "hero," "heroism," or "heroic," because their meaning varies from person to person and from society to society, depending on the attributes or behaviors deemed commendable. Courage? Strength? Physical prowess? Selflessness? Self-sacrifice? Determination? Ambition? Intelligence? Wisdom? Compassion? Opinions will differ, and fictional depictions of success or failure consequent on particular behaviors inevitably shape our assessments. For the Homeric understanding of *hērōs* (pl. *hērōes*), see Nagy 1979, 67–117, 159–61, 171, and 342.

2. Barker 2009. See also Havelock 1978, 123–38, and Cairns 2018, 388–405.

3. I am grateful to an anonymous reader for Yale University Press for pointing out that no other ordinary warrior in the *Iliad* ever challenges authority in this way, and that Thersites's audacity itself exemplifies the disruption resulting from Agamemnon's treatment of Achilles.

4. Barker sees in the *Iliad* a "movement towards the establishment of a divine assembly with ordered dissent under Zeus' ultimate authority" (2009, 77). Although divine assemblies "appear as little more than showcases for Zeus' power" (75), they nevertheless exhibit a shift "not only to speech and discussion but also to a communal setting" (77), where "Zeus now sits in judgement in an assembly directing events to their peaceful resolution" (78).

5. Hephaestus's damaged leg may be the sole example of divine vulnerability to permanent physical injury. The *Iliad* presents his lameness as evidence of the impossibility of successfully challenging Zeus (*Il.* 1.589–93). But sources vary. Some suggest that his injury was present at birth. Others suggest that it was a consequence of his having angered Hera. For various archaic versions, see Gantz 1993, 74–76. Barker explains that the gods' laughter reduces the tension and that "the story of the gods fighting belongs to the past" (2009, 75).

6. M. W. Blundell 1989, 26–31. On the "heroic ideal" in Homer, see also Solmsen 1954, 1–5; Havelock 1978, 97–98, 108; and Redfield 1994, esp. 99–127.

7. On Homeric morality, see especially Dodds 1951; Adkins 1960, 1971, and 1987; Long 1970; Gagarin 1987; van Wees 1992, 25–166; Zanker 1992 and 1994, 1–71; Williams 1993; Seaford 1994, 1–29; Finkelberg 1998; Donlan 1999; Cairns 2018.

8. I have discussed these issues more fully in Anhalt 2017. Achilles ultimately avenges his friend's death by killing his killer, but he becomes supernaturally monstrous in the process. At the *Iliad*'s conclusion, not vengeance but a shared moment of empathy with the father of his friend's killer finally begins to ease Achilles's devastating grief and restores his humanity.

9. Unlike Thersites, a Greek seer in a previous assembly at the beginning of the *Iliad* understands clearly the danger he faces in telling King Agamemnon the

truth. Achilles calls in this seer to find out why Apollo has sent a plague against the army, but the seer is reluctant to speak, since he knows that his information will anger Agamemnon. Only under Achilles's protection can the seer reveal the truth (*Il.* 1.74–91).

10. Regarding Thersites's *akosmos* (disorderly/rebellious) speech, see Martin 1989, esp. 17, and Barker 2009, 56–60, 65. In contrast to the hierarchical speech structure evident in Homer, democratic Athens in the fifth century BCE purported, at least, to permit anyone to speak (Ober 2003, 6–7; Saxonhouse 2006, 1–3). But cf. Aristophanes's mocking depiction of the gulf between the aspiration and the reality in his comic play the *Acharnians* (425 BCE).

11. Barker argues that "the scene of laughter has the effect of co-opting the onlookers back into the hierarchy" (2009, 60) but also "opens the audience up to criticism even as they are invited to sanction the reassertion of authority" (58).

12. E.g., Sophocles's *Ajax*. See Anhalt 2017, 146–48.

13. For varying views of the relationship between divine and human agency, see, for example, Willcock 1970, 6–7; Havelock 1978, 42, 50; Nussbaum 1986, 3–4; Austin 1987, 63–70; Gaskin 1990, 6; Morrison 1997; and Pucci 2002. Schein considers the gods "an *ex post facto* explanation, not a cause or agent" of events (1984, 57–61) and not incompatible with human moral responsibility. Hammer, by contrast, finds the relationship between chance and human agency to be determined by the characters' own cultural assumptions and their preoccupation with the instability of status (1998, 140). Andersen observes that "academic research shows that religious belief leads people to think that almost nothing happens accidentally or randomly" (2017, 262). I argue simply that Homer's narrative affords the audience a broader, more objective understanding of chance versus choice than the mortal characters within the epic have.

14. See Cook 2003. Regarding "multiple determination" or "double motivation," see for example Lesky 2001 (orig. pub. 1961); Dodds 1951, 1–18; Adkins 1960, 2–3, 22–23; Willcock 1970, 1–10; and Edwards 1987, 135. Redfield suggests that the concept of "Zeus's will" encapsulates the understanding of the poet and the characters that "since it happened, Zeus must have willed it" (1994, 105).

For discussions of Athena's appearance to Achilles in *Iliad* I and its implications for human responsibility, see for example Dodds 1951, 14–15; Snell 1953; Edwards 1987, 180–81; Williams 1993, 21–31; and Ahrensdorf 2014, 38–39. Schein finds Athena's presence "psychologically plausible" as evidence of Achilles's second thoughts (1984, 57–58). Similarly, Cook notes the correspondence between Athena's advice and Achilles's own calculation (2003, 191–92).

15. The ancient Greek attitude toward myth and history is complex. See, for example, M. I. Finley 1965; Veyne 1988; Graf 1993; Calame 1996; Gotteland

2001, 89–102; Konstan and Raaflaub 2009; Hertel 2011; and Herren 2017, 1–26 and 83–96. Schein identifies "fate" as the "poetic tradition" (1984, 63–64), while Redfield explains that for Homer's original audiences, "Fate is history" (1994, 133). Regarding poets' variations of plot and emphases, Burian observes that "myth is subject to interpretation and revision, but not to complete overturn, because it is also history" (1997, 185; and similarly Edmunds 2014, 12).

16. D'Aulaires 1962, 9.

17. Snell explains that Greek religion did not establish a specific ethical code (1953, 25–26), and Adkins maintains that the gods in the Homeric epics are not just (1960, 62). See also, for example, Guthrie 1950, 117–27; Griffin 1980, 179–202; Clay 1983, 133–48, and 1989, 55–56; Burkert 1985, 119–215; Edwards 1987, 131–42; and Pucci 2002. Many scholars identify the gods as moral examples against which to measure human actions (e.g., Griffin 1980, 162; Schein 1984, 51–57, 61; Pucci 2002; Kearns 2004, 71; and Ahrensdorf 2014, 25–72). On moral distinctions between the two epics, see Havelock 1978, 123–92; Lloyd-Jones 1983, 28–32; and Kearns 2004, 67–69.

18. Homer does not mention this tale until almost the end of the *Iliad* (*Il.* 24.25–30). See Gantz 1993, 567; and Pucci 2002, 25–26.

19. Following a seer's instructions and led by their queen, the Trojan women perform a generous sacrifice to Athena. The women pray for the destruction of a most fearsome Greek warrior, and they ask the goddess to pity the Trojan citadel and the wives and children of Troy. But, the narrator informs us, "Pallas Athena refused" (*Il.* 6.311).

20. Zeus makes this point explicitly in *Od.* 1.32–43 (see chapter 2).

21. Zeus's promise to grant Achilles's request to let the Trojans prevail is simply another way of saying that as long as their best warrior refuses to fight, the Greeks will of course fare badly against the Trojans.

22. See Cook 2003. For a survey of scholarship regarding Agamemnon's motives, see Knox and Russo 1989. Regarding Homeric psychology, see, for example, Gill 1996, 29–41.

23. Like Agamemnon, Troy's king Priam also blames the gods for his and his people's troubles. He tells Helen, "As far as I'm concerned, you aren't responsible. As I see it, the gods are the cause. They aroused against me this war of many tears" (*Il.* 3.164–65). But the Trojans have no legitimate claim for retaining Helen or for jeopardizing their city and its populace. They are flagrantly violating two crucial moral principles understood by the ancient Greeks as guaranteed by Zeus: the reciprocal responsibilities of *xenia* (guest-friendship), and the obligations of sworn oaths (Zanker 1994, 31–35). See also Kane 1996, 19 and n9; Muellner 1996, 37–51; and Ahrensdorf 2014, 33–34. On the importance of *xenia*, see Walsh

2005, 24–25. On oaths, see Sommerstein and Torrance 2014. Zeus's guarantee may be simply another way of saying that violations of these two moral principles have predictably negative consequences.

Stealing Helen from her husband while being entertained as a guest in their house, Paris egregiously violated his obligations to his hosts under the system of *xenia*. Subsequently, the Trojans blatantly violate an oath by refusing to return Helen following a supernaturally aborted duel between Paris and Helen's Greek husband, Menelaus (*Il.* 3.86–110). Mid-duel, the goddess Aphrodite magically whisks Paris off the battlefield and deposits him back in the bedchamber he shares with Helen (*Il.* 3.369–82). Aphrodite's blatant favoritism underscores the illegitimacy of Paris's claim to Helen. Although Homer doesn't mention the story of the Judgment of Paris here, Homer's audience knows that Paris made a choice, prioritizing sex (Aphrodite) over power (Hera) and wisdom (Athena). The chief men of the Trojans feel that Helen's beauty justifies the war, but even they think that the Trojans should just let her go back to the Greeks (*Il.* 3.156–60). The Trojan leaders' failure to return Helen seems, to the audience, foolish and self-destructive.

The Greeks understand the duel between Menelaus and Paris as a fight to the death (*Il.* 3.101–2, 281–91, 320–23), whereas the Trojans merely swear that whoever "wins" will get to keep Helen (*Il.* 3.71–72, 92, 136–38, 253–55). But even by their own understanding of the oath, the Trojans violate it: Zeus, the divine guarantor of oaths, corroborates Agamemnon's claim that Menelaus was victorious (*Il.* 3.457 and 4.13), and Paris himself acknowledges that Menelaus "won" (*Il.* 3.439). It does seem surprising that in ten years of warfare no one previously thought to have wife stealer and husband settle their dispute over Helen one-on-one. But the story of this belated man-to-man fight recapitulates for the audience the war's trivial origins and the Trojans' moral failings (Leaf 1886, 87). See Schein 1984, 20–22; and Kozak 2014a and b.

24. Anhalt 2017, 95–114.

25. Barker discusses Agamemnon's "obsession with power" and his counterproductive efforts to retain it (2009, 42–45). On Homeric ideals of leadership and kingship, see Cairns 2018. For a comprehensive and thorough treatment of Agamemnon in the *Iliad* and *Odyssey*, see Porter 2019.

CHAPTER 2

1. On *dike*, see Havelock 1978. See also chapter 6.

2. For the *Odyssey*'s portrait of slavery, see especially Thalmann 1998, 48–107.

3. Unlike autocracy, as Snyder explains, democratic government has the ability to provide a principle of succession (2018, 38–66), since "the meaning of each democratic election is a promise of the next one" (251).

4. At the *Odyssey*'s conclusion, another Ithacan reiterates this criticism of the community's failure to stop the suitors' abusive behavior (*Od.* 24.455–61).

5. Wilson translates this multifaceted adjective as "complicated" (2018). My understanding of the *Telemachy*, "the story of the exploits of Telemachus" (the *Odyssey*'s first four books), derives directly from Scott 1987. The *Odyssey*'s title, signaling as its subject one man's achievements, contrasts with the title of the *Iliad*, meaning "the story of Ilion (Troy),"—i.e., events concerning the fate of an entire city. The opening lines announce the story's subject: Odysseus and his circuitous journey home to Ithaca following the Trojan War. Odysseus is "striving for his life and for the homecoming of his companions" (*Od.* 1 5) and "desiring his return home and his wife" (*Od.* 1.13). Odysseus's determination to return home powers the epic, but the title character does not appear until book 5, while books 1 through 4 present his son's adventures, not his. Scott explains that the *Telemachy* establishes the social and political context for Odysseus's adventures.

Cf. Peradotto's argument that the *Odyssey*'s opening lines encapsulate the role of books 1 through 4 in presenting Telemachus's search for "an identifying description of the father he knows literally only by name" (1990, 119). See also Graziosi's discussion of the *Odyssey*'s central themes (2016, 95–107). Peradotto discusses the significance of the adjective *polutropos* at *Od.* 1.1 (1990, 94–119). Observing that *polutropos* can be read actively or passively (114), Peradotto explains that it emphasizes "mutability, plurality, variability, transitions, the crossing of borders, the wearing of masks, the assumption of multiple roles." Peradotto notes further that this descriptor is only ever also applied to Hermes, Odysseus's great grandfather (116). See also Pucci 1987, esp. 127–14.

6. Although the concept of the *polis* as a "citizen-community" larger than a single family or tribe may not yet have existed when the *Odyssey* first took shape, the contrasts between life with a good ruler and life without one suggest that the *Odyssey* is already depicting the risks, as well as the advantages, of life in a human community.

7. Identifying all of these parallels between Pylos and Sparta and the precise antitheses on Ithaca, Scott observes that they collectively define Odysseus's conception of "home." Odysseus's return to his family and community and his reinstatement as king will enable his palace in Ithaca to "offer the full rewards of human existence portrayed in the palaces of Nestor and Menelaus" (1987, 136).

8. The *Iliad* similarly emphasizes the vital importance of *xenia*. A guest's violation of his host's hospitality by stealing or seducing the host's wife caused the Trojan War itself. In the middle of battle, a Greek and a Trojan warrior, discovering that their ancestors had been guest-friends, decide to exchange armor and affirm the guest-friendship relationship into the next generation (*Iliad* 6.119–236. See Anhalt 2017, 30–32, 39–41.)

9. The *Telemachy* (*Od.* 1–4) follows a pattern typical of archaic oral poetry known as "ring-composition."

10. Scott 1987.

11. Many scholars identify the Homeric *basileus* (king) as a sort of warlord or tribal leader possessing authority derived both from heredity and from personal achievement (e.g., M. I. Finley 1954; Donlan 1979 and 1993; Raaflaub 1989 and 1993; and van Wees 1992). See also Thalmann 1998, 9 and *passim*.

12. On the relationship between poet and Muse, see Nagy 1979, 16–17; Redfield 1994, 39–45; Rabel 1997, 23; Pucci 2002, 19–20; de Jong 2006; and Halliwell 2011, 25–26, 55–77. Within the *Iliad*, the Muses function as a source of memory, enabling the narrator to recall catalogues of troops, ships, or fallen warriors (*Il.* 2.484–93, 2.761–62, 11.218–20, 14.508–10, 16.112–13). Nussbaum explains that the Homeric epic poet "associates knowing with the ability to enumerate: the Muses give him their knowledge of the warring armies by imparting a catalogue of their numbers and divisions" (1986, 107). Only once do the Muses take action against a human being, wounding a man and depriving him of his musical ability because he challenges them (*Il.* 2.594–600; Gantz 1993, 55)

13. Discussions of the oral tradition abound. See especially Schein 1984, 1–18; Nagy 1990, 17–18, 1992, and 1996; Meier 1993, 14; Seaford 1994, 144–54; Barker 2009, 10; Dué and Ebbott 2010, 4–29; Halliwell 2011, 58–62; and Elmer 2013. An authoritative written text of the *Iliad* and *Odyssey* was not commissioned until the middle of the sixth century BCE. Nagy argues for an "evolutionary model of Homeric poetry culminating in a static phase that lasts about two centuries, framed by a relatively formative stage in the latter part of the eighth century and an increasingly definitive stage in the middle of the sixth" (1992, 52).

For the relationship between Greek mythology and ancient Greek religious faith and ritual, see, for example, Veyne 1988; Versnel 1990 and 2011, 539–59; Seaford 1994; Mastronarde 2010, 15–18; and Parker 2011.

14. Martin distinguishes ancient Greek mythical tales from the sacred texts of other peoples: "Because creative artists like poets and vase painters could stylize and invent details or even new episodes to enhance their narratives about gods, the resulting mythic material is more flexible and individualized than iron-clad dogmas set out in a sacred book that might make exclusive claims to spiritual truths," such as "the sacred texts of modern monotheistic religions" (1989, 61–62). On the independence of Homeric epic from the constraints of literature produced at the demand of a powerful mortal or supernatural ruler, see also Russo 1968; Nagler 1974; Austin 1975; Finnegan 1977; Edwards 1987; and Raaflaub 1989, to cite only a few.

15. Scholars dispute whether Homeric epic affirmed or challenged traditional aristocratic values; see especially Hammer 2002, 144–69. Parry argues that oral poetry

presents a fixed, stable, universally accepted set of cultural assumptions (1971, 390), and Tandy maintains that the Homeric epics systematically affirmed and maintained "a self-conscious aristocratic class" (1997, 152–88; and similarly Thalmann 1998, 1–10, 275; Haller 2013, 164; and Herren 2017, 25–26). But others disagree, many suggesting that the epics had a broad and not narrowly aristocratic audience: e.g., Kirk 1962, 275; Scully 1990; and Donlan 1993. Schein considers the *Iliad* "an ironic meditation" on "traditional themes" (1984, 1), and Raaflaub argues that although archaic poetry was by and for aristocrats, it both promoted and challenged aristocratic values (1993, 75). Hammer characterizes epic "as public poetry that was engaged in reflection on the activity of organizing community life" (2002, 11, similarly 48). For the relationship between poet and audience, see also Scodel 2002.

16. The *Odyssey*'s first word, *anēr* (man), versus *menis* (wrath), the *Iliad*'s first word, identifies this epic's subject as not a passion but a person and focuses attention on the consequences of human priorities and choices. Unlike in English, Greek word inflections and syntax permit a sentence to begin with the direct object: *andra* (man) in the *Odyssey*, *menin* (wrath) in the *Iliad*.

17. Raaflaub 2016, 128.

18. Athena initiates events in the divine council on Olympus, it's true. But as goddess of strategic cunning and ingenuity, she embodies Odysseus's specific skill set. Her concern for Odysseus in this opening scene begins to delineate more fully her close connection to Odysseus, previously hinted at in the *Iliad*. Athena favors Odysseus and feels sorry for him. Her wish that he be able to return home aligns perfectly with his own desire. (But cf. Ahrensdorf's view that Odysseus is not particularly eager to return home [2014, 216–23]). Poseidon, angry at Odysseus for blinding his son the Cyclops, is preventing his return. We are getting the story out of chronological order. Later, Odysseus himself will tell how—and why—he blinded the Cyclops (see chapter 4), but as the *Odyssey* begins, Odysseus has already done this—*and boasted about it*—and is enduring the consequences. Although Zeus now agrees that Poseidon must give up his anger and that Calypso must release Odysseus so that he can return home, Odysseus, as we will soon discover, is responsible for his own predicament.

19. See Nagy's definition of *kleos* (1979, 15–18).

20. Felson suggests that by telling Telemachus that Odysseus is being held by "savage men" rather than being detained by Calypso, Athena prevents Telemachus "from seeing his father's absence as a desertion" (1994, 76). See also Beard's discussion of Telemachus's rebuke of Penelope following Athena's visit (2017, 3–8).

21. Regarding tensions between Helen and Menelaus in their marriage and storytelling, see Olson 1989; Katz 1991, 78–79; Felson 1994, 81–82; Doherty 1995, 86; and Bergren 2008, 111–26.

22. On the *Odyssey*'s references to the story of Agamemnon and Orestes as a model for Odysseus and Telemachus, see Felson 1994, 93–107. Alden, too, discusses the significance of the stories that Telemachus hears (2017, 154–71).

23. Historically, in the absence of a prior transformation of social values away from acceptance of autocracy, the removal of an autocrat and even the implementation of democratic institutions produce dire consequences including, at times, atrocities (Chua 2003). Removal of an autocrat may impede rather than promote the development of "constitutional liberalism" (Zakaria 2007). Discussing the Arab Spring of 2011, Worth suggests that although mass protests can produce regime change, this often means simply the substitution of one autocrat for another (2016). By 2015, Worth observes, "the whole region seemed to be sinking into a dismayingly familiar chaos, with dictators (or would-be dictators) and jihadi groups killing and yet somehow sustaining each other in a weird symbiosis. . . . The only thing being democratized was violence" (2016, 224).

24. Felson identifies epic poetry itself as a form of *xenia*, reciprocally creating *homophrosyne* (like-mindedness) between singer and audience (1994, 137–44).

CHAPTER 3

1. Andersen 2017. Andersen uses the term "magical thinkers." Albright cites a recent *Reader's Digest* survey in which "the four people most trusted by Americans were all fictional role players—movie actors—with Tom Hanks heading the list. Evidently the individuals we most believe in aren't real" (2018, 236).

2. Schein points out that of the nonhuman female characters, Calypso alone appears both in Odysseus's tales and in the third-person narrative (1995, 17).

3. Suggesting that Calypso's name means "Concealer," Schein observes that female figures in Odysseus's tales are "often monstrous and their menace is literally or symbolically sexual—specific instances of the general danger of being swallowed, engulfed, concealed, or obliterated, against which he constantly struggles" (1995, 19–20). Felson, too, identifies Calypso as "the concealer" (e.g., 1994, 45) and argues that the decision to leave Calypso's island "enables Odysseus to coalesce as a self" (49). Similarly, Bergren identifies Odysseus's "escape from Calypso" as "a symbolic rebirth of the *psychē*" (2008, 58–78). Peradotto, by contrast, argues that Calypso's function is to immobilize Odysseus (1990, 102–5).

4. Rood discusses Odysseus's capacity both to build a raft and to sing an epic tale of his own experience (2008, 40).

5. In the *Iliad*, the same article of clothing identifies the reverse dependency: the community's need of the high-achieving individual for its survival. Upon learning of her husband Hector's death, the Trojan princess Andromache knows

that her city is doomed. Throwing to the ground her *kredemnon* (headband) in grief, Andromache symbolically prefigures the fall of Troy itself (*Il.* 22.460–72). As when battlements fall, Hector's death makes his city, community, and family vulnerable to destruction. Individuals comprising the community depend on the high-achieving individual for their survival. But cf. Pucci's identification of the sexual overtones of the goddess's offer of a *kredemnon* to Odysseus (1987, 64). Scully identifies the metaphorical association between *kredemnon* and *polis* (1990, 31–33). See also Canevaro 2018, 240–43.

6. On folktale and fairy-tale elements in the *Odyssey*, see especially Schein 2016a (orig. 1970) and 2016b (orig. 2002); Denys 1973; Peradotto 1990, 32–93; Reinhardt 1996; West 1997; W. Hansen 2002 and 2014; and Edmunds 2016.

7. Odysseus will later implicitly challenge the Phaeacian king's analogy (or expose its irony) by reporting that the Cyclops Polyphemus told him that the Cyclopes don't care for Zeus or the gods and that they claim to be more powerful than gods (9.275–76). See also chapter 4.

8. On Odysseus's encounter with Nausicaa and his resistance to marrying her, see Felson 1994, 46–48.

9. Cf. Thalmann's discussion of the tensions between hospitality and competition on Scheria (1998, 141–53).

10. Peradotto points out that Demodocus's tale of Odysseus can be "pure entertainment" for the Phaeacians because its contents are unconnected to their own lives. By contrast, Odysseus's tales do have relevance for them: Poseidon's hatred of Odysseus connects his story to theirs, and Odysseus's account of the Cyclops and of Aeolus complicates their decision about how to treat him, since the two tales contrast the dangers of mistreating strangers with the costs of helping someone hated by the gods (1990, 91–92). On the competition between Demodocus and Odysseus and Zeus as the implicit subject of Demodocus's third song, see Nagy 2010, 96–102.

11. E.g., Felson 1994, 81–82.

12. On Odysseus's reaction to Demodocus's songs, see especially Nagy 1979, 13–65; Pucci 1987, 214–27; Ahrensdorf 2014, 224–25; and Alden 2017, 200–221.

13. In the *Iliad*, for example, Zeus delights in viewing stories of mortal conflict (Anhalt 2017, 100–102).

14. The tale of Ares and Aphrodite celebrates the victory of cleverness over strength (Peradotto 1990, 56). See also Felson 1994, 134–35. Regarding associations between Hephaestus and Odysseus and the significance of this tale for the larger narrative (foreshadowing the reunion of Odysseus and Penelope), see Zeitlin 1996. 33–42, 50–51.

CHAPTER 4

1. E.g., describing modern Russian propaganda and its promotion of political fiction, Snyder identifies the "calculated effort to undo logic and factuality" (2018, 151. See also 160–216).

2. See Andersen's disturbing analysis of the extraordinary American propensity to blur the distinction between reality and fantasy and to mistake the latter for the former (2017). Ancient Greek, however, directly associates truth with memory, since, as Martin observes, the Greek *alethea* (true things) is literally "what is not forgotten" (2016, 34). Herren maintains that the ancient Greeks "prided themselves in discerning fact from fiction" (2017, 91). Snyder insists that "freedom depends upon citizens who are able to make a distinction between what is true and what they want to hear. Authoritarianism arrives not because people say that they want it, but because they lose the ability to distinguish between facts and desires" (2018, 251). Moreover, "Authoritarianism begins when we can no longer tell the difference between the true and the appealing. At the same time, the cynic who decides that there is no truth at all is the citizen who welcomes the tyrant" (280).

3. Most discusses Odysseus's objectives in books 9 through 12 (1989). Felson notes that the narrator authenticates only the episodes involving Calypso, the Cyclops, and the sun god (1994, 49). Schein observes that Odysseus's tales in books 9 through 12 "constitute *his* [italics Schein's] not the poem's version of heroic experience" (1995, 19). See also Alden's discussion of the purposes of Odysseus's first-person narrative and his "cover stories" in the *Odyssey*'s second half (2017, 222–303).

4. Doherty argues that female power in the *Odyssey* serves both "to reinforce a male-dominated gender system" and also, to some extent, to "elude or subvert this kind of cooptation" (1995. 88). See also Ford 1992, 86–87.

5. See Felson 1994, 131–32.

6. E.g., the narrator and the gods vouch for Odysseus's true identity at *Od.* 1.11–21, 5.7–17, and 13.287–310.

7. E.g., Herodotus 1.5 and Thucydides 1.1 and 1.21–22. Unlike Thucydides, Herodotus doesn't exclude myth entirely from his tales and also includes supernatural elements (oracles, dreams, portents). Herren (2017, 83–96) provides a good recent discussion of the Greeks' understanding of the relationship between history and myth, arguing that "the process of ordering, classifying, and rationalizing the earliest figures of Greek myth began in the fifth century with figures such as Hecateus of Miletus, Pherecydes the Athenian, Herodorus, and Hellanicus" (87).

8. Scott 1987, 134.

9. Raaflaub defines the contrast as between the Phaeacians' "ideal *polis*" and the Cyclopes' "non-*polis*") 2016, 129–30).

10. See Vidal-Naquet 1986. Nussbaum identifies the Cyclopes' defect as a lack of education (1986, 253).

11. *Iliad* 5.59–64 identifies shipbuilding as a *kakon* (evil) for all the Trojans, including the man who built the ship on which Paris sailed to Greece. The Greeks' homeward voyage proves disastrous for many of the victors as well (e.g., *Od.* 3.130–36, 286–300; 4.81–96, 487–511).

12. Oddly, in the Cyclops's cave, Odysseus makes the very same mistake that he criticizes his men for making after sacking the Ciconians' city (*Od.* 9.43ff.): he thought then that they should flee immediately, but his men wanted to linger. In consequence, all suffered and many died.

13. The trick is twice as clever in Greek. *Ou tis* means "no one," but in a question to which the speaker expects the answer "no," and in the "if" clause of a condition, the Greek for "no one" is *mē tis* "not anyone":

"No one (*mē tis*) is stealing your flocks, are they?"
"No one (*mē tis*) is killing you by stratagem or by force, are they?"
"If . . . no one (*mē tis*) is overpowering you . . ."

And the answer is *Outis* "no one," the name Odysseus cleverly supplied. The Cyclops intends, "(A man called) 'No one' is killing me by treachery *or* by force" (*Od.* 9. 408), but the other Cyclopes hear, "No one is killing me by treachery *nor* by force." The Greek permits either translation.

When Odysseus exults in the success of his plan, he calls it *mētis* (wisdom, skill, cunning, craft, enterprise). This sounds very like *mē tis*, though it's one word instead of two and is pronounced with perhaps just a slight difference. *Mē tis* (no one) has an acute accent over the first syllable, suggesting that it may have been pronounced with a slightly rising pitch; whereas *mētis* (wisdom, cunning) has a circumflex, suggesting a rising and falling of the pitch on the same syllable.

Athena earlier identifies *mētis* as central to Odysseus's character, and also necessary for his son's success. Disguised as Mentor and advising Telemachus to seek news of his father, she observes that the young man appears not entirely devoid of his father's *mētis* (*Od.* 2. 279). On the *Outis/mētis* wordplay, see Austin 1972; Detienne and Vernant 1978, esp. chapter 4; Pucci 1986; Winkler 1990, 143–45; and Peradotto 1990, 143–70. But cf. Peradotto's argument that this episode demonstrates the poet's cleverness in presenting his own *mētis* as that of Odysseus (46–47). Perodotto connects *Outis* with *outaō* (to pierce; 149–51), and suggests, moreover, that the name correlates with the associations of *polutropos* and is, paradoxically, antithetical to the pursuit of *kleos* (154–55).

14. For the meaning of Odysseus's name, see Dimock 1963 and 1989, 246–63; Peradotto 1990, esp. 94–142; and Alden 2017, 185–93.

15. Nagy 2007.

16. The "shades of the departed dead" (*Od.* 11.37) have "powerless heads," literally, heads without *menos* (will, spirit, martial might, courage; *Od.* 11. 49). The spirit of the seer Teiresias describes the underworld as "a place that is *aterpea* [lacking delights or pleasures]" (*Od.* 11.94). The verb *terpō*, meaning "to delight" and "to cheer," and in the middle voice "to enjoy oneself" and "to take pleasure in," describes precisely the positive experience of life in the well ordered human communities of Pylos and Sparta (e.g., *Od.* 3.70, 4.17, 4.47). On Homer's portrait of the underworld, see also Gazis 2018 and Grey 2019.

17. The *Iliad* previously introduced the contrast between Achilles's honesty and Odysseus's crafty deceptions (e.g., *Il.* 9.312–13; and see Anhalt 2017, 57–58, 64). Achilles's surprise at seeing Odysseus, of all people, in the underworld corroborates Odysseus's depiction of post-death existence as being devoid of all pleasures. Achilles can't imagine how or why Odysseus would opt to come to the underworld (*Od.* 11.473–76). We might misunderstand the implications of this encounter and assume that Odysseus is showing us a regretful Achilles, who so hates being dead that he admits he made a mistake in choosing to die young. But Achilles has not chosen to die young. In the *Iliad*, he chooses to avenge his beloved friend's death, and he does not care if that means that he will die young (*Il.* 18.98–126). In telling Odysseus that even a most miserable life is preferable to being dead, the spirit of Achilles does not express regret for his own decision; he emphasizes the nobility of his choice. Having chosen to do what he considered right, no matter the cost, Achilles has no regrets, but he now knows clearly that death holds no delights whatsoever. Odysseus is letting us know that he now knows this, too.

Even if Achilles were admitting that his own choice was a mistake (and his words do not support this interpretation), Odysseus is narrating this story. His Achilles is not identical to the Achilles portrayed by the *Iliad*'s narrator. The *Odyssey*'s Odysseus puts these words into the mouth of *this* Achilles. Odysseus, as the *Odyssey* portrays him, is using this characterization of Achilles to validate his own priorities.

18. Anhalt 2017, 80–114. Identifying Achilles's name as a combination of *akhos* and *laos*, Nagy decodes the name to mean a protagonist who brings suffering to his people (1979, 69–74).

19. But cf. Pucci 1987, 98–109. Pucci argues that the text has "the goal of deluding the reader into assuming the truth of what he reads" (108). Even if a text could have a "goal," in this instance which "truth" would that be? Odysseus's words? The narrator's? Instead of validating one "truth," the *Odyssey* compels the reader to compare and contrast Odysseus's tales with those told by the narrator and by other characters.

20. See Winkler's discussion of the utility and necessity of secrecy, lying, and misdirection in the *Odyssey,* and parallels in the culture of late-nineteenth-century rural Greece (1990, 134–37).

21. *Odyssey* 17–24 will continue to portray deception and lying as essential to Odysseus's survival (see chapter 5).

22. Hundreds of years after the *Odyssey* first took shape (c. 700 BCE), in the Athenian democracy of the fifth-century BCE, lying and deception began to appear much more morally problematic. Aeschylus's *Oresteia* exposes dishonesty and treachery as manipulative and destructive (see chapter 6). Other fifth-century tragedies also explicitly criticize the clever capacity for deceit. E.g., Euripides's *Hecuba* (see Anhalt 2017, 172–74, 177) and *Andromache* (see Hesk 2000, 64–84), and Sophocles's *Philoctetes* (see Hesk 2000, 188–201).

23. Athena claims that she shares Odysseus's talent for *mētis* (wisdom, cunning) and *kerdea* (gains, profits, shrewd counsels; *Od.* 13.299). On the relationship between Athena and Odysseus, see Pucci 1987, 22–23, 33–43, 99–109. On *mētis*, see Nagy 1979, 47–49. Felson views the reunion of Odysseus and Athena as a preview of the reunion of Odysseus and Penelope (1994, 50). For Athena's role in the *Odyssey,* see especially Murnaghan 1995.

24. But cf. Hesk's observation that, although the Greeks admired *mētis,* not all forms of deception constitute *mētis* and not all *mētis* involves deception (2000, 10).

25. On these and other possibilities, see Alden 2017, 300–303, versus Peradotto 1990, 144–45. Peradotto rejects Alden's suggestion of *eparitos* (chosen, picked man), as inconsistent with the narrative. Peradotto associates all of the fake names in *Odyssey* 24 with the dual active and passive sense of *odussamenos.*

26. Peradotto examines the significance of Odysseus's choice of Idomeneus and Crete (1990, 109–10).

27. On deception and misdirection in the *Odyssey*, see especially Winkler 1990, 129–61.

28. Telemachus's adventures in Pylos and Sparta occur while we learn of Odysseus's adventures in books 5–14. With Athena's help, Telemachus evades the suitors' ambush; he worries about it, but the attack never materializes (*Od.* 15.292–300).

29. Thalmann, discussing the *Odyssey*'s portrait of Eumaeus and Philoitius (1998, 84–100), defines the "pseudo-kinship" relationship between the swineherd and Telemachus as "the disguising of the relationship of slavery as something else" (89).

30. Viewing this scene as evidence of "the decisive importance of the voice above all other signs in the epic tradition," Pucci maintains that Telemachus "lets himself be persuaded" and "chooses to believe" Odysseus (1987, 95–97). Not surprisingly, several cinematic reinterpretations of the *Odyssey* involve an imposter

returning and claiming to be Odysseus; e.g., *Le Retour de Martin Guerre* (1982), *Sommersby* (1993), and *O Brother, Where Art Thou?* (2000).

31. Telemachus responds, "My mother says that I am his son. But I at any rate don't know. For not ever does anyone himself know his own birth/origin" (*Od.* 1.215–16). See also Thalmann's discussion of ambiguities and tensions in the relationship between Telemachus and Odysseus (1998, 206–23).

32. Kahneman explains "cognitive ease" (2011, 59–70).

CHAPTER 5

1. The *Iliad* portrays women as prizes of honor and as catalysts of male conflict. The quarrel between Agamemnon and Achilles, originating in one man's decision to appropriate another man's woman, echoes the cause of the Trojan War itself: the Trojan prince Paris's theft of Helen from her Greek husband King Menelaus. As prizes to be won in battle, like tripods, cooking bowls, or armor, female captives lack autonomy and individuality, remaining silent markers of male achievement. The narrative perhaps evokes some sympathy for Helen, showing her ambivalence and her failed effort to resist the force of Aphrodite (e.g., *Iliad* 3.390–420). But she remains essentially a pawn in the male competition for honor.

The *Iliad* also depicts women as devastated widows and grieving mothers (e.g., Andromache, Hecuba). In battle scenes, the embedded stories and similes evoke sympathy for even minor warriors by showing the pain that their death causes to the women in their lives. The grief of Hector's wife and mother emphasizes the terrible tragedy of Hector's death. By detailing women's grief at losing loved ones, the *Iliad* cultivates an appreciation for the value and significance of every individual human life and the tragedy of each individual death, but the emphasis is on male individuals, male lives, male deaths. On male competition for women in Homeric society, see Thalmann 1998, 193–206. Excellent discussions of the depiction of women in the Homeric epics include Foley 1978. 1995, 2005; Katz 1981; Schein 1995; Felson and Slatkin 2004; Nappi 2015; Edmunds 2016, 103–61; and Canevaro 2018. Regarding the historicity of the *Odyssey*'s portrait of women, see Graham 1995.

2. On Odysseus's slave women, see Thalmann 1998, 49–74. Thalmann argues that "for all women, sexual fidelity is the standard by which loyalty to Odysseus is measured" (73).

3. Cf. Felson's discussion of the negative consequences of Helen's story on her household and her relationship with Menelaus (1994, 81–82, 98–99, 133–34).

4. On disguise and recognition in the *Odyssey* and Odysseus's scar and name, see especially Pucci 1987, 83–97; and Peradotto 1990, 120–42.

5. Felson explains that Penelope functions as both "subject" and "object" (1994,

3–14). See also Anhalt 2002. On the role of objects in depicting female characters in epic, see Canevaro 2018, esp. 55–107.

6. On Penelope as "weaver," see especially Felson 1994, 15–42; Clayton 2004; and Bergren 2008.

7. See Felson 1994, 28–29 and 54–55. Schein notes that we have only Odysseus's word on this (1995, 24). Good discussions of Penelope's cleverness include Murnaghan 1986 and Winkler 1990, 129–61.

8. Thalmann (1998, 172–73). Thalmann views the contest of the bow as emblematic of the tensions between the *oikos* (household) and the community (109–73). On Penelope's motives, see also Woodhouse 1930, 82–83; Harsh 1950, 13; Amory 1963, 116; Winkler 1990, 155; Felson 1994, 16–17 and 137; Peradotto 1990, 85; and Foley 2001, 136.

9. Aorist indicative of *eidō*.

10. On the reunion of Odysseus and Penelope, see Harsh 1950; Amory 1963; Russo 1982; Peradotto 1990, 155–61; Winkler 1990, 145–61; Zeitlin 1996, 19–52; and Bergren 2008, 215–41. Zeitlin suggests that the possibility of moving the bed symbolically evokes the possibility of another man supplanting Odysseus (1996, 26–27). Felson argues that Penelope's role in this scene undermines the traditional gender hierarchy (1994, 56–64).

11. See Foley's discussion of Penelope's moral agency (2001, 126–44). Foley explains that "both sexes can publicly demonstrate *arete* (excellence or virtue) and achieve *kleos* (fame) for their actions, although they exercise their capacities for virtue in different contexts and achieve fame by different routes" (127). But contrast Schein's argument that in this simile, Odysseus redefines the meaning of *kleos* from "supremacy in battle" to Penelope's "mental toughness and faithfulness" (1995, 23–34). See also Cairns 2018, 384–86.

12. See Foley 1978 for discussion of this and other "reverse similes" in the *Odyssey*. On *Od.* 23.31–40, see also Murnaghan 1987, 141–43; Suzuki 1989, 90; Winkler 1990, 160–61; Katz 1991, 184–87; Zeitlin 1996, 51–52; Silk 2004, 39.

13. Discussing Athena's role in the epic, Murnaghan explains that in the *Odyssey*, "female power is channeled into the reestablishment of a patriarchal order" (1995, 63). Murnaghan contrasts Athena's "manipulative" control of Penelope with the "extraordinary partnership" that the goddess manifests with Odysseus (66–73).

14. Schein discusses the bow's function of alluding to Hercules (2016b).

15. Felson argues, conversely, that Telemachus's development illuminates Penelope's character (1994, 67–91). See also Beard's discussion of Telemachus's silencing of Penelope in *Od.* 1 (2017, 3–17, 97).

16. See especially Katz 1991, 3–19 and 155–95. Felson maintains that Penelope is "actively weaving her destiny" (1994, 18) and "acting for her own sake as well

as . . . to ensure Odysseus' glory and safety" (19). Schein argues that the *Odyssey* portrays Penelope's fidelity and ingenuity as "existing for the sake of Odysseus and as an adjunct to his heroic identity," while the epic also calls that interpretation into question (1995. 21) and partially undermines "the standard patriarchal reading" (25–26).

Felson argues that in referencing Helen, "Penelope exonerates Helen to exonerate herself" (1994, 40), but Zeitlin maintains that the reference appears "like an unconscious vindication of Helen" (1995, 144). In addition, the reference might seem to undermine Penelope's own claim to admirable fidelity (1996. 48–52, with bibliography).

17. The *Odyssey* as a whole does not affirm the negative attitude toward all women expressed by Agamemnon's shade (Felson 1994, 93–95).

18. Saxonhouse 1985, 17–36. Contrasting Penelope and Odysseus as moral agents, Foley explains that on the surface the *Odyssey* presents women having "the same moral capacities as men," (i.e., for *aretē* and *kleos*), but that in fact, women in the epic "do not have the same degree of moral autonomy and self-sufficiency as men" (1995. 95–96).

19. Zeitlin observes that these tears recall Odysseus's weeping on Scheria (*Odyssey* 8), which catalyzed his identification of himself among the Phaeacians (1995, 145, and 1996, 51–52).

20. On the *homophrosyne* (like-mindedness) of Odysseus and Penelope, see especially Winkler 1990, 142–61; and Felson 1994, 44–65. Schein suggests that the "mental similarity" between Odysseus and Penelope exemplifies "the kind of harmony in marriage that Odysseus wishes for Nausikaa at 6.181–85" (1995, 21). But contrast Thalmann's argument that in the final analysis, Penelope subordinates herself to Odysseus (1998, 232–37). Felson, however, suggests that the relationship between Penelope and Odysseus shows not an equality between genders, but an alternation between domination and subordination (1994, 6–9). Foley argues that Penelope "is both constrained and willing . . . to sacrifice her own needs for the benefit of others" (1995, 108). But in fact, Penelope's needs and the needs of others align; her choices promote the removal of the oppressive suitors and the restoration of order in her home.

21. Cf. Thalmann's discussion of contrasts between Homeric and modern honor-based societies (1998, 123–24).

22. E.g., Snyder asserts as the fundamental fascist concept the notion "that politics begins from 'friend or foe'" (2018, 61). He explains that "fascism is the falsehood that the enemy chosen by a leader must be the enemy for all" (280).

23. Schein, however, argues that "clearly the poem expects its audience and readers to approve of the slaughter of the suitors" (2016b. 50).

24. On *hybris* in epic and tragedy, see Fisher 1992. While English contrasts *hubris*, understood as "pride" or "arrogance," with "humility," the ancient Greek antithesis of *hybris* is *sophrosyne*, a broad concept of correct moral action (Fisher 1992, 111–18). Fisher discusses the greater prevalence of *hybris* words in the *Odyssey* than in the *Iliad* and their emphasis in condemning the suitors' conduct (151–84). Sommerstein explains that *hybris* is mistakenly understood as referring to "a state of mind," whereas in reality it refers to the "degrading and contemptuous treatment of fellow human beings" (2013, 1 and n2 with bibliography).

25. On Odysseus's decision to spare the singer, see Pucci 1987, 228–35.

26. Anhalt 2017, 95–99.

27. Cf. Felson 1994, 109–23. Felson argues that by individualizing the suitors, the *Odyssey* makes Penelope more responsible for their deaths and "partially exonerates them by making a few respectable characters blame society for indulging these youths and tolerating their misbehavior" (111).

28. Felson, however, argues that Telemachus "goes too far" in punishing the slave women (1994, 86–87).

29. The swineherd attributes the slaves' neglect of their responsibilities to Zeus for taking away half of a man's *aretē* (excellence) when he becomes a slave (*Od.* 17.322–23). But nothing in the narrative supports this view. In fact, the swineherd himself constitutes a living contradiction of it; he remains noble in his loyalty to Odysseus despite having been born a free man and then kidnapped and sold into slavery (*Od.* 15.398–484).

30. Katz argues that Melantho's mistreatment of Odysseus "displaces the question of sexual misconduct from Penelope onto her faithless serving women and thus functions to absolve Penelope from the suspicion of wrongdoing" (1991, 132). See also Thalmann's discussion of Melantho (1998, 70–74) and the goatherd Melanthios (83–84).

31. Odysseus's calculating, calibrated anger, presented as constructive in the *Odyssey*, contrasts with the rage of Achilles, presented as irrational and destructive in the *Iliad*. Odysseus acts with self-restraint and forethought, punishing the guilty while sparing the innocent. His violent revenge seems to restore order and happiness for his family, his community, and himself. By contrast, in the *Iliad*, Achilles's unreflective, unrestrained rage proves self-defeating. His excessive, indiscriminate rage-fueled violence brings devastation on his community and himself. Killing, maiming, and torturing his enemies without discrimination or limit, Achilles achieves results that neither he nor anyone else could possibly desire (Anhalt 2017, 102–14). On parallels and contrasts between Odysseus and Achilles, see also Pucci 1987, 135–47 and 165–73.

32. E.g., Murnaghan argues that Athena's victory over Poseidon "is associated with civilization as Odysseus both returns to civilization and restores civilized

values on Ithaka" (1995, 65, 77–78). Thalmann, however, argues that Odysseus's vengeance prioritizes the *oikos* (household) over the community (1998, 171–237), since Odysseus's "authority is imposed on Ithakan society as a whole" (171). Thalmann views this conclusion as incongruous and paradoxical, symbolized by "the bloodshed within the hall, normally the scene of peaceful feasting" and by the competition between beggars, normally the recipients of hospitality (171). For Thalmann, Odysseus's violent revenge exposes "the implicit dissonance between the competitive aspect of honor and the peaceful, temporary incorporation of outsiders through hospitality" (172).

33. Christensen observes that the epic puts the audience in the position of judging, since Athena's intervention "artificially closes the theme of strife" and "the *Odyssey*'s abrupt resolution invite[s] reflection and debate" (2018, 28–29).

34. Odysseus's dismissal of infinite material compensation mirrors Achilles's rejection of Agamemnon's offer of reparations (*Il.* 9.378–87). The *Iliad* also suggests that savage slaughter cannot soothe the emotional wound either; Achilles's rage only escalates as he exacts his increasingly bloody vengeance (books 19–22).

35. Literally: "Let no man be *athemistios* [lawless, unrighteous, wicked]"—-i.e., lacking *themis*, knowledge and observance of what is lawful, customary, right.

36. Dimock 1963; and Peradotto 1990, 120–42 and 165–67.

37. Achilles sacrifices his humanity in the pursuit of vengeance (Anhalt 2017, 102–7).

38. Twenty-first-century "honor killings" similarly often result from an offense against some man's wife, sister, or daughter. Feeling directly attacked, the woman's male relatives may retaliate against the attacker, but they are also likely to punish the woman. (And, like Odysseus ordering the killing of the slave women, the perpetrators do not care whether the woman was raped or complicit.) The woman's value derives from her relation to her male relatives and her function as a marker of her male relatives' status.

39. Graziosi maintains, however, that Zeus's intervention at the epic's conclusion presents "collective amnesia as the only way to restore peace on Ithaca" (2016, 103). This appears most unlikely, given the importance of memory in Homeric epic and the fact that the word for "truth," *alētheia*, means also "not forgetting."

CHAPTER 6

1. Knox 1979, 126–127. In a political sense, the word could also mean "revolutionary."

2. Good introductions to Aeschylus and the trilogy include Fagles 1975; Goward 2005; Mitchell-Boyask 2009; Marshall 2017; and Taplin 2018. My understanding of the *Oresteia* derives especially from Herington 1986, 111–56. The *Oresteia*,

meaning "the story of Orestes" (as the *Odyssey* means "the story of Odysseus"), presents a continuous plot in three tragedies. The final play in the original tetralogy, the "satyr" drama *Proteus*, has not survived (Fagles 1975, 94; Herington 1986. 64). See also Winnington-Ingram 1983; Nussbaum 1986, 33–47; Meier 1993, 33–34.

3. Lloyd-Jones 1983, 29.

4. On Aeschylus's reworking of Homer's tale of Orestes, see especially Goldhill 1986, 147–54; Olson 1990; Felson 1994, 93–107; Mitchell-Boyask 2009, 19–27; Alden 2017, 77–100; and Taplin 2018, 137–40. For various versions of the tale, see also Gantz 1993, 664–75; Goward 2005, 43–46; Marshall 2017, 21–26; and Taplin 2018, 141–50. Zeus, complaining that mortals blame gods for self-induced sufferings, cites Orestes's example, explaining that Aegisthus deservedly paid the penalty for ignoring the gods' explicit warning not to marry Clytemnestra or kill Agamemnon (*Od.* 1.28–43). Athena uses Orestes's example to motivate Odysseus's son to destroy his mother's suitors and, like Orestes, win a good reputation (*Od.* 1.297–302). Similarly, Nestor praises Orestes's killing of Aegisthus and extols the value of having a son who can avenge his father's murder (*Od.* 3.193–98). Nestor's repetition of Athena's words is formulaic (*Od.* 3.199–200, and 1.301–2), but it also emphasizes the complete lack of controversy in the *Odyssey* about the correctness of Orestes's actions. (See also *Od.* 3.232–35 and 254–312; 4.90–93 and 512–47; 24.95–97 and 199–202.)

5. Herington 1986, 131–33; and similarly Meier 1993, 104; and Taplin 2018, xiv–xvi.

6. Herington 1986, 62–63 and 125–26. On *dike* (justice) in Aeschylus, see especially Havelock 1978, 277–95; Goldhill 1986, 20–23, 33–56; Meier 1993, 74–78; and Mitchell-Boyask 2009, 98–100. Defining the *Oresteia*'s movement from hierarchical family ties to civic ties, Goldhilll discusses the trilogy's "re-evaluation of kinship" (2012, 238–39).

7. Havelock identifies the substitution of persuasion for violence in the *Oresteia*'s conclusion (1978, 279–80). On Aeschylus's concept of learning by suffering and the potential of conflict to be constructive, see Fagles 1975, 20, 25–26; Nussbaum 1986, 44–46; Euben 1990, 69–94; and Meier 1993, 121–23. Christensen finds a constructive form of competition already present in Homer and Hesiod, not only within the worlds depicted in the epics but also in the constructive rivalry between epics (2018, 3, 33–34).

8. See, for example, Rinon 2008. On the relationship between tragedy and archaic beliefs, see especially Burian 1997 and Cairns 2013. For the Athenian context and production of tragedy, see especially Pickard-Cambridge 1953; Winkler and Zeitlin 1990; Meier 1993, 44–61; Csapo and Slater 1994; Easterling 1997; Mitchell-Boyask 2009, 34–43; and E. Hall 2010, 1–11. The origins of the genre

remain obscure. Knox discusses the use of mythical subjects in tragedy and the emphasis on human beings (1979, 4–24), explaining that "tragic myth, for the fifth-century Greeks, was the story of their past, their history—for early times the only history they knew" (11). Tragic performances became an official part of the Great Dionysia, a yearly Athenian festival in honor of Dionysos, c. 534 BCE. That year, the tragic performer Thespis won first prize. Herington offers an overview of the early Athenian theater and the role of the poet-playwright (1986. 32–41). Swift 2016 provides a good recent introduction to this distinctively Athenian genre and its themes. Murnaghan suggests that the *Odyssey*'s depiction of Penelope's relationship with her female servants anticipates the later choral performances of Athenian tragedy (2018).

9. Good discussions of tragic themes in the Homeric epics include Redfield 1994 and Rinon 2008. Specifying formal features of tragedy already visible in the *Iliad* and *Odyssey*, de Jong identifies Homer as "the first tragedian" (2016).

10. Carter 2007, 4–7 and 158–60. Nussbaum characterizes Athenian tragedy as an invitation to the audience to participate in "a contested place of moral struggle (1986, xxvii). Meier defines tragedy as an "institutionalized discussion" of issues of communal concern and "a precondition for rational politics" (1993, 42–43). Explaining that Athenian religious festivals included "the public airing of criticism and doubts," Meier considers tragedy "the Greek way of dealing communally with communal questions" (48). Similarly, Cartledge 1997, 18–22. On religious issues in the *Oresteia*, see especially Sourvinou-Inwood 2003, 231–51.

11. Meier emphasizes the unprecedentedly broad political participation (1993, 1–7), the application of rationality to traditional myth (esp. 36–43), and the novel power and responsibility of individual citizens (e.g., 97–101).

12. Andersen argues convincingly that the moral relativism of the academy over the past several decades has empowered reality deniers of all political persuasions by suggesting that every fantastical, unfalsifiable conviction is as true or correct as any other (2017, 189–97).

13. J. S. Mill recognizes that "the tendency of all opinions to become sectarian is not cured by the freest discussion, but is often heightened and exacerbated thereby: the truth which ought to have been, but was not, seen, being rejected all the more violently because proclaimed by persons regarded as opponents. But it is not on the impassioned partisan, it is on the calmer and more disinterested bystander, that this collision of opinions works its salutary effect" (1859, 115).

14. See Macleod's discussion of *dike* (justice) in the *Oresteia* (1982). Lattimore observes that the *Agamemnon* pits "not so much right against wrong as right against right, each person insisting on his right with the force of passion" (1972, 74).

15. We may be accustomed to thinking of free choice and constraint as antithetical, but the play suggests that in sacrificing his daughter, Agamemnon acted freely and also was not really free to choose (Nussbaum 1986, 33–34). His warriors would have starved otherwise. Of course, Agamemnon's goal was not to save the warriors but to lead them to Troy, where many died and many others died afterward on the way home. The chorus claims that in making his choice, Agamemnon "put on himself the leather strap [of the yoke] of *anangke* [necessity, constraint]" (*Ag.* 218). That is, he actively chose to do something that he was constrained to do anyway. Lloyd-Jones argues that Zeus-sent *Atē* prevents Agamemnon from having any choice in the matter (1962), but Nussbaum identifies the sacrifice of Iphigenia as both "necessary" and "blameworthy" (1986, 33), because Zeus puts Agamemnon, "a previously guiltless man, in a situation in which there is open to him no guilt-free course" (34, citing Lloyd-Jones 1962, 191–92). See also Fagles 1975, 26.

16. Nussbaum 1986, 35–38. The chorus blames Agamemnon not for the sacrifice, but for "the change of thought and passion accompanying the killing," since Agamemnon treats his own child as if she were a sacrificial beast and acts without regrets (36–37). Nussbaum identifies the "yokestrap of necessity" as an image for "Agamemnon's inference from the necessity of the act to its rightness" (36). Similarly, Hammond maintains that "the collaboration of god and man, whether or not man is aware of it, does not deprive man of his ability to choose" (1972, 93). Nussbaum explains that before making his decision, Agamemnon realizes that either choice results in evil, but that *after* choosing, he entertains the possibility that the result may not be evil, with the consequence that "an act that we were prepared to view as the lesser of two hideous wrongs and impieties has now become for him pious and right, as though by some art of decision-making he has resolved the conflict and disposed of the other 'heavy doom.'" Moreover, Agamemnon seems to believe that if he has made the right decision, then "it is appropriate to want it, even to be enthusiastic about it. From 'which of these is without evils?' he has moved to 'May all turn out well'" (Nussbaum 1986, 35–36). See also Garvie 2010, 33–41.

17. The first two plays of the trilogy allude elsewhere to the theme of speech silenced, distorted, or deceiving (e.g., *Ag.* 36–39 and 1639–40; *L.B.* 264–68, 555, 581–82, 770–73, 812–17). The *Eumenides* exemplifies the value of open debate (e.g., *Eum.* 436–42, 575–75). Ober identifies the centrality of freedom of speech to the concept of citizenship and to the ideal of self-rule in democratic Athens (1989, 296; and 2003, 6–7). See also Saxonhouse 2006, 1–3 and *passim*; and Carter 2007, 71–73.

18. Herington 1986, 119–21. Herington explains that in this scene, "the arrogance and folly in the heart of Troy's conqueror are given magnificent external

expression" (120). Garvie similarly observes that "for the first time we *see* him committing *hybris*" (2010, 38). On *hybris* in the *Oresteia*, see also Fisher 1992, 270–97. Fisher cites Winnington-Ingram's view of "*hybris* in Aeschylus (and Sophocles) as the abuse of power committed by those prepared to indulge to excess the pursuit of honour and success in which their society's values encouraged them to engage" (296, citing Winnington-Ingram 1980, 97–100; and 1983, 311ff.). Winnington-Ingram defines *hybris* (abuse of power) as the antithesis of *sophrosyne* (moderation, discretion, self-control, temperance, chastity, etc.; 1983, 98–99). Goldhill identifies an opposition between *hybris* and *dikē* (1986, 35–36).

Goheen discusses the "ambiguous blood color" of the tapestries and its significance (1972. 107–15), arguing that the color evokes "fear for the blood already spilled and for the possibility of blood to come" (110). Zeitlin reads this scene as emblematic of Agamemnon's "secret affinity with the Trojan king Priam and with barbarian values of luxury and gratification of desires" (1996. 92). See also Foley 2001, 208–10; Garvie 2010, 37–38; and E. Hall 2010, 214–15.

19. But cf. Goheen's argument that Clytemnestra's persuasive force dramatizes "what the Chorus has sung as the way retribution overtakes the sinner, *Peithō* (Persuasion), the agent of *Atē* (Ruin) conducts him to his doom, unable longer himself to control his destiny" (1972, 115–16).

20. Herington 1986, 123–24. Foley discusses Clytemnestra's perverse exultation (2001, 210–11) and Garvie her "blasphemy" at the play's conclusion (2010, 40). Alden examines Clytemnestra's reversal of funerary ritual (2017, 94–100). See also Winnington-Ingram 1983, 105–14; and Herington 1986, 113–14.

21. Beard identifies Aeschylus's Clytemnestra as epitomizing "the unquestionable mess that women make of power in Greek myth" (2017, 59), arguing that "the patriarchal order is only restored when Clytemnestra's children conspire to kill her" (60).

22. In the *Libation Bearers*, however, Clytemnestra does not seem to care very much for her surviving two children (e.g., *L.B.* 737–40).

23. E.g., Arriving home triumphant, Agamemnon thinks it *dikē* to address first the gods who were in part the cause of [or accomplices in] his homecoming, saluting them for "the just things [*dikaiōn*] which I did to the city of Priam" (*Ag.* 810–13). Clytemnestra calls her murder of her husband *dikē* (*Ag.* 1432, 1525–29). The chorus recognizes that vengeance is reciprocal, predicting that "*dikē* [justice] is sharpening its blade" for more bloodshed (*Ag.* 1535–36) and realizing that it is unclear where justice lies, since "reproach comes against reproaches. It's difficult to judge. [Someone] plunders him who is plundering, and the killer pays in full" (*Ag.* 1560–62). Nevertheless, Aegisthus exultantly greets "the kindly, justice-bearing [*dikēphorou*] light of day" (*Ag.* 1577).

24. Herington 1986, 119–20 and 144. Herington finds complete "moral confusion" in the *Agamemnon* (111), but contrast Hammond's claim that "the *Agamemnon* ends with the triumph of Justice" (1972, 99). Foley maintains that the play emphasizes that it is "impossible for a woman to be a true agent of justice" (2001, 229).

25. Lebeck 1971, 25–36; Herington 1986, 120–22; Nussbaum 1986, 44–47; Meier 1993, 120–21; Garvie 2010, 34–35. For centuries, the *Odyssey* had emphasized the importance of interpreting, understanding, and learning from experience (see chapter 5).

26. Defending the necessity of "freedom of opinion" and "freedom of the expression of opinion," J. S. Mill argues, "If any opinion is compelled to silence, that opinion may, for aught we can certainly know, be true. To deny this is to assume our own infallibility." Moreover, "though the silenced opinion be an error, it may, and very commonly does, contain a portion of truth; and since the general or prevailing opinion on any subject is rarely or never the whole truth, it is only by collision of adverse opinions that the remainder of the truth has any chance of being supplied" (1859, 115–16).

27. E.g., the Chorus (*L. B.* 121–23, 306–15, 400–404); Electra (*L.B.* 142–44), Orestes (*L.B.* 269–97, 990, 1027–28). Herington suggests, however, that unlike the *Agamemnon*'s characters, Orestes and Electra in the *Libation Bearers* do "seem to possess an intuition, still unformulated, of a justice that transcends revenge" (1986, 131–33).

28. Herington 1986, 124–34; Garvie 2010, 51; E. Hall 2010, 218. Foley finds less symmetry, arguing that the *Libation Bearers* "redefines Clytemnestra's act and highlights the monstrosity of the wife's crime against her husband" (2001, 331).

29. See Fagles's assessment of the chorus in each play, elderly men of Argos in the *Agamemnon*, captive slave women in the *Libation Bearers*, and Furies in the *Eumenides* (1975, 67). Garvie notes the unusualness of a tragic chorus intervening in the plot (2010, 43–49). See also E. Hall 2010, 219.

On the parable of the lion cub, see Fagles 1975, 29–30; and Knox 1979, 27–38. Knox identifies the cub as the embodiment of "the repetitive pattern imposed . . . by the system of private vengeance" (36–37). Meier views the tale of the cub as emblematic of an effort to violate "the distinction between civilization and the wild" which will inevitably provoke vengeance (1993, 125). Taplin suggests that "the initial response to pay back violence with violence is 'hard-wired' in animals, not excluding humans" (2018, xix).

30. Herington 1986, 133–43; Meier 1993, 109–12.

31. Herington 1986, 134–56. But cf. Garvie's assumption that Athena brings jurors with her (2010, 57–59).

260 NOTES TO CHAPTER 6

The *Iliad* offers a prototype of a legal procedure for addressing a case of murder: Achilles's immortal shield, crafted by the god Hephaestus, includes a depiction of a city at peace, containing desirable elements of communal life (marriage festivals, singing, dancing, flute and lyre music, an arbitration procedure). In this peacetime scene, a *histor* (arbitrator) presides over a case of murder (*Il.* 18.497–508). The victim, kinsman of the murdered man, in rejecting an offer of material compensation, reflects the feeling angrily expressed by Achilles and Odysseus elsewhere that no form of material compensation could possibly satisfy their desire for revenge (*Il.* 9.374–409; and *Od.* 22.61–65). The arbitration procedure, however, suggests that a nonviolent solution better serves the community's interests.

32. Fagles observes that "Apollo's values—Law and Order—are undermined by his methods of enforcement: he would slaughter the Furies to preserve his sense of justice, he is murderously self-righteous. And the Furies calmly, rationally expose him in debate. First he justifies matricide in terms of vengeance, then he pardons it with absolution" (1975, 75). On the appropriateness of Athena as the mediator between Apollo and the Furies, see Fagles 1975, 76–77; and Herington 1986, 142–43. An anonymous reader for Yale University Press notes that Athena's preference for the masculine in all things, save marriage, enables her to mediate without passing judgement.

33. Fagles 1975, 77–83. On the significance of the trumpet blast, see also Rosenmeyer 1982, 342–43. Originally, *dikē* simply meant "way." In the trilogy, each character claims that his or her *dikē* "way" is right. But by the fifth century BCE, *dikē* also meant a "trial by jury." Instead of celebrating retaliatory atrocities as admirable triumphs, the community as a whole determines *dikē* by holding a trial (Herington 1986, 143–45).

34. Herington emphasizes Aeschylus's sympathetic portrait of ordinary characters (1986, 113–19, 129–30).

35. Herington 1986, 143–57, esp. 150–55. Herington also observes that in human debates "between adversaries opposed on grounds of deeply felt principle, unfortunately for humanity, simple reasoning rarely seems to achieve much" (141).

36. See Ready 2011, 123 and 63n127. On lions in Homeric similes, see Alden 2005.

37. Taplin 2018, xxi–xxii.

38. Lattimore argues that the trilogy transforms the story of Atreus and his descendants "into a grand parable of progress," as Athena turns "persuasion (flattery), the deadly magic of the earlier plays," into a constructive force, impelling the Furies "to accept of their own free will a new and better place in the world" (1972, 88). Fagles suggests that the trilogy might be deemed a "rite of passage from savagery to civilization" (1975, 19), arguing that it concludes "in a great mutual victory"

(86). Winnington-Ingram finds that the trilogy dramatizes the movement "from the vendetta to the court of law" (1983, 127). Herington explains that Athena's persuasion transforms the Furies from "utterly revolting creatures" into "highly articulate conservatives," who finally become "fertility goddesses with the power to blight or prosper the life of nature at their will" (1986, 152–53). Athena's last speech has not survived but, given the play's title, she must have changed the Furies' name from Erinyes (Furies) to Eumenides (well-minded ones or kindly ones; 155–56).

Such "positive" interpretations of the trilogy's trajectory remain controversial, however. Rosenmeyer finds the message of the *Eumenides* more complex, deeming it not "legal, much less ethical or philosophical, but pragmatic" (1982, 342–53). See also Macleod's discussion of the communal nature of the trilogy's resolution (1982, 136–38). Garvie finds the resolution more apparent than real (2010, 60). Murnaghan argues that the conclusion of the *Eumenides* combines "both the acknowledgement of female strength and the establishment of hierarchies in which the female is subordinate to the male" (1995, 61), since the Furies "accept an honored but subordinate role in the reconstituted social order" (63). Similarly, Zeitlin reads the *Oresteia* as a "definitive masculine triumph" over matriarchy (1996, 87–119). Zeitlin sees in the trilogy's conclusion "a hierarchization of values" (87), arguing that "the *Oresteia* stands squarely within the misogynistic tradition that pervades Greek thought," and that "if Aeschylus is concerned with world building, the cornerstone of his architecture is the control of women, the social and cultural prerequisite for the construction of civilization" (88). Foley, too, finds that "the trilogy moves gradually toward asserting the familiar male-dominated order" (2001, 232) threatened by "any autonomous action by a woman" (234). E. Hall similarly observes that in the *Eumenides,* the concluding emphasis on the rule of law in Athens includes the subordination of women (2010, 223–27). The pervasive, established subjugation of women in Athens in the fifth-century BCE would scarcely seem to require dramatic emphasis, however, and undeniably the Furies, no less than Athens itself, also benefit from the new arrangement.

39. For the political resonance of the *Eumenides* in the fifth century BCE, see Herington 1986, 63, 146–50; Meier 1993, 25–41 and 97–130; Mitchell-Boyask 2009, 97–107; Garvie 2010, 53–54; and Sommerstein 2010, 281–89. By establishing the Council of the Areopagus as the permanent court for murder trials, Athena validates the recent reduction of this council's powers (Herington 1986, 150). Having overthrown their last tyrant by 508 BCE, the Athenians initially retained many aristocratic safeguards against direct popular voting. (On Cleisthenes's constitution, see Herodotus 5.66–69, and Aristotle *Constitution of the Athenians* 21.) The Council of the Areopagus (Hill of Ares), named for the

council's meeting place, consisted of ex-magistrates, still at that time mostly from noble and wealthy families. The council provided a conservative check on the Assembly, preparing legislation and guiding the Assembly's decisions. When the ostracism of the conservatives' leader (461 BCE) left the conservative opposition weak and disorganized, the democrats pushed through a radical program of constitutional reforms. These reforms preserved the Council of the Areopagus as the court for murder trials, but stripped it of its legislative role. Instead, the *Boulē*, a council of regular citizens appointed by lottery, and the *Ekklesia*, the Assembly of all Athenian citizens, now determined the laws.

The *Eumenides* also validates a radical, highly controversial foreign policy shift. The leader of the conservative faction had favored continued alliance with Sparta. But after ostracizing him, the Athenians broke their long-standing treaty with Sparta and made one with Sparta's ancient enemy Argos. In the play, Orestes proclaims the Argive commitment to the alliance, promising an alliance between his people of Argos and the Athenians for all time (*Eum.* 289–91).

The almost immediate assassination of the leader of the radical democrats attests that the new constitutional reforms and foreign policy reversal remained controversial and potentially explosive. By removing the legislative authority of the Council of the Areopagus and reducing it to presiding over murder trials, the new, radically democratic legislation gave each Athenian citizen direct responsibility for determining and implementing justice. Herington observes that Athens in 458 BCE was becoming "a world wherein, literally, *the onus of judging rests on the human being*, even when he must judge between gods" (1986, 147; italics in original).

40. For Lloyd-Jones, the play presents the judicial process as not supplanting but assisting the Furies (1983, 91–95). Similarly, Carter 2007, 31. On Athena's use of persuasion and the transformation of the Furies, see Fagles 1975, 33, 84–85; Rosenmeyer 1982, 350–53; Goldhill 1986, 29–30; Meier 1993, 105–6, 130, 134–37; Mitchell-Boyask 2009, 89–96; and Garvie 2010, 59–60. Rynearson identifies Athena's persuasion of the Erinyes as a form of "wooing" (2013). On the symbolism of the crimson color at the play's conclusion, see Herington 1986, 155–56.

CHAPTER 7

1. Although commonly called "the Theban Plays," or "the Theban Trilogy," these plays are not in fact a trilogy, not having been produced in the same year. Sophocles did not even write the pieces of this story in mythical chronological sequence (i.e., the tale of Oedipus, then Oedipus at Colonus, then Antigone). He wrote *Antigone* first (c. 443 BCE); then *Oedipus*, often called by its Latin title *Oedipus Rex*, about fifteen years later; and *Oedipus at Colonus*, describing events occurring prior to the events in *Antigone*, some two decades after that (c. 405 BCE, produced

posthumously 401 BCE). On the date of the *Antigone*, see Cairns 2016, 1–3.

2. Describing his visit to the underworld, Odysseus says:

"And I saw the mother of Oidipodes [Oedipus], the noble Epikaste [Iocasta],
Who unwittingly did a terrible deed, marrying her own son.
And he married her having killed his own father.
But the gods instantly [*aphar*] made these things notorious among men.
But he ruled over the Cadmeians in lovely Thebes,
enduring the troubles, because of the destructive plans of the gods.
And she went down to the realm of the powerful doorkeeper Hades,
Fastening a noose, hung high from the lofty crossbeam,
Held fast by her anguish. And she left to him afterward very many troubles,
As many as a mother's avenging spirits accomplish." (*Od.* 11.271–80).

Gantz observes that this description suggests that Oedipus and Iocasta could not have had time to produce four children. The *Iliad* mentions a warrior who "once went to Thebes and the tomb of the fallen Oedipus and was victorious there over all the Cadmeians" *(Il.* 23.679–80). (The alliterative *dedoupotos Oidipodao / es taphon* means, literally, "to the tomb of Oedipus, fallen with a thud.") Identifying the verb with death in warfare, or by violence rather than by old age, Gantz infers from the passage funeral games held in Oedipus's honor. Hesiod mentions demigods battling in Thebes over Oedipus's sheep flocks (*Erg.* 162–63) (1993. 296, 500–502). See also Cairns 2016, 3–10.

In Sophocles's *Oedipus* (c. 428 BCE), Oedipus uncovers the truth about himself. Not the gods, as Homer's Odysseus claims, but Oedipus's own intellect, courage, and determination reveal the facts.

3. The Roman Republic lasted 450 years. The US republic has endured nearly 250.

4. Gantz 1993, 490–95, 519–22. Aeschylus wrote a *Laius* and an *Oedipus*, both now lost. Euripides also wrote an *Oedipus*, of which only scant fragments survive. In Sophocles's *Oedipus at Colonus* (posth. 401 BCE), Oedipus dies and will be buried not in Thebes but somewhere near Athens, and the secrecy of the site of his tomb (not its future celebrated prominence) is a crucial plot point (*OC* 1518ff.). Gantz identifies Sophocles's version as the earliest surviving literary source for Oedipus's death at Colonus, perhaps reflecting a recent Attic tradition (296, 502, citing Severyns 1928). An *Antigone* by Euripides also has not survived. Sophocles's *Antigone* begins where Aeschylus's *Seven against Thebes* (467 BCE) ends, as Antigone and her sister Ismene mourn their brothers' deaths. No earlier surviving source focuses on Antigone's burial of her brother. In some later ancient sources, Ismene was killed before her brother attacked Thebes, and Haemon was killed by the Sphynx (495, 519–21). For an excellent introduction to the *Antigone*, see Cairns 2016.

5. On *hybris* in the *Antigone* and Creon's "increasingly authoritarian" behavior, see Fisher 1992, 308–12. Liapis notes the archaic association of *hybris* with "the overturning of political order" (2013, 92).

6. For my understanding of this play, I am deeply indebted to Richard Garner's wisdom, insight, and eloquence. I also rely considerably on Meier 1993, 187–203.

7. See Burian 2010, esp. 283.

8. For Hegel's reading of the play as an opposition between "the family" and "the state" and modern critical responses to that view, see Burian 2010. Finding Hegel the first to see Antigone's identity as a woman as essential to understanding the play (273), Burian explains that Hegel "made Antigone the embodiment of family and its right, in conflict with Creon, the representative of the law of the state" (271).

Creon values the *polis* and its laws over kinship and chthonic law (e.g., Markell 2003, 62–73), but he cannot be viewed as the ideal embodiment of the state and the rule of law (e.g., Euben 1997, 139–78, esp. 157). Burian, too, rejects Hegel's idealization of Antigone and Creon as perfect exemplars of opposing but equally valid principles, since Creon fails to represent the state adequately, and Antigone offers a similarly ambivalent model of "the family" (2010, 256–60). Burian also notes that many critics unjustifiably idealize Antigone as "an exemplary figure," a female "heroine" in the male Aristotelian mode, while others view her as "the representative of a distinctly female consciousness, the elemental power of kinship based on blood" (271–72). Butler maintains that "Antigone represents not kinship in its ideal form but its deformation and displacement" (2000, 24), and Brendese identifies Antigone as "anti-generational" both in her name and in her rejection of childbearing (2010, 125). Liapis, however, argues that the play depicts "the defeat of the *polis* and its institutions by the individual, self-contained, and self-destructive *oikos*" (2013, 107). See also Carter's discussion of the relationship between *oikos* and *polis* in tragedy (2007, 74–78). On ancient and modern reception of the *Antigone*, see Cairns 2016, 115–53.

Whitman dismisses 904–20 as a "glaring example of an actor's interpolation" (1951, 92–93). But see Burian 2010, 272, 280–81 and n93 on the critical response to these lines. See also Winnington-Ingram 1980, 145; Foley 2001, 175–79; Goldhill 2012, 245; and Garvie 2016, 37–38.

Discussing Antigone's opening address to Ismene, Goldhill concludes that "what we share, since Hegel, is the question of *where* the conflict in the *Antigone* is, the political question of what is shared"—a question introduced "from the first word of the play . . . a passionate and overdetermined appeal . . . *ō koinon*" (2012, 248).

9. E.g., Thucydides's account of the civil war in Corcyra (427 BCE), where factional loyalties eroded and perverted all other values and relationships (3.82–84).

10. See Wininngton-Ingram 1980, 117–49; Cairns 2016, 93–104; and Garvie 2016, 31–41.

11. M. W. Blundell 1989, 26–31.

12. Ryan observes that "the division of the world into friends and enemies was a defining characteristic of fascism" (2012, 913). Snyder explains, "That politics begins from 'friend or foe' is the basic fascist idea, formulated by the Nazi legal theorist Carl Schmitt and endorsed and propagated by [Ivan] Ilyin" (2018, 61). Albright notes that Hitler could conceive of only two options, as he himself insisted: "either the victory of the Aryan side or its annihilation and the victory of the Jews" (2018, 40).

Winnington-Ingram (1980, 121–28) suggests, however, that Creon's arguments would have resonated favorably with an Athenian citizen in the fifth century BCE (123) and that his denial of burial to Polynices might seem morally "repugnant but justifiable on political grounds" (121). Liapis, too, maintains that a fifth-century audience would very likely have had sympathy for the legitimacy of Creon's arguments and aims (2013, 109). Discussing Creon's conception of sovereignty, Liapis explains that in placing the city's interests above all (96–97), and in his conviction that he is "the designated representative of the body politic" (98), Creon defines "good leadership" as requiring "absolute obedience" (100). Eventually, Creon exemplifies the destructiveness of his own clan (102–7).

13. Carter 2007, 146–55. Carter rejects as anachronistic the modern liberal view of Antigone as a "freedom fighter."

14. The *Antigone* critiques, without dismissing, the ancient conception that "the city is one's principal source of safety" (Carter 2007, 103–14). The *Iliad* repeatedly foreshadows the fall of Troy as a calamity, depicting the destruction of defensive walls and their defenders as catastrophic (e.g., *Il.* 6.447–65, 12.2–37 and 451–471, and 22.84–85 and 477–515). Many of Euripides's plays make the point as well (e.g., *Hecuba, Trojan Women, Bacchae*).

15. Burian 2010, 283. Burian explains that "Antigone's 'No!' is not a rejection of state power as such, but of its misuse" (2010, 264). Similarly, Liapis contends that Antigone cannot be understood as a defender of human dignity against despotic repression, because she opposes only Creon's ban on burying her brother (2013, 83–86).

16. Meier 1993, 197–98; Carter 2007, 112 and 116; and Burian 2010, 274.

17. Many scholars have recognized that Creon's motives are not irreligious, nor are Antigone's motives apolitical. E.g., Whitman 1951, 85–88; Foley 2001, 173–89; Burian 2010, 272 and 278; and Liapis 2013, 95.

18. In choosing to bury Eteocles but not Polynices, Creon prioritizes "his obligation to the state over any family duty" (Burian 2010, 276). And yet, as

Cairns observes, as Antigone's nearest male relative, Creon, is now both the head of her household and her guardian (2016, 43).

19. Winnington-Ingram rejects any reductive interpretation of the play as "a simple contrast between villainy on the one hand, sweetness and light on the other" (1980, 128), but he points out that Antigone confronts her own death "nobly," whereas Creon crumbles. Regarding the play's concluding symmetries, see especially Segal 1995, 119–37. Segal observes that "Creon, having misunderstood the nature of community in his 'tyrannical' conception of ruling a city (733–739), performs at the end a funerary ritual in which he is virtually the sole mourner of his house. His situation, therefore, comes to mirror that of Antigone, who, in her isolated performance of the rites for Polyneices, is also the sole mourner of a ruined house" (131). Brendese similarly points out that Creon's anxiety regarding Antigone's threat to his manhood (*Ant.* 528–29) foreshadows a reversal in which he ultimately assumes the traditionally female role of mourning dead relatives (2010, 123). Burian identifies the "intransigence" of both Creon and Antigone (2010, 286), explaining that Antigone "reminds the *polis* of a fundamental obligation that, in the person of its ruler Creon, it resists to its own peril" (272), while, paradoxically, "Creon's notion that every value must be subordinated to the good of the *polis* harms the *polis*" (276).

Goldhill, discussing contrasts between the relationship between the two sisters and the relationship between the two brothers, notes Antigone's "rejection of sisterhood" (2012. 231–49). In threatening to hate her sister (*Ant.* 86, 93), Antigone reflects the dysfunction of her family, the House of Laius: a family riven, as Sophocles's original audience knew, by curses and kindred killings (Liapis 2013). Liapis, too, rejects a polarized reading of Creon as a tyrant and Antigone as a martyr (2013, 108).

20. Carter 2007, 147–48. Garvie explains that Sophocles's original audience "would be inclined to look askance at Antigone, a woman who interferes in men's concerns, and who defies the laws of the city (2016, 34–35). Beard discusses the frequent portrayal of women in Greek myth as "abusers rather than users of power" (2017, 58–61).

21. More favorable views of Antigone abound, however. E.g., Whitman asserts that she "has the full measure of self-destructive heroism," arguing that "her political *aretē*, her vision of the divine law on which every true government must be formed, gives her a new dimension." He maintains that "she combines the virtues of Ajax and Odysseus in a chiseled magnificence that even Sophocles never surpassed." Moreover, "like Ajax, she chooses to die well rather than live badly" (1951, 88). Cairns argues that the play ultimately vindicates Antigone (2016, 38–39, 53, 90–92), and Garvie contends that "it is the emotional, irrational Antigone, not

the intellectual, rational Creon, who turns out to be right" (2016, 39).

Irigaray discusses Antigone as an exemplar of constructive feminist action (1985, 217–19). Foley, too, views Antigone favorably, suggesting that she challenges Creon's ethical approach and calls into question fifth-century Athenian methods and priorities despite her "temperament" and her "disruptive character and emotions" (1996 and 2001, 172–200). E. Hall maintains that the play shows Antigone to be "absolutely right" and emphasizes that it is necessary "to *listen* to dissenting voices" (2010, 307–8; emphasis in original). Many followers of Hegel's reading view Antigone as morally right and Creon as wrong (Burian 2010, 260–62); and Burian sees in Antigone, possibly, "the seed of principled, non-violent civil disobedience" (287). Brendese, however, suggests that "Antigone's act of resistance appears as a necessary condition of possibility for democracy, but not a sufficient one" (2010, 124; citing Euben 1990, 96–130).

For a recent synopsis and critique of feminist and Hegelian interpretations of *Antigone*, see Goldlhill 2012, 233–35, 245–48. Goldhill seeks to explain "why silencing Ismene is itself a revealing and worrying political gesture" (235) and criticizes feminists such as Butler and Irigaray for providing a "reenactment of Antigone's dismissive attitude towards her sister, rather than an analysis of it" (246).

22. Defining Creon's character as "typical" of ancient Greek tyrants—i.e., short-tempered, rejecting criticism, suspecting corruption, resenting women, demanding subservience—Whitman adds that "he is a tyrant who cloaks himself in the oligarchic watchwords of 'good order' and 'obedience to law'" (1951, 90; and similarly Winnington-Ingram 1980, 125). Regarding Creon's tyrannical behavior and the antipathy this might have evoked in a fifth-century audience, see Zeitlin 1986, 102; and Euben 1997, 157. Some scholars argue that Creon attempts to do the right thing but becomes tyrannical when challenged (e.g., Ostwald 1986, 148–61). Burian, however, points out that Creon's very first speech shows "signs of autocratic leanings" (2010, 277n86). Moreover, the claims of Antigone and Creon that her actions have popular support (*Ant.* 504–5, 692–95) "remind us that for democratic Athens, at any rate, valid law involves the consent of the community" (Burian 2010, 279). Observing that the play takes place on Creon's first day as king, E. Hall notes that Creon ironically affirms the truth of his own assertion that a man's true character becomes apparent only when he rules (2010, 306). Brendese sees both Antigone and Creon as problematic, noting that their "Oedipal deafness to others issues strong warnings of perilous consequences for democracy" (2010. 124). Brendese contrasts Haemon's "ability to listen and remember," while noting that Haemon ultimately abandons hope of his father ever being able to hear (124–25 and n60). Goldhill observes that, somewhat paradoxically, "Antigone's sense of *philia* is as polarized as Creon's

and as impossible: if you disagree with her you are hated, even if you are a sister. If you are a brother you are loved, even when you attack the state" (2012, 241). Garvie suggests that Creon appears progressively more tyrannical (2016, 32–33), while Liapis maintains that the play presents an evolving view of both Creon and Antigone, encouraging the audience "to reassess their original evaluations" of both (2013, 82). But cf. Cairns's discussion of the archaic view of fate and forces beyond human control (2016, 88–92).

23. Cf. Foley 2001, 172–200. Foley argues that Antigone "offers an alternative mode of ethical reasoning to that adopted by Creon" (172).

24. Sophocles portrays Ismene as a good woman adhering to standards for women of her time: obedient, unwilling to challenge male authority. The standard persisted. E.g., Whitman describes Ismene as "a norm with which we could find no fault" (1951, 89). Edmund Burke, however, famously claimed that "all that is required for the triumph of Evil is that good men do nothing." Accepting injustice, just "going along to get along," as Ismene does, permitted many atrocities in the twentieth century and continues to do so in the twenty-first.

25. For the Athenian audience's probable acceptance of Creon's denial of burial within the city but openness to the possibility of burial elsewhere, see Sourvinou-Inwood. 1989. Fisher similarly suggests that Creon transgresses in forbidding burial of any kind, even outside the borders of Thebes (1992, 311). While the failure to bury Polynices offends the gods below, strictly speaking, only burial within the city limits would offend Zeus and the city's other gods, not burial per se (Carter 2007, 112; Burian 2010, 276 and n85). Liapis, however, finds this argument inadmissible, since burial outside the city's limits is never proposed in the play (2013, 89–90). See also Cairns 2016, 37–42.

26. After the First World War, for example, the British defined the territory of Iraq somewhat arbitrarily, without sufficiently considering divisive ethnic and religious allegiances in the new nation. These divisions continue to prevent Iraqis from developing a secure and functioning nation-state based on an appreciation for their obligations to one another as fellow citizens. Rigid sectarian allegiances instead produce devastating violence in Iraq and beyond. This problem—or some version of it—persists in many other parts of the world as well. (e.g., *Economist*, June 9, 2012: "The last time Kenyans went to the polls to elect a president [in 2007], the ensuing dispute left 1,500 people dead and 300,000 displaced. The chaos, much of it orchestrated by leading politicians, tore the seams of Kenya's patchwork of more than 40 tribes, with violence erupting largely along tribal lines. Tribalism, plainly, was still the bane of Kenyan politics.")

The problem admits no easy resolution. Goldhill identifies a fundamental opposition between the hierarchical structure of the family under the *kurios* (master) and the "horizontal relationships" and "equality before the law" established by democratic government (2012, 237).

27. Sophocles's *Ajax* (c. 448 BCE), produced less than a decade before the *Antigone*, explores the challenge that this necessary variability and the newer democratic conception of group consensus poses to the traditional conception of "friends" and "enemies" or "good" and "bad" as immutable categories. The *Ajax* emphasizes that new democratic procedures can produce violent reactions in people who have been operating with fixed, unchanging standards of right and wrong. The title character is appalled to realize that friends can sometimes become enemies, and enemies friends. Like Creon in the *Antigone*, Ajax believes that these categories endure even in death. The *Ajax* suggests, however, that the traditional absolute allegiance to friendship derives from a misconception, because the categories of "friend" and "enemy" prove unstable. Democratic politics can make a virtue of this instability, enabling us to recognize fellow citizens as friends and even sometimes to compromise or make common cause with former enemies. At the same time, the *Ajax* emphasizes that, since a majority vote can produce a manifest injustice, the moral flexibility and compromise necessary to group decision-making can and must incorporate some absolute respect for objective standards of justice and compassion. (See especially Knox 1979, 125–60; Winnington-Ingram 1980, 128–36; and Anhalt 2017, 115–48).

28. See Andersen 2017.

29. See especially Aristotle's *Constitution of the Athenians*; Hignett 1952; and Kagan 1969. The *Oresteia* (458 BCE) and *Antigone* (c. 443 BCE) each appeared shortly after the ostracism of a current leader of the conservative political opposition. Ostracism was, in effect, an unpopularity contest. All eligible citizens could vote, and the man earning the most votes had to leave Athens for ten years. The ostracism of the conservative leader Cimon, son of Miltiades (461 BCE), permitted the implementation of more radical democratic institutional reforms. The ostracism of the conservative leader Thucydides (not the historian), son of Melesias (443 BCE), left this new, radically democratic government and its leader, Pericles, politically ascendant (Stockton 1990, 33–39). On ostracism, see Kagan 1961 and Forsdyke 2005).

30. Meier 1993, 198–203.

31. Ober discusses "majoritarian tyranny" (2017b, 14–22, 70, and 180).

32. By contrast, the *Prometheus Bound* presents Prometheus as the great benefactor of human beings because he gave men fire and, through it, all human science and technology. (The authorship and date of this play remain uncertain. See Griffith 1977 and 1984; Conacher 1980, 140–74; Saïd 1985; Flintoff 1986; Gantz 1993, 158 and n14, 199–200 and n3; Bassi 2010, 84 and nn41–45, including

additional bibliography; and Sommerstein 2010, 228–34).

33. Euben explains that *deinon* "indicates mastery and control, resourcefulness and daring, culture and civilization," but also "what is terrible and fearful, monstrous and evil, self-annihilating and powerless in the face of implacable fate" (1997, 172).

34. Whitman devalues the goal of reconciling the two sets of standards, identifying the concluding sentiment of the First Choral Ode merely with the viewpoint of the chorus, and dismissing it as "the little pietism at the end," arguing that "the chorus, in contrast to the heroic individual, ordinarily chooses safety. Its members have no moral position" (1951, 91). Burian, however, observes that the ode's conclusion identifies "the danger of making wrong choices" (2010, 279). Raaflaub explains that "the poet saw—and feared—man's potential for almost unlimited achievement as well as self-destruction" (2016, 128). See also Cairns 2016, 31–32, 59–66.

35. Ober identifies criticism and change as essential features of democratic government, explaining that "the claim that revisability is among democracy's attractions and strengths suggests that it is actually in the self-interest of a democracy (unlike brittle, nonrevisable authoritarian regimes) to defend and even to seek to enlarge space for criticism" (1994, 150). Ober not only finds a "symbiosis between democracy and criticism" (151), but also maintains that "criticism is a precondition of revision" (170), suggesting that the critic can help "to guarantee the potential revisability of the democratic regime through the performative act of constructing an alternative political paradigm" (170). See also Ober 1996.

Works Cited

GREEK TEXTS AND COMMENTARIES

Allen, T. W. 1908. *Homeri Opera*. Vols. 3 and 4. Oxford: Oxford University Press.

Denniston, J. D., and D. Page. 1957. *Aeschylus: Agamemnon*. Oxford: Oxford University Press.

Leaf, W., ed. 1886. *The Iliad*. 2 vols. London: Macmillan.

Monro, D. B., and T. W. Allen. 1902. *Homeri Opera*. Vols. 1 and 2. Oxford: Oxford University Press.

Page, D. L. 1972. *Aeschyli Septem Quae Supersunt Tragoedias*. Oxford: Oxford University Press.

Pearson, A. C. 1924. *Sophoclis Fabulae*. Oxford: Oxford University Press.

SECONDARY SOURCES

Adkins, A. W. H. 1960. *Merit and Responsibility: A Study in Greek Values*. Oxford: Clarendon.

———. 1971. "Homeric Values and Homeric Society." *Journal of Hellenic Studies* 91:1–14.

———. 1987. "Gagarin and the 'Morality' of Homer." *Classical Philology* 82:311–22.

Adler, E. 2016. *Classics, the Culture Wars, and Beyond*. Ann Arbor: University of Michigan Press.

Ahrensdorf, P. J. 2014. *Homer on the Gods and Human Virtue: Creating the Foundations of Classical Civilization*. Cambridge and New York: Cambridge University Press.

Alaux, J. 2011. "Acting Myth: Athenian Drama." In *A Companion to Greek Mythology*, edited by K. Dowden and N. Livingstone, 141–56. Malden, MA: Wiley-Blackwell.

Albright, M. 2918. *Fascism: A Warning*. With Bill Woodward. New York: HarperCollins.

Alden, M. J. 2005. "Lions in Paradise: Lion Similes in the *Iliad* and the Lion Cubs of *Il.* 18.318–22." *Classical Quarterly* 55, no. 2: 335–42.

———. 2017. *Para-Narratives in the Odyssey: Stories in the Frame.* Oxford: Oxford University Press.

Amory, A. 1963. "The Reunion of Odysseus and Penelope." In *Essays on the Odyssey*, edited by C. H. Taylor, 100–121. Bloomington: University of Indiana Press.

Andersen, K. 2017. *Fantasyland: How America Went Haywire: A 500-Year History.* New York: Random House.

Andreyev, Y. 1991. "Greece of the Eleventh to Ninth Centuries BC in the Homeric Epics." In *Early Antiquity*, edited by I. M. Diakanoff, translated by A Kirjanov, 328–48. Chicago: University of Chicago Press.

Anhalt, E. K. 2002. "A Matter of Perspective: Penelope and the Nightingale in *Odyssey* 19.512–534." *Classical Journal* 97, no. 2: 145–59.

———. 2017. *Enraged: Why Violent Times Need Ancient Greek Myths.* New Haven: Yale University Press.

Arnason, J. P., and P. Murphy, eds. 2001. *Agon, Logos, Polis: The Greek Achievement and Its Aftermath.* Stuttgart: Franz Steiner Verlag.

Arnason, J. P., K. A. Raaflaub, and P. Wagner, eds. 2013. *The Greek Polis and the Invention of Democracy: A Politico-Cultural Transformation and Its Interpretations.* Malden, MA: Wiley-Blackwell.

Austin, N. 1972. "Name Magic in the *Odyssey*." *California Studies in Classical Antiquity* 5:1–19.

———. 1975. *Archery at the Dark of the Moon: Poetic Problems in Homer's Odyssey.* Berkeley: University of California Press.

———. 1987. "Homeric Icons." In *Approaches to Teaching Homer's Iliad and Odyssey*, edited by K. Myrsiades. New York: Modern Language Association of America, 63–70. Portions copyright 1983 by Washington and Lee University, reprinted from *Shenandoah: The Washington and Lee University Review.*

———. 2011. "Homer Who?" *Arion* 19, no. 2: 121–53.

Barker, E. T. E. 2009. *Entering the Agon: Dissent and Authority in Homer, Historiography, and Tragedy.* Oxford: Oxford University Press.

Bassi, K. 2010. "Making Prometheus Speak: Dialogue, Torture, and the Power of Secrets in *Prometheus Bound*." In *When Worlds Elide: Classics, Politics, Culture*, edited by K. Bassi and J. P. Euben, 77–109. Lanham, MD: Rowman and Littlefield.

Beard, M. 2017. *Women & Power: A Manifesto.* New York: Liveright / W. W. Norton.

Beck, D. 2005. *Homeric Conversation*. Hellenic Studies Series 14. Washington: Center for Hellenic Studies, Harvard University Press.

Bergren, A. 2008. *Weaving Truth: Essays on Language and the Female in Greek Thought*. Hellenic Studies Series 19. Washington: Center for Hellenic Studies.

Blok, J. 2017. *Citizenship in Classical Athens*. Cambridge and New York: Cambridge University Press.

Bloxham, J. 2018. *Ancient Greece and American Conservatism: Classical Influence on the Modern Right*. London and New York: I. B. Tauris, 2018.

Blundell, M. W. 1989. *Helping Friends and Harming Enemies: A Study in Sophocles and Greek Ethics*. Cambridge: Cambridge University Press.

Blundell, S. 1995. *Women in Ancient Greece*. Cambridge, MA: Harvard University Press.

Boedeker, D., and K. A. Raaflaub. 2005. "Tragedy and City." In *A Companion to Tragedy*, edited by R. Bushnell, 109–27. Oxford, UK, and Malden, MA: Wiley-Blackwell.

Boegehold, A. L., and A. C. Scafuro, eds. 1994. *Athenian Identity and Civic Ideology*. Baltimore: Johns Hopkins University Press.

Brendese, P. J. 2010. "For Love of the Impossible: *Antigone*, Memory, and the Politics of Possibility." In *When Worlds Elide: Classics, Politics, Culture*, edited by K. Bassi and J. P. Euben, 111–35. Lanham, MD: Rowman and Littlefield.

Burian, P. 1997. "Myth into *Muthos*: The Shaping of Tragic Plot." In *The Cambridge Companion to Greek Tragedy*, edited by P. E. Easterling, 178–208. Cambridge: Cambridge University Press.

———. 2010. "Gender and the City: Antigone from Hegel to Butler and Back." In *When Worlds Elide: Classics, Politics, Culture*, edited by K. Bassi and J. P. Euben, 255–99. Lanham, MD: Rowman and Littlefield.

———. 2011. "Athenian Tragedy as Democratic Discourse." In *Why Athens? A Reappraisal of Tragic Politics* edited by D. M. Carter, 95–119. Oxford: Oxford University Press.

Burkert, W. 1985. *Greek Religion*. Translated by J. Raffan. Cambridge, MA: Harvard University Press.

Butler, J. 2000. *Antigone's Claim: Kinship between Life and Death*. New York: Columbia University Press.

Cairns, D. L. 2005. "Values." In *A Companion to Greek Tragedy*, edited by J. Gregory, 305–20. Malden, MA: Wiley-Blackwell.

———. 2016. *Sophocles: Antigone*. Bloomsbury Companions to Greek and Roman Tragedy. London and New York: Bloomsbury Academic.

———. 2018. "Homeric Values and the Virtues of Kingship." In *The Homeric Ep-

ics and the Chinese Book of Songs: Foundational Texts Compared, edited by F.-H. Mutschler, 381–409. Newcastle, UK: Cambridge Scholars Publishing.

Cairns, D. L., ed. 2001. *Oxford Readings in Homer's Iliad*. Oxford and New York: Oxford University Press.

———. 2013. *Tragedy and Archaic Greek Thought*. Swansea: Classical Press of Wales.

Calame, C. 1996. *Mythe et histoire dans l'antiquité grecque: La création symbolique d'une colonie*. Lausanne, Switzerland: Editions Payot.

Canevaro, L. G. 2018. *Women of Substance in Homeric Epic: Objects, Gender, Agency*. Oxford and New York: Oxford University Press.

Carter, D. M. 2007. *The Politics of Greek Tragedy*. Exeter, UK: Liverpool University Press.

Cartledge, P. 1997. "'Deep Plays': Theatre as Process in Greek Civic Life." In *The Cambridge Companion to Greek Tragedy*, edited by P. E. Easterling, 3–35. Cambridge: Cambridge University Press.

———. 2016. *Democracy: A Life*. Oxford and New York: Oxford University Press.

Chua, A. 2003. *World on Fire: How Exporting Free Market Democracy Breeds Ethnic Hatred and Global Instability*. New York: Random House.

Christensen, J. P. 2018. "*Eris* and *Epos*: Competition, Composition, and the Domestication of Strife." In *Yearbook of Ancient Greek Epic*, edited by J. L. Ready, 1–39. Leiden and Boston: Brill.

Clay, J. S. 1983. *The Wrath of Athena: Gods and Men in the Odyssey*. Princeton, NJ: Princeton University Press.

———. 1989. *The Politics of Olympus*. Princeton, NJ: Princeton University Press.

Clayton, B. 2004. *A Penelopean Poetics: Reweaving the Feminine in Homer's Odyssey*. Lanham, MD: Lexington Books.

Cohen, B., ed. 1995. *The Distaff Side: Representing the Female in Homer's Odyssey*. Oxford and New York: Oxford University Press.

Conacher, D. J. 1980. *Aeschylus' Prometheus Bound: A Literary Commentary*. Toronto: University of Toronto Press.

Cook, E. F. 1995. *The "Odyssey" in Athens: Myths of Cultural Origins*. Myth and Poetics. Ithaca, NY: Cornell University Press.

———. 2003. "Agamemnon's Test of the Army in *Iliad* Book 2 and the Function of Homeric *Akhos*." *American Journal of Philology* 124:165–98.

Csapo, E. 2005. *Theories of Mythology*. Malden, MA: Wiley-Blackwell.

Csapo, E. and W. Slater. 1994. *The Context of Ancient Drama*. Ann Arbor: University of Michigan Press.

Davies, J. K. 1993. *Democracy and Classical Greece*. 2nd Edition. Cambridge, MA: Harvard University Press.

D'Aulaire, I., and E. P. D'Aulaire. 1962. *D'Aulaires' Book of Greek Myths*. New York: Doubleday.

Denys, P. 1973. *Folktales in Homer's Odyssey*. Cambridge, MA: Harvard University Press.

Dimock, G., Jr.. 1963. "The Name of Odysseus." In *Essays on the Odyssey*, edited by C. H. Taylor, 54–73. Bloomington: University of Indiana Press. Originally published in *Hudson Review* 9 (1956): 52–70.]

———. 1989. *The Unity of the Odyssey*. Amherst: University of Massachusetts Press.

Detienne, M. and J.-P. Vernant. 1978. *Cunning Intelligence in Greek Culture and Society*, translated by J. Lloyd. Atlantic Highlands, NJ: Humanities Press.

Dickinson, O. 2006. *The Aegean from Bronze Age to Iron Age: Continuity and Change between the Twelfth and Eighth Centuries BC*. London: Routledge.

Dmitriev, Sviatoslav. 2018. *The Birth of the Athenian Community: From Solon to Cleisthenes*. Abingdon, UK, and New York: Routledge.

Dodds, E. R. 1951. *The Greeks and the Irrational*. Berkeley: University of California Press.

Doherty, L. E. 1995. "Sirens, Muses, and Female Narrators in the *Odyssey*." In *The Distaff Side: Representing the Female in Homer's Odyssey*, edited by B. Cohen, 81–92. Oxford and New York: Oxford University Press.

Donlan, W. 1979. "The Structure of Authority in the *Iliad*." *Arethusa* 12:51–70.

———.1985. "The Social Groups of Dark Age Greece." *Classical Philology* 80:293–308.

———.1993. "Dueling with Gifts in the *Iliad*: As the Audience Saw It," *Colby Quarterly* 29, no. 3: 155–72.

———. 1999. *The Aristocratic Ideal and Selected Papers*. Wauconda, IL: Bolchazy-Carducci.

Dowden, K., and N. Livingstone. 2011. "Thinking through Myth, Thinking Myth Through." In *A Companion to Greek Mythology*, edited by K. Dowden and N. Livingstone, 3–23. Malden, MA: Wiley-Blackwell.

DuBois, P. 2001. *Trojan Horses: Saving the Classics from Conservatives*. New York: New York University Press.

———. 2010. *Out of Athens: The New Ancient Greeks*. Cambridge, MA: Harvard University Press.

Dué, C., and Ebbott, M. 2010. *Iliad 10 and the Poetics of Ambush*. Hellenic Studies Series 39. Washington: Center for Hellenic Studies, Harvard University Press.

Dunn, J. 1979. *Western Political Theory in the Face of the Future*. Cambridge: Cambridge University Press.

———. 1992. *Democracy: The Unfinished Journey, 508 BCE to AD 1993*. Oxford: Oxford University Press.

———. 2005a. *Setting the People Free: The Story of Democracy*. London: Atlantic Books.

———. 2005b. *Democracy: A History*. New York: Atlantic Monthly Press.

Easterling, P. E. 1991. "Men's *Kléos* and Women's *Góos*: Female Voices in the *Iliad*." *Journal of Modern Greek Studies* 9, no. 2: 145–51.

Easterling, P. E., ed. 1997. *The Cambridge Companion to Greek Tragedy*. Cambridge: Cambridge University Press.

Edmunds, L. 1989. "Commentary on Raaflaub." In *Proceedings of the Boston Area Colloquium in Ancient Philosophy*, vol. 4, edited by J. Cleary and D. Shartin. New York: University Press of America.

———. 2016. *Stealing Helen: The Myth of the Abducted Wife in Comparative Perspective*. Princeton: Princeton University Press.

Edmunds, L., ed. 2014. *Approaches to Greek Myth*. 2nd edition. Baltimore: Johns Hopkins University Press.

Edwards, M. W. 1987. *Homer, Poet of the Iliad*. Baltimore: Johns Hopkins University Press.

Euben, J. P. 1990. *The Tragedy of Political Theory: The Road Not Taken*. Princeton, NJ: Princeton University Press.

———. 1997. *Corrupting Youth: Political Education, Democratic Culture, and Political Theory*. Princeton, NJ: Princeton University Press.

Euben, J. P., J. Wallach, and J. Ober, eds. 1994. *Athenian Political Thought and the Reconstruction of American Democracy*. Ithaca, NY: Cornell University Press.

Fabre-Serris, J. and A. Keith, eds. 2015. *Women and War in Antiquity*. Baltimore: Johns Hopkins University Press.

Fagles, R. 1975. "The Serpent and the Eagle." In Aeschylus, *The Oresteia*, translated by R. Fagles, 13–98. New York: Viking Press. Reprint of 1966 original.

Fantham, E., H. P. Foley, N. B. Kampen, S. B. Pomeroy, and H. A. Shapiro, eds. 1994. *Women in the Classical World*. New York: Oxford University Press.

Felson, N. 1994. *Regarding Penelope: From Character to Poetics*. Norman: University of Oklahoma Press.

Felson, N., and L. M. Slatkin. 2004. "Gender and Homeric Epic." In *The Cambridge Companion to Homer*, edited by R. Fowler, 91–114. Cambridge: Cambridge University Press.

Felson-Rubin, N. 1987. "Penelope's Perspective: Character from Plot." In *Homer: Beyond Oral Poetry: Recent Trends in Homeric Interpretation*, edited by J. M. Bremer, I. J. F. de Jong, and J. Kalff, 61–83. Amsterdam: B. R. Grüner.

Finkelberg, M. 1998. "*Timē* and *Aretē* in Homer." *Classical Quarterly* 48:14–28.

———. 2018. "The Formation of the Homeric Epics." In *The Homeric Epics and the Chinese Book of Songs: Foundational Texts Compared*, edited by F.-H. Mutschler, 15–38. Newcastle, UK: Cambridge Scholars Publishing.

Finley, J. H., Jr. 1967. "Politics and Early Attic Tragedy." *Harvard Studies in Classical Philology* 71:1–13.

Finley, M. I. 1954 (2nd ed. 1979). *The World of Odysseus*. New York: Viking.

———. 1965. "Myth, Memory, and History." *History and Theory* 4:281–302.

———, ed. 1968. *Slavery in Classical Antiquity: Views and Controversies*, 2nd ed. Cambridge: W. Heffer and Sons.

———. 1973 (2nd ed. 1985). *Democracy Ancient and Modern*. New Brunswick, NJ: Rutgers University Press.

———. 1980. *Ancient Slavery and Modern Ideology*. New York: Viking Press.

———. 1987. *Classical Slavery*. London: Routledge.

Finnegan, R. 1977. *Oral Poetry: Its Nature, Significance, and Social Context*. Cambridge: Cambridge University Press.

Fisher, N. R. E. 1992. *Hybris: A Study in the Values of Honour and Shame in Ancient Greece*. Warminster, UK: Aris and Phillips.

Flintoff, E. 1986. "The Date of the *Prometheus Bound*." *Mnemosyne* 39:82–91.

Foley, H. P. 1978. "'Reverse Similes' and Sex Roles in the Odyssey." *Arethusa* 11:7–26.

———. 1981a. "The Conception of Women in Athenian Drama." In *Reflections of Women in Antiquity*, edited by H. P. Foley, 127–68. New York: Gordon and Breach.

———. 1995. "Penelope as Moral Agent." In *The Distaff Side: Representing the Female in Homer's Odyssey*, edited by B. Cohen, 93–115. Oxford and New York: Oxford University Press.

———. 1996. "Antigone as Moral Agent." In *Tragedy and the Tragic: Greek Theater and Beyond*, edited by M. S. Silk, 49–73. Oxford: Clarendon Press.

———. 2001. *Female Acts in Greek Tragedy*. Princeton, NJ: Princeton University Press.

———. 2005. "Women in Ancient Epic," in *A Companion to Ancient Epic*, edited by J. M. Foley, 105–18. Malden, MA: Blackwell.

Foley, H. P., ed. 1981b. *Reflections of Women in Antiquity*. New York: Gordon and Breach.

Ford, A. 1992. *Homer: The Poetry of the Past*. Ithaca, NY, and New York: Cornell University Press.

Forrest, W. G. 1966. *The Emergence of Greek Democracy, 800–400 BC*. New York: McGraw-Hill.

Forsdyke, S. 2005. *Exile, Ostracism, and Democracy: The Politics of Expulsion in Ancient Greece*. Princeton, NJ: Princeton University Press.

Foster, E. 2010. *Thucydides, Pericles, and Periclean Imperialism*. Cambridge: Cambridge University Press.

Fowler, R. 2004. "The Homeric Question." In *The Cambridge Companion to Homer*, edited by R. Fowler, 220–32. Cambridge: Cambridge University Press.

Friedrich, R. 2019. *Postoral Homer: Orality and Literacy in the Homer Epic*. Hermes Einzelschriften, Band 112. Stuttgart: Franz Steiner Verlag.

Gagarin, M. 1987. "Morality in Homer." *Classical Philology* 82:285–306.

Gantz, T. 1993. *Early Greek Myth: A Guide to Literary and Artistic Sources*. 2 vols. Baltimore and London: Johns Hopkins University Press.

Garlan, Y. 1988. *Slavery in Ancient Greece*. Translated by J. Lloyd. Ithaca, NY: Cornell University Press.

Garner, R. 1990. *From Homer to Tragedy: The Art of Allusion in Greek Poetry*. London: Routledge.

Garvie, A. F. 2010. *The Plays of Aeschylus*. London: Bristol Classical Press.

———. 2016. *The Plays of Sophocles*, 2nd ed. Originally published 2005. London and New York: Bloomsbury Academic.

Gaskin, R. 1990. "Do Homeric Heroes Make Real Decisions?" *Classical Quarterly* 40:1–15.

Gazis, G. A. 2018. *Homer and the Poetics of Hades*. Oxford and New York: Oxford University Press.

Gill, C. 1996. *Personality in Greek Epic, Tragedy, and Philosophy: The Self in Dialogue*. Oxford: Clarendon.

Goheen, R. F. 1972. "Aspects of Dramatic Symbolism: Three Studies in the *Oresteia*." In *Aeschylus: A Collection of Critical Essays*, edited by M. H. McCall, Jr., 106–23. Englewood Cliffs, NJ: Prentice-Hall.

Goldhill, S. 1986. *Reading Greek Tragedy*. Cambridge: Cambridge University Press.

———. 1990. "The Great Dionysia and Civic Ideology." In *Nothing to Do with Dionysos? Athenian Drama in Its Social Context*, edited by J. J. Winkler and F. I. Zeitlin, 97–129. Princeton, NJ: Princeton University Press. Originally published in *Journal of Hellenic Studies* 107 (1987): 58–76.

———. 2000. "Civic Ideology and the Problem of Difference: The Politics of Aeschylean Tragedy, Once Again." *Journal of Hellenic Studies* 120:34–56.

———. 2004. *Love, Sex & Tragedy: How the Ancient World Shapes Our Lives*. Chicago: University of Chicago Press.

———. 2009. "The Audience on Stage: Rhetoric, Emotion, and Judgment in

Sophoclean Theater." In *Sophocles and the Greek Tragic Tradition*, edited by S. Goldhill and E. Hall, 27–47. Cambridge: Cambridge University Press.

———. 2012. *Sophocles and the Language of Tragedy*. Oxford: Oxford University Press.

Goldhill, S., and E. Hall, eds. 2009. *Sophocles and the Greek Tragic Tradition*. Cambridge: Cambridge University Press.

Gonzalez, J. M. 2013. *The Epic Rhapsode and His Craft: Homeric Performance in a Diachronic Perspective*. Washington: Center for Hellenic Studies.

Gotteland, S. 2001. *Mythe et rhétorique: Les examples mythiques dans le discours politique de l' Athènes classique*. Paris: Les Belles lettres.

Goward, B. 2005. *Aeschylus: Agamemnon*. London: Gerald Duckworth.

Graf, F. 1993. *Greek Mythology: An Introduction*. Translated by T. Marier. Baltimore: Johns Hopkins University Press.

———. 2011. "Myth and Hellenic Identities." In *A Companion to Greek Mythology*, edited by K. Dowden and N. Livingstone, 211–26. Malden, MA: Wiley-Blackwell.

Graham, A. J. 1995. "The *Odyssey*, History, and Women." In *The Distaff Side: Representing the Female in Homer's Odyssey*, edited by B. Cohen, 3–16. Oxford and New York: Oxford University Press.

Graziosi, B. 2016. *Homer*. Oxford: Oxford University Press.

Gregory, J. 2012. "Sophocles and Education" In *Brill's Companion to Sophocles*, edited by A. Markantonatos, 515–35. Leiden: Brill.

Grethlein, J. 2010. *The Greeks and Their Past: Poetry, Oratory and History in the Fifth Century* BCE. Cambridge: Cambridge University Press.

Grey, S. F. 2019. "The Afterlife in Homer's *Odyssey*." In *Imagining the Afterlife in the Ancient World*, edited by J. Harrison, 101–16. London and New York: Routledge.

Griffin, J. 1980. *Homer on Life and Death*. Oxford: Clarendon.

Griffith, M. 1977. *The Authenticity of Prometheus Bound*. Cambridge: Cambridge University Press.

———. 1984 "The Vocabulary of *Prometheus Bound*." *Classical Quarterly* 34:282–91.

———. 1995. "Brilliant Dynasts: Power and Politics in the *Oresteia*." *Classical Antiquity* 14:62–129.

Guthrie, W. K. C. 1950. *The Greeks and Their Gods*. Boston: Beacon Press.

Hale, M. R. 2017. "Regenerating the World: the French Revolution, Civic Festivals, and the Forging of Modern American Democracy, 1793-1795." *Journal of American History* 103:891–920.

Hall, E. 1989. *Inventing the Barbarian: Greek Self-Definition through Tragedy.* Oxford: Clarendon.

———. 2010. *Greek Tragedy: Suffering under the Sun.* Oxford: Oxford University Press.

Hall, J. M. 2007. *A History of the Archaic Greek World, ca. 1200–479* BCE. Malden, MA: Blackwell.

Haller, B. S. 2013. "Dolios in *Odyssey* 4 and 24: Penelope's Plotting and Alternative Narratives of Odysseus' *Nostos.*" *Transactions of the American Philological Association* 143:263–92.

Halliwell, S. 2011. *Between Ecstasy and Truth: Interpretations of Greek Poetics from Homer to Longinus.* Oxford: Oxford University Press.

Hammer, D. C. 1998. "The Cultural Construction of Chance in the *Iliad.*" *Arethusa* 31, no. 2: 125–48.

———. 2002. *The Iliad as Politics: The Performance of Political Thought.* Norman: University of Oklahoma Press.

Hammond, N. G. L. 1972. "Personal Freedom and Its Limitations in the *Oresteia.*" In *Aeschylus: A Collection of Critical Essays,* edited by M. H. McCall, Jr., 90–105. Englewood Cliffs, NJ: Prentice-Hall.

Hanink, J. 2017. *The Classical Debt: Greek Antiquity in an Era of Austerity.* Cambridge, MA: Harvard University Press.

Hansen, M. H. 1991. *The Athenian Democracy in the Age of Demosthenes.* Oxford: Blackwell.

———. 1992. "The Tradition of the Athenian Democracy, A.D. 1750–1990." *Greece & Rome* 39:14–30.

———. 1996. "The Ancient Athenian and the Modern Liberal View of Liberty as a Democratic Ideal." In *Demokratia: A Conversation on Democracies, Ancient and Modern,* edited by J. Ober and C. W. Hedrick, Jr., 91–104. Princeton, NJ: Princeton University Press.

Hansen, W. 2002. *Ariadne's Thread: A Guide to International Stories in Classical Literature.* Ithaca, NY: Cornell University Press.

———. 2014. "Odysseus and the Oar: a Comparative Approach to a Greek Legend." In *Approaches to Greek Myth,* edited by L. Edmunds, 245–79. Baltimore: Johns Hopkins University Press.

Hanson, V. D. 2001. "Democratic Warfare, Ancient and Modern." In *War and Democracy: A Comparative Study of the Korean War and the Peloponnesian War,* edited by D. McCann and B. S. Strauss, 3–33. Armonk, NY: M. E. Sharpe.

Hanson, V. D., and J. Heath. 1998. *Who Killed Homer? The Demise of Classical Education and the Recovery of Greek Wisdom.* New York: Free Press.

Hanson, V. D., J. Heath, and B. S. Thornton. 2000. *Bonfire of the Humanities:*

Rescuing the Classics in an Impoverished Age. Wilmington, DE: Intercollegiate Studies Institute.

Harsh, P. 1950. "Penelope and Odysseus in *Od.* 19." *American Journal of Philology* 71:1–21.

Havelock, E. A. 1978. *The Greek Concept of Justice from Its Shadow in Homer to Its Substance in Plato.* Cambridge, MA: Harvard University Press.

Herington, C. J. 1985. *Poetry into Drama: Early Tragedy and the Greek Poetic Tradition.* Berkeley: University of California Press.

———. 1986. *Aeschylus.* New Haven and London: Yale University Press.

Herren, M. 2017. *The Anatomy of Myth: The Art of Interpretation from the Presocratics to the Church Fathers.* Oxford: Oxford University Press.

Hertel, D. 2011 "The Myth of History: The Case of Troy." In *A Companion to Greek Mythology,* edited by K. Dowden and N. Livingstone, 425–41. Malden, MA: Wiley-Blackwell.

Hesk, J. 2000. *Deception and Democracy in Classical Athens.* Cambridge: Cambridge University Press.

Hignett, C. 1952. *A History of the Athenian Constitution to the End of the Fifth Century B.C.* Oxford: Oxford University Press.

Hunt, P. 2018. "Ancient Greece as a Slave Society." In *What Is a Slave Society? The Practice of Slavery in Global Perspective,* edited by N. Lenski and C. M. Cameron, 61–85. Cambridge and New York: Cambridge University Press.

Irigaray, L. 1985. *Speculum of the Other Woman.* Translated by G. Gill. Ithaca, NY: Cornell University Press.

Jones, A. H. M. 1986. *Athenian Democracy.* Baltimore: Johns Hopkins University Press. Originally published 1957.

Jong, I. J. F. de. 2006. "The Homeric Narrator and His Own *kleos.*" *Mnemosyne* 59:188–207.

———. 2016. "Homer: The First Tragedian." *Greece & Rome* 63, no. 2: 149–62.

Just, R. 1989. *Women in Athenian Law and Life.* London and New York: Routledge.

Kagan, D. 1961. "The Origins and Purposes of Ostracism." *Hesperia* 30:393–401.

———. 1969. *The Outbreak of the Peloponnesian War.* Ithaca, NY: Cornell University Press.

———. 1974. *The Archidamian War.* Ithaca, NY: Cornell University Press.

———. 1981. *The Peace of Nicias and the Sicilian Expedition.* Ithaca, NY: Cornell University Press.

———. 1987. *The Fall of the Athenian Empire.* Ithaca, NY: Cornell University Press.

———. 1991. *Pericles of Athens and the Birth of Democracy.* New York: Free Press.

Kahneman, D. 2011. *Thinking Fast and Slow*. New York: Farrar, Straus, and Giroux.

Kane, R. L. 1996. "Ajax and the Sword of Hector: Sophocles' *Ajax* 815–822." *Hermes* 124:17–28.

Kasimis, D. 2018. *The Perpetual Immigrant and the Limits of Athenian Democracy*. Cambridge and New York: Cambridge University Press.

Katz, M. A. 1981. "The Divided World of *Iliad* VI." In *Reflections of Women in Antiquity*, edited by H. P. Foley, 19–44. New York: Gordon and Breach.

———. 1991. *Penelope's Renown: Meaning and Indeterminacy in the Odyssey*. Princeton, NJ: Princeton University Press.

———. 1999. "Women and Democracy in Ancient Greece." In *Contextualizing Classics: Ideology, Performance, Dialogue*, edited by T. M. Falkner, N. Felson, and D. Konstan, 41–68. Lanham, MD: Rowman and Littlefield.

Kearns, E. 2004. "The Gods in the Homeric Epics." In *The Cambridge Companion to Homer*, edited by R Fowler, 59–73. Cambridge: Cambridge University Press.

Kirk, G. S. 1962. *The Songs of Homer*. Cambridge: Cambridge University Press.

———. 1976. *Homer and the Oral Tradition*. Cambridge: Cambridge University Press.

Knox, B. 1957. *Oedipus at Thebes*. New Haven: Yale University Press.

———. 1979. *Word and Action: Essays on the Ancient Theater*. Baltimore: Johns Hopkins University Press.

Knox, R., and J. Russo. 1989. "Agamemnon's Test: *Iliad* 2.73–75." *Classical Antiquity* 8:351–58.

Konstan, D., and K. A. Raaflaub, eds. 2009. *Epic and History*. Malden, MA: Wiley-Blackwell.

Kozak, L. A. 2014a. "Oaths between Warriors in Epic and Tragedy." In *Oaths and Swearing in Ancient Greece*, edited by A. H. Sommerstein and I. C. Torrance, 60–66. Berlin: Walter de Gruyter.

———. 2014b. "Oaths and Characterization: Two Homeric Case Studies." In *Oaths and Swearing in Ancient Greece*, edited by A. H. Sommerstein and I. C. Torrance, 213–29. Berlin: Walter de Gruyter.

Kurke, L. 1998. "The Cultural Impact of (on) Democracy: Decentering Tragedy." In *Democracy 2500? Questions and Challenges*, edited by I. Morris and K. A. Raaflaub, 155–69. Dubuque, IA: Kendall-Hunt.

Lattimore, R. 1972. "Introduction to the *Oresteia*." In *Aeschylus: A Collection of Critical Essays*, edited by M. H. McCall, Jr., 73–89. Englewood Cliffs, NJ: Prentice-Hall.

Lebeck, A. 1971. *The Oresteia: A Study in Language and Structure*. Washington: Center for Hellenic Studies.

Lefkowitz, M. R. 1986. *Women in Greek Myth*. Baltimore: Johns Hopkins University Press.

———. 2012. *The Lives of the Greek Poets*. 2nd ed. Baltimore: Johns Hopkins University Press.

Lesky, A. 2001. "Divine and Human Causation in Homeric Epic." Reprinted in *Oxford Readings in Homer's Iliad*, edited by D. L. Cairns, 170–202. Oxford: Oxford University Press. Abridged, translated version of 1961 original.

Levitsky, S., and D. Ziblatt. 2018. *How Democracies Die*. New York: Penguin Random House LLC.

Lewis, S. 2009. *Greek Tyranny*. Liverpool, UK: Liverpool University Press.

Liapis, V. 2013. "Creon the Labdacid: Political Confrontation and the Doomed *Oikos* in Sophocles' *Antigone*." In *Tragedy and Archaic Greek Thought*, edited by D. L. Cairns, 81–18. Swansea: Classical Press of Wales.

Livingstone, N. 2011. "Instructing Myth: From Homer to the Sophists." In *A Companion to Greek Mythology*, edited by K. Dowden and N. Livingstone, 125–139. Malden, MA: Wiley-Blackwell.

Lloyd-Jones, H. 1962. "The Guilt of Agamemnon." *Classical Quarterly* 12:187–99.

———. 1983. *The Justice of Zeus*. 2nd edition. Berkeley: University of California Press.

Long, A. A. 1970. "Morals and Values in Homer." *Journal of Hellenic Studies* 90:121–39.

Lord, A. B. 1960. *The Singer of Tales*. Cambridge: Harvard University Press.

———. 1991. *Epic Singers and Oral Tradition*. Ithaca, NY: Cornell University Press.

———. 1995. *The Singer Resumes the Tale*, edited by M. L. Lord. Ithaca, NY: Cornell University Press.

Luraghi, N. 2015. "Anatomy of the Monster: the Discourse of Tyranny in Ancient Greece." In *Antimonarchic Discourse in Antiquity*, edited by H. Börm, 66–84. Stuttgart: Franz Steiner Verlag.

———. 2018. "The Discourse of Tyranny and the Greek Roots of the Bad King." In *Evil Lords: Theories and Representations of Tyranny from Antiquity to the Renaissance*, edited by N. Panou and H. Schadee, 11–26. Oxford and New York: Oxford University Press.

Macleod, C. W. 1982. "Politics and the *Oresteia*." *Journal of Hellenic Studies* 102:124–44.

Markell, P. 2003. *Bound by Recognition*. Princeton, NJ: Princeton University Press.

Marks, J. 2003. "Alternative Odysseys: The Case of Thoas and Odysseus." *Transactions of the American Philological Association* 133:209–26.

Marshall, C. W. 2017. *Aeschylus: Libation Bearers*. London and New York: Bloomsbury Academic.

Martin, R. P. 1989. *The Language of Heroes: Speech and Performance in the Iliad.* Ithaca, NY: Cornell University Press.

———. 2016. *Classical Mythology: The Basics.* New York and London: Routledge.

Mastronarde, D. J. 2010. *The Art of Euripides: Dramatic Technique and Social Context.* Cambridge: Cambridge University Press.

McCall, M. H., Jr., ed. 1972. *Aeschylus: A Collection of Critical Essays.* Englewood Cliffs, NJ: Prentice-Hall.

McGlew, J. 1993. *Tyranny and Political Culture in Ancient Greece.* Ithaca, NY: Cornell University Press.

Meier, C. 1993. *The Political Art of Greek Tragedy.* Translated by A. Webber. Baltimore: Johns Hopkins University Press.

———. 2012. *A Culture of Freedom: Ancient Greece and the Origins of Europe.* Oxford: Oxford University Press.

Melton, B. L. 2013. "Appropriations of Cicero and Cato in the Making of American Civic Identity." In *Classics in the Modern World: A "Democratic Turn"?,* edited by L. Hardwick and S. Harrison, 79–88. Oxford: Oxford University Press.

Mill, J. S. 1859. *On Liberty.* Reprinted 1976. New York: Penguin Books.

Mitchell-Boyask, R. 2009. *Aeschylus: Eumenides.* London: Gerald Duckworth.

Morris, I. 1996. "The Strong Principle of Equality and the Archaic Origins of Greek Democracy." In *Demokratia: A Conversation on Democracies, Ancient and Modern,* edited by J. Ober and C. W. Hedrick, Jr., 19–48. Princeton, NJ: Princeton University Press.

Morrison, J. V. 1997. "*Kerostasia,* the Dictates of Fate, and the Will of Zeus in the *Iliad.*" *Arethusa* 30, no. 2: 276–96.

Most, G. 1989. "The Structure and Function of Odysseus' *Apologia.*" *Transactions of the American Philological Association* 119:15–30.

Muellner. L. 1996. *The Anger of Achilles: Mēnis in Greek Epic.* Ithaca, NY: Cornell University Press.

Murnaghan, S. 1986. "Penelope's *Agonoia*: Knowledge, Power, and Gender in the *Odyssey.*" *Helios* 13, no. 2: 103–16.

———. 1987. *Disguise and Recognition in the Odyssey.* Princeton, NJ: Princeton University Press.

———. 1995. "The Plan of Athena." In *The Distaff Side: Representing the Female in Homer's Odyssey,* edited by B. Cohen, 61–80. Oxford and New York: Oxford University Press.

———. 2018. "Penelope as Tragic Heroine: Choral Dynamics in Homeric Epic." In *Yearbook of Ancient Greek Epic,* edited by J. L. Ready, 165–89. Leiden and Boston: Brill.

Nagler, M. N. 1974. *Spontaneity and Tradition: A Study in the Oral Art of Homer*. Berkeley: University of California Press.

Nagy, G. 1979. *The Best of the Achaeans: Concepts of the Hero in Archaic Greek Poetry*. 2nd ed. Baltimore: Johns Hopkins University Press. Revised 1999.

———. 1990. *Pindar's Homer: The Lyric Possession of an Epic Past*. Baltimore: Johns Hopkins University Press.

———. 1992. "Homeric Questions." *Transactions of the American Philological Association* 122:17–60.

———.1996. *Homeric Questions*. Austin: University of Texas Press.

———. 2002. *Plato's Rhapsody and Homer's Music: The Poetcs of the Panathenaic Festival in Classical Athens*. Cambridge, MA, and Athens: Center for Hellenic Studies.

———. 2007. "Homer and Greek Myth." In *The Cambridge Companion to Greek Mythology*, edited by R. D. Woodard, 52–82. Cambridge: Cambridge University Press.

———. 2010. *Homer the Pre-Classic*. Berkeley and Los Angeles: University of California Press.

Nappi, M. 2015. "Women and War in the *Iliad*." In *Women and War in Antiquity*, edited by J. Fabre-Serris and A. Keith, 34–51. Baltimore: Johns Hopkins University Press.

Nussbaum, M. C. 1986. *The Fragility of Goodness: Luck and Ethics in Greek Tragedy and Philosophy*. Cambridge, MA: Cambridge University Press.

———1997. *Cultivating Humanity: A Classical Defense of Reform in Liberal Education*. Cambridge, MA: Harvard University Press.

———2010. *Not for Profit: Why Democracy Needs the Humanities*. Princeton, NJ: Princeton University Press.

Ober, J. 1989. *Mass and Elite in Democratic Athens: Rhetoric, Ideology, and the Power of the People*. Princeton, NJ: Princeton University Press.

———. 1994. "How to Criticize Democracy in Late Fifth- and Fourth-Century Athens." In *Athenian Political Thought and the Reconstruction of American Democracy*, edited by J. P. Euben, J. Wallach, and J. Ober, 149–171. Ithaca, NY: Cornell University Press.

———. 1996. *The Athenian Revolution: Essays on Ancient Greek Democracy and Political Theory*. Princeton, NJ: Princeton University Press.

———. 1998. "Revolution Matters: Democracy as Demotic Action (a Response to Kurt A. Raaflaub)." In *Democracy 2500? Questions and Challenges*, edited by I. Morris and K. A. Rauflaub, 67–86. Dubuque, IA: Kendall-Hunt.

———. 2003. "Conditions for Athenian Democracy." In *The Making and Unmaking of Democracy: Lessons from History and World Politics*, edited by T. K. Rabb and E. N. Suleman, 2–22. London: Routledge.

———. 2008. *Democracy and Knowledge: Innovation and Learning in Classical Athens*. Princeton, NJ: Princeton University Press.

———. 2015. *The Rise and Fall of Classical Greece*. Princeton, NJ: Princeton University Press.

———. 2017. "Mass and Elite Revisited." In *Mass and Elite in the Greek and Roman Worlds: From Sparta to Late Antiquity*, edited by R. Evans, 1–11. New York: Routledge.

———. 2017b. *Demopolis: Democracy before Liberalism in Theory and Practice (The Seeley Lectures)*. Cambridge: Cambridge University Press.

Ober, J., and C. W. Hedrick, Jr., eds. 1996. *Demokratia: A Conversation on Democracies, Ancient and Modern*. Princeton, NJ: Princeton University Press.

Olson, D. 1989. "The Stories of Helen and Menelaus (*Odyssey* 4.240–289) and the Return of Odysseus." *American Journal of Philology* 110, no. 3, 387–94.

———. 1990. "The Stories of Agamemnon in Homer's *Odyssey*." *Transactions of the American Philological Association* 120:57–71.

Osborne, R. 1996. *Greece in the Making 1200–479 BC*. New York: Routledge.

———. 2010. *Athens and Athenian Democracy*. Cambridge: Cambridge University Press.

Ostwald, M. 1986. *From Popular Sovereignty to the Sovereignty of Law: Law, Society, and Politics in Fifth-Century Athens*. Berkeley: University of California Press.

Page, D. L. 1959. *History and the Homeric Iliad*. Berkeley: University of California Press.

Panou, N. and H. Schadee, eds. 2018. *Evil Lords: Theories and Representations of Tyranny from Antiquity to the Renaissance*. Oxford and New York: Oxford University Press.

Parker, R. 2011. *On Greek Religion*. Ithaca, NJ: Cornell University Press.

Parry, M. 1971. *The Making of Homeric Verse: The Collected Papers of Millman Parry*. Edited by A. Parry. Oxford: Clarendon.

Peradotto, J. 1990. *Man in the Middle Voice: Name and Narrative in the Odyssey*. Princeton, NJ: Princeton University Press.

Pickard-Cambridge, A. 1953. *The Dramatic Festivals of Athens*. Oxford: Clarendon Press.

Podlecki, A. J. 1966. "Creon and Herodotus." *Transactions of the American Philological Association* 97:359–71.

———. 1986. "*Polis* and Monarch in Early Attic Tragedy." In *Greek Tragedy and Political Theory*, edited by J. P. Euben, 76–100. Berkeley: University of California Press.

Pomeroy, S. 1975. *Goddesses, Whores, Wives, and Slaves: Women in Classical Antiquity*. New York: Schocken.

Porter, A. 2019. *Agamemnon, the Pathetic Despot: Reading Characterization in Homer.* Cambridge, MA: Harvard University Press.

Pozzi, D. C., and J. M. Wickersham, eds. 1991. *Myth and the Polis.* Ithaca, NY: Cornell University Press.

Pucci, P. 1986. "Les Figures de la Mētis dans l'*Odyssée.*" *Metis* 1:7–28.

———. 1987. *Odysseus Polutropos: Intertextual Readings in the Odyssey and the Iliad.* Ithaca, NY, and New York: Cornell University Press.

———. 2002. "Theology and Poetics in the *Iliad.*" *Arethusa* 35, no. 1: 17–34.

Raaflaub, K. A. 1989. "Homer and the Beginning of Political Thought in Greece." *Proceedings of the Boston Area Colloquium Series in Ancient Philosophy* 4:1–25.

———. 1993. "Homer to Solon: The Rise of the *Polis:* The Written Sources." In *The Ancient Greek City State*, edited by M. H. Hansen, 41–105. Copenhagen: Royal Danish Academy of Sciences and Letters.

———. 1994. "Democracy, Power, and Imperialism in Fifth-Century Athens." In *Athenian Political Thought and the Reconstruction of American Democracy*, edited by J. P. Euben, J. Wallach, and J. Ober, 103–46. Ithaca, NY: Cornell University Press.

———. 1997. "Homeric Society." In *A New Companion to Homer*, edited by I. Morris and B. Powell, 624–48. Leiden: Brill.

———. 1998. "Power in the Hands of the People: Foundations of Athenian Democracy." In *Democracy 2500? Questions and Challenges*, edited by I. Morris and K. A. Rauflaub, 31–66. Dubuque, IA: Kendall-Hunt.

———. 2000: "Poets, Lawgivers, and the Beginning of Political Reflection in Archaic Greece," in *The Cambridge History of Greek and Roman Political Thought*, edited by C. Rowe and M. Schofield, 23–59. Cambridge: Cambridge University Press.

———. 2001. "Father of All, Destroyer of All: War in Late Fifth-Century Athenian Discourse and Ideology." In *War and Democracy: A Comparative Study of the Korean War and the Peloponnesian War*, edited by D. McCann and B. S. Strauss, 307–56. Armonk, NY: M. E. Sharpe.

———. 2003. "Stick and Glue: The Function of Tyranny in Fifth-Century Athenian Democracy." In *Popular Tyranny*, edited by K. A. Morgan, 59–93. Austin: University of Texas Press.

———. 2004. *The Discovery of Freedom in Ancient Greece.* Translated by R. Franciscono. Chicago: University of Chicago Press. First English edition, revised and updated from the German.

———. 2012. "Sophocles and Political Thought." In Brill's *Companion to Sophocles*, edited by A. Markantonatos, 471–88. Leiden, Netherlands: Brill.

———. 2015. "Ancient Greece: The Historical Needle's Eye of Modern Politics and Political Thought." *Classical World* 109:3–37.

————. 2016. "Ancient Greece: Man the Measure of All Things." In *The Adventures of the Human Intellect: Self, Society, and the Divine in Ancient World Cultures*, edited by K. A. Raaflaub, 127–148. Malden, MA: Wiley-Blackwell.

Raaflaub, K. A., J. Ober, et al., eds. 2007. *Origins of Democracy in Ancient Greece.* Berkeley: University of California Press.

Rabel, R. J. 1997. *Plot and Point of View in the Iliad.* Ann Arbor: University of Michigan Press.

Rabinowitz, N. S. 1992. "Tragedy and the Politics of Containment." In *Pornography and Representation in Greece and Rome*, edited by A. Richlin, 36–52. Oxford and New York: Oxford University Press.

————. 2008. *Greek Tragedy.* Malden, MA: Wiley-Blackwell.

Rahe, P. A. 1992. *Republics Ancient and Modern.* Chapel Hill: University of North Carolina Press, 1992.

Ready, J. L. 2011. *Character, Narrator, and Simile in the Iliad.* Cambridge: Cambridge University Press.

————. 2015. "The Textualization of Homeric Epic by Means of Dictation." *Transactions of the American Philological Association* 145:1–75.

Redfield, J. M. 1994. 2nd ed. *Nature and Culture in the Iliad: The Tragedy of Hector.* Durham, NC: Duke University Press. Originally published 1975.

Reece, S. 1993. *The Stranger's Welcome: Oral Theory and the Aesthetics of the Homeric Hospitality Scene.* Ann Arbor: University of Michigan Press.

Rehm, R. 2016. 2nd ed. *Understanding Greek Tragic Theatre.* Originally published 1992. London; New York: Routledge,

Reinhardt, K. 1996. "The Adventures in the *Odyssey*," translated by H. Flower, in *Reading the Odyssey: Selected Interpretive Essays*, edited by S. Schein. Princeton, NJ: Princeton University Press.

Rhodes, P. J. 2003. "Nothing to Do with Democracy: Athenian Drama and the *Polis*." *Journal of Hellenic Studies* 123:104–19.

————. 2004. *Athenian Democracy.* Oxford: Oxford University Press.

Richard, C. J. 1994. *The Founders and the Classics: Greece, Rome, and the American Enlightenment.* Cambridge: Harvard University Press.

————. 2009. *Greeks and Romans Bearing Gifts: How the Ancients Inspired the Founding Fathers.* Lanham, MD: Rowman and Littlefield.

Richardson, S. 2006. "The Devious Narrator of the *Odyssey*." *Classical Journal* 101:337–59.

Rinon, Y. 2008. "A Tragic Pattern in the *Iliad*." *Harvard Studies in Classical Philology* 104:45–91.

Robinson, E. W. 1997. *The First Democracies: Early Popular Government outside Athens.* Stuttgart: Franz Steiner Verlag.

Rood, N. 2008. "Craft Similes and the Construction of Heroes in the *Iliad*." *Harvard Studies in Classical Philology* 104:19–43.

Roselli, D. K. 2011. *Theater of the People: Spectators and Society in Ancient Athens*. Austin: University of Texas Press.

Rosenbloom, D. 1995. "Myth, History, and Hegemony in Aeschylus." In *History, Tragedy, Theory: Dialogues on Athenian Drama*, edited by B. Goff, 91–130. Austin: University of Texas Press.

Rosenmeyer, T. 1982. *The Art of Aeschylus*. Berkeley: University of California Press.

Rosivach, V. 2014. "Classical Athens: Predatory Democracy? Hidden Oligarchy? Neither? Both?" *New England Classical Journal* 41, no. 3: 168–94.

Russo, J. 1968. "Homer against His Tradition." *Arion* 7:275–95.

———. 1982. "Interview and Aftermath: Dream, Fantasy, and Intuition in *Odyssey* 19 and 20." *American Journal of Philology* 103:4–18.

Ryan, A. 2012. *A History of Political Thought: From Herodotus to the Present*. 2 vols. New York and London: W. W. Norton.

Rynearson, N. 2013. "Courting the Erinyes: Persuasion, Sacrifice, and Seduction in Aeschylus' Eumenides." *Transactions of the American Philological Association* 143: 1-22.

Saïd, S. 1985. *Sophiste et tyran ou le problème du Prométhée enchaîné*. Collection Études et Commentaires, 95. Paris: Klincksieck.

———. 1998. "Tragedy and Politics," in *Democracy, Empire and the Arts in Fifth-Century Athens*. Center for Hellenic Studies, Colloquia 2, edited by D. Boedeker and K. A. Raaflaub, 275–95. Cambridge, MA: Harvard University Press.

Samons, L. J. II. 2004. *What's Wrong with Democracy? From Athenian Practice to American Worship*. Berkeley: University of California Press.

Saxonhouse, A. W. 1985. *Women in the History of Political Thought: Ancient Greece to Machiavelli*. New York: Praeger Publishers

———. 2006. *Free Speech and Democracy in Ancient Athens*. Cambridge: Cambridge University Press.

Schein, S. L. 1984. *The Mortal Hero: An Introduction to Homer's Iliad*. Berkeley: University of California Press.

———. 1995. "Female Representation and Interpreting the *Odyssey*." In *The Distaff Side: Representing the Female in Homer's Odyssey*, edited by B. Cohen, 17–27. Oxford and New York: Oxford University Press.

———. 2016a. "Odysseus and Polyphemos in the *Odyssey*." In *Homeric Epic and Its Reception: Interpretive Essays*, 27–38. Oxford: Oxford University Press. Originally published in *Greek, Roman, and Byzantine Studies* 11 (1970): 73–83.

———. 2016b. "Mythological Allusion in the *Odyssey*: Herakles and the Bow of Odysseus." In *Homeric Epic and Its Reception: Interpretive Essays*, 39–54. Oxford: Oxford University Press. Lightly revised version of a chapter originally published in 2002 in *Omero tremila anni dopo*, edited by F. Montanari and P. Ascheri. Rome: Edizioni di Storia e Letteratura.

Scodel, R. 2002. *Listening to Homer: Tradition, Narrative, and Audience*. Ann Arbor: University of Michigan Press.

———. 2010. *An Introduction to Greek Tragedy*. Cambridge: Cambridge University Press.

Scott, W. C. 1987. "Teaching Homer from the Top Down: The *Telemachy*." In *Approaches to Teaching Homer's Iliad and Odyssey*, edited by K. Myrsiades, 132–36. New York: Modern Language Association of America.

Scully, S. 1990. *Homer and the Sacred City*. Ithaca, NY: Cornell University Press.

Seaford, R. 1994. *Reciprocity and Ritual: Homer and Tragedy in the Developing City-State*. Oxford: Clarendon.

Segal, C. P. 1995. *Sophocles' Tragic World: Divinity, Nature, Society*. Cambridge, MA: Harvard University Press.

Severyns, A. 1928. *Le cycle épique dans l'école d'Aristarque*. Liège, Belgium: Vaillant-Carmanne; and Paris: E. Champion.

Silk, M. S. 2004 "The *Odyssey* and Its Explorations." In *The Cambridge Companion to Homer*, edited by R. Fowler, 31–44. Cambridge: Cambridge University Press.

Snell, B. 1953. *The Discovery of the Mind: The Greek Origins of European Thought*. Translated by T. G. Rosenmeyer. Cambridge, MA: Harvard University Press.

Snyder, T. 2018. *The Road to Unfreedom: Russia, Europe, America*. New York: Tim Duggan Books.

Solmsen, F. 1954. "The 'Gift' of Speech in Homer and Hesiod." *Transactions and Proceedings of the American Philological Association* 85:1–15.

Sommerstein, A. H. 2010. *Aeschylean Tragedy*. London: Gerald Duckworth.

———. 2013. "*Atē* in Aeschylus." In *Tragedy and Archaic Greek Thought*, edited by D. L. Cairns, 1–16. Swansea: Classical Press of Wales.

Sommerstein, A. H., and I. C. Torrance. 2014, eds. *Oaths and Swearing in Ancient Greece*. Berlin: Walter de Gruyter.

Sourvinou-Inwood, C. 1989. "Reading Sophocles' *Antigone*." *Journal of Hellenic Studies* 109:134–48.

———. 2003. *Tragedy and Athenian Religion*. Lanham, MD: Rowman and Littlefield.

Stewart, E. 2017. *Greek Tragedy on the Move: The Birth of a Panhellenic Art Form c. 500–300 BC*. Oxford and New York: Oxford University Press.

Stockton, D. 1990. *The Classical Athenian Democracy*. Oxford: Oxford University Press.

Suzuki, M. 1989. *Metamorphoses of Helen: Authority, Difference, and the Epic.* Ithaca, NY, and London: Cornell University Press.

Swift, L. 2016. *Greek Tragedy: Themes and Contexts.* London and New York: Bloomsbury Academic.

Tandy, D. 1997. *Warriors into Traders: The Power of the Market in Early Greece.* Berkeley: University of California Press.

Taplin, O., trans. 2018. *The Oresteia.* New York and London: W.W. Norton.

Thalmann, W. G. 1998. *The Swineherd and the Bow: Representations of Class in the Odyssey.* Ithaca, NY: Cornell University Press.

Thomas, R. 1995. "The Place of the Poet in Archaic Society." In *The Greek World,* edited by A. Powell, 104–29. London: Routledge.

Torrance, I. C. 2013. *Metapoetry in Euripides.* Oxford: Oxford University Press.

Van Wees, H. 1992. *Status Warriors: War, Violence, and Society in Homer and History.* Amsterdam: Gieben.

Vernant, J.-P., and P. Vidal-Naquet. 1988. *Myth and Tragedy in Ancient Greece.* Translated by J. Lloyd. New York: Zone Books. Originally published as *Mythe et tragédie en Grèce ancienne* (1972) and *Mythe et tragédie en Grèce ancienne deux* (1986).

Versnel, H. S. 1990. "What's Sauce for the Goose Is Sauce for the Gander: Myth and Ritual Old and New." In *Approaches to Greek Myth,* edited by L. Edmunds, 84–151. Baltimore: Johns Hopkins University Press. 2nd ed. 2014.

———. 2011. *Coping with the Gods: Wayward Readings in Greek Theology.* Leiden, Netherlands: Brill.

Veyne, P. 1988. *Did the Greeks Believe in Their Myths? An Essay on the Constitutive Imagination.* Translated by P. Wissing. Chicago: University of Chicago Press. Originally published in 1983 as *Les Grecs ont-ils cru a leurs mythes?*

Vickers, B. 1973. *Towards Greek Tragedy.* London: Longman.

Vidal-Naquet, P. 1986. "Land and Sacrifice in the Odyssey," in *The Black Hunter,* translated by A. Szegedy-Maszak, 15–38. Baltimore: Johns Hopkins University Press.

Walsh, T. R. 2005. *Fighting Words and Feuding Words: Anger and the Homeric Poems.* Lanham, MD: Rowman and Littlefield.

West, M. L. 1997. *The East Face of Helicon: West Asiatic Elements in Greek Poetry and Myth.* London: Oxford University Press.

———. 2011. *The Making of the Iliad: Disquisition and Analytical Commentary.* Oxford: Oxford University Press.

———. 2017. *The Making of the Odyssey.* Oxford and New York: Oxford University Press.

Whitman, C. H. 1951. *Sophocles: A Study of Heroic Humanism.* Cambridge, MA: Harvard University Press.

Willcock, M. M. 1970. "Some Aspects of the Gods in the *Iliad.*" *Bulletin of the*

Institute of Classical Studies 17:1–10. Also in *Essays on the Iliad: Selected Modern Criticism*, edited by J. Wright, 58–69. Bloomington: Indiana University Press, 1978.

Williams, B. 1993. *Shame and Necessity*. Sather's Classical Lectures, vol. 57. Berkeley: University of California Press.

Wilson, E., trans. 2018. *Homer: The Odyssey*. New York: W. W. Norton.

Winkler, J. J. 1990. *The Constraints of Desire: The Anthropology of Sex and Gender in Ancient Greece*. New York: Routledge.

Winkler, J. J. and Zeitlin, F., eds. 1990. *Nothing to Do with Dionysos? Athenian Drama in Its Social Context*. Princeton, NJ: Princeton University Press.

Winnington-Ingram, R. P. 1980. *Sophocles: An Interpretation*. Cambridge: Cambridge University Press.

———. 1983. *Studies in Aeschylus*. Cambridge: Cambridge University Press.

Wood, G. S. 1972. *The Creation of the American Republic, 1776–1787*. New York: W. W. Norton.

Woodard, R., ed. 2007. *The Cambridge Companion to Greek Mythology*. Cambridge: Cambridge University Press.

Woodhouse, W. J. 1930. *The Composition of Homer's Odyssey*. Oxford: Clarendon Press.

Worth, R. 2016. *A Rage for Order: The Middle East in Turmoil, from Tahrir Square to Isis*. New York: Farrar, Straus, and Giroux.

Zakaria, F. 2007. *The Future of Freedom: Illiberal Democracy at Home and Abroad*. New York: W. W. Norton. First published 2003.

Zanker, G. 1992. "Sophocles' Ajax and the Heroic Values of the *Iliad*." *Classical Quarterly* 42:20–25.

———. 1994. *The Heart of Achilles: Characterization and Ethics in the Iliad*. Ann Arbor: University of Michigan Press.

Zeitlin, F. I. 1986. "Thebes: Theater of Self and Society in Athenian Drama." In *Greek Tragedy and Political Theory*, edited by J. P. Euben, 101–41. Berkeley: University of California Press.

———. 1990. "Playing the Other: Theater, Theatricality, and the Feminine in Greek Drama." In *Nothing to Do with Dionysos? Athenian Drama in Its Social Context*, edited by J. J. Winkler and F. I. Zeitlin, 63–93. Princeton, NJ: Princeton University Press.

———. 1995. "Figuring Fidelity in Homer's Odyssey." In *The Distaff Side: Representing the Female in Homer's Odyssey*, edited by B. Cohen, 117–52. Oxford and New York: Oxford University Press.

———. 1996. *Playing the Other: Gender and Society in Classical Greek Literature*. Chicago: University of Chicago Press.

Zuckerberg, D. 2018. *Not All Dead White Men: Classics and Misogyny in the Digital Age*. Cambridge, MA, and London: Harvard University Press.

Index

Paris, 14, 30, 47, 74, 110, 157, 159–60,
163, 239–40n23, 247n11, 250n1
Parry, M., 242–43n15
Peitho, 183
Penelope, 37, 39, 40–42, 47, 50, 68,
85, 97–98, 120, 124, 144, 146–49,
151, 162–63, 165, 250–51n5, 251n15,
253n30; bed, moving of, 134–35,
142, 251n10; bow, contest of, 130–
31, 136, 141; empirical knowledge,
141–42; female servants, 255–56n8;
fidelity of, 251–52n16; grief of, 44,
125, 127–28; humanity of, 141;
ingenuity of, 141–42; *kleos*, 143,
145; loyalty of, 125, 134, 141, 145;
male competition, as object for,
140–41; moral agency of, 251n11;
nightingale tale, 128–29; Odysseus, "extraordinary partnership"
with, 251n13; Odysseus, relationship between, 252n20; skepticism
of, 142, 145; suitors of, 51–52, 74,
103–4, 125–34, 140–41, 253n27;
suitors, in underworld, 135–36;
weaving trick, 136, 141, 251–52n16
Peradotto, J., 233–34n17, 244n3,
245n10, 249n25; *polutropos*, significance of, 241n5, 247n13
Pericles, 232n10, 269n29; "Funeral
Oration," 219
persuasion, 182–84; persuasive speech,
183
Phaeacians, 69, 71–74, 77, 81–82,
87–90, 91, 100, 104–6, 108–9,
111–12, 114, 245n10; struggle, lack
of, 83–85
Pherecydes the Athenian, 246n7
Philoctetes (Sophocles), 249n22
philia, 267–68n22
philoi (friends), 2, 118, 193, 195, 202–3,
206, 212
Philoitius, 249n29

polarization, 11, 217
poleis (citizen-communities), 3–4
polis, 204–6, 212, 221–22, 234n18,
264n8, 266n19; as citizen community, 231n7, 241n6
political authority, 49–50; obligations
toward governed, 65
Polynices, 187, 197, 265n12, 265–
66n18, 266n19, 268n25
popular will, 3; mob potential, concern
of, 230n5; ochlocracy, enshrining
of, 219
populism, 218, 221; rise of, 3
Porter, A., 233–34n17
Poseidon, 35–37, 43–44, 54, 69–
71, 73, 95–96, 108, 112, 243n18,
245n10, 253–54n32
Priam, 87, 98, 156, 162, 177, 239–
40n23, 257–58n18, 258n23
Prometheus, 269–70n32
Prometheus Bound (Aeschylus), 269–
70n32
Proteus, 48, 107
Pucci, P., 244–45n5, 248n19, 249–
50n30
Pylades, 168–69

Raaflaub, K. A., 229–30n2, 230n5,
231n7, 231n8, 235n20, 242–43n15,
246n9, 270n34
Rabel, R. J., 235n21
rational thought, 76, 84, 113, 209
reality: v. fantasy, 209–10
reality TV, 121
reciprocity, 54–56, 222, 231n7; reciprocal values, 115–16; self-interest,
63–64
Redfield, J. M., 235n20, 238n14, 238–
39n15
responsibility, 4, 28, 61, 115–16, 136,
153, 163, 195, 238n13; acknowledging of, 197, 200, 215, 223; and